Financial Elements of Contracts

Financial Elements of Contracts

Drafting, Monitoring and Compliance Audits

Sidney Philip Blum

OXFORD

UNIVERSITY PRESS

Oxford University Press, Inc., publishes works that further Oxford University's objective of excellence in research, scholarship, and education.

Oxford   New York
Auckland   Cape Town   Dar es Salaam   Hong Kong   Karachi   Kuala Lumpur   Madrid   Melbourne
Mexico City   Nairobi   New Delhi   Shanghai   Taipei   Toronto

With offices in
Argentina   Austria   Brazil   Chile   Czech Republic   France   Greece   Guatemala   Hungary   Italy
Japan   Poland   Portugal   Singapore   South Korea   Switzerland   Thailand   Turkey   Ukraine
Vietnam

Library of Congress Cataloging-in-Publication Data
Blum, Sidney Philip, 1964–
   Financial elements of contracts : drafting, monitoring and compliance audits / Sidney Philip Blum.
      p. cm.
   Includes bibliographical references and index.
   ISBN 978-0-19-538863-3 ((pbk.) : alk. paper)
   1. Contracts—United States. 2. Corporations—Accounting—Law and legislation—United States.
   3. Disclosure in accounting—United States. 4. United States. Sarbanes-Oxley Act of 2002. I. Title.
   KF801.B59 2010
   346.7302—dc22   2009035330

1 2 3 4 5 6 7 8 9
Printed in the United States of America on acid-free paper

Note to Readers
This publication is designed to provide accurate and authoritative information in regard to the subject matter
covered. It is based upon sources believed to be accurate and reliable and is intended to be current as of the
time it was written. It is sold with the understanding that the publisher is not engaged in rendering legal,
accounting, or other professional services. If legal advice or other expert assistance is required, the services
of a competent professional person should be sought. Also, to confirm that the information has not been
affected or changed by recent developments, traditional legal research techniques should be used, including
checking primary sources where appropriate.

(Based on the Declaration of Principles jointly adopted by a Committee of the
American Bar Association and a Committee of Publishers and Associations.)

You may order this or any other Oxford University Press publication by
visiting the Oxford University Press website at www.oup.com

To my loving wife Rachel and my very special daughters

—Jessica, Gabriella, and Marissa

Contents

ABOUT THE AUTHOR   xiii

INTRODUCTION   xv

CHAPTER 1: **An Overview of Self-Reporting Contracts**   1

    1.1. An Environment That Encourages Misreporting   2
    1.2. Economics of Self-Reporting   3
    1.3. Plan the Relationship with the Third Party   4
        1.3.1. Phase 1: Business Strategy   4
        1.3.2. Phase 2: Contract Execution   6
        1.3.3. Phase 3: Continuous Internal Monitoring
               and Contract Management   7
        1.3.4. Phase 4: Periodic Monitoring Audits   8
        1.3.5. Phase 5: Exit Strategy   11
        1.3.6. Looking to the Future   12

CHAPTER 2: **Why You Need to Monitor Self-Reporting Contractees**   15

    2.1. Effective Licensee Monitoring—A Summary   16
        2.1.1. Calculating Royalties on the Disposition of All
               Licensed Product(s)   16
        2.1.2. Maintenance Procedures for Licensee's
               Internal Records   18
        2.1.3. Information to be Provided in Royalty Statements 18
        2.1.4. Establishing a License Monitoring Program   19
        2.1.5. Royalty Audits   20
        2.1.6. Periodic Reports   21
        2.1.7. Effective Licensee Monitoring   22
    2.2. Intellectual Property Compliance Around the World   23
    2.3. Digital Content: A Burgeoning Global Royalty Market   23
    2.4. Emerging Regional Trends   24
        2.4.1. Asia   24
        2.4.2. North America   25
        2.4.3. Europe—Middle East—Africa   26

2.5. Sarbanes-Oxley Act of 2002 and Third-Party Monitoring   27

    2.5.1. SOX Section 302: Internal Control Certifications   31

    2.5.2. SOX Section 404: Assessment of Internal Control   32

    2.5.3. SOX Section 802: Criminal Penalties
        for Violation of SOX   34

CHAPTER 3: **Types of Self-Reporting Contracts and Reporting Risks**   35

  3.1. Advertising Agency Contracts   38

    3.1.1. Contract Description   38

    3.1.2. Key Terms and Conditions That Auditors Care About   39

    3.1.3. Reporting Areas and Associated Risks   42

    3.1.4. Documents to Consider Requesting in the Contract
        to Allow for Adequate External Monitoring   43

  3.2. Construction Contracts   45

    3.2.1. Contract Description   45

    3.2.2. Key Terms and Conditions That Auditors Care About   48

    3.2.3. The Variable Cost Contract Monitoring Process   53

    3.2.4. When to Conduct Self-Monitoring and an Audit   58

    3.2.5. Key Documents That a Construction Company Should
        Be Contractually Required to Retain for Construcion
        Contract Monitoring and Why   59

  3.3. Digital Distribution Contracts   60

    3.3.1. Contract Description   60

    3.3.2. Digital Distribution Self-Reporting Areas of Concern   64

    3.3.3. Summary of Digital Distribution Risks   67

    3.3.4. Some Areas to Monitor in Digital Distribution
        Agreements   67

  3.4. Distribution and Reseller Contracts   69

    3.4.1. Contract Description   69

    3.4.2. Key Terms and Conditions That Auditors Care About   75

    3.4.3. Sample Key Terms and Conditions From
        a Distribution Agreement   77

  3.5. Franchisee Contracts   80

    3.5.1. Contract Description   80

    3.5.2. Key Terms and Conditions That Auditors Care About   82

    3.5.3. Reporting Areas and Associated Risks   92

    3.5.4. Documents to Consider Requesting in the Contract
        to Allow for Adequate External Monitoring   93

  3.6. Joint Venture and Partner Contract   94

    3.6.1. Contract Description   94

    3.6.2. Key Terms and Conditions That Auditors Care About   94

    3.6.3. Documents to Consider Requesting in the Contract
        to Allow for Adequate External Monitoring   101

  3.7. Most-Favored-Nation Contracts   101

    3.7.1. Contract Description   101

    3.7.2. Key Terms and Conditions That Auditors Care About   102

3.7.3. Reporting Areas and Associated Risks 104

3.7.4. Documents to Consider Requesting in the Contract
to Allow for Adequate External Monitoring 105

3.7.5. Example of Most-Favored-Nations Contract Language 106

3.8. Manufacturing Contracts 108

3.8.1. Contract Description 108

3.8.2. Key Terms and Conditions That Auditors Care About 108

3.8.3. Documents to Consider Requesting in the Contract
to Allow for Monitoring 120

3.9. Royalty/Licensing Contracts 121

3.9.1. Contract Description 121

3.9.2. Key Terms and Conditions That Auditors Care About 123

3.9.3. Documents to Consider Requesting in the Contract
to Allow for Adequate External Monitoring 131

3.10. Software/End User License Contracts 132

3.10.1. Contract Description 132

3.10.2. Key Terms and Conditions That Auditors
Care About 134

3.10.3. Reporting Areas and Associated Risks 135

CHAPTER 4: **Roles in Third-Party Monitoring** 139

4.1. Establishing Roles 140

4.2. Key Decision-Makers 141

4.3. Influencers 141

4.3.1. Step #1: Who's Job Is It to Run the Monitoring Program? 142

4.3.2. Step #2: Questions to Ask to Determine the Level
of Effort in Monitoring the Licensees 144

4.3.3. Determining the Roles in Monitoring
Third-Party Licensees 146

4.3.4. In-House Lawyer's Role 152

4.3.5. Program Coordination Licensor's Role in an Audit 153

4.3.6. Licensee's Role in an Audit 153

CHAPTER 5: **Justification and Implementation of a Contract
Monitoring program (CMP)** 155

5.1. Introduction 157

5.1.1. Create a CMP 158

5.1.2. CMP Justification 158

5.1.3. CMP Scope 161

5.1.4. CMP Objectives 161

5.1.5. CMP Policy Statement 163

5.1.6. CMP Board Resolution 163

5.1.7. Running the CMP Program—Legal or Finance? 165

5.1.8. Overcoming Objections to Monitoring Third Parties 165

5.1.9. Selection of the Third Party for Monitoring
and/or Audit 166

5.1.10. Selection and Contracting with the Auditor 170

5.1.11. Notification Letters to Third Parties of the CMP 178

5.1.12. Notification Letter to the Third Party of an Impending Audit 179

5.1.13. Red Flags Indicators of Underreporting and Reacting to Those Indicators 180

5.1.14. Information to the Auditor 184

5.1.15. The Lawyer's Role in Third-Party Audits 184

5.1.16. What to Do with the Audit Report 187

5.1.17. Reporting to Management on the Program's Success and Evaluation—The Contract Monitoring Program (CMP) 189

5.1.18. Annual Reminder of CMP to the Self-Reporting Party 189

CHAPTER 6: **Writing the Contract: Financial Terms and Conditions** 191

6.1. Advertising: External Expenditure Commitments 194

6.2. Advertising: As a Payment to the Licensors 196

6.3. Closeouts 197

6.4. Counterfeiting Protection 199

6.5. Cost Recovery 201

6.6. Deduction and Discount Limitations 204

6.7. Exchange Rates 208

6.8. Granting the Right 209

6.9. Gross Sales 212

6.10. Insurance 215

6.11. Interest (Late Fees) Penalties 216

6.12. Inventory 219

6.13. Minimum Guarantees 222

6.14. Most-Favored-Nation 224

6.15. Net Sales 226

6.16. Non-Disclosure Agreements 229

6.17. Price Controls 230

6.18. Record Keeping 230

6.19. Related Party Sales 235

6.20. Reporting 237

6.21. Returns 241

6.22. Right to Audit 242

6.23. Royalty Calculations 245

6.24. Royalty Payment 249

6.25. Territory 251

6.26. Termination 253

6.27. Posttermination Rights 255

6.27.1. Effect of Termination 258

6.28. Tax Deductions—On Royalty Payments 260

6.29. Tax Deductions—As a Reduction From Gross Sales 260

6.30. Unauthorized Use of Licensed Product 261

CHAPTER 7: **Best Practices for a Licensee**   263

    7.1. Some Top Best Practices for a Licensee   264

    7.2. Why Licensees Underreport Royalties   269

    7.3. IP Inventory Monitoring   272

    7.4. Preparing for the Royalty Audit   273

    7.5. Non-Disclosure Agreement (NDA)   276

    7.6. Communications with the Licensor   276

    7.7. Creating the Control Environment   276

    7.8. How to Avoid Being Audited   277

APPENDICES

    APPENDIX I   **Sample License Agreement**   279

    APPENDIX II   **Registration of Manufacturer**   327

    APPENDIX III   **Royalty Statement**   329

    APPENDIX IV   **Settlement Letter (California)**   331

    APPENDIX V   **Non-Disclosure Agreement**   333

    APPENDIX VI   **Third-Party Risk-Ranking Matrix**   337

    APPENDIX VII   **Notification of a Third-Party Audit Program**   341

    APPENDIX VIII   **Notification of an Audit**   343

INDEX   345

About the Author

Sidney P. Blum, CPA, CFE, CrFA, FACFEI, DABFA, CPEA, and CFF is globally recognized as a leading authority in third-party auditing with contract compliance experience in such diverse areas as royalty, channel/distribution, filmed entertainment, digital distribution, advertising, participation, residual, construction and most-favored-nation. Mr. Blum's background includes serving clients in a vast number of industries, such as media and entertainment, consumer products, semiconductor, high technology, software, manufacturing, distribution, and oil and gas.

Mr. Blum graduated Cum Laude from California State University, Northridge with a degree in Business Administration and an option in Accounting Theory and Practice.

Mr. Blum has been gathering information for this book for over twenty years and first started writing procedures for third-party inspections as a staff auditor with the Big 8 accounting firm, Ernst & Whinney. While at Ernst & Whinney, Mr. Blum focused on third-party audits for the media and entertainment industries, including the Screen Actors Guild, Directors Guild, Motion Picture Pension Plan, Writers Guild, and major studios. He also performed numerous movie production and distribution audits as well as numerous forensic investigations.

After leaving Ernst & Whinney, Mr. Blum began five years of third-party vendor, construction, time and material, and cost-plus contract auditing for Occidental Petroleum and Unocal.

Mr. Blum then joined the Walt Disney Company as a royalty audit manager where he consolidated much of his learning over the years and worked to develop the royalty audit programs for Disney's video/DVD unit, gaming division, and the Internet division.

Mr. Blum then rejoined Ernst & Whinney, renamed Ernst & Young thanks to mergers, and eventually consolidated his writings to create the royalty audit methodology for the firm. After more than five years with Ernst & Young, Mr. Blum accepted a Partnership with another Big 4 accounting firm, KPMG. He was hired to help start KPMG's Contract Compliance Services practice. At KPMG, Mr. Blum reconsolidated his experiences and wrote the overall global third-party auditing methodology along with the product specific methodologies for royalties, advertising and third-party vendors, all based on his prior writings and years of experience performing this work.

Since writing the methodologies for two of the Big 4 firms, thanks to crosspollination by employee movement between the firms, his procedures and methodologies for third-party auditing have been adopted by all Big 4 firms.

Mr. Blum is now recognized as a leading authority on third-party auditing, especially related to royalties. He has been called the father/creator of today's leading royalty auditing methods.

Over the years, Mr. Blum's clients have included some of the world's largest companies along with many niche industries. His third-party audit clients have included some of the largest companies in biotechnology, media & entertainment, hardware, software, music, microchips, medical supplies, oil & gas, construction and apparel.

Professional Certifications
  Certified Public Accountant
  - California
  - New York
  American Institute of Certified Public Accountants
  - Certified in Financial Forensics
  Association of Certified Fraud Examiners
  - Certified Fraud Examiner
  American College of Forensic Examiners Institute
  - Fellow
  American Board of Forensic Accounting
  - Diplomate
  Board of Environmental, Health & Safety Auditors
  - Certified Environmental Auditor
  - Certified Health & Safety Auditor
  - Certified Forensic Accountant

Hobbies
  Worldwide travel (81 countries visited)
  Road bicycling
  Home remodeling
  Russian literature

Foremost, he is a loving husband to Rachel and proud father to his three daughters Jessica, Gabriella and Marissa.

Introduction

In twenty years of enforcing "right-to-audit" provisions in a vast array of industries, for some of the largest licensors and for various Fortune 500 companies, I have never seen a well-written contract that adequately addresses the financial considerations of the arrangement and provides adequate recourse to the party that receives the information. This often leads to litigation and costly audits. This book provides extremely valuable information about how to properly protect a party receiving self-reported information and identifies the opportunities for reasonable penalties when the contact is violated. It also explains the role of a litigator during a royalty audit.

Contracts where the second party to a contract "self-reports" financial and other information to the first party of the contract are, for the purposes of this book, called a "self-reporting party." These trust based contracts require the reporting of important financial and other information such as royalties under an intellectual property license or expenses under a time and material agreement. Companies that self-report this information nearly always provide grossly inaccurate information, often ranging from 10 percent to 200 percent depending on the industry. While the reasons for the misreporting are vast, they are primarily caused by poorly written contracts coupled with responsible parties not adequately monitoring the reports of the self-reporting party. By applying the principles in this book, transactional attorneys will learn to write improved contracts that control the financial risks, and litigation attorneys will know how to better investigate a self-reporting party through an audit.

This book will provide great value to all parties in self-reporting relationships, including licensors, licensees, attorneys, and accountants. A focus is placed on intellectual property contracts and monitoring the resultant royalty streams, but it will also touch on a magnitude of other self-reporting contracts.

Early in my career at the "Big 8" accounting firm of Ernst & Whinney, I learned as a financial statement auditor to never trust financial statements. The combination of complex accounting rules and either ignorant or dishonest chief financial officers (CFOs) and assemblers of accounting statements resulted in nearly every audit discovering significant adjustments to the originally reported numbers. These adjustments of internally reported financial numbers were often "material" in nature, generally meaning a value in excess of 10 percent of the company's financial statement's reported revenues or assets. With audited financial numbers being materially correct after often large adjustments proposed by auditors, you can now understand the high risk of financial misreporting by a self-reporting party where the information they are reporting is often not material or not subject to the scrutiny of the financial statement auditors. Even if the financial information is audited, it is only inspected to about 10 percent of accuracy compared to the overall sales or asset information. This margin of error is not acceptable to companies that receive self-reported information from a party associated only by contract.

Early in my career, thanks to the poor financial statements that I found that most companies produced, I had a reputation as the "hacker" because by the time I had completed my audit, the CFO had resigned or been fired, and just about every company went from operating in the black to the red. So the day Enron collapsed, I was not surprised but rather wondered what took so long as I had seen similar financial irregularities in every company I had ever audited. Then, Congress and the Securities and Exchange Commission finally reacted with the Sarbanes-Oxley Act of 2002 to try to get companies to clean up their financial statements, and the result was a record number of financial restatements, billions of dollars of stock losses, and CFOs being fired. The result of the Sarbanes-Oxley Act is to increase the onus on companies to monitor expense and/or revenue information being reported by an unrelated self-reporting party.

Does that mean accountants have cleaned up their act and that we can trust financial data they have audited? After all, we certified public accountants (CPAs) like to think of ourselves as individuals above corruption. The American Institute of Certified Public Accountants (AICPA) mission refers to such noble ends as "integrity, objectivity, competence" (but, interestingly, the mission does not state to make certain financial statements are reasonably accurate). And the AICPA has recognized repeatedly the importance of the need for the competent CPA to help bring stability in troubled economic times. It is also noted on the AICPA Web site, "AICPA Professional Ethics Executive Committee and Strategic Planning Committee are both focusing on ways to reinforce our commitment to ethics and excellence" in an August 2002 speech by then-Chair James Castello. So, six years after this speech and the continual collapse of major lending institutions (Countrywide, Indymac Bank, and WAMU) that had financial statements that greatly overstated their value, have we gotten to the point that we can always trust audited financial statements? The answer is a resounding "no." People are still people. Greed, laziness, corruption, lack of caring, stupidity . . . call it what you will. Financial information is generally misreported.

With the expanding global economy, company mangers need to keep in mind that increased governance demands by stockholders and the government and the risk of not properly monitoring self-reporting relationships exposes companies to financial loss and misconduct investigation.

To understand the risk of not properly contracting and monitoring self-reporting relationships, it is first best to understand that financial statement auditors work in a world of "materiality." This means that from the start, auditors and accountants know that the financial statements don't need to be 100 percent accurate; they just need to be somewhat close. Materiality is better defined as if the accounting numbers as presented don't affect the decision-making of the reader (i.e., the bank or stockholders), then the numbers are close enough. The guideline for how close is close enough used by most financial statement auditors is 10 percent. So if the financial statements report $920 million of income and it was really $1 billion, well, that is close enough. Who cares about a little $80 million understatement? Well, if your company receives a share of that $80 million understatement, then you care.

What all this leads to is an appreciation that companies that report financial data get it close generally but are almost always wrong in the information they report. (After more than twenty years of auditing, I am still looking for the company that gets it right the first time). And being off 10 percent is generally acceptable on a material basis; however, if you are concerned about accuracy of reporting that is much less than materiality, then you are now warned: unless your contract with the other party is extremely well-written, then you are doomed to be reading inaccurate financial reports and therefore suffering the consequences.

[Now keeping the 10 percent acceptable misstatement in mind, it is easy to understand why audits completed under the 5 percent misstatement cost recovery provision usually result in cost recoveries.]

Here is an illustrative example of materiality versus a royalty report and why royalty reports, nearly 100 percent of the time, underreport royalties:

Financial Statement Sales	$ 100,000,000
Financial Statement Materiality (10%)	$ 10,000,000
Royalty Bearing Product Sales	$ 5,000,000
Royalty Due @ 7.5%	$ 375,000
Royalty Actually Reported	$ 250,000
Underreporting	$ 125,000

As the royalty bearing statement sales of $5 million are less than the $10 million of materiality inspected by the financial statement auditors, there may be a lack of scrutiny. This allows for errors in the statement of the royalty liability; so the licensor is underpaid $125,000 because the payment is below everyone's radar. The licensee's financial statement auditors are satisfied as the misreported royalty is only $125,000, as the underreporting is well below materiality of $10 million. However, no licensor would be happy with an underreporting of $125,000; it's just the number is too small for the financial statement auditors to care about so the licensor cannot rely on a correction due to a financial statement auditors demand. As the licensor cannot or should not rely on the financial statement auditor of the licensee to protect the licensor, the licensor instead must hire a royalty auditor who does not work in a world of materiality but rather in a world of return on investment. The royalty auditor is concerned about the $125,000 while the financial statement auditor does not care in this example.

I have never seen accurate self-reported financial data! I have never seen a contract that properly governs the financial reporting requirements of the self-reporting party and clearly lays out the penalties for each violation of the contract!

With billions of dollars being self-reported and billions of dollars of self-reporting errors, this book is desperately needed. Lawyers and licensors are great at the boilerplate terms and conditions, but when it comes to the financial controls to be placed on the self-reporting party and the penalties to be paid when those financial controls are not met, today's contracts get a grade of "D" at best. As I once quipped to a group of lawyers from a prestigious law firm, perhaps the contracts are so poorly written by the transactional attorneys so they can keep their brethren litigation attorneys fully employed. [Not that I mind—as a royalty auditor and expert witness, it also keeps me fully employed!]

Self-reporting parties misreport if they know there is no monitoring programs such as an audit. This can cost a company 10 percent to 200 percent of reported amounts.

It seems that many contract writers and business developers forget the main reason that contracts relying on self-reporting by another party are written—to make money or reduce costs. Unfortunately, as lawyers do not have the insight into, or understanding of accounting, including "what can go wrong will go wrong," they are challenged to write tight contracts that govern the financial risks that also balance continuing operational needs.

To most writers of contracts, it is generally about just getting the deal done and then praying that everything will work out right and that honesty will prevail. Well, forget it. Every dollar the self-reporting party misreports is profit to their bottom line. [Interestingly enough, in hundreds of examinations the rule seems to always be the same—royalties are underreported and expenses are overreported. It is almost never the other way around.]

When times are tough, or even not so tough, the easiest extra dollar saved comes from misreporting to a self-reporting relationship.

Contracts that require a third party to self-report activity are, as a characteristic of human nature, subject to misreporting by the third party regardless of the nature of the agreement. The reasons for the misreporting are wide in range but generally fall into one of three categories: moral corruption, lack of due care, or ignorance. Generally, misreporting results from all three of these categories, just to a different degree.

When businesses enter into a self-reporting contract, usually all sides plan to follow the intent and actual wording of the agreement. Unfortunately, the individuals who negotiate and sign the agreement are rarely the same as the monitors and reporters under the agreements. The intention of the agreement is often not matched to actual activities or is inflexible toward the contracting party, so there are constant violations. The agreements often lack clear definitions, so the intention of the words or contract language is often misconstrued by both sides to the agreement.

Understanding that all self-reporting financial arrangements are subject to and most likely to result in errors helps the contract negotiator better establish a reporting environment that all parties can follow. With the self-reporting arrangement, one rule to follow when it comes to financial arrangements can be expressed by the insightful words of Albert Einstein, "everything should be made as simple as possible, but no simpler." Most contracts have very simple financial terms that don't provide adequate definitions of financial restrictions and obligations, thus leading to large financial disputes. This is often seen when the word "reasonable" is used as a limiting factor as opposed to an exacting quantity, such as trade discount deductions are limited to 10 percent as opposed to the very weak trade discount deductions are limited to reasonable industry standards.

Ultimately, the goal of good financial terms within a contract is to increase the likelihood that all parties know their responsibilities for financial compliance and the reasonable penalties, should they not comply. I say "reasonable" because too many contracts go right to termination to solve issues as opposed to a penalty that is practical and will allow the parties to continue business.

The common excuse I hear for a poorly written contract is, "we will lose the deal if we don't sign the contract as is and we will worry about the details later." Unfortunately, the rush to close the deal immediately will lead to future disputes, making the parties in the negotiation wonder why they didn't spent a couple more hours hammering out the details for monitoring and remediation of contraction violation. I have seen countless instances where poorly written contracts that fail to mention reasonable remedies for the various contract violations have resulted in extremely costly lawsuits (though one could say this is a good employment strategy for lawyers because we know there is plenty of money to be made in intellectual property ("IP") and other contractual dispute litigation).

This book works to identify simple, straightforward contract language that helps to encourage contractual compliance. By reading this book, the transactional attorneys will do a better job of writing contracts and thus better serve their employer/client. The litigators will learn about partnering with a highly skilled auditor/expert witness to help them investigate the third party and understand the weaknesses of many contracts that are under dispute.

> Companies need to put the same amount of energy into monitoring a contract as they do into establishing the business relationship and writing the contract.

CHAPTER

1

An Overview of Self-Reporting Contracts

1.1. An Environment That Encourages Misreporting   2

1.2. Economics of Self-Reporting   3

1.3. Plan the Relationship with the Third Party   4

    1.3.1. Phase 1: Business Strategy   4

    1.3.2. Phase 2: Contract Execution   6

    1.3.3. Phase 3: Continuous Internal Monitoring and Contract Management   7

    1.3.4. Phase 4: Periodic Monitoring Audits   8

    1.3.5. Phase 5: Exit Strategy   11

    1.3.6. Looking to the Future   12

1.1. An Environment That Encourages Misreporting

Licensees know the following when it comes to paying royalties:

- Licensors rarely conduct royalty audits.
- Not maintaining records and minimally cooperating with a royalty audit greatly reduces the odds of having to pay findings from a royalty audit.
- Poorly written financial terms and the complete lack of financial penalties encourage licensees to underpay royalties.
- Even if a royalty audit finds amounts have been underpaid, it is generally simple to settle for pennies on the dollar as many licensors are too concerned about damaging the relationship.
- Many licensors treat royalty revenues as "icing on the cake" instead of as an important income flow.

So why do licensees pay the proper amounts on time? The answer is that they don't. Licensees purposely underpay royalties. And I mean **all** licensees underpay, not just some. It is just a matter of if you can catch the licensee.

No licensee pays all royalties due. Active monitoring is a deterrent to underreporting and noncompliance. (PS: I know lawyers hate to use the word "all," but I have yet to be proven wrong. I am certain there are some licensees with little to no sales who just pay minimum guarantees . . . I just don't audit them as there is not much risk of underreporting).

Lawyers, in turn, tend to write contracts that go straight to termination and fail to grasp the ongoing business necessity with the self-reporting third party. Lawyers need to learn to think like business people and substitute "remedies" for "termination." Remedies are generally clear monetary penalties to be paid should the third party violate various contract provisions other than the most basic areas of overcharging of costs or underreporting of revenues that are to be shared. An example of when "termination" is often the penalty identified in the contract, as opposed to a monetary penalty, comes when the self-reporting policy fails to buy general or product liability insurance that names the other party as additionally insured. In reality, I have never seen a company terminate an agreement because the self-reporting party did not buy adequate insurance; however, no remedy is listed in the agreement.

The practical solution for not buying general or product liability insurance is that the self-reporting party must pay the equivalent amount to the licensor.

Another example is for the selling of unlicensed product. The penalty should be clearly stated that all revenues from these sales of unlicensed product will go to the licensor as opposed to termination (now this might become a bit more complicated if there is an exclusive license agreement with another party that was violated . . . then the question arises who gets to keep the penalty for violating the agreement . . . the other licensee who had the exclusive agreement or the licensor).

1.2. Economics of Self-Reporting

Since Enron, investors have demanded more accurate financial reporting and a higher degree of corporate governance. This increased oversight has focused on internally created reports and neglected self-reporting relationships. In order to meet today's global business needs, companies need to better understand their sources of income and expenses that are controlled by third parties.

Self-reporting relationships primarily rely on trust as guided by a contract. These contracts are numerous and include such areas as royalty, time and material, advertising, distribution, research and development, cost sharing, revenue sharing, and the list goes on. The value of such self-reporting contracts range from small dollars to billions of dollars. Larger self-reporting contracts where billions of dollars are at stake can vary from time and material, such as those of the United States Agency for International Development spending billions for the reconstruction of Iraq or for medical royalties, such as the money Amgen receives from licensing its Epogen pharmaceutical.

What represents high risks for underreporting revenues and overpayment of expenses is still generally neglected by companies. The self-reporting economy is estimated to be between $300 billion and $500 billion, that calculates roughly to $30 billion to $50 billion in reporting errors. Yet, despite these errors, contractors bury their heads in the sand.

With the United States Sarbanes-Oxley Act of 2002 (SOX), Japan SOX, and with other nations clamping down on financial statements, companies should take the time to increase their corporate governance over third-party relationships by reexamining all of their self-reporting contracts. Strong contracts and monitoring are a vital part of presenting fair financial statements and meeting legal responsibilities.

With increased legal risks comes the added burden of many companies needing to work in a global economy. So the self-reporting third party is no longer just down the street; it is often halfway across the world, speaking a different language, and under a different currency. This leads to greatly increased risks of reporting errors because oversight is often nonexistent or highly dysfunctional. With complex financial arrangements and international relationships, the risk of regulatory and contractual noncompliance due to poorly written contracts is at a high level that is only destined to get worse.

1.3. Plan the Relationship with the Third Party

In creating a contractual relationship with third-party reporting, consideration must be given to the nature of the agreement and how the various phases of the relationship process will be monitored. The various phases are:

1. Business strategy
2. Contract execution
3. Continuous internal monitoring and contract management
4. Periodic monitoring audits
5. Exit strategy

1.3.1. Phase 1: Business Strategy

Outsourcing operations to a third party that must self-report is an important business strategy decision. The loss of control over the operations creates substantial business risk. This outsourcing is most often doomed for failure, or to at least problems, unless information exchange between the organizations is adequately controlled. Information to be exchanged must be clearly identified in the contract.

This received information is often rife with errors that are difficult to identify due to a variety of factors, not the least of which are language barriers, business ethic and operating differences, cultural challenges, and technical skills and abilities. Reliance must be placed on the self-reporting company's internal controls that are often not to the standard of the monitoring company's. These problems at the self-reporting company are nearly impossible to detect without adequate information flows from the self-reporting company.

The business strategy to outsource operations, therefore, must consider the controls it will have over information flow. Such considerations may include:

- How will the self-reported company ensure controls are adequate to properly collect financial data and report on the accuracy of that information? For example, does the self-reporting company have adequate financial software in place to accurately capture and report on the information needed by the monitoring company?

- Are the business strategies of the two companies aligned to promote adequate and proper information flow?
- Are there business incentives to encourage the self-reporting party to comply with the needs of the monitoring company, both in terms of reward and penalties for noncompliance?
- Will the higher risks created by using an outsourced company be offset by the value gained?
- Have the risks of noncompliance, inadequate information, or incorrect information flow been considered when selecting the self-reporting company?

Overall, will the contract be able to control these risks to an acceptable level?

Companies must decide early on in the contracting process how intensively they wish to monitor the self-reporting company, as this will affect the terms and conditions that will allow the company to perform the monitoring.

Basic considerations are:

1. Ability of the company to monitor.
   a. Is the third party nearby or far away? If far away, who will do the monitoring and what information needs to be included because of the distance, such as exchange rate detail?
   b. Are there sufficient financial and human resources available to have a viable monitoring program? While a company might not have the resources today, it should consider putting in all contractual protections and document production requirements so the program can be established in the future. This will also help reduce future litigation costs associated with document production.
2. What is the appetite of the company to inspect the records of the self-reporting company? Despite all the known issues associated with self-reporters, many companies elect not to monitor the third party as they are concerned about upsetting the continuous business relationship or believe any findings from such monitoring or auditing would not be worth the efforts of the monitoring. Such risk acceptance is extremely common with today's businesses. It is common because companies work very hard to establish business relationships and often place a high degree of reliance on the self-reporting party, and it is not within the benefit of the individuals associated with writing the contract and/or business development to create distress during the contracting process at the risk of upsetting or losing the agreement. However, most self-reporting companies expect to be subject to inspection so the fear of inspecting your business partner is business ignorance.
3. Do the individuals writing the contact have an appreciation of the needs of the monitoring processes? The individuals writing the contract

understand the business strategy of why they are writing the contract but don't have an appreciation for the importance of the continuous monitoring.

> Companies should put the same effort into contract monitoring as they do for establishing the contract.

1.3.2. Phase 2: Contract Execution

Contracts are generally not written adequately to protect financial interests because the business developers and lawyers who write the contracts do not have the accounting, audit, and forensic background to understand the many different ways a self-reporting company may manipulate their reporting responsibilities. Rarely is the accounting department requested to review the financial terms of the agreement, and even if requested to do so, few in-house accountants have the technical skills to appreciate how a self-reporting company may accidentally or purposely misrepresent reported information.

The basic tenets when it comes to financial control in writing a self-reporting contract: is the limitation clearly and numerically written, and is there an adequate penalty if it is not achieved? For example, extremely commonly used language in calculating net sales from gross sales in a royalty relationship is "deductions for normal trade discounts may be taken." The problem with this language is that "normal" is vague and will be interpreted different by the licensor and the licensee. By simply stating a percentage limitation, better control can be placed over the licensee, so the preferred language would allow "trade discounts not to exceed 10 percent off of the highest selling price of the product." This method of clearly communicating expectations results in better reporting and better relationships between the contracting parties.

In creating a robust contract, it is important to use the resources of a highly skilled attorney who understands where financial arrangements may be abused or misconstrued. The skilled attorney may seek out assistance from an auditor to examine the contract to identify where financial limitations are not adequately defined.

While the negotiation of these financial limitations is often painful to the business developers looking to close the deal, it can avoid much more troublesome future business disputes and extremely costly litigation. No companies go into a contract with litigation as the intended result, but knowing that self-reporting relationships often lead to litigation should provide enough incentive for companies to take the extra steps necessary to protect themselves in a well-written contract. Questions to ask yourself when writing a contract include:

- Are the reporting terms reasonable?
- Are the reporting terms clear, understandable, and not subject to interpretation?
- Will the reports of the self-reporting party provide sufficient detail information to allow for proper monitoring without physical audit of the books and records of the third party?
- Does the third party have the ability to comply with the controls established in the contract?
- Are penalties for noncompliance sufficient to be an incentive for the third party to properly report?
- Are there other tools in the agreement that will allow for the proper monitoring of the third party?

Monitoring of contracts is done internally by reviewing the reports provided by the third party and externally by enforcement of the right-to-audit provision. Sufficient energy must be spent to clearly identify how the contract will be monitored before signing the agreement.

For internal monitoring, clear delineation of responsible parties should be reached prior to signing the contract. Each responsible party should state what they need from the reporting party in order for them to fulfill their obligations. Then this requested information, if appropriate, should be formalized in the agreement.

For external monitoring, the contract must have a "right-to-audit" clause that clearly gives sufficient power to the auditor to access all vital provisions of the contract. When negotiating audit rights, it should be made clear the purpose of the audit is to avoid future business disputes and ensure a system of "trust but verify." From the outset, it is imperative to communicate to the self-reporting party that the "right-to-audit" provision will be enacted as part of normal operating procedures and is not punitive.

1.3.3. Phase 3: Continuous Internal Monitoring and Contract Management

A company must first identify who is going to monitor the self-reporting party's contractual compliance. Then the attorney must work with the party that is to monitor the self-reporting party to determine what information is needed to monitor the self-reporting party's contractual compliance. This needed information must be clearly written into the contract's terms and conditions. Such information is often received in a statement so it is best to include such a statement to be completed by the third party in an attachment to the contract. Information that is commonly requested to be included in statements is covered in a later chapter.

As a part of the continuous internal monitoring, the monitoring company must identify the "red flags" that could indicate a contract noncompliance issue or a going-concern issue at the licensee. Examples of red flags that are covered in more detail include failure to submit timely statements, unexpected royalty payment decreases, or, conversely, expense increases, unauthorized new products, and miscalculations in the statements.

1.3.4. Phase 4: Periodic Monitoring Audits

Periodic monitoring audits conducted under the "right-to-audit" provision of the contract are a common business practice to demonstrate concern, influence, and control over the self-reporting party, and, if done correctly, to enhance the business relationship. Such work is often defined by the type of audit being conducted, such as a "royalty audit," "distribution audit," "advertising agency audit," or "construction audit." Care must be taken to understand this is not an "audit" as defined by "Generally Accepted Accounting Standards," which is to express an opinion over the fairness of the financial presentation of the information. Nor are the goals similar to that of other types of the loosely used word of "audit," such as a tax audit, quality control audit, or other type of audit. In fact, if a certified public accountant (CPA) performs the work under a "right-to-audit" provision, then he must be careful not to call it an "audit" or "review" as these have specific legal definitions for an accountant not generally contemplated under the "right-to-audit" provisions of the contract. If it is called a royalty audit by the CPA, then it is important the CPA clarify the work is not an audit under accounting definitions, but rather contractual definitions of an "audit."

Also, "right-to-audit" provisions often mention that the work is to be done by an independent accountant, and here again, this language often used by the writers of the contract is not done in consideration of Generally Accepted Accounting Standards governing independence but rather refers more to a neutral party, as better defined by the role of an expert witness. There are substantial differences for a CPA when considering independence versus neutrality.

The audits, as contemplated by the "right-to-audit" provisions, can be reactive or proactive. Reactive audits tend to be in response to an incident identified by the monitoring party, such as royalties not being paid. These audits tend to yield higher returns to the monitoring company as they are based on information indicating a known weakness in controls at the self-reporting company. However, reactive audits are often started too late to provide adequate benefit or recoveries to the monitoring party. This is the scenario where settling for pennies on the dollar often kicks in.

Conversely, a proactive monitoring program initiates an audit before there is a concern or substantial risks are identified. Such a program starts an audit as part of normal business operations. While the findings may be lower than a reactionary audit, the recoveries are often higher because these identify concerns earlier in the business relationship, thereby allowing for a more timely and equitable solution as the reporting party is not yet at a point of distress that caused the red-flag indicators to go off, thus causing a reactionary audit. Proactive monitoring programs also have the additional following benefits:

- The third party does not feel singled out if it is clearly identified that this is part of normal business operations of the monitoring party.
- Business relations are generally still positive so the self-reporting party is more likely to cooperate with the audit.
- Management is more likely to buy into the program as it is created at the start of the contracting process and is not an audit performed in a panic, requiring multiple inputs from various different organizational functions (i.e., legal, operations, business development, accounting, internal audit).
- The program can be budgeted and adequately planned for financial and human resource allocation. This is a structured approach to the monitoring process.
- A well-designed program increases corporate governance, which in turn can help demonstrate to external auditors and other interested parties compliance with the Sarbanes-Oxley Act of 2002.
- Transparency is brought to the contract.
- It helps create stronger internal controls for both the monitoring company and the self-reporting company.
- It can be a tool for identifying potential contract weaknesses before they become a problem.
- It allows for the gathering of important intelligence of the self-reporting party.
- It facilitates ongoing positive communications.

Cost becomes a key consideration when determining the type of monitoring audit that will be performed. But with various options available from low to high cost, the cost should not prevent a monitoring program. These types of audit will be discussed in more detail in a following chapter; however, they are described here briefly:

- *Desktop*: This audit involves sending out a list of questions and document requests to the third party to provide certain information not normally provided in periodic statements required under the contract. This work is generally focused in one or two areas of concern and is performed remotely (not at the self-reporting party's offices). For example, if merchandise returns appear high for one reporting period on a royalty statement, a request may be made to the self-reporting third party to provide support for all returns during the month and the offsetting original sales documentation. This work can be done at a very low cost and often does not trigger the "right-to-audit" provision of the agreement so the periodic inspection rights are preserved if audits are limited to once in a certain period, such as annually.

- *Short*: A short audit is more of a "kick-the-tires" type of audit. Generally limited to one or two days, it focuses on low-hanging fruit or areas where errors are most likely to occur, such as in a royalty audit where you look for differences between the sales ledger and the royalty statements. The benefit of a short audit is that if a quick finding is made, the work scope can quickly be increased and a more extensive evaluation started. The downside of this approach is the lack of cooperation by the self-reporting party that was misinformed the engagement would be simple and the inevitable delays and inefficiencies caused by the self-reporting party not being prepared for a more intense audit in addition to the missed findings from a more detailed audit. The upside of this approach over the desktop review is that if the findings exceed the cost recovery provision of an agreement that has properly included them, then the cost of the audit may be recoverable.

- *Extensive*: An extensive evaluation of the self-reporting entity is a full-blown project. This can be inexpensive (relatively speaking) ranging from less than $10,000 to $150,000 in 2008 dollars. The range is based on numerous factors such as skills of the auditor, complexity of the contract, number of transactions, cooperation of the self-reporting company, accuracy of information, number of contract violations, value of the violations, location of records, availability of the records including soft versus hard copy, and numerous other factors. These projects allow the auditor to make an intensive review of compliance and often results in the highest findings. The general rule of thumb to be followed for this type of work falls under the concept of "return on investment" or ROI. Additional costs are spent on the project provided the recoverable findings exceed the costs. Key is the word "recoverable" because often findings are not recovered so the costs will be too great for the return. Findings generally are not recoverable when:
  - Management takes a decision not to seek recovery.
  - The findings are not strongly supported by the agreement due to its ambiguous or missing terms and conditions. *This is often the result of the poorly written contract—an issue that is a basis for this book.*
  - The third party refuses to make good on the findings, and the monitoring party determines the costs to recovery these findings are too great in terms of financial costs or business relationship costs.

- *Litigation*: Audits performed for parties that are in litigation or in a serious dispute are often costly and can be extremely time consuming. For example, as of the time of the writing of this book, I am involved as the royalty auditor for a licensor/licensee dispute involving findings that could total well above $20 million. The dispute is in mediation. The two parties constantly refuse to cooperate, and significant motions are being written to compel the audit and have documents submitted in a suitable format. This audit is costing over $100,000 and has been ongoing for more than three years. The litigation attorneys are making the most of fighting over this audit and enjoying substantial fees for their services. Many of the arguments and wasted time of the litigators could have been minimized if the original contract was much better written and if the counsel had been trained in the purpose of an audit and the extent of what an auditor typical does to test reported information. Had this audit been performed by parties not in litigation, the savings could have been perhaps 70 percent, and the time period for the work shrunk from years to months.

1.3.5. Phase 5: Exit Strategy

While the business strategy for starting a relationship is often well discussed, though not necessarily well planned, the exit strategy for ending the self-reporting relationship through a smooth transition is often overlooked.

The most troublesome agreement for a licensor that I have audited was an Evergreen license that was poorly written in many aspects including, not the least, its failure to expire. While this pharmaceutical agreement with a 10 percent royalty on net sales was small at first, the licensee's sales eventually grew to over $20 billion dollars. Needless to say, the two parties have been battling for years in high publicity litigations over multiple contentious issues. Of course, the licensor has tried desperately to take the license back to no avail as it has lost these many billions of dollars of sales and profits.

Many other agreements simply have automatic multiple-year renewal options that merely favor the licensee (the self-reporting party). These automatic renewals that go on for ten plus years are common in the apparel industry, and in my opinion, should be avoided as they do not allow for the modification of agreements to match the changing business needs of our fast-moving economy.

For the pharmaceutical licensor client involved in litigation, it obviously had a great dislike for the licensee, but because the exit strategy was not well planned, it could not sever the relationship with the licensee and seek a better business partner or bring the medication in-house. Needless to say, royalty audits and other monitoring activity of the licensee was greatly interrupted if not completely confounded because every attempt for discovery dragged for months while the sides argued in mediation on immaterial aspects of dispute that seemed only to prolong the pain of the licensor and the licensee.

The lesson learned is that leaving the exit strategy to chance or simple termination of the agreement (without consideration to items such as sell-off periods, IP technology destruction) often leads to grey market activity, expensive and time consuming disputes, irreconcilable differences, lost time, and futile attempts to reconstruct the meaning of the exit strategy of the original contract drafters who generally are not longer employed by any of the parties.

Successful exit strategies are negotiated when the contract is written. Identification of separation points that benefit both parties should be considered with a drop-dead date for ultimate termination.

In conclusion, too many contracts only have a termination clause that does not allow the contracting parties to consider changes in market conditions. This, in turn, leads to protracted litigation as the parties fight over termination.

1.3.6. Looking to the Future

Those who write the contracts generally do not understand the basic management aspects of the agreement nor do they understand the financial risks of misreporting caused by the third party's weak internal controls and lack of incentive to properly report. This leads to the inevitable lost revenues and higher costs. A contract that provides adequate control over the self-reporting relationship is the key to maximizing revenue, minimizing costs, and avoiding litigation when the all-too-common disputes occur. A company loses control of basic operating revenues and costs under any contract that relies on a third party to honestly self-report information, and this loss of control is generally not understood by the contracting parties.

Companies are constantly under strict pressure to improve internal controls. Civil and criminal penalties are the potential future relief for stockholders and investors who have lost capital due to management that has not met its due diligence governance obligations. The United States has codified penalties in the Sarbanes-Oxley Act of 2002 for companies that are regulated by the Securities and Exchange Commission. Talk abounds that similar Sarbanes-Oxley controls will be pushed onto nonpublic companies. Smart financial statement auditors are coming to realize that material errors can occur for some companies that rely on third-party reporting, so adequate governance through a properly constructed contract is critical. Lessons learned from Sarbanes-Oxley continue to spread around the globe, making it imperative that all parties to the contract strictly follow plain and clear financial terms and conditions. Likewise, the contracts must clearly state the penalties of noncompliance with certain provisions so that management can calculate the risk of noncompliance. Just stating that the contract will be terminated in case of a minor violation is neither practical nor realistic and impedes proper risk management over the contract. With the global economy comes increased risk for misunderstanding and misreporting. Ethics vary from region to region. Increased risks need to be addressed in contracts so that boilerplate terms and conditions are becoming less useful, especially as less-developed entities attempt to comply with antiquated accounting computer systems that do not allow compliance with a contract's reporting terms and conditions. The writers of contracts generally fail to understand these reporting limitations of the self-reporting policy so they do not adjust the financial reporting terms to meet the compliance constants of the self-reporting party.

When drafting reporting requires for a self-reporting party, consideration must be given to that party's internal controls. While ideally you would like the self-reporting party to at least have the same internal controls of your own organization, this is often impractical to monitor and measure. Therefore, a risk-based approach must be taken to writing the compliance terms on the self-reporting party.

As a company plans for its future, it must first inventory all of its self-reporting relationships and assess the company's risk tolerance for reporting errors. There are many different factors that must be considered in determining risks of self-reporting, but generally, chief among these is economic loss. If the risks are high, then management must examine how it is controlling those risks through properly structured contracts, internal monitoring, audits, and its litigation threshold. Managing high-risk self-reporting arrangement is a key operational component that many companies overlook as they are too busy running internal operations. The good transactional attorney is aware of management's lack of focus on third-party monitoring so he works to help identify the tools that management needs and then includes them in the contract, taking into consideration the self-reporting entity's capabilities. The good litigation attorney is aware of a self-reporting contract's weaknesses and strengths and knows how to use an auditor during discovery to maximize value for the client.

Why You Need to Monitor Self-Reporting Contractees

2.1. Effective Licensee Monitoring—A Summary   16

    2.1.1. Calculating Royalties on the Disposition of All Licensed Product(s)   16

    2.1.2. Maintenance Procedures for Licensee's Internal Records   18

    2.1.3. Information to be Provided in Royalty Statements   18

    2.1.4. Establishing a License Monitoring Program   19

    2.1.5. Royalty Audits   20

    2.1.6. Periodic Reports   21

    2.1.7. Effective Licensee Monitoring   22

2.2. Intellectual Property Compliance Around the World   23

2.3. Digital Content: A Burgeoning Global Royalty Market   23

2.4. Emerging Regional Trends   24

    2.4.1. Asia   24

    2.4.2. North America   25

    2.4.3. Europe—Middle East—Africa   26

2.5. Sarbanes-Oxley Act of 2002 and Third-Party Monitoring   27

    2.5.1. SOX Section 302: Internal Control Certifications   31

    2.5.2. SOX Section 404: Assessment of Internal Control   32

    2.5.3. SOX Section 802: Criminal Penalties for Violation of SOX   34

2.1. Effective Licensee Monitoring—A Summary

While there are many types of self-reporting arrangements, the monitoring of royalty paying licensees is perhaps the leading area where abuses are found. With well over $100 billion dollars of royalties paid annually, the value of underreported royalties could easily top more than $10 billion. This section will summarize what is included in much more detail in this book that is related to the effective monitoring of licensees.

Both novice and seasoned licensors make the same critical mistake of not adequately instructing the licensee how to calculate the royalty and preserve supporting records. The emphasis to close the deal and rely on the honesty of the self-reporting licensee to report royalties properly and to maintain documents usually costs the licensor significant income. Experience shows that the typical licensee underreports revenues sufficient to trigger the cost recovery provision of the licensee agreement. Licensees with better record keeping and royalty accounting practices make more accurate and higher royalty payments, reducing the need for royalty audits and the inevitable negotiations to recover underpaid royalties and audit costs. Prior to executing a license agreement, the following questions should be considered:

- How will I make certain the licensee understands her responsibility to self-report the royalty income properly?
- How will I be comfortable that the licensee has complied with the license agreement?

There are four important royalty reporting items to be communicated to the licensee prior to executing a license agreement:

- Method of calculating royalties on the disposition of all licensed product(s)
- The licensee's responsibility to maintain internal records that support the creation and disposition of licensed product(s) (i.e., inventory and sales records)
- Information to be provided in royalty statements
- Information to be provided in periodic reports regarding the status of the licensee's operations

2.1.1. Calculating Royalties on the Disposition of All Licensed Product(s)

Authors of license agreements generally do not have financial experience and are, therefore, unable to properly identify the very specific financial records that should be considered for retention. They are also unable to contemplate how a licensee might interpret seemingly simple royalty calculations in various ways that inevitably lead to underreported royalties. For example, many licensees consider gross revenues to be calculated after discounts, returns, and taxes, while they actually should be an accounting consideration before any deductions. Therefore, many licensees underreport revenues when these deductions are not limited. Seasoned intellectual property attorneys may also miss the detail required in the license agreement that instructs both the licensee's entry-level accounting clerk as well as management on how exactly to calculate the royalty for all licensed product dispositions. Most license agreements tend only to address the payment of royalties from net sales, generally defined as the gross of invoiced sales minus certain deductions and any product returns. Also, these agreements do not often cover other nonsale dispositions of licensed property such as free goods, missing goods, and intellectual property used internally by the licensee for things like research and development or personal consumption.

A well-written agreement must cover all potential uses of licensed products and define restrictions on each prospective disposition and its associated royalty, if any, to be paid to the licensor. Consider the seemingly simple area of free goods. Many agreements are either silent on the topic or when limits are placed on them, the term free good is not defined. The lack of both of these limits and a definition of free goods commonly results in licensees providing the free goods to a customer in exchange for promised higher purchases of nonlicensed goods or other favors that result in reduced royalty payments.

The following are commonly missed instructions to licensees for calculating royalties:

- Unaccounted for, free, internally used, and other property dispositions not included in sales shall bear a royalty based on the highest net selling price for the licensed property.
- Consideration should be given to not allowing free goods (unless there are strong restrictions).
- Licensed products are not to be sold bundled with nonlicensed ones. If they are, the total bundled selling price shall be fully allocated to the licensed product.
- The gross sales price shall be the invoiced price before any deductions.
- Product returns shall not be subtracted from gross revenues or shall be limited to a small percentage of gross revenues.
- A licensed subcomponent shall have the royalty paid that is based on the sales price of the total working end product.
- All deductions must be specifically defined by the agreement. For example, taxes must be specifically listed on the invoice and identified by category, e.g., value added or sales, etc. Further, refunds or offsets of

value-added taxes (common in most countries but rarely acknowledged by licensees) must be offset against deductions.

A leading practice is to have the licensor's royalty auditor review the license agreement prior to signing to identify loopholes that may allow the licensee to miscalculate the royalty.

2.1.2. Maintenance Procedures for Licensee's Internal Records

Licensees rarely maintain the proper records to support their royalty calculations. Usually the licensee's internal record retention requirements do not consider the needs of the licensor or auditor. Even when records are required to be maintained by the license agreement, there is rarely a penalty should the licensee not retain the records. In the initial license agreement and annually thereafter, consideration should be given to reminding the licensee in writing of its obligation to maintain financial records to support the royalty statements.

If records are not retained, the licensor should give consideration to requiring that the licensee pay liquidated damages, generally defined with a minimum and maximum range, e.g., between 20 percent and 100 percent of the royalties owed. And such liquidated damages should be considered to be further defined as not less than a specific dollar amount or at the minimum guarantee. In the end, the lowest amount is usually claimed.

2.1.3. Information to be Provided in Royalty Statements

Licensees tend to provide minimal information in royalty statements. From their perspective, the more information provided to the licensor, the more opportunity the licensor has to identify potential underreporting. The initial license agreement should also consider inclusion of an appendix with the royalty statement the licensee must complete and the information to be provided in periodic reports. The licensor should consider constantly monitoring of the licensee's operations to identify red flags of concern that could diminish the value of the licensed property. A customized, signed checklist should be submitted with each royalty statement that provides the licensor with an update of the licensee's operations. Certain responses provided by the licensee may trigger a detailed assessment of the licensee's contract compliance.

In a royalty statement, the licensee should provide the following information as a minimum requirement:

- Signed certification by a company executive that the statement is in compliance with the licensee agreement

- Gross sales by licensed product and territory if international sales are involved
- Deductions by licensed product (each deduction should be separately listed)
- Returns by licensed product
- Net sales by licensed product
- Royalty to be paid based on net sales and exchange rates (including their country source)

In addition, royalty statements should consider covering the movement of the licensed property, including the gross number of units sold, the gross number of units returned, the gross number of free units, and the gross number of other unit dispositions.

2.1.4. Establishing a License Monitoring Program

A licensor must establish a licensee monitoring program to assess on a continual basis if the licensee is properly self-reporting royalties and complying with other key contract terms and conditions. With many organizations in the United States, now following Sarbanes-Oxley 404, the need to have a licensee monitoring program is more critical than ever.

Licensors have relied far too heavily on their licensees' own ability to provide accurate self-reporting or to adhere with various other contract provisions. In relinquishing contract oversight to the licensee, licensors fail to see that licensees have been reducing the number of staff responsible for overseeing license compliance or have been giving this responsibility to less experienced workers. More troubling, as awareness of staff cutbacks spreads, so does the risk rise that licensees will purposely underreport royalties, knowing the chances of getting caught are low. Licensors are generally not monitoring licensee operational changes. Cutting internal monitoring capabilities may prove especially risky in situations where licensees have international operations, and the licensor lacks the resources to monitor worldwide sales. It is important to understand that underreporting royalties appears to be more of the norm than the exception. An overwhelming majority of royalty compliance projects result in tangible recoveries. This often results in a no-cost project to the licensor if the license agreement has a cost recovery provision (for example, passing on the cost to the licensee should the underreporting in any one period exceed the lesser of 3 percent of reported royalties or $5,000).

Due to the complex nature of licensing contracts and the prevailing reliance on licensees to report and pay royalties accurately without substantiating backup documentation, the only way licensors can assess that royalties are correct and can ensure contract compliance is to establish a proactive licensee compliance program. Because the potential additional revenue from uncovering underreported royalties and license fees is greater than program costs, leading companies implement a systematic program with three major goals: (1) increase licensee awareness of their obligations, (2) assess licensee compliance with their obligations, and (3) inform the licensee of leading practices.

These three goals are accomplished by two methods: internal monitoring and external monitoring through royalty audits. Internal monitoring is generally very limited in scope and relies on an analytical review of the royalty statements that search for predetermined risk warning red flags that indicate licensee underreporting of royalties. Usually a red flag warning will dictate the need for a royalty audit.

2.1.5. Royalty Audits

Royalty audits can be an effective deterrent to licensee abuses, and those conducting the audits can perform several important roles: they can help to preserve, and even enhance, the licensor/licensee relationship; they know how to secure the greatest recoveries at the lowest cost; they provide valuable insights and advice on how to reduce future contract violations; and they often discover underreported royalties that are many times greater than that of auditors lacking this particular expertise.

Take the case of a leading company that initially assigned its internal audit team to perform three biannual audits of its licensees. The work findings from the internal auditors yielded about $20,000. After hiring highly experienced external advisers to conduct the next biannual royalty compliance project, the findings ranged from approximately US$200,000 to US$500,000 per licensee. In addition to recouping these funds, the process helped the licensee and licensor strengthen their internal controls and clarify their reporting requirements through rewritten license agreements. In another case, a university received US$15,000 in royalties from its licensee, but an external royalty compliance project completed in 2004 found more than US$23 million more was due. The university requested the audit, thinking they had been underpaid around $50,000. In this case, the licensee had sublicensed the technology's intellectual property to a third party for a flat fee of $75 million that appeared as a line item in the general ledger as "other revenue" and was never entered into the sales journal, so the sale was never on an invoice. The agreement called for royalties to be based on "invoiced sales" so the licensee had attempted to work around this royalty obligation. A royalty auditor, merely following the agreement and looking at the sales journal and invoices, as described in the narrowly focused agreement, would never had found this finding.

The importance of the royalty auditor's background and approach cannot be overemphasized. Ambiguous contracts are subject to varying degrees of interpretation, and underreported royalties are often so well-hidden that only a very experienced royalty auditor can find the funds and successfully present the claim. Even the most sophisticated companies may underreport royalty income as a result of contract ambiguities or the efforts of inexperienced or overzealous personnel to meet predetermined operating goals. While the auditor does not interpret the agreement, they can point out weakness in language for licensor/licensee discussion along with opportunities for contract amendments and rewrites to improve the internal control environment and relationship.

A dedicated royalty auditor will be alert to these and other problems and will look beyond collections and revenue recovery issues to identify reporting problems. The auditor also can help put controls in place on both the licensor and the licensee that address the root causes of the reporting issues without damaging or undermining valuable business relationships. Unfortunately, too many licensors fear upsetting the relationship and therefore do not execute their rights to audit. This is a real risk if using a nondedicated auditor to perform the royalty audit. Financial statement and internal auditors may not understand the business relationships that go beyond and often exceed the importance of monetary findings. There are several important steps to consider when developing strategies to monitor intellectual property. The first step is to identify which licensees present the highest risk based on their internal monitoring capabilities and then, if necessary, conduct a royalty audit. But it is equally important for the royalty auditor to review:

- Processes and controls to offer improvement ideas to both licensees and licensor
- Existing agreements to ensure compliance and reporting requirements
- Agreement structures to reduce underpayments by licensees
- Contract-administration processes to benchmark against best-in-class standards

2.1.6. Periodic Reports

Licensees should be required to report periodically in addition to the royalty statement, yet the requirement for periodic reports is almost never found in license agreements. Periodic reports are essential for a licensor to monitor the self-reporting licensee. A periodic report (for example, returned quarterly with the royalty statement) might include the following questions:

- Have there been any changes to the following since the last royalty statement: personnel completing the royalty statement calculation, accounting systems, and/or new or discontinued licensed products?
- Have you begun selling in any new territories?

- Has the company declared bankruptcy, or is it in financial difficulty?
- Have there been any reorganizations related to personnel who calculate the royalty?
- Have there been any layoffs?
- Have you changed the way you calculate the royalty?
- Are you in the process of, or will you be merging with another company in the near future?
- Have you identified any areas of potential noncompliance with the agreement?

2.1.7. Effective Licensee Monitoring

Businesses that include proper contract language instructing a licensee on how to calculate a royalty; on the specific documents to retain; and, in addition, have a proactive licensee monitoring program are best positioned to achieve higher royalty revenues at reduced monitoring costs without damaging business relationships. Specific records a licensor should suggest the licensee consider as required for retention might include:

Inventory-related records:

- Annual year-end inventory records
- Annual inventory roll forwards for each licensed product or product category
- Inventory count records
- Purchasing records
- Free goods shipped from inventory, including the names of the recipients
- Catalogues
- All records of disposals other than sales

Sales ledger records:

- Gross sales
- Deductions
- Original invoices

Financial records:

- Annual audited financial statements
- General ledger
- Calculation of royalties

2.2. Intellectual Property Compliance Around the World

Significant new royalty contract opportunities have emerged in Asia, South America, and Eastern Europe with the expanding global economy, and in sync, underreported royalty revenues from nondomestic licensees are rising at a dramatic rate. As a result, there is a resulting trend toward a potential substantial loss of income to licensors based on royalty compliance inspections performed by its member firms.

The causes for the rapid rise in underreported royalties are broad in scope, ranging from legitimate business-process constraints emanating from sometimes overly complex global contracts to weaker controls and intellectual property laws in expanding international economies.

Regardless of the causes of the underreporting, economic losses abound from the flourishing black-and-grey market distribution channels. What's more, licensee monitoring has grown increasingly difficult as businesses become more dispersed and as products can be sold in unmonitored global markets.

E-mails and phone calls to overseas licensees can often go unanswered, and sales figures from retailers may not be reliable or even obtainable from many regions. With significant licensee operations in hard-to-reach manufacturing locales throughout many regions that are notorious for black-and-grey-market activities, contract compliance professionals may be challenged more than ever to perform under the "right-to-audit" provisions included in many license agreements.

2.3. Digital Content: A Burgeoning Global Royalty Market

As royalties from digital content have helped to enrich many media companies for several years, contract compliance professionals are being deployed globally and more frequently to assess royalty payments from digitally distributed intellectual property, such as video games, ring-tones, wallpapers, video clips, full-length music tracks, and similar media. Monitoring royalties related to digital content presents its own unique challenges.

Some licensees may be so concerned with being "first-to-market" or with the quantity of goods distributed that they can neglect creating effective accounting systems to properly capture complete downloads and allocate royalties appropriately. Recovering lost royalties from licensees—sometimes in excess of 20 percent of reported royalties, in the author's experience—requires specially trained contract compliance professionals.

Licensees underreport digital media distributions and royalties for a number of reasons. These issues are often overlooked by accountants without proper intellectual property royalty auditing training. Licensees can frequently use third parties to distribute digital content. These third parties may not be subject to the right-to-audit provisions listed in contracts between licensees and licensors. It may also be unclear as to whether the licensee or the third-party distributor has the responsibility to pay royalties to the licensor.

Licensors do not or cannot process the metadata provided by licensees to describe key aspects of their digital content. Metadata accuracy affects the licensors' own ability to pay royalties to their content-creator partners (i.e., recording artists, song writers, game developers, etc.).

A licensee's self-reported royalty documentation may include only summaries of digital content sold, creating difficulty in retaining sufficient detailed delivery and revenue information to support royalty payments to licensors. Royalty payments to licensors may be calculated on the basis of assumptions. Licensors and/or third parties may inappropriately exclude unidentified revenue from royalty payments to licensors. Digital media licensing agreements may not appropriately address items such as undelivered content, free samples, and product bundles. Licensing agreements may restrict distribution of digital content to certain regions or localities. Tracking compliance with these restrictions can be complex.

2.4. Emerging Regional Trends

Digital content royalties is just one area of concern for consumer product licensors. Global companies are facing a number of emerging regional challenges in monitoring their licensees.

2.4.1. Asia

Typically, for reasons ranging from the extent to which agreements work bilaterally to tradition, Asian licensees have been reluctant to allow licensors to examine their financial records through trained professionals. Such reluctance exists despite requirements or incentives for an examination and a specific obligation in their contract. Identification by licensors of significant incidences of noncompliance or large financial consequences does not encourage field examinations in many instances.

In some cases, licensees have imposed conditions on license or royalty compliance examinations, such as restricting the records that may be accessed; limiting the time allocated to conduct fieldwork; and requiring examination of records in cities other than where the documents are normally prepared and maintained, thereby denying access to the staff that had prepared the source documents.

In Asia, royalty compliance examinations have been seen as something that U.S. and European companies are likely to perform for Asian companies. But the author has seen instances where Asian companies are examining other Asian companies. Indeed, some Asian licensors have sought to examine European- and U.S.-based licensees.

In Japan where many companies have both licensors and licensees, some have been willing to respect their agreement to be subject to a royalty compliance examination despite concerns that such an exam would border on mistrust. More and more, Japanese companies are requiring that compliance be tested, with litigation and arbitration to follow, if necessary. South Korean companies are also moving in this direction.

Some companies have advised their licensees that royalty compliance exams will be performed and that noncooperation will bring consequences. This approach may work where a licensee needs the licensor more than the other way around. However, Stonefield Josephson considers the tactic extreme and ill-advised in Asia.

A number of licensors are working to change these attitudes. Many have sought to educate the licensee that good corporate governance simply doesn't allow them to assume an "honesty system" will work, much in the same way that many companies typically require contracts before entering into transactions or demand letters of credit before shipping goods to customers. They have explained the need to take some measure to verify compliance. In other words "trust, but verify."

Unfortunately, in a large number of cases, licensors' concerns about compliance in Asia have some basis, with the identification of large sums undeclared. Examinations can be conducted successfully within Asia without unduly straining the relationship, especially if the program is managed carefully by both the licensor and the experienced contract compliance professional who performs the royalty compliance examination.

2.4.2. North America

The breadth and scale of self-reporting programs placed in operation by licensors has had a favorable impact on the quality and accuracy of self-reporting to those licensors. In the absence of such proactive monitoring programs in North America, the author's first-time royalty audits commonly identify underreported royalties in excess of 20 percent and occasionally, underreported royalties in excess of 100 percent.

The reasons for underreporting may be centered on aggressive contract interpretation, poorly written contracts that lack penalties to encourage proper and timely payments, royalty statements prepared by untrained employees, and a lack of licensee focus on their need to accurately self-report revenues and resulting royalties.

Licensors tend to see an immediate impact when they place a broad monitoring program into operation, with a positive "coattail" impact even on those licensees that are not included in the initial wave of examinations, as word spreads quickly among licensees that the licensor has enacted a royalty compliance program.

When starting a proactive royalty compliance program, it is important that the licensor communicates to all licensees the intent and scope of the program so as to maintain relationships and so the program is perceived as thorough, impartial, and fair.

Generally speaking, North America licensors can fall into three primary groups:

1. Companies that proactively conduct ongoing royalty compliance examinations as part of normal business operations and that budget for recoveries over costs each year
2. Companies that are reactive, conducting fewer than a handful of royalty compliance examinations and only after a determining that the licensee is underreporting
3. Companies that don't monitor licensees through royalty compliance examinations

Extreme care should be taken to help ensure the royalty compliance professionals selected are specifically trained in third-party royalty auditing as licensors rarely have more than one chance to examine the records of the licensee, and the resulting recoveries resulting from the skills of different auditors can be remarkably different. When companies select royalty auditors, this cost can be offset by an agreement's cost recovery provision. Such provisions are trending toward cost recovery at underreporting the lesser of 5 percent or $10,000 in any one reporting period. Some provisions have replaced 5 percent with 3 percent, and the most common mistake is to have cost recovery based on the entire period reviewed, as opposed to any one reporting statement.

Additionally, companies with material revenues from self-reporting third-party licensees may now be required to enact royalty compliance programs to meet Sarbanes-Oxley Act requirements.

2.4.3. Europe—Middle East—Africa

While many licensees are based in Western Europe and North America, their factory operations increasingly have shifted to Eastern Europe in search of lower labor costs and other financial incentives. As this manufacturing shift occurs, the author has found that professionals unfamiliar with traditional Western accounting internal controls and reporting are preparing royalty reports that almost always fail to properly account for manufactured licensed product, sales, and resultant royalties. Most often, experience shows that these misstatements appear to be an honest misreading of complex foreign language contracts. Many times the errors are by individuals who have never seen a copy of the agreement and, therefore, are generally unaware of the unique restrictions that can affect the royalty due to the licensor, i.e., on returns, minimum selling prices, related party sales, shrinkage, calculation of gross revenues, and price protection, etc.

Securing records from licensees in a reviewable format can be difficult in Eastern Europe, as the local practices and accounting rules can affect how information is captured, retained, and presented.

Therefore, using a local royalty contract compliance professional skilled in local language, accounting practices, customs, tax laws, record retention requirements, and industry practices is recommended for a successful royalty compliance examination in Eastern Europe.

In the European Union, licensors may have to exercise their "rights of audit" to protect their intellectual property (IP) in countries that may not have a long tradition of proper IP protection. But royalty compliance examinations are not the only tool, especially in Eastern Europe. Licensors may wish to consider a broader strategy to protect IP by lobbying government officials to protect the rights of consumer product licensors. This is particularly important in regions where counterfeiting is a significant source of local employment.

Globalization has opened up many new markets for licensors. However, weak contracts not properly addressing collection penalties and right-to-audit needs, cultural differences and language barriers, and misunderstandings of regulations have made the efficient collection of royalties from licensees a challenge in many ways.

2.5. Sarbanes-Oxley Act of 2002 and Third-Party Monitoring

The Public Company Accounting Reform and Investor Protection Act of 2002 (aka Sarbanes-Oxley Act of 2002) ("SOX") was federal legislation enacted to protect against corporate accounting malfeasance after the Enron fiasco and the collapse of the Big 5 accounting firm, Arthur Andersen. SOX established and strengthened standards for United States public companies with an emphasis on the responsibilities of executive management, boards, and their independent accountants. SOX does not apply to private companies.

There are eleven sections within SOX, including such areas as enhanced corporate board responsibilities, sign-off requirements for executive management, independent accountant testing (known as SOX 404), internal control risk assessment, auditor independence, improved financial disclosures, and criminal penalties.

The Public Company Accounting Oversight Board ("PCAOB"), or lovingly called "Pe-ca-boo," is a government agency established to oversee accounting firms performing work as independent auditors over public companies.

There are two basic guidelines under the Securities and Exchange Commissions interpretive guidance:

- "Management's evaluation of evidence about the operation of its controls should be based on its assessment of risk"
- "Management should evaluate whether it has implemented controls that adequately address the risk that a material misstatement of the financial statements would not be prevented or detected in a timely manner"

When drafting a contract, lawyers must be aware of the self-reporting requirements that will allow all parties to comply with SOX. Considerations to be made are:

- Are controls within the agreement adequate to address the risk of material misstatement of either party's financial statements? Typical points where internal controls may fail in the self-reporting environment, thereby causing a material misstatement are:
  - Management override.
  - Complexity of agreements. [Personally, as a royalty auditor, I like complex agreements as the more complex, the more likely I will make monetary findings for my client, and I will need to be hired to help investigate the contract's compliance.]
  - Subjective judgment due to poorly written or ambiguous terms and conditions.
  - Changes in key personnel.
  - Change in information technology.
  - Mergers/acquisitions/restructuring.
  - Reliance on subcontractors or other entities. [As information is processed through each layer, there is an increased chance for errors. Information from subcontracts is received, processed, and regurgitated in new formats, and the input controls need to work with the output controls so what goes in is the same as what goes out, perhaps just in a different category. This is important for both transactional and litigation attorneys to understand.]
- Is the agreement flexible enough to allow for monitoring controls to be adjusted throughout the agreement's life?

- Is there an understanding of what "material" errors may occur (material to the financial statements of the contracting entities, as opposed to the agreement itself)? Material means the financial error is so large that it would affect the decision of the reviewer.
- Is monitoring adequate to identify materiality incorrect or fraudulent reports? Considerations to be made related to fraudulent reporting are:
  - ◌ Self-reporting entities locations and number of business units involved in the process where the self-reporting errors may occur.
  - ◌ Has the self-reporting entity established a central point of control for the reports, and does that central point of control review information provided by other units of the organization or just consolidate the information? My experience has been that most licensees that consolidate information from various related entities generally do not examine the information for reasonableness. This consolidation is often done by a low level clerk without review.
  - ◌ Has the management of the party receiving the information, such as the licensor, considered the risk factors of each individual self-reporting party as opposed to a generic assessment for all contracts? Boilerplate agreements that do not address individual risks of each self-reporting entity are likely to have issues.
  - ◌ Is there an understanding of the internal controls at the self-reporting party that might fail? Has the risk of the failure been identified/ classified (low, medium, high)? Are back-ups built into the agreement to monitor these risks? Such risks might be unreported sales; however, by also monitoring inventory production and inventory physical count levels, missing inventory and unreported sales might be identified.
  - ◌ Is the monitoring increased for high-risk, self-reporting contracts and decreased for low-risk self-reporting contracts?
- Is there a right-to-audit provision?
- Will executive management certifying compliance with SOX have adequate information to make an informed decision?
- Are the self-reporting party's internal controls adequate to properly report on critical information? This includes the self-reporting third party's management, monitoring, information technology environment, complexity of the agreement, internal control environment, country/accounting rules, change controls, and reporting history, amongst other items.

There are three sections of SOX that lawyers s need to be especially aware of when drafting self-reporting contracts that may reach a level of financial materiality (affects more than 5 percent of a company's sales or assets is generally considered a safe point for materiality consideration, given that 10 percent is often the financial materiality target).

SOX is important for both parties to the contract if the agreement is of a material nature. The receiver of the information must make certain that they are receiving adequate information from the self-reporting third party to properly disclose any future lost revenues or unexpected future costs that could affect the stability or viability of the company receiving the information. This information may need to be disclosed as notes to the company's financial statements or may affect balance sheet items, such as the value of assets or liabilities. For example, if a public company licensor is receiving 20 percent of its revenue from a licensee and that licensee has just had an event that could affect the licensee as a going concern (aka bankruptcy, fire, strike, government seizure), then there must be adequate monitoring in place to make certain the licensor is notified in a timely manner that this revenue stream could be lost so a proper disclosure can be made.

As a real-life example, one of the largest licensee manufacturers of TVs and DVDs in Eastern Europe had a suspicious fire that destroyed their tremendously large factory. Eight months after the fire and after two royalty reports had not been received (along with millions of dollars of expected royalty payments), the publicly held licensor decided to get tough with the licensee and ordered me to conduct a contract compliance audit. Not till I arrived at the corporate headquarters was there a disclosure of the fire and the licensor had come to learn this materiality important revenue stream had been lost. By time the disclosure was made to the public, nearly a year had passed. Under SOX, this could place the executive management of the licensor at risk for criminal penalty.

Likewise, the self-reporting public company must have a contract that is clear of its obligations under the agreement. Taking a look at SOX from a licensee's perspective, it must clearly understand its financial reporting obligations and have adequate internal controls in place to make certain the royalty liability is recognized and paid in a timely manner.

As stated throughout this book, licensees commonly underreport by more than 10 percent and often more than 100 percent. Therefore, if a public company licensee has underreported a 10 percent royalty obligation by more than 100 percent there is a chance this unreported liability can be material to the financial records of the licensee. Financial statement auditors are generally oblivious to this unrecorded material liability as they don't understand licensing agreements and are not skilled in royalty auditing. Financial auditors generally just take the word of the licensee that there is no underreporting. It is not until a royalty audit is conducted that a disclosure is made of the material liability to the licensor.

[Quick lesson for the litigator representing a licensor: often a licensee will state their independent financial statement auditor has reviewed the license agreement and the payments, statements and everything else is correct as the information has been audited. Don't believe the payments are correct! Remember, independent auditors are concerned with "material" correctness based on the licensee's financial records. That means usually, if the numbers are 90 percent accurate, that is sufficient. So if any one number in the financial statements can be off 10 percent, then chances are, the royalty payments are not so material that an auditor would even look at them as they represent less than 10 percent of the company's expenses. Further, the fresh-out-of-college auditor conducting the financial statement audit will most likely not have the experience to read contracts to determine compliance.]

Here is another real life example. I was hired by a public company licensee that had just been audited by one of the four major music labels. I was to be an expert witness in the licensee's defense. The music label's auditors had made a claim for millions of dollars that were material to the licensee. The licensee had not been interpreting the license agreement in the same manner as the music label. The brunt of the claim came from the licensee's lack of record keeping and reporting as required by the license agreement. Because of the lack of record keeping, a very large monetary claim was made for the periods of missing financial/sales records. Had the licensee been properly maintaining its internal controls over proper financial record keeping, had the agreement more clearly identify the records the licensee was obligated to maintain, and had the licensor done a better job to make certain the licensee was reporting quarterly, a major lawsuit could have been avoided. The licensee had to disclosure this lawsuit and the potential liability in its financial notes; however, one could argue that the liability from many years earlier should have been disclosed much sooner and should, therefore, have resulted in an adjustment to the prior year financial statements to reflect the liability. Restatement of financial statements almost always lead to SEC or PCAOB investigations and, under SOX, could lead to criminal prosecution. Further, because the licensee failed to maintain records for one music label, word quickly spread of the first music label's findings and shortly thereafter, the other major music labels were auditing the licensee. This placed a significant burden on the licensee's management and forced the licensee out of the music distribution industry. Because multiple claims were being made against the licensee, all licensors had to settle for less money than had just one licensor conducted an audit. If the licensor had adequate internal controls in place, including a well-worded license agreement and proper monitoring, then the audit would not have been required or the findings would have been substantially less, and the licensor would have received more money from the licensee, along with avoiding the costs of litigation and sharing what money was available with other music labels who also made audit claims.

2.5.1. SOX Section 302: Internal Control Certifications

SOX Section 302 requires adequate internal controls to ensure materially correct financial disclosures. The ultimate responsibility for the accuracy and completeness of the financial disclosures rests with the signing officers, generally the chief financial officer and often the chief operating officer. By signing, these offices certify they are responsible for establishing and maintaining internal controls and have designed such internal controls to ensure that material information relating to the company and its consolidated subsidiaries is materially correct.

Prior to signing this certification, as further stated in the code, the signing officers need to have evaluated the effectiveness of the company's internal controls as of a date within 90 days prior to the report and have presented in the report their conclusions about the effectiveness of their internal controls based on their evaluation as of that date. Under Section 302, the focus is disclosure controls as opposed to financial reporting controls.

As the certifying officers do not have the capacity themselves to perform the tests to access if the controls are adequate, reliance is generally placed on accounting staff, internal auditors, or external consultant to report on the adequacy of the controls to management. As stated, these generalists generally are not trained to understand the reporting, monitoring, and liabilities associated with self-reporting relationships and often will pass on the agreements, if read at all, and inform management that the controls are adequate.

The external auditors will then review the certification by management, along with the supporting work papers and conduct tests of the support for accuracy. This higher level testing has a low likelihood of discovering additional system weaknesses. The external auditors will opine on if the internal controls over financial reporting are adequate to prevent a material misstatement of the financial statements and related disclosures, as discussed in more detail in the next section.

2.5.2. SOX Section 404: Assessment of Internal Control

SOX Section 404 requires management and the external auditor to report on the adequacy of the company's internal control over financial reporting ("ICFR"). Section 404, laughingly referred to as the full employment act for auditors, requires a report on internal controls to be included in the annual report to the Securities and Exchange Commission. According to the regulation, the report "contains an assessment, as of the end of the most recent fiscal year of the Company, of the effectiveness of the internal control structure and procedures of the issuer for financial reporting." The code further states that the report covers "the responsibility of management for establishing and maintaining an adequate internal control structure and procedures for financial reporting."

By adopting the internal control framework established by the Committee of Sponsoring Organizations of the Treadway Commission ("COSO"), management can help identify and monitor these risks. According to COSO's Web site (www.coso.org), they are "dedicated to guiding executive management and governance entities toward the establishment of more effective, efficient, and ethical business operations on a global basis." "COSO is recognized the world over for providing guidance on critical aspects of organizational governance, business ethics, internal control, enterprise risk management, fraud, and financial reporting."

An advanced self-reporting contract would require a self-reporting entity to follow the guidance of COSO, even it that self-reporting company is not a public entity. The underlying purpose of COSO is to help prevent fraudulent financial reporting.

COSO has issued various types of guidance to help a company improve internal controls over financial reporting that should reduce errors in financial reporting. While the guidance is geared toward public financial statements, the same internal controls used to produce more accurate financial statements can also be used to create more reliable royalty and other statements from the self-reporting party.

As with any financial control environment, the internal controls of the self-reporting party are constantly changing. Most frequently, these changes are in information systems or personnel. Either of these changes generally led to reporting errors. When a company selects a new accounting system, self-reporting requirements are almost never a consideration. As such, what we see in monitoring is that the new system is installed, and the third-party is no longer able to comply with its contractual requirements.

For example, an apparel licensee was using an accounting system called "AIMS." AIMS stands for "Accounting Information and Management System." This licensee was able to provide inventory count information. Midway through the contract, the licensee switched accounting systems and was no longer able to provide historical inventory level information, thereby making it nearly impossible to access the movement of the licensed intellectually property contained within the relevant inventory. Had this small licensee had adequate internal controls in place, including SOX testing or been following COSO guidance, then this contract violation of not being able to track inventory could have been identified before becoming a relationship issue between the licensor and licensee.

As recently as July 2007, the Public Company Accounting Oversight Board (PCAOB) updated SOX guidance by issuing Auditing Standard No. 5 for public accounting firms. This standard, that replaced the initial 2004 Auditing Standard No. 2, instructs management and external auditors to perform a top-down risk assessment as opposed to assessing all areas of potential financial risk regardless of materiality. By performing a top-down approach, management has wide discretion in the SOX compliance approach as the scope is now based on management's assessments of risks and evidence gathered during the examination.

A United States public company must now take into account PCAOB Auditing Standard No. 5 when examining self-reporting contract arrangements. Unfortunately, few have, as the financial statement auditors have historically not provided much guidance in this area due to naivety.

Auditing Standard No. 5 requires management to:

Assess both the design and operating effectiveness of selected internal controls related to significant accounts and relevant assertions, in the context of material misstatement risks;

Understand the flow of transactions, including IT aspects, sufficient enough to identify points at which a misstatement could arise;

Evaluate company-level (entity-level) controls, which correspond to the components of the COSO framework;

Perform a fraud risk assessment;

Evaluate controls designed to prevent or detect fraud, including management override of controls;

Evaluate controls over the period-end financial reporting process;

Scale the assessment based on the size and complexity of the company;

Rely on management's work based on factors such as competency, objectivity, and risk;

Conclude on the adequacy of internal control over financial reporting.

There are certain limitations for compliance of SOX requirements based on company assets. This compliance requirement is a moving target as smaller public companies constantly seek relief from SOX requirements due to the large financial compliance burden.

2.5.3. SOX Section 802: Criminal Penalties for Violation of SOX

Section 802(a) of SOX, 18 U.S.C. § 1519 states:

Whoever knowingly alters, destroys, mutilates, conceals, covers up, falsifies, or makes a false entry in any record, document, or tangible object with the intent to impede, obstruct, or influence the investigation or proper administration of any matter within the jurisdiction of any department or agency of the United States or any case filed under title 11, or in relation to or contemplation of any such matter or case, shall be fined under this title, imprisoned not more than 20 years, or both.

CHAPTER
3

Types of Self-Reporting Contracts and Reporting Risks

3.1. Advertising Agency Contracts   38

    3.1.1. Contract Description   38

    3.1.2. Key Terms and Conditions That Auditors Care About   39

    3.1.3. Reporting Areas and Associated Risks   42

    3.1.4. Documents to Consider Requesting in the Contract
         to Allow for Adequate External Monitoring   43

3.2. Construction Contracts   45

    3.2.1. Contract Description   45

    3.2.2. Key Terms and Conditions That Auditors Care About   48

    3.2.3. The Variable Cost Contract Monitoring Process   53

    3.2.4. When to Conduct Self-Monitoring and an Audit   58

    3.2.5. Key Documents That a Construction Company Should
         Be Contractually Required to Retain for Construcion
         Contract Monitoring and Why   59

3.3. Digital Distribution Contracts   60

    3.3.1. Contract Description   60

    3.3.2. Digital Distribution Self-Reporting Areas of Concern   64

    3.3.3. Summary of Digital Distribution Risks   67

    3.3.4. Some Areas to Monitor in Digital Distribution
         Agreements   67

3.4. Distribution and Reseller Contracts   69

    3.4.1. Contract Description   69

         3.4.1.1. Understanding a Channel   69

         3.4.1.2. Retailer to OEM Reporting   71

         3.4.1.3. Incentive/Rebate Programs   72

3.4.1.4. Special Contract Considerations for
Distribution Agreements   75

3.4.2. Key Terms and Conditions That Auditors Care About   75

3.4.3. Sample Key Terms and Conditions From a
Distribution Agreement   77

3.5. Franchisee Contracts   80

3.5.1. Contract Description   80

3.5.2. Key Terms and Conditions That Auditors Care About   82

3.5.3. Reporting Areas and Associated Risks   92

3.5.4. Documents to Consider Requesting in the Contract
to Allow for Adequate External Monitoring   93

3.6. Joint Venture and Partner Contract   94

3.6.1. Contract Description   94

3.6.2. Key Terms and Conditions That Auditors Care About   94

3.6.3. Documents to Consider Requesting in the Contract
to Allow for Adequate External Monitoring   101

3.7. Most-Favored-Nation Contracts   101

3.7.1. Contract Description   101

3.7.2. Key Terms and Conditions That Auditors Care About   102

3.7.3. Reporting Areas and Associated Risks   104

3.7.4. Documents to Consider Requesting in the Contract
to Allow for Adequate External Monitoring   105

3.7.5. Example of Most-Favored-Nations Contract Language   106

3.8. Manufacturing Contracts   108

3.8.1. Contract Description   108

3.8.2. Key Terms and Conditions That Auditors Care About   108

3.8.3. Documents to Consider Requesting in the Contract
to Allow for Monitoring   120

3.9. Royalty/Licensing Contracts   121

3.9.1. Contract Description   121

3.9.1.1. The Licensor   121

3.9.1.2. The Licensee   122

3.9.2. Key Terms and Conditions That Auditors Care About   123

3.9.3. Documents to Consider Requesting in the Contract
to Allow for Adequate External Monitoring   131

3.10. Software/End User License Contracts   132

    3.10.1. Contract Description   132

    3.10.2. Key Terms and Conditions That Auditors
            Care About   134

    3.10.3. Reporting Areas and Associated Risks   135

        3.10.3.1. Causes of Contract Violations   136

        3.10.3.2. Problem Areas   137

        3.10.3.3. Documents to Consider Requesting in
                 the Contract to Allow for Adequate
                 External Monitoring   137

There are many different types of self-reporting agreements. It would be impractical to address them all in this book. Each has its own complexities and issues. The following are some of the more generic self-reporting arrangements:

Example Self-Reporting Contracts by Industry

	Con. Products	Gov.	High Tech	Hospitals/ Research Facilities	Media & Enter.	Mfg.	Not for profit	Pharma	Real Estate	Service
Advertising	X		X	X	x		X	X	X	X
Construction	X	X	X	X	X	X	X	X	X	X
Co-promotion	X		X	X	X	X	X	X	X	X
Cost Plus		X		X	X	X	X	X	X	X
Digital Distribution	X		X		X					
Distribution	X		X		X	X		X		
Franchisee	X					X	X			X
Joint Venture	X	X	X	X	X	X	X	X	X	X
Most Favored Nation	X	X	X	X	X	X	X	X	X	X
Participations					X					
Production/ Mfg.	X	X			X	X		X		X
Reseller	X		X			X		X		
Revenue Sharing	X		X	X	X	X	X	X	X	X
Royalty	X		X	X	X		X	X		
End-User License	X		X							
Time & Material		X	X	X	X	X	X	X	X	X

3.1. Advertising Agency Contracts

3.1.1. Contract Description

An advertising agency contract authorizes an advertising agency to plan, design, and/or carry out an advertising campaign for its client. The purpose of an advertising campaign is to inform the public about a company, product, service, point of view, individual, service, or event. Advertising agencies provide guidance on where to spend advertising dollars, such as the

Internet, magazines, radio, newspaper, and television. The agencies self-report to their clients advertising expenditures, advertising placements, and internal production costs that are time- and material- based. Monitoring the expenditures and advertising placements is a critical function of the client, especially given the tens of millions of dollars many companies spend on advertising. Additionally, specialized advertising expenditure costs need to be monitored where companies pay based on the unique media. For example:

- Internet: Pay-Per-Click
- TV/Radio Broadcast: Minimum viewership (Neilson rating), time of day, local versus national placement, competing advertisements, and nature of show/viewing audience
- Magazine/TV: Minimum circulation and location within the publication

3.1.2. Key Terms and Conditions That Auditors Care About

The following key terms and conditions have been included in advertising service agreements for different companies. This list is designed to draw attention to those terms unique to Advertising Agency Contracts.

1. **Agency Services:** This section refers to the service agreement between the client and the advertising agency and explains who is appointed to perform services, advertising plans, local agreements, and subcontracting conditions. Most services are divided into the following categories:
   i. Media
      - The advertising agency negotiates with the appropriate media outlet (i.e., television network, publication, radio station, etc.) to purchase airtime or publication space as needed to carry out the agreed-upon media plan.
   ii. Production
      - Advertising agencies conceive and produce materials appropriate to the approved media plan and bill the client accordingly.
   iii. Service
      - The advertising agency performs all necessary and related services to properly carry out the media plan and fulfill its obligations outlined in the service agreement.
2. **Agency Obligations:** This section outlines the standards of the services to be performed such as the legality of advertising materials, the sensitivity to different countries and locations where the advertisement might be run, approval of advertisements to be used, as well as reimbursable and nonreimbursable costs incurred on the project.

3. **Agency Compensation**: Details the general types of compensation: a) commission, b) fee, and c) retainer. The type of service rendered usually dictates the way the agency is compensated.

a) Commission

Commissions are commonly done with media services/billing. A media commission is calculated either by gross billing or net billing. The traditional media commission is 15 percent. Typically, the advertising agency will negotiate with the appropriate media outlet and arrange for space and time as needed to carry out the agreed-upon media plan.

As an example of net billing, an advertising agency places an ad through a media outlet that sells ad space for $1,000. The advertising agency would then receive a bill from the media outlet with the following line items:

Advertisement	$1,000
Commission @ 15 percent	$150
Balance Due	$ 850

The advertising agency would then bill the client the full $1000 and keep the $150 commission. Note that the $150 is a 15 percent mark *down* from $1,000. If the advertising agency were to mark *up* the $850 to $1000, the increase would effectively result in a 17.65 percent commission.

As an example of gross billing, the agency charges the client separately for all work done beyond the traditional account service (i.e., extra production or work outside the scope of the account service agreement). Such services are simply marked up 17.65 percent, and the agency would send the client the following bill:

Advertisement	$ 850
Service Fee @ 17.65 percent	$150
Balance Due	$1000

b) Fee

For all but the largest advertising agencies, fee or "production" billing has been the trend. In this arrangement, rates vary with the level of service provided. For example, the following rates might apply:

Senior Creative or principal	$200/hour
Mid-level creative, media, account service	$150/hour
Junior creative and administrative	$75/hour

Often the advertising agency simply works as a third party to the producers of the advertisement, and the client compensates the agency based on production costs without any markup as they are incurred by the agency. Production costs typically include, but are not limited to, comprehensive layouts, finished art, photography, use rights, testimonial, slide film, auditioning, storage, studio facilities, network integration, color changes, and production supervision by nonagency personnel. In this example, time and expense reports should be kept by the agency in the event that the client chooses to exercise its "right to audit" clause in the agreement.

c) Retainer

Retainer (guaranteed fee) agreements work well for service agreements where the advertising agency is able to provide immediate or ongoing service for a client who needs it. Many clients work on a monthly retainer to ensure that ongoing service is available. An example might be a client who pays $5000 per month to an advertising agency to handle all public relations issues.

4. **Audits:** This section outlines the expectations regarding a "right-to-audit" clause; for example:

"The Agency's independent Certified Public Accounting firm shall, each year after its annual review of the Agency's books, records and accounts, certify that such records are kept in accordance with generally accepted accounting principles—to be satisfied by the agency's auditors unqualified audit opinion, and shall at <CLIENT>'s request confirm that it has reviewed the <CLIENT> cost analysis system and confirm that the report submitted to <CLIENT> has been prepared in accordance with these records, and that direct and indirect costs have been consistently applied to all clients of the Agency. Additional costs resulting there from shall be borne by and billed to the <CLIENT> entity requesting such certificate.

<CLIENT> or its appointed agent shall have the right, upon reasonable request, to review Agency's books, records and accounting practices, as they pertain to services rendered to <CLIENT>, which Agency agrees to make

available to <CLIENT>, during normal working hours, on an agreed worksheet format. Agency shall maintain complete records, including but not limited to, all Direct Labor Costs, the cost of all materials and services purchased, and work subcontracted to other parties. Such records shall be maintained in such a manner as may be readily audited. Agency will also make available such information as may be required to verify that indirect cost allocation has been properly and consistently applied. Such records, including all supporting documents, shall be available at all reasonable times but not more frequently than quarterly for audit by <CLIENT>, unless <CLIENT> has reason to believe Agency has breached its obligations under this Agreement, or an audit firm engaged by <CLIENT> during the term of this Agreement and for one year following the termination of this Agreement, or until all disputes between <CLIENT> and Agency have been resolved, whichever is later. <CLIENT> shall ensure that any review pursuant to this sub clause and the results thereof are kept confidential."

Contracts with right-to-audit provisions may include:

- Creative Advertising
- Media Planning/Buying
- Direct Marketing
- Promotions/Events Marketing
- Health Science
- Multicultural
- Public Relations
- Interactive/Internet Marketing
- Sports Marketing
- Co-promotion

5. **Exhibits:** This section lists various documents to supplement the service agreement:

- List of corresponding <CLIENT> and agency entities
- Compensation

3.1.3. Reporting Areas and Associated Risks

Monitoring advertising expenditures and examining for "proof of performance" by self-reporting advertising agencies should be a part of every organization's basic operation. Every organization investing millions of dollars through advertising agencies should implement their right-to-audit.

The major risk categories for self-reporting errors with advertising agency contracts are:

General Billing	Creative Services
• Existence of executed contracts	• Legal clearance procedures for creative work
• Fees and commissions	
• Adherence to contract billing terms	• Licenses for intellectual property
• Discounts and rebates owed clients	• Production of advertising
• Travel and entertainment policy	• Competitive bidding procedures
• Examination of direct client expenses	• Use of independent contractors

Media Services	General Operations
• Execution of approved media plans	• Agency segregation of duties
• Media buying effectiveness	• Internal controls
• Confirmation that advertisement was placed	• Existence of disaster recovery plan
	• Insurance coverage
• Vendor credit procedures for nonexecuted advertisements	• Conflict of interest compliance
	• Tracking of budget vs. actual
• Post-buy analysis procedures	• Policies and procedures
• Co-op advertising	

These categories result in the following typical audit findings that are not properly reported by the advertising agency:

- Expenditures through unauthorized media or locations
- Expenditures for unauthorized items such as personal benefits to agency employees
- Undisclosed use of related party advertisers charging excessively high fees
- Use of unproductive advertising dollars
- Non-placement of advertisements
- Bundled sales costs
- Excessive entertainment and other out of pocket expenditures.
- Unreported rebates/kickbacks

3.1.4. Documents to Consider Requesting in the Contract to Allow for Adequate External Monitoring

Based on the potential findings, it may be beneficial to secure some of the following documents with periodic expense statements from the advertising agency so that management can make a better decision if to pursue an audit or litigation for recovery of costs.

Media Billing

i. Approved media plans
ii. Budget to actual costs
iii. List of disbursements relating to media plans
iv. Listing of all credits received
v. Third-party invoices and support of media placement
vi. Copy of print advertisement as evidence that advertisement was placed
vii. Cancelled checks

Production

a. Approved work plan
b. List of all disbursements and supporting documentation
c. The timesheets of employees who worked on production/creative services
d. Cancelled checks

Service Cost

a. Approved work plan
b. Calculation of service costs
c. Total hours and salary reported by advertising agreement in support of service costs
d. Individual payroll information, including hours worked and confirmation of when overtime was paid

As part of the monitoring/litigation process, the monitoring company may wish to be able to have sufficient monitoring tools in place through the contract or other methods to answer the following questions:

a. What is your organizational structure?
b. How many contracts with <<Client>> are in force for the year 200X?
c. Do you maintain copies of all current contracts?
d. Are there any side agreements or other amendments?
e. What is your understanding of the contract billing terms?
f. How do you ensure adherence to those terms?
g. How are media plans approved, and who approves them?
h. What is the process over media planning, buying, monitoring, and billing?
i. What is the process over allocating the appropriate resources to the <<Client>>'s projects?
j. What is the process over recording time and expenses to the <<Client>>'s projects?

k. Do you have any travel or entertainment policies, and if so, what are they?

l. Is there a management review of expense and/or services prior to invoicing <<Client>>?

m. How do you track the budget vs. the actual charges?

n. What legal clearance procedures are in place for creative work?

o. What is the process over calculating the total service costs, including truing up the estimate to actual?

p. What is the process over reporting to <<Client>>?

q. Do you use independent contractors?

r. Are competitive bids required, and who approves the bids?

s. What are the performance requirements for contracted third parties?

t. What are the penalties and other provisions for nonperformance?

u. Are there procedures established to monitor third-party compliance with other contractual provisions (insurance, controls, etc.)?

3.2. Construction Contracts

3.2.1. Contract Description

A construction contract is for the construction of a physical asset. It can also be for the destruction, demolition, repair, or restoration of a physical asset. Construction contracts are subject to the overcharging of construction costs by the self-reporting entity ("contractor"). Just about every construction contract with variable charging of costs results in overcharges. Construction projects are among the most complex of all contractual arrangements where overcharges and therefore recoveries can occur. Comprehensive contracts must be written to prevent overcharges. It is for this reason that many accounting firms, specialty firms, and various government entities have very busy and successful teams of auditors specializing in construction auditing. These teams of auditors should more than pay for themselves in costs recovered from the third-party self-reporting contractor. And with audit cost recovery provisions, it is extremely attractive for clients to audit contractors. Construction overcharges occur in every way imaginable due to the complexity of construction contracts and the ease with which one can overcharge a client under variable fee contracts.

There are several different types of construction contracts, each with its own particular self-reporting issues. Some of these different contracts are "time and material," "cost-plus," "guaranteed maximum price," "unit price," and "fixed-fee" (aka "lump-sum"). While all construction contracts should be monitored and audited, this book will emphasis agreements where noncompliance with the contract is rampant—namely, contracts that are not fixed-fee.

This does not mean fixed-fee contracts should not be monitored or audited. In fact, monitoring of fixed-fee arrangements should be conducted to assess the following:

- Substandard goods and services.
  - Contractors are known to use substandard products, cut corners by using inferior construction techniques, or use personnel not adequately trained as required by the agreement. Such cost cutting can be very costly to the buyer, and such shortcuts need to be identified and fixed or costs recovered.
- If change orders were required or if duplicate work was included within the original order's bid amount.
- If change orders or emergency work was performed in accordance with rates as originally identified in the initial contract.
- If costs were paid for by the buyer yet charged by the contractor.
- If the contractor and subcontractors maintained adequate insurance and performance bonds throughout the course of the project.
- If project percentage of completion calculations and payment milestones were adequately met prior to seeking payment. This may be a timing difference resulting in interest rate recoveries based on the time value of the early payment.
- If the final deliverable performs as required, but there were savings experienced by the contractor through value engineering (the use of alternative technology to reduce costs but does not reduce the quality or function of the specific task), then the contract should specify how savings between the value engineering should be shared with the buyer. Without this specification, the savings tend to all go to the contractor.

Generally speaking, costs that are commonly overcharged are labor, materials, overhead, and failure to report rebates and incentives (aka kickbacks). These overcharges appear in all areas where there are variable charges, such as from working drawings, topographies, administration, and construction. The reasons for the overcharges are not always the fault of the contractor. Often the cause is a poorly written contract or contract management where design and construction requirements are unclear or keep changing; out-of-scope work is allowed without contract amendment, quality or delivery dates are not defined; and/or record-keeping requirements are not defined.

The following examines two types of contacts: "cost-plus" and "time and material."

1. Cost-Plus Contracts: A cost-plus contract (sometimes referred to as a cost-reimbursement contract) involves one where the client pays for the actual costs of the construction project plus a profit, generally a percentage of costs or a fixed amount over costs. As these contracts almost always have the profit as a percentage of costs, there is an incentive for the contractor to overstate costs for two reasons: one, to get money for costs that were not incurred on the project; and two, the more they spend, the more profit the contractor gets. This leads to the incentive for the contractor to slow down work and have employees work longer hours. To offset these costs runoffs, there are often incentives to keep costs down, resulting in higher profits to the contractor. Without these incentives to keep costs down, you are basically guaranteeing overcharges by the contractor. It is generally best to avoid cost-plus contracts as there is often an incentive for the contractor to overcharge.

A cost-plus contract is generally used if there are many uncertainties for the project so the extent of costs or even the scope of work that needs to be completed cannot be clearly defined. For example, the number of labor hours, quantity or type of equipment, supplies, or challenges of construction cannot be anticipated. These contracts are often used when there are emergency construction contracts (the other option being time and material contracts).

As an actual example, a pipeline broke in Central California along the coast, and hundreds of barrels of oil leaked into a sensitive nature preserve. A contractor was hired under a cost-plus arrangement to repair the pipe and clean an area of oil that was indeterminable. The cost recovery audit identified many instances of excessive charges to the project, and the contractor had clearly run up costs to make a higher profit. For example, a crane was rented by the contractor for thirty days at over $2500 a day, and the crane was never used on the project. We knew the crane was never used because a crane operator was never hired, so the crane just sat idle at the construction site with no intention to put it to use. Later examination showed the crane owner was a relative of the contractor, so we had reason to believe that kickbacks were involved with false invoicing.

Because of the nature of cost-plus contracts, it is extremely important for the contractor to maintain complete and accurate records. The extent of these records should be clearly identified in the construction contract. These records must be detailed as to all costs incurred, the reasons for the costs, and should include detailed items such as who worked on the project, their skills, the hours/days worked and what they exactly did on the project.

There are four different types of cost-plus contracts. All of the contracts are subject to significant overcharges by the contractor for the "cost" portion of the agreement. These different types are based on the different profit incentive plans. These are:

a. *Cost plus a percentage of costs:* These contracts should almost always be audited as there is limited incentive for the contractor to control costs and actually an incentive for the contractor to overcharge. These contracts are even prohibited by United States federal regulations due to the overcharging that occurs. Still many companies use these, most likely because of the ignorance of management.

b. *Cost plus a fixed fee:* This cost-plus contract relies on a profit paid, regardless of the costs of the project.

c. *Cost plus an incentive fee:* This cost-plus contract is among the most popular as it rewards the contractor for controlling costs and/or completing on time. These projects generally involve a target for total costs with the profit being reduced with cost overruns and the profit increased with cost savings. These contracts should still be closely monitored because cash to the contractor for inappropriate cost charges can result in a greater benefit to the contractor than the incentive to control costs.

d. *Cost plus an award fee:* The contract, often combined with the cost plus an incentive fee contract, awards a contractor for meeting technical specifications in a project's construction. For example, an award may be paid for a boat that exceeds certain criteria for speed, cargo capacity, size, range, and mobility.

3.2.2. Key Terms and Conditions That Auditors Care About

For construction audits, the auditor is primarily concerned about agreeing cost reimbursement requests to supporting documentation. Additionally, the auditor asks the question "does the work performed fall under the scope of the contract?" The contract needs to be written to allow the auditor to perform this work.

The following explores in detail what an auditor is attempting to accomplish when performing an audit so the contract can be written to support this activity.

The first place to start is the objectives of a contract audit. Typical objectives are to determine if:

- A properly executed contract and amendments were executed for the work performed.
- The contract was written in such a manner as to clearly identify the scope of the authorized work and the contract pricing.
- Work performed prior to the execution of the contract was properly authorized.
- The work performed was in accordance with the contract's terms and conditions.
- Contract payments are properly supported and agree with the contract.
- Expenditures are reasonable and agree to price lists.
- Kickbacks are identified and rebates are reported.

Construction contracts are often time sensitive with start dates, end dates, reward dates, and other completion target dates that are in different accounting periods and often occur over the life of different accounting systems that track the construction costs.

Because many contractors are serving multiple clients and contracts simultaneously, it is very important for the contractor to have accounting systems and internal controls that make certain only authorized costs are charged to the project. Weak internal controls result in many instances leading to costs that are charged to the wrong project. The charging to wrong projects is particularly important to identify if the costs of construction are passed onto the client. This is generally not a concern under a fixed price contract, which is why this book does not address fixed price contracts (this may become a concern under a fixed priced contract if there are amendments to the fixed priced contract, and the basis for the pricing to the amendment are prior actual costs). There are often incentives for contractors to move costs from a less profitable project to a more profitable one.

Because construction contracts can span a long period of time and larger contracts can exceed billions of dollars, consideration must be made to perform external and internal monitoring through the life of the contract and after contract conclusion. This "work-in-progress" monitoring is often timed to the contractor achieving certain milestones or requesting certain milestone payments. Payments to contractors are often based on "percentage of completion." The role of the internal or external monitor of the contractor is to make certain that charges are in accordance with the contact, have actually been incurred, are reasonable, are supportable, and are appropriate.

For a construction cost recovery audit, an auditor will generally look at the following areas. Therefore, the contract must make certain that controls are in place to allow the auditor to perform their job:

i. Basic controlling provisions of the contract:
   a. Guarantees
   b. Penalties
   c. Incentives
   d. Postponement
   e. Cancellation
   f. Scope
   g. Change orders/method
   h. Responsibility for additional expenses, such as:
      i. Weather
      ii. Strikes
      iii. War
      iv. Scope changes
      v. Management changes
      vi. Inflation

    ii. Costs charged to the contract.

For this audit work to be successful, the contact should require the contactor to maintain an electronic accounting system of records; have a separate accounting ledger for costs charged to each individual contract; and require that all payroll, invoices, purchase orders, personnel, cash disbursement, cash receipt, general ledgers, financial statements, and other books and records be retained for at least three years after completion of the agreement (often after release of the performance bond). The auditor then compares the information provided by the contactor to the actual construction contract for appropriateness.

Further, the contact should specify the auditor be allowed to interview key members of management and others involved in the project such as architects, engineers, site and construction managers, general contractors, and subcontractors.

    Additionally, the auditor may be comparing costs to regulatory limitations, especially if the audit is performed under Yellow Book standards. Yellow Book standards are for audits of government agencies.

    Another example are tests to determine if only statutorily allowed taxes and employee benefits are charged to the project.

    The mantra of the auditor is "follow the money." Looking at cash inflow and outflows is important to identify:

    a. Billing system.

    b. How costs are charged to the project.

    c. When cost are allowed to be charged to the project (i.e., when the subcontractor is paid, when the subcontractor's invoice is received by the contractor, or when the purchase order is issued to the subcontractor). Generally, it is best to require that costs may only be charged to the project after the costs have been incurred.

  iii. Quality control.

  iv. Project change order controls.

    a. Have all change orders been properly approved by the client?

    b. Are the items in the charge order included in the original scope so there is a duplicate payment?

    c. Are charges against one change order included in the original contract or other change orders?

   v. Project close out.

  vi. Licensing compliance.

 vii. Fraud.

viii. Visit to the construction site:

    a. A visit to the construction site is very helpful to identify if charges to the contract for materials reflect actual materials. Further, a timely visit while work is still in progress can help identify if the client is being charged for excess equipment such as items not on-site or not being used on the project. Therefore, it is important the contract allow multiple on-site visits by the auditor. This is different from other contracts where limitations are often placed on the auditor, such as one visit a year.

b. While on-site, the auditor must be allowed to interview key personnel and review documents included on-site such as drawings/schematics, payroll records, and journals. This on-site visit might also include a questionnaire to the project manager to identify the status of the project and activity that could indicate overcharges, such as reduction in scope, return of goods, excess/ideal equipment.

c. The auditor should inspect uninstalled inventory to identify surplus goods where refunds may be due.

The auditor should also consider the use of a specialist during construction audits.

Cost recovery construction audits are generally conducted under one of three professional standards. It is important to know these different standards, especially in light of many attorneys stating that a contract audit needs to be conducted by "an independent certified public accountant." Though in reality, the contract writers don't really mean an independent CPA, but rather a CPA. By knowing the standards or definitions of "audit" the lawyer can better understand the roles the auditor plays in construction contracts. The most unique of the three standards to construction contracts are Yellow Book standards that are the standards to be followed when conducting contract audits of government agencies. Also, what should be noted is that none of these standards are "audits" as defined by the American Institute of Certified Public Accountants (AICPA). Per the AICPA, an audit is an opinion on the fair presentation of a financial statement. The monitoring of a third party rarely reaches the requirements of an audit and the "right to audit" does not refer to an audit as defined by the AICPA but instead refers to an inspection under one of the following three standards of the AICPA:

a. Attestation Standards. (aka: Agreed Upon Procedures)

Attestation Standards are about as close as an auditor gets to performing a financial audit without conducting an audit as defined by the AICPA. The most basic rules for a CPA conducting an engagement under Attestation Standards are independence from both parties to the contract, the technical skills to conduct the work, and the ability to conduct the work with due care. The work must also be adequately planned, and the auditor must gather sufficient evidential matter to support any conclusions or findings.

The work performed under Attestation Standards is a particular type for contracts, and it is called "Agreed Upon Procedures" (AUP). Under an AUP report, the auditor will require any party reading and planning to rely on the report to agree to the adequacy and sufficiency of the procedures for the reader's purposes. The procedures performed by the auditor must be clearly identified in the report, and the auditor must be careful to use specific wording that does not challenge their independence. However, independence does not necessarily mean neutrality as the auditor often only requires the engaging party to agree to the procedures, and therefore the auditor is performing the procedures as requested by the investigating party as opposed to the inspected self-reporting third party.

b. Yellow Book Standards

Yellow Book Standards, also known as "Government Auditing Standards," in the most simple sense, are like Attestation Standards but for audits of government entities. These standards are issued by the Comptroller General of the United States Government Accountability Office (GAO). These standards contain requirements for Attestation/Agreed Upon Procedure engagements and performance audits. There are four general standards under Yellow Book for auditors: independence, professional judgment, competence, and quality control and assurance. The basic rule of thumb is that if you follow AICPA Attestation Standards, then you will be complying with Yellow Book Standards.

Therefore, any contract with a government agency where the funding is provided by the government or is subject to government oversight should require the auditor to be Yellow Book certified, which means to have taken a certain number of continuing education hours within the prior year related to Yellow Book audits.

c. Consulting Standards

Most third party inspections are conducted under Consulting Standards, including those where the contract states the auditor should be independent. An auditor performing under consulting standards is not working under independence standards (though the auditor should not have any conflicts with the party being inspected). Under a consulting engagement, the auditor makes findings and recommendations in accordance with the directions provided by the engaging party. This work often involves counseling the client, working as an advocate for the client, and requires lower levels of documentation of the work performed.

Under consulting standards, when performing a contract audit, as the auditor is not independent, the auditor may choose to ignore findings that are not to the benefit of the client if so instructed to do so by the client.

Under all of these standards, the report is generally just to be released to the client. Releasing the entire report to the third party being investigated exposes the auditor to litigation from the third party (this risk can be offset by obtaining a release of liability prior to providing the report).

There are other standards, such as for audits in accordance with the *International Standards for the Professional Practice of Internal Auditing* as published by the Institute of Internal Auditors (IIA); however, these standards are not governed by law and are therefore not covered in this book.

A construction contract review, after consideration of the terms of the agreement, tends to be focused on cost and the recovery of overcharges. Costs should be specifically tied to the contract, along with direct overhead cost allocations. The overhead allocations are variable and therefore subject to a high risk of abuse. The basic tenet, barring strict contractual guidelines, is for costs to be allocated in a systematic basis that is common throughout all construction company projects. Abuses in overhead allocation tend to be found when fixed fee projects do not receive allocations of overhead while those with variable reimbursement terms receive all the costs allocations.

Other areas where improper costs are infrequently seen include charges of nonoperating costs, such as taxes, advertising, selling, training, demurrage, construction errors, government penalties for code and other violations (unless specifically allowed for in the contract), idle equipment, and general overhead. Because of the challenges some companies face in identifying direct versus general overhead, it is best to specifically identify the direct overhead that may be charged to the contract.

Unfortunately, many companies fall prey to contract amendments that are too eagerly signed by distressed buyers based on contractor errors. Often, poor planning is the claimed cause of the amendment and therefore greater care needs to be made in the initial contracting process, including identifying some level of variables for the unknown that may occur and not result in increased costs. Areas with increased costs and needing amendments tend to appear as design changes resulting in unplanned construction costs. Not surprising, amendments always tend to increase costs. Costs savings through change of scope are often not reported by the construction company, resulting in the need of savvy oversight.

3.2.3. The Variable Cost Contract Monitoring Process

All Big 4 accounting firms, most all national accounting firms, and many niche accounting firms have full-time staff dedicated to conducting construction audits. Additionally, just about any large corporation with sizeable construction and an internal audit department dedicates significant resources to audit all major construction with the expectation that the recoveries from this work will pay for the costs of the audit several times over and possibly the entire budget of the internal audit department as well. Properly run construction audits are a profit maker for internal audit departments that help them support the need for their existence. And of course, just about any variable cost construction project performed for the government will be subject to an audit. When so many people are involved in construction contract auditing, it is a clear sign that abuses abound, and there is money to be recovered. Surprisingly, though, many construction projects where significant recoveries can be achieved are never audited. The lack of auditing and self-monitoring, along with weak contracts, helps promote abuses in the construction industry.

The fact that construction audits result in so much money being recovered is a clear indicator there is a breakdown in the control environment. This weakness seems to be caused by the initial contract. Contracts tend to identify allowable costs and the scope of the project, but they forget the monitoring aspects of the construction contract. Even multibillion dollar construction contracts often do not establish internal monitoring guidelines for the construction company. While internal monitoring is only a band-aid approach to a major bleed of excess costs, it can at least result in a construction company that is more aware that monitoring will be occurring and can also result in sufficient reduced costs to make the inclusion of self-monitoring requirements worth the few lines in a the contract. In fact, some government construction contracts require the government or an independent auditor to test project costs to make certain they comply with government cost standards (FERC). Such requirements for self monitoring are rarely, if ever, implemented in the private sector and could result in significant benefits to the buyer.

While cost recovery is important, monitoring of construction contracts also typically includes an assessment of the project quality as not all costs are recovered just through overcharges on invoices or inappropriate allocations. Costs can also be recovered for low-quality work or excessive work beyond the needs of the buyer.

One major reason for the overcharges with variable construction contracts is that many exclude right-to-audit provisions. Those that do include right-to-audit provisions often do not make the penalties adequate enough to discourage overcharges. For a mature industry, the contracts in use to allow for adequate monitoring are often well behind the times.

As with any third-party auditing, the lawyer should be advising management of the needs to make sure that properly skilled auditors are assigned to audit the construction contracts. Because of vague contract terms and complex construction agreements, construction audits can be confusing and significant recoveries can be overlooked by inexperience auditors. Inexperienced auditors are often found in today's internal audit departments given the high turnover of staff, including those that are "wet behind the ears" and "fresh" out of college. At a minimum, any auditor planning to perform a construction audit should have formalized training in construction contract auditing prior to beginning work. The auditor, working with counsel, should also know when accounting skills are inadequate to properly evaluate contract compliance, and under these circumstances, highly skilled external professionals such as engineers should be employed during the evaluation process.

Findings from construction contract audits tend to repeat themselves. Therefore, with this knowledge, lawyers should use this as an opportunity to shape contract terms and conditions that 1) reduce the chances of such findings occurring and 2) allow for easier monitoring of the contracts. The findings that are often seen include:

- *Not recognizing volume or other rebates from suppliers.* These rebates are often paid to the construction company after a project is completed, sometimes more than a year later, and may be reported as other revenue thereby passing cost records. Rebates should be prorated back to the buyers. Reviewing supplier agreements and incentive programs is the first step in identifying these potential rebates (aka: kickbacks). Also reviewing revenue records is a good second approach.
- *Not recognizing construction bond deposits.*
- *Charges for equipment that was never used or was idle.* Some equipment, such as cranes, requires an operator. External monitoring can be conducted by comparing equipment operating dates and hours to operator hours (i.e., was the construction crane operator working the same hours as the construction crane?). Therefore, the contract should require the construction company to provide adequate detail regarding equipment usage by day/hour and employee work hours by day to allow for such third-party monitoring.
- *Charges for material that was not used.* Construction companies overorder materials. What happens to this material is that it is often returned for credit or used on the next project. While returned materials can be easier to identify through credits, material shipped to another project is a bit more complicated. There are a variety of methods to compare material orders to usage; however, these are often dependent on the construction company being required to have adequate controls in place that track material usage. Such controls to track material usage should be specified in the agreement; unfortunately, they never seem to be. Therefore, auditors need to use a bit of skill to identify when excess material has been shipped off-site to an unrelated project. There is usually a record of such shipments that need to be tracked down.
- *Charges for labor costs that are not incurred.* Everyone has seen construction sites that appear to have a lot of people standing around, doing nothing. With a cost-plus contract, that should not be a surprise. So how do you identify when there is excess labor on-site? Like other areas, there are several different approaches, all dependent on the contract requiring the construction company to maintain adequate records for monitoring. Such testing may include comparing the workers on-site to the daily log of construction activity, comparing equipment usage hours to operators on staff (i.e., one bulldozer per operator) and identifying if

the construction dates makes sense (i.e., was the construction charge incurred on a Sunday when such work is in an area where Sunday construction is prohibited?).

- ***Charges for costs not permitted under the agreement.*** As stated previously these would include items such as general overhead and unrelated costs. A periodic detailed cost ledger provided by the construction company can help identify these costs. Therefore, consideration should be made to requiring such cost detail ledgers to be supplied with reimbursement requests.

- ***Duplicate charges.*** Contracts should require adequate supporting documentation behind invoices to identify duplicate charges. In labor, this would be, at a minimum, employee names, work dates, title, and work hours. In materials, this would be, at a minimum, a description, original invoice number, date that costs were incurred, and amount.

- ***Not giving credit for prepayments.*** Advances are often paid. Surprisingly, such advances might not be applied against invoices, especially if held over for a period of time.

- ***Duplication of work scope in change orders and the original contract.*** Change orders may duplicate original materials, and services contemplated under prior change orders and the original contract, yet the change orders re-charge for this material. The original contract and subsequent change orders should be clearly written to help avoid these duplicate listings of chargeable items.

- ***Inflated burden.***

- ***Substandard products/materials/people.*** There is a large incentive for contractors to use substandard product, especially if product costs are identified on a price list in the contract. Use of inadequately trained workers can be costly not only in terms of payment for the wrong skill sets, but also in the quality of the finished product. Contracts must clearly identify the penalties should substandard products, materials, or people be used on a project, including reimbursements for costs to mitigate the damages caused, and if no physical damages, at a minimum, the savings experienced by the contractor should be forwarded to the buyer.

- ***Substandard technical skills.*** Substandard technical skills are identified when a certain skill level is expected to perform a procedure, and a craftsman of less-than-required skills performs the work. This is often found through review of personnel records and job titles. Therefore, contractors should be required to maintain payroll records that allow for an easy cross-reference of job titles, and such information should be included in invoice support.

- ***Inadequate monitoring of subcontractor invoices.*** General contractors often don't make an effort to review the invoices of subcontractors as they can have an incentive to not reduce a subcontractor's invoice if the contractor charges a percentage fee over the subcontractor's costs. Better agreements require the auditing of the subcontractor by the general contractor and allow auditing by the ultimate buyer of the project. Additionally, the general contractor may have specific requirements for the monitoring that they are obligated to perform of subcontractor activity, such as comparison of subcontractor invoices to rate sheets, change orders, and time cards. Further, the subcontractors should have the same record retention and reporting requirements as the general contractor.

- *Change orders not executed.* Verbal agreements often lead to costly arguments and significant disputes. Contracts should not only state clearly that all agreements should be in writing but should also require that should there be any disputes regarding charges not included in a written agreement, then the buyer's decision regarding the authorization of the charges are final. Additionally, the change-order process should be clearly identified in the agreement. As some projects encounter "emergency" scope changes that make a written change order not practical in the short run, the contract should clearly define what constitutes an emergency and should identify both the time limit to secure a written change order as well as the consequences should the written emergency change order not be executed within the defined time limit.
- *Sales tax recovery.* Many states have provisions that allow for the recovery of sales taxes. It is often not within the incentive of the contractor to recover sales taxes as such recovery must flow to the buyer (or alternatively, the contractor recoveries sales taxes and pockets the recovery). To help secure recovery of sales taxes, the buyer may wish to be in charge of paying all sales taxes.
- *Double charging of costs that are included in overhead.* Direct costs must be reviewed to determine if costs that are already included in overhead charge percentages have been double charged as a direct cost. This is more common in cost-plus arrangements.
- *Subcontractors are related parties.* It seems like every contractor has a brother, cousin, or a close friend whom they hire as a subcontractor. These subcontractors can easily overcharge costs that are passed onto the buyer. Such overcharges can be kicked back to the subcontractor or hidden through complex transactions such as the subcontractor hiring the contractor on another project at inflated fees (or just hiring the contractor with the contractor performing no work to be paid). To help combat such abuse, the contract should clearly identify that subcontractors that are related parties must be approved by the buyer; otherwise, the charges from the related party will not be reimbursed. Further, a more aggressive requirement would identify a most favored nation provision where the contractor is required to secure services at the most favorable rates available in the market, and any inflated prices identified

by the buyer shall be reimbursed to the buyer plus interest or other penalties.

3.2.4. When to Conduct Self-Monitoring and an Audit

Like other contracts, self-monitoring should be a continuous process from the moment the first obligations are being incurred by the contractor. Therefore, like other contracts, it is essential that the contract provide the tools to the buyer to allow for adequate monitoring of the contractor. This includes the detailed reports identified earlier and the access to key construction personnel.

Large construction contracts should almost always be audited as a key part of self-monitoring due to the high degree of opportunities for overcharges and inadequate completion of the project's initial specifications. While many audit clauses allow for one audit per year, construction contracts would be better written to allow for continuous auditing of the project without periodic restrictions due to the limited time frame of the projects and the lack of repetitive processes experienced in other contract arrangements, such as licensing.

There exists varying opinions on when to conduct a construction audit; however, all parties at least seem to agree there should be an audit soon after or near completion of the construction project. While such audits near completion of a large project may miss some late charges (which, surprising, it is not uncommon for charges to come in a year after the completion of when the cost was incurred), the benefit of having personnel who understand the retained documents and actual construction performed during the project can be invaluable to the auditor as he researches documents and asks questions. One leading approach is to conduct a majority of the audit near the completion of the project, for example, when 95 percent or more of the project is completed and then a final project audit after it is relatively certain all significant variable costs have been charged. The second audit for the remaining balance can face challenges of personnel not being available to answer questions, so it is best to conduct the audit as soon as there is a level of comfort that most all charges have been invoiced.

In addition to the end-of-project construction audit, for significant projects, especially those with costs incurred over one year, at least one annual audit should be conducted. Conducting at least annual audits (instead of just waiting for the end of the project) increases the chances of recoveries and better investigations with more knowledgeable contractors being available as they are closer to the date the costs were incurred.

One of the most critical times to conduct a construction audit is prior to the final payment, even if a reservation of rights is included with the final payment. As long as the buyer has cash in hand, they have some level of control when the final audit identifies the overcharges. Certainly the timing of such an audit is critical to help avoid penalties for late payment to the contractor.

To help avoid such penalties, it is beneficial to note in the right-to-audit provision for a construction contract that the final payment is subject to a final audit. Such final audit provisions generally require the audit to be conducted within a certain time frame, such as within thirty days of the contractor's submitted documentation for 90 percent of project completion.

3.2.5. Key Documents That a Construction Company Should Be Contractually Required to Retain for Construction Contract Monitoring and Why

The following are some items that a construction company might be specifically required to maintain:

1. Key procedures in the processing, controlling, and monitoring of work performed under the contract. Such procedures may include:
   a. Overhead allocation
   b. Project cost allocations
2. Historical accounting books and records.
3. Cost estimates.
4. Bid submittal.
5. Executed contract and change orders.
6. Calculation behind progress invoices.
7. Calculation of any retentions/reserves.
8. Time cards and approval of time cards or other approval of overtime and work documentation.
9. Personnel, including training, qualification, and certification records.
10. Proof of insurance naming companies to be additionally insured.
11. Evidence of performance bond.
12. Certifications of work completion from specified professional during specific project phases.
13. Evidence of following proper procedures for change orders.
14. Evidence of material and equipment receipt, installation, and function.
15. Evidence of lien releases and other potential encumbrances or restrictions.
16. Permits.
17. Resolution of government inspections.
18. Contracts with suppliers.
19. Identification of potential reimbursements..
20. Overtime work is preapproved.
21. Support for all charges in the form of third party invoices and contracts.
    a. Evidence of completion prior to payment of each invoice

22. List of authorized approvers of purchase orders and invoices.
23. Cash disbursement subsidiary ledgers.
24. Job cost ledgers.
25. Payroll journals.
26. Cancelled checks.
27. Bank statements.
28. Budget to actual records.
29. Subcontractor contracts (that include right-to-audit provisions).
30. Inspection Reports, including raw materials (quantity and quality), work in progress, and completion. If remediation is required, the reports of such remediation.
31. Support for all billing to the buyer.
32. Subcontractor bid selection procedures, requests for proposals, bid submittals, selection sheets indicating why the vendor was selected, and the contract.
33. Subcontractor invoices and provided support.
34. Personal expense records, even if not charged to the project (you may want to see if there were any favors paid to buyer personnel).

Further, the construction company should be contractually required to maintain a system of duty segregation related to purchasing, accounts payable, and cash to help minimize defalcations.

3.3. Digital Distribution Contracts

3.3.1. Contract Description

A digital distribution contract is for the distribution of media and entertainment, generally though the Internet, cable, or wireless networks. Much of the products being distributed is software, music, ringtones, games, or filmed entertainment. Contracts with self-reporting relationships include those with wireless phone companies, cable companies, satellite companies, advertisers, software companies, game box manufacturers, content aggregators, content distributions, equipment manufacturers, MP3 players, IPTV, an ever-growing list of telecommunication companies, content owners, and talent. Each party requires a different financial stream to be tracked. Yet, it can be particularly difficult to track the accuracy of products distributed digitally because of the lack of a physical asset. Reliance must be made on the ability of the distributor to accurately track all distributions. There are many complexities involved in this tracking, with highlights including the number of units distributed both to the same receiving party and multiple parties, monies received from the distributions, completeness of distribution records, and accuracy of distribution information. Many digital distribution contracts do not adequately address the detailed information that should be captured and reported to enable the content owner to remotely monitor the accuracy of the reported information.

The digital distributors are often start-up companies with limited experience in creating sufficient financial controls to track records. Those who think they have set up adequate controls don't learn of their inaccuracy until questions are raised about the historical information. Technology companies with experience in producing items in hard copy often struggle to switch to digital distribution. On top of financial record management come the issues of digital rights management (the control over the end users use of the licensed product). Many companies, in their continued effort to make the sale, are not properly addressing the operational risks and challenges to be found in constantly changing digital strategies. The monitoring of third-party distributors requires controls both over financial reporting and the intellectual property being distributed. Too many distributors argue that financial and intellectual property controls make it difficult to maximize revenue streams, hence the real risk for misreporting.

Distributors must be instructed in contracts to take an enterprise-wide approach to identifying and managing digital risks, including how the distributors must report on their compliance. Only a strong internal control environment will allow the proper execution of the business strategies for protection to all parties involved.

Understanding the risks of misreporting starts with understanding that digital distributors are vast in number and each with their own internal control environments. With predigital licensing deals that made hard products such as DVDs, the rules were basically the same between all producers; namely, count the number of DVDs, and understand the inventory control environment over them. With this predigital hard item environment, there were physical items purchased and physical items shipped, all easily traceable and recordable through individual, unique SKU numbers.

Now with digital distribution, every distribution company seems to have its own method to track downloads through different operating systems and software programs often developed in-house. Some are sophisticated, some are complex, but all are full of errors explained by the armies of IT programmers working around the clock to make the software better. The transition to digital has changed the basic business model, creating large opportunities along with risks. The desire to quickly make the detail without sufficient controls is par for the course with digital distribution as managers must make quick decisions to face the rapidly changing environment.

As companies grow and digitally transform, they need to balance their digital opportunities with the right control environments as this is an important part of implementing a successful strategy. Companies in the digital world have a tendency to be hot one day and have their bubble burst the next, so the prudent content owner keeps a careful eye on its licensees. Quarterly reporting is not wise. Monthly reporting of results to the content owner, made easier through electronic data capture and reporting, should be the practice, as opposed to quarterly paper reporting used in other licensing industries.

A comprehensive understanding of the risks, changing environments, unknowns, and interrelationships between the various players in digital distribution are required before the proper contract can be written. Contracts must be flexible to allow for changing environments yet, should encourage the licensee to act in a prudent manner and to seek approval before using new and unique distribution channels. The brick and mortar approach to slowly reacting to the changing environment will not work with ongoing digital transformations. Companies must react quickly to build contracts that make certain that self-reporting third parties are capturing all revenues from content and service provided and that the digital distribution activities are appropriate. Without this control, evolving business models will fail to meet the needs of the content owner. Finding the right balance between control, flexibility, and monitoring is important.

Contracts must be written to manage all four stages of the digital life cycle: content creation, content management, content distribution, and content transaction. Each stage possesses unique challenges of self-monitoring. Understanding these unique challenges is the first step in designing the proper contract to control the associated risks. This is further complicated as the different stages become blurred, and the risks change faster than contracts can be amended.

Managing digital content requires a risk-control system that is aligned with the four stages of the digital life cycle and that can identify the key digital challenges and interdependencies. Understanding the digital life cycle and the various environments so that a risk control system can be established, as memorialized in a contract, should result in controls to identify, assess, manage, and monitor the operational challenges, interdependencies, and risks associated with executing a digital strategy. The strategy and contract language should consider the following:

- An enterprise-wide understanding of where control breakdowns could occur and required associated controls to help prevent those risks from occurring.
- Assigning to senior level executives the responsibility for contract compliance, thereby providing a top-down control to make certain the digital strategy also includes a strategy for monitoring and reporting.
- Flexibility to address the varying objectives and business challenges that might occur with each unique business opportunity.
- Controls over third-party activities downstream (i.e., subdistributors) activities extending the reach of the content owner not only to the

contractee, but over all parties that may have access to the intellectual property and therefore affect the business development.

The following are some of the different players in the digital environment that have a role in self-reporting. These roles are ever changing with new parties being created and distribution steams being identified:

- Content creators. "Musicians, songwriters, game developers, software developers, actors, writers." These individuals are among the most active monitors of self-reporting relationships and, because of their almost universal inability to individually monitor the licensees of their content, they rely as a group on guilds, agencies, and private companies created under federal regulations to monitor the licensees. Entertainment industry monitoring companies include the following, among others: the Screen Actors Guild, Directors Guild of America, Motion Picture Pension Plan, the Harry Fox Agency (music) and SoundExchange (though technically not licensing when using music under federal regulation, which is monitored by SoundExchange). The contracts and reporting requirements allowing talent to monitor digital distribution is generally subject to intense negotiations. This generally leaves little power to the talent to effect the internal control environment of the licensees, and therefore the power of digital distribution risk control tends to rest with the distributors, not the content owners.
- Content owners. "Music labels, film studios, game studios/producers, publishers, news organizations, software companies." These companies play a dual role. They are both licensors and licensees. These companies must report to the content creators and tend to have very sophisticated systems in place to accumulate the financial data to be reported; yet, despite being under constant audit, these same companies continue to inaccurately report information to the content creators. These same companies tend to aggressive audit licensees who are distributing their digital content. For entertainment companies, the distributors who need to be monitored tend to be Internet, cable TV, satellite TV, or cellular telephone companies. Each one of these distribution channels has its own unique challenges as addressed in following sections.
- Network and Device Manufacturers. These companies create the technology that allow for end user enjoyment of the digital content. These companies, usually referred to as OEMs (original equipment manufacturers), are generally under license to produce enabling equipment and must pay a royalty for the right to use the associated intellectual property. These companies have a tendency to underreport royalties from 20 percent to 50 percent and therefore require constant scrutiny.
- Advertisers. Advertising over the Internet is a vehicle used to encourage digital distribution. Advertisers often must pay based on the success of

their advertisements. The more money or viewers they receive through their advertisement, the more money they must pay. The charges for this success are often billed to the advertiser. It is prudent therefore for the advertiser to monitor the Internet portal to make certain what they are charged is in compliance with the agreement. Such advertising agency audits, as discussed in another section, are wise and often well worth the effort.

- Content Distributors. The Internet portals and wireless cell phone companies distribute product, thereby controlling the communication and distribution to the end user. The Internet portal then is also responsible for collection of sales revenues, end user satisfaction, and public perception. These companies, as mentioned earlier, often start quickly and don't have the internal controls in place to properly self-report as required by the agreement. These companies also tend to work with various content owners and don't adequate identify the different monitoring requirements of each content owner.
- Content Aggregators. These companies work with content owners and distributors to provide a vehicle for multiple parties to have their data consolidated and distributed more efficiently. These companies can provide the tracking support for digital distribution, including up to and including cash collections and resultant royalty payments to the content owner.

3.3.2. Digital Distribution Self-Reporting Areas of Concern

The following are areas where controls must be established to avoid some of the risks associated with self-reporting and digital distribution:

- "New digital products." As products change, the self-reporting party often fails to update the agreement, or the updated agreement does not address the risks associated with the new digital product because there are too many unknowns.
- "New distribution sublicensees." Licensees often don't do all the distribution by themselves; more likely than not, they sublicense distribution rights. The key term and conditions missing related to sublicenses are 1) sublicensees do not require licensor pre-approval or 2) the licensor does not have the right to audit the records of the sublicensee or receive audit reports from the licensee's audit of the sublicensee. Generally, the content owner/licensor fails to instruct the licensee of its monitor roles over sublicenses.
- "Separate and specific content rights for product types and distribution channels." A catchall agreement generally does not work for digital distribution. Therefore, it is important the contract be structured to require

the licensee to seek approval for all new distribution channels and the licensee be required to report, within the standard reporting structure, all methods of distribution.

- "Revenue share models that are not royalty based." Just monitoring if royalties are properly being paid is hard enough, and now companies have new agreements in place that continue to create new revenue sharing arrangements. Like any new revenue stream, it is important that a complete understanding of what can go wrong will go wrong is required, and the contract addresses these areas.
- "Royalties based on evolving business models: i.e., subscription and streaming." As distribution channels change and distributors must work under different licensing agreements with varying terms and conditions for royalty payments, there are bound to be royalty miscalculations, often more than 10 percent of reported royalties. Underreporting occurs frequently with both streaming and subscription services.
- "Timeliness of reporting and payment." The one area with a lower level of risk is the timeliness of reporting and payment. Most content owners or other report recipients keep close tabs on the timely delivery of royalty statements and royalty payments as this is perhaps the easiest item for the content owner to monitor. The greatest areas for improvement tend to be the information that is actually reported. Does the information flow provide sufficient data for the content owner to properly monitor the activities of both the licensee and the sublicense? It would be best if the content owner had access to the raw data from the sublicensee; however, because of confidentiality restrictions caused by the sublicensee distribution for many different content owners, the odds of receiving this sublicensee raw data that may include confidential information of other content owners is minimal.
- "Accuracy of reporting." The accuracy of the reports is, of course, of the greatest concern to the report recipient. As discussed throughout this book, accuracy can be monitored through analytical analysis, that is, comparing reports to each other for unusual variances. However, only through an audit can a true appreciation for the accuracy of the report be properly accessed.
- "Completeness of reporting." It is important that the report recipient carefully read each report. I have often seen incomplete reports, yet the report reader has done nothing about the missing information, usually because of the assumption that if a cell in the report is blank, then there must be nothing to report. When reports cells are blank, the recipient must assess if that would be expected. For example, if the reporting company is allowed under the contract to make deductions and such deductions are to be detailed in the report, if a report is received without deductions, it is probably safe to say the deductions were made on gross numbers reported prior to insertion in the report.

Therefore, the report reader should question if deductions were actually made or why no deductions are included on the report. It is rare that a self-reporting company does not take advantage of allowed deductions, so it is best to have stronger monitoring for unusual items on the report instead of ignoring them. Just hoping the self-reporting entity that failed to make allowed deductions is foolhardy.

- "Approvals on product usage." Inappropriate digital distribution of product is a common occurrence, especially in music. The three most common errors are (1) distribution of music before the authorization date, (2) distribution of music after the authorization date, and (3) distribution of single track songs when they are only to be distributed as an album. All digital distribution contracts should have distribution and product limitations; the key is to clearly identify the remedy should inappropriate distribution occur. Usually the penalty (or alternative royalty due) is all revenues from the inappropriate distribution plus interest and audit cost recovery.

- "Rights are identified and covered for each product-type and distribution channel." Ownership of digitally produced entertainment can change. It is important that the right for distribution is tracked to the highest degree possible, as the penalty for inappropriate distribution via litigation can be substantial. Controls must clearly be put into place in the contract that require all parties to continually monitor content ownership, and the penalties should be spelled out if distribution continues if there is no longer ownership. The penalties should include indemnification amongst other remedies.

- "Controls are in place over accounting and distribution prior to contract execution." Assurances should be made prior to contract execution that controls over accounting and distribution are in place prior to contract execution. This might include a precontract audit or the requirement for the distributor (or subdistributors) to obtain an independent certification/evaluation of their controls. Writing into the contract the internal controls that must be in place at contract start and throughout the life of the agreement is a useful tool to clearly identify the expectations of the self-reporting entity. Such controls can be general as to allow flexibility for changes in the reporting environment, yet strong enough to ensure some reliance on the reported records. Some controls might include annual financial statements audits, SAS 70 reports (a report over the information technology controls prepared by a CPA), segregation of duties, information emergency recovery and back-up procedures, confidentiality, written certification of reports by company executives, and explanations of variances between reporting periods.

3.3.3. Summary of Digital Distribution Risks

- Incorrect interpretation of contracts
- Failure to adopt changes to licensing policies
- Transferring licenses between entities
- Failure to pay the correct/sufficient royalty fees
- Unclear terms relating to new technology
- Distribution of intellectual property without sufficient end user license/ deployment restrictions
- Inaccurate royalty or discount application
- Intentional or unintentional errors
- Excluded license sales (products and business units)
- Not meeting minimum royalty requirements
- Untimely reporting or past due payments
- Poor license management and record keeping by customer
- Personnel in charge of installations are unaware of licensing terms or do not track current license usage
- Inconsistent application of agreement terms
- Lack of strong internal controls to accurately track and report fees
- Inconsistent or inadequate reporting

3.3.4. Some Areas to Monitor in Digital Distribution Agreements

In constructing the digital distribution license contract, the digital rights holder should make certain the license agreement with the publisher, distributor, Web portal, etc. . . . adequately addresses the following digital distribution specific areas. Sufficient information should be received to allow the licensor to perform trend analysis; identify reporting gaps (such as missing portals, dates, times, products); monitor pricing, identify sales volumes and discounts or credits; identify inappropriate bundling or selling single tracks from albums; identify unlicensed product, re-perform the licensee's royalty calculation, etc. . . .

1. A very important area that digital contracts often don't address is the ability of the right holder/licensor to monitor the activity of subdistributors. The subdistributor is the distributor for the licensee. Reliance cannot be placed on the licensee to monitor their distributors (the licensor's subdistributor). The license/distribution agreement should require the licensee to include in their contract the right of the licensor to audit the subdistributor and recover audit costs as with any distribution agreement. Furthermore, the licensor should be allowed direct access to

the reports provided by the subdistributor to the licensee. While the licensor may rarely ever look at the subdistributor reports, the ability to have direct access to the subdistributor's report is very important, as many reporting errors occur when the licensee processes the subdistributors information to create the report to the licensor.

The greatest challenge to gaining access to the subdistributor report by the licensor is the confidential information that may be claimed by the distributor. The subdistributor's report will generally have sales volume of more than just the licensor. Therefore, this confidentiality issue must be addressed generally by requiring the sublicensor to segregate the sales by licensor or by providing licensing rights of the sublicensor directly by the licensor.

Another approach is to require the licensee to annually audit the subdistributor by an auditor jointly selected by the licensor/licensee.

2. The royalty reporting format should align with the data processing needs of the licensor. The key tracking mechanism should be identified in the contract and by exhibit in the royalty report.

3. The licensee should be required to provide a reconciliation showing the data received from sublicensees and how that data was processed to identify the reportable amounts to the licensor. This will help the licensor track subdistributors being used by the licensee.

4. The licensed use of the digitally distributed product must be identified. For example, with music distribution, is bundling allowed, are albums allowed to be split into single tracks, is international music fee or streaming permitted, how are ringtones to be distributed, or are tracks over a certain number of minutes to be counted as more than one song for royalty payment?

5. What are the purchase options the licensee is licensed to use? For example, are they subscription, à la carte, credit bundles, prepaid cards, or single track?

6. The system back-up requirements should be addressed. This includes remote back-up locations and the requirement that the licensee and subdistributors be able to recover from any disaster within a specified time period. A "disaster recovery plan" should be submitted to the licensor for evaluation.

7. The licensee should be required to inform the licensor when there is a platform change as records may be lost in this process. A platform change may affect reporting methods, and alternative monitoring may be required, such as new format royalty reports. A change in platform might also spark a royalty audit before the old platform goes off line.

8. What controls must be in place by the licensee and subdistributors to adequate monitor sales, including the various issues that might occur, such as multiple content orders (ordering the same product more than once by the same customer), the controls that must be in place to

determine the point a download is royalty bearing (such as the use of a key to turn on the content download), what constitutes a failed order so no royalty is due and the effect on royalty payments, the timing of the sales of subdistributors and by when subdistributor sales must be reported on the royalty report to the licensor, allowable deductions including various credits that may be issued from customer satisfaction to challenges if data was successfully downloaded, maximum time that distributors and subdistributors must implement price code changes, how subscription revenues are to be apportioned, how unused credits from prepaid cards are to be applied, etc . . .

9. System configuration requirements to identify licensor content versus other content.
10. Transaction logs in electronic format that should accompany royalty statements. The detailed information to be included in the transaction log should be identified, such as the order source, territory, product type, record number, MS ISDN, price, time, and date.
11. Sales/distributions by portals so that completeness of reported information can be monitored.
12. Detailed information that allows the tracing from the transaction logs to the reported royalties.

3.4. Distribution and Reseller Contracts

3.4.1. Contract Description

There are many different types of distribution contracts such as those for physical products and for digital products such as software and music. This section refers only to physical products as there is a separate section describing digital distribution.

3.4.1.1. Understanding a Channel

Distribution and reseller contracts allow a method or "channel" for goods to effectively and efficiently flow from the manufacturer to the end user. These agreements allow the manufacturer to focus on its core strength of manufacturing while leaving the distribution to a third party that has the connections, facilities, assets, and knowledge to find and deliver the goods to a wide network of customers. The offset of the strength of getting the manufacturer's goods to the end user is the embedded weaknesses of the data flow returning from the point of sale to the end user and back to the manufacturer. This is especially true if the manufacturer benefits in sharing revenue with the end user or pays incentives/rebates to the distributor to encourage the final sale of the products. The missing information from data flow gaps creates problems for the customer/end user, distributor, and the manufacturer, and, therefore it is to the benefit of all to have adequate third-party monitoring.

In regard to third-party monitoring, the key is to improve information flow through a properly designed process as dictated through a well-written agreement. The flow of information from the end user through the channel to the Original Equipment Manufacturer (OEM) helps maintain control over the OEM's brand, reduce the risks distributors face in reporting violations, and helps to ensure customers are properly protected by securing original products backed with OEM warranties.

In writing a distribution contract, it is best to first understand the distribution channel—namely, the route of the products from the OEM to the end user and the return of information from the end user to the OEM. Typically, there are two distribution channels, one where the OEM sells directly to the retailer who then sells to the end user, and the second where the OEM sells to a distributor or in turn sells to the retailer who in turn sells to the end user. As would be expected, as product and information flows through each independent entity, the product or information is subject to manipulation and loss. The goal is to maintain a solid leak proof channel so that information and product flows are secure. This helps all members of the channel as each part is interdependent on another. If the OEM is unable to track its goods through to the end user, then the OEM faces many risks, such as dissatisfied customers and lost sales, an inability to track warranty obligations, lack of controls over rebates and refunds, and quality control tracking challenges—not to mention lost revenue sharing if the OEM shares in the benefits of retailer revenues or the retailer has a right to seek price protection if goods are not sold at a sufficient dollar value. An important part of channel control is to make certain that OEM produced product make it to the trusted retailers as opposed to inferior grey market counterfeit product.

For low-value items, strict channel controls are of lower risk. The higher the value of the product, the more risks associated with grey market activity and the needs to monitor rebates, exchanges, or retailers who are authorized to sell the product. Related to retailer control, most channel agreements dictate to the distributor to whom they may sell the OEM's product. This control is essential for brand protection. For example, a seller of a high-end shirt that is sold at Nordstrom most likely does not want the same shirt simultaneously sold at a closeout store such as Marshalls. To help control where a distributor may sell products, the agreement should specifically state the names of the authorized retailers and establish an approval protocol to add new retailers. Penalties for selling to unauthorized retailers or unauthorized distributors should be clearly identified in the agreement. Further, the agreement must make certain the distributor is required to report on all sales regardless if the OEM shares in the revenue benefit of the distributor's sales. Some distributors may sell to different retailers depending on the status of the product.

For example, an older product that used to sell in Nordstrom may be sold to Marshalls after a certain point when clearance of the slow moving merchandise is in the best interest of the distributor and the OEM. In such cases, contracts should avoid wording such as "obsolete" to describe when a good may be sold as closeout. Instead, the contract should specifically describe when a second tier or closeout retailer can be used, such as subject to approval by the OEM, when the product is no longer in the current catalog, or as of a specific date, such as ninety days after initial sale (sometimes called the "street date").

Understanding how to design the contract to dictate information flows depends on the nature of the information to be exchanged and the cost/benefit to secure the information. There are multiple costs associated with the flow of data centered about human and electronic capital. Many distributors and retailers might see limited to no benefit in tracking data for the OEM, and therefore their efforts will not be at a level required by the OEM to meet the OEM's business requirements. Incentives built into tracking requirements of distributors and retailers are often required to make certain that data is adequately and properly captured for the OEM's benefit. The incentives can be positive or negative reinforcements. Negative reinforcements include penalty provisions for misreporting such as paying for the cost of an audit and interest on excess refund claims. Positive reinforcement can be identifying system or monitoring efficiencies in reporting, establishing standardization for reporting and controls, using incentive or rebate programs for accurate reporting, and increasing end user confidence, thereby increasing brand and retailer loyalty through positive end user communications and warranty protection.

At the end of the day, if the end user secures original products in a timely manner that are undamaged or, if damaged, the end-user is able to easily have access to warranty protection or exchanges, not only will the end user benefit but so also will the OEM, distributor, and retailer.

3.4.1.2. Retailer to OEM Reporting

The point of sales or "POS" refers to when the good transfers from the retailer to the end user. This sale is generally captured electronically and reported through electronic data interchange (EDI). While POS reporting is common, and we like to think of computer systems as always properly adding up the number, because of human control over POS systems, there tends to be many data capture errors, especially if there are a high volume of transactions, multiple systems or multiple points of sale, or the systems and retailers are in more than one time zone. The POS system is only as good as the system programmer. Unfortunately, many POS systems do not capture the data needed by the monitor to adequately track vital information, as POS systems are often designed to meet the needs of the retailer and not the needs of the OEM.

For example, for items ranging from video game sales to high technology equipment, an OEM will want to track items, such as sales date, serial number, and personal customer information or demographics. Of the three items just mentioned, the retailer might not be interested in tracking the serial number as that is more of a warranty issue or problem for the OEM, especially if the retailer secures the product through a distributor.

If the OEM can contractually receive data directly from the retailer's system, the ability of the OEM to gather end user data is dramatically enhanced generally to the benefit of the OEM, retailer, and the end user (for warranty issues but perhaps not for privacy issues). Information that OEM often secures through the retailer's POS system is sales date, sales dollar amount, sales quantity, store location, customer demographics, inventory stock number, discounts or coupons, and for higher priced items, serial numbers but perhaps not the name of the actual end user.

In writing the contract to control information flow, after identifying the required information, the next best step is to identify how the information gathered will be beneficial to all entities in the channel from OEM to retailer. By working with the distributor or retailer to buy into the common needs for the data, a contract's reporting requirements and subsequent monitoring activity will be eased with a greater amount of compliance. This value-added approach or positive reinforcement, as described previously, is a key part of a successful channel information flow relationship.

Buying into the benefit of information sharing does not stop with each party understanding the benefit of the data but should be backed by monetary contributions by each member in the channel. Putting skin into the game helps encourage compliance, thereby easier monitoring. The retailer and distributor should not see channel monitoring as just a cost of business but as a key attribute to controlling operations, reducing costs, and ultimately creating a better customer relationship that will drive sales.

3.4.1.3. Incentive/Rebate Programs

Incentive programs are important tools to stimulate sales. Before such programs can be enacted; however, the monitoring controls over the program must be established, or otherwise abuse is certain to follow. Because of abuse, many incentive programs that include monetary payments to distributors or retailers result in audits of the distributor's or retailer's records. Therefore, given the proven history of audit findings, a key control for an incentive program is adequate internal controls supported by a strong contract that allows detailed monitoring of the third party. Most common errors made due to contract or monitoring control weaknesses are areas associated with duplicate claims, claims on unauthorized products, claims for products sold at an insufficient price, or sales outside of the incentive program territory or retailers. Keeping where these errors occur, the contract drafter should consider how to write the contract to allow for monitoring to prevent these abuses.

For more expensive items, the serial number is the most important tool for tracking and monitoring for unauthorized rebate requests. As stated, serial numbers can be territory, customer, and even rebate or incentive program specific so that a claim for an unauthorized serial number can be quickly identified and rejected. The additional key control is to make certain the same serial number cannot have more than one claim. Incentive programs without serial number controls are generally subject to multiple claims on the same product sale.

Some incentive programs and controls include:

1. *Price Protection.* Price protection is used by OEMs to encourage retailers not to return goods by guaranteeing a certain profit or price to the retailer. For example, suppose a retailer has a slow moving DVD it cannot sell for $10 (the required amount to cover costs), and it wishes to return the DVD to the OEM. The OEM does not want the DVD returned, so the OEM will price protect the DVD by stating that instead of returning the DVD, for any DVD you sell for less than $10 but not lower than $8, we will pay the difference between the selling price and the $10. So if the DVD sells for $8.50, the OEM pays the retailer $1.50 to make the retailer whole at $10.

   Price protection programs are subject to significant abuse and must be closely monitored. Abuse examples include the return of price protected goods that are not reported to the OEM, an overstatement of the price protection claim, claims of price protection on goods that were not sold or sold outside of the price protection eligible date range.

   Price protection monitoring requires access to both sales and inventory data. Price protection is generally based on a certain number of units remaining in inventory as of a certain day. The OEM must have assurances that this inventory actually exists, and it is not gray market product. An inventory roll forward comparing units sold to the retailer and units the retailer sold to the end users to identify actual ending inventory on hand, subject to price protection, is a key control tool. Price protection programs should be minimal, and efforts in the contracting process to control excess purchases from the retailer should be considered. When price protection is being used, the OEM is hurt in two ways: 1) having to pay the price protection and 2) the brand image suffers as the market price to the end user goes down.

2. *POS Instant Rebates.* Instant rebate costs at the Point of Sale (POS) may be covered by the OEM. If the OEM covers the cost or instant discounting, there are several risks of overclaims; namely, a) the retailer does not pass the rebate onto the buyer, b) the transaction is cancelled, c) there is a return of the product in subsequent periods, d) sale reporting is

delayed from a pre-rebate period to a rebate period, or e) duplicate claims are submitted for the same product.

Each one of these instant rebate risks should be considered and addressed in the contract and/or special program agreement. Contractual controls for each should address the necessary documentation to be retained for each sale. As a starting point, the following should be required to be retained by the retailer: point of sale records, including buyer's name (if allowed by law, in order to receive the instant rebate); gross sales price, date of transaction; store location; register number; payment type (for comparing amount paid by the client to the gross sales price); item description; model number; and serial number of the item receiving the instant discount. Equal information should be retained for returns. Additionally, detailed inventory records need to be retained by the retailer, showing quantities eligible for rebate purchased, sales, destructions, shrinkage, returns, date, serial number, quantity, value, and location.

3. *Volume Discounts.* Volume discounts are among the most popular and are generally dependent on sales or purchase quantities. The highest risk with volume discounts comes from distributors who sell to retailers and manipulate sales dates to increase sales within a volume incentive period, thereby making claims for benefits for sales that actually occurred in other periods outside the volume incentive program period. Basically, distributors record sales on the wrong dates or delay sales to the volume rebate period (e.g., perhaps items are shipped outside the volume discount period, but the invoice is created within the volume discount period). Another trick is to receive an advance payment for future sales and record the advance as a sale, when in fact the advance is a liability until the product actually exchanges hands. Discounts are often paid at year end, so particular attention needs to be paid to sales and purchase cut-off dates. As such, contracts should clearly specify the dates the discounts apply, to what merchandise, if it is dollar or quantity based, records to be maintained to allow for date verification of sales, and penalties should a company attempt to manipulate data by reporting the sale in the wrong period. Contracts should also say that the sale takes place on the date the goods are shipped to the customer, thus reducing the chances of sales invoice date manipulation or recording advances as sales.

Volume discount support to be maintained is very similar to other areas, such as complete inventory records and especially to a requirement for a physical inventory count as of the last date of the volume discount period. The OEM might even wish to have an auditor present to count the inventory on the last day of the volume discount period to verify there is not an overclaim for sales. Care must also be taken to look for large quantities of sales before the cut-off date that are returned after this date to falsely inflate sales and therefore secure a higher rebate. As such, the contract should specify that sales records must be available for inspection both during the period in question and after the period in question. Further, the agreement might also want to state that returns within a certain number of days after the end of the volume discount period, such as thirty days, must be netted against associated sales that occurred during the volume discount period.

3.4.1.4. Special Contract Considerations for Distribution Agreements

The prior section has touched on some special contract provisions to control channel partners. This section will outline provisions that are often overlooked and could be of help in the monitoring process:

1. Incentives to report accurately.
2. Requirement to use a common POS system that reports directly to the OEM when needed (i.e., daily, weekly, monthly).
3. Costs or penalties for not reporting accurately.
4. Audit rights.
5. System reporting anomalies that should be investigated and how such investigations are to be reported such as spikes or sudden drops in sales data. For example, a "gap analysis" is to be performed by the retailer if there is a period without sales of a particular stock number that tends to be active.
6. Raw data that must be retained to support EDI and the length of retention (one and a half years minimum with three years as better).
7. Ratio reports to be run, such as inventory turns.
8. Inventory roll forwards to be provided quarterly.
9. Procedures for approving new retailers.
10. Procedures to follow before selling at closeout prices.
11. Controls to prevent gray market activity from entering the channel (i.e., serial number, POS location/date, model number validation).
12. Territorial controls (these can be established by serial numbers, customer demographic reports, and retail locations).
13. Controls to prevent duplicate issuance of serial numbers.
14. Retailer and distributor specific serial number controls. So if the retailer or distributor is given specific serial numbers they are permitted to sell. This often identifies when distributors are selling amongst themselves.
15. Excess rebates to the same end user.

3.4.2. Key Terms and Conditions That Auditors Care About:

Auditing the channel is an important tool when relying on self-reported data from resellers and distributors. Industry expectations are strong that there will be auditing. Auditing is often done as either a detailed assessment or a cursory review based on a variety of risk factors identified by the OEM. The auditor must first consider the following terms and conditions before deciding the audit procedures that will occur (provided, of course, that there is a contract between the OEM and distributor or retailer):

1. Right-to-audit period and clause (generally in the partner contract and often duplicated in incentive program terms and conditions).
2. Minimum advance notice requirement or a statement allowing for unannounced audits and the requirement for the distributor to support the audit.
3. Right of access to data during an audit and other queries (if not an audit, such as specific document requests such as year-end inventory records).
4. Inventory control and reporting requirements, including reporting requirements of the distributors, subdistributors, and retailers.
5. Terms and conditions of incentive programs, including reporting requirements.
6. Sales/returns and reporting requirements (return controls should include the need to verify serial numbers of returned goods to sold goods, including a verification of the credit price to the original sales price).
7. EDI requirements, including frequency of reporting and system security (if EDI is not used, then other reporting methods, such as Web site reporting, e-mails, hard copy, CD data, and how to be delivered such as via overnight courier).
8. Systems in place to control monitoring and reporting, including require POS systems.
9. Financial reconciliation controls.
10. Right to validate end users.
11. Serial number or other product tracking requirements, including the need to supply serial numbers for warranty protection and incentive claims. Also, controls of the distributor or retailer that must be in place to prevent different transactions using the same serial number (i.e., the same serial number product can only be returned once for each sale) should be included.
12. Product sourcing requirements.
13. Territory.
14. Products.
15. Authorized customers.
16. Methods to deauthorize customers/retailers.
17. Methods to approve new customers/retailers.
18. Penalties.
19. Interest.

20. Grey market controls.
21. Records to be maintained to support incentive programs and the period during which those records need to be maintained. This should include how these records are to be maintained, such as raw, unscrubbed data.
22. Records to be submitted with incentive claims (i.e., POS data, end user data, reseller purchase order number, transaction date, model number, serial number, reseller name, invoice number, shipping date, claim form number, sales representative, authorization number).

3.4.3. Sample Key Terms and Conditions From a Distribution Agreement

"Whereas, OEM is desirous of granting an exclusive distributorship to Distributor for sales of products and services within exclusively assigned territories specified in Attachment B attached hereto and incorporated herein by reference (and they hereinafter being called the "Territory" and Distributor are desirous of undertaking responsibility of sales and services within said Territory;

WHEREAS, Distributor has sufficient facilities, resources, and personnel to adequately sell products and services within said territory and perform its obligations under this Agreement and is not precluded by any existing arrangements, contractual or otherwise, from entering into this Agreement.

NOW, THEREFORE, in consideration of the foregoing and in consideration of the mutual covenants hereinafter set forth, it is agreed by and between the parties hereto as follows:

1. *Product.*
   All medical devices of OEM approved for sale by the Food and Drug Administration for sale in the Territory excluding XXXX products.
2. *Units.*
   Model numbers as identified in Attachment C pursuance to the terms and conditions hereof.
3. *Territory.*
   United States and Canada.
4. *Term.*
   Twenty-four months, commencing with the first delivery of OEM products to Distributor. Upon expiration, or earlier termination, all products still in Distributor's possession shall remain subject to the terms of the agreement, and the parties shall remain obligated to perform their respective obligations through the expiration of the respective term and disposition of the units for each such Product in accordance with this agreement.

5. *Rights.*

OEM hereby grants the Distributor the exclusive right to enter into agreements for the sale of OEM's products and related services specified in Attachment B within the Territory with customers who carry on business in the Territory (hereinafter referred to as "customer"), subject to the terms and conditions herein. Notwithstanding, Distributor shall obtain written approval from the Vice President—Distribution, OEM, for all customer requests beyond the sale of product and service of authorized product prior to the execution of any Agreement by Distributor with its customers. The Distributor shall have the right to sell OEM products and services as specified in Attachment A and as may be updated and changed by OEM from time to time. Distributor shall have no right to appoint others to be distributors or subdistributors of OEM's products and services without OEM's prior written consent, and any such attempted appointment, without prior written consent, shall be void and without effect.

The relationship of OEM and the Distributor under this Agreement shall be, and shall at all times remain, one of independent contractor and not that of franchisor and franchisee, employer and employee, joint ventures, partners, affiliates, or principal and agent. Except as otherwise provided for in this Agreement neither OEM nor the Distributor shall have any authority to assume or create any obligation on the other's behalf with respect to the products and services or otherwise, and neither OEM nor the Distributor shall take any action that has the effect of creating the appearance of its having such authority.

6. *Guarantee Upfront Fee.*

Within 30 days after effective date of this agreement, Distributor shall pay OEM a Guarantee Upfront Fee of $xx,xxxx, which is recoupable to the extent provided below, but otherwise not subject to refund, set off or withholding: $x for each Unit sold is recoupable from the Net Distribution Revenues payable to OEM for such Unit.

7. *Duties of Distributor.*

Distributor shall use its best efforts to promote and solicit orders for the sales of OEM's products and services within the Territory at prices established by OEM and as agreed with Distributor to vary from time to time. Distributor shall prepare and forward to OEM reports of its sales prior to the shipment of Products and delivery of Services by OEM.

The Distributor shall solicit orders whereby customers shall purchase from the Distributor the right and sublicense to use the products and services through Distributor sublicense agreements which shall contain terms and conditions similar to those set forth in OEM's then existing Sales Agreements as the same may be amended from time to time. A copy of the most recent edition of OEM's Sales Agreement is attached hereto as Schedule A. Distributor will not vary such terms and conditions in its agreements with customers without the prior written authorization from OEM, which terms of variance shall be presented to OEM. The Distributor and its customers shall not have any rights to use the products and services except through the customer's acquisition of the rights to use pursuant to this Section. The license hereby granted to the Distributor authorizes the Distributor to (I) sublicense the products and services and (II) use the products and services for demonstrating and servicing customers of OEM products and services and for no other purposes. A copy of the Distributor's prospective customer agreements to be executed by customers are included in Schedule B. Such agreements shall contain language protecting OEM's confidential information as described in Section 21 below and OEM's copyright and trade secret rights under both U.S. and international law. A copy of each executed agreement must be retained by Distributor and forwarded to OEM by mail or overnight courier for delivery within thirty (30) days of the date signed by customer.

OEM hereby grants to Distributor and Distributor hereby accepts, subject to the terms and conditions set forth in this Agreement, an exclusive and non-transferable license to sublicense to customers located in the Territory OEM products and services specified in Attachment B.

Distributor shall separately track each Unit sale by type of customer transaction (e.g., rush, advance purchase, promotional) for each Distribution location by customer. Distributor shall keep accurate accounts, books, and records in relation to all its obligations hereunder including inventory and sales records involving the OEM's products which shall be sufficient to enable the OEM to check the accuracy of the Distributor with regard to Distributor's obligations under this Agreement.

8. *Audit Rights.*

[See example of audit right wording in Appendix to this book.]

9. *Sales Representative.*

OEM hereby designates the Distributor as its authorized sales representative for the Products listed on Schedule A in the Territories and the Distributor agrees to provide the following services to customers of the products and services:

9.1: Sales, returns, credits and invoicing.

9.2: Rebate processing.

9.3: Fulfillment of special customer requests.

9.4: Notification to OEM of warranty issues.

9.5: Warranty repair as preauthorized by OEM.

The foregoing services of the Distributor shall not relieve OEM of its obligation to promptly fulfill its obligations under its warranty program reported by customers if accompanied by valid and properly documented information including invoice. The method of warranty repair for reported defects is selected solely by OEM.

In the event any customer for any reason, during the term of this Agreement and any subsequent renewal periods, ceases to be entitled to the use or possession of the Products, Distributor shall take immediate action to insure that the products and services are completely removed from the premises of customer. Distributor shall promptly obtain and furnish OEM with a copy of a letter from such customer certifying complete removal and return of products and services.

10. *Duties of OEM.*

During the term of this Agreement, OEM agrees to provide to Distributor's customers all products and services as indicated in the Distributor's agreement with its customers.

OEM shall provide all technical sales support required and shall not unreasonably withhold requests for on-site technical support as determined by Distributor to support new sales and for the warranty period.

OEM shall provide legal services and consulting to Distributor for activities directly related to the sale of OEM products and services.

OEM shall on the first day of each calendar month pay Distributor a monthly retainer in the amount of $XXXXXX to conducts any and all sales activities under this Agreement.

11. *No Purchases Elsewhere.*

Distributor will not obtain OEM products from any other source during the applicable Distribution period.

12. *Advertising Allowance.*

To the extent Distributor spends money promoting OEM products to customers, retailers and the general public, Distributor shall be entitled to an allowance for such verifiable expenditures in an amount of up to 5 percent of Net Distribution Revenues, but will not in any way reduce the Guaranteed Upfront Fees or monthly retainer fees. Distributor shall adequately document and report such expenditures with each distribution report.

13. *Distribution Report.*

Distributor shall report to OEM (or its designee) weekly for each OEM product units sold, gross revenues, discounts, net sales price, freight, sales by model number, serial number of sold products, advertising expenditures, distribution expenses and other revenues and expenses in accordance with the format included in Schedule C."

3.5. Franchisee Contracts

3.5.1. Contract Description

Franchisee contracts govern a franchisee's distribution of franchisor products or services though independent retail operations. Franchising has been an American fixture since Isaac Singer franchised the Singer sewing machine in the early 1850s. On the most basic level, the "franchisor" provides goodwill associated with the franchisor's trademark to the "franchisee." Depending on the level of service and the industry, the franchisor can provide many different services to the franchisee, including all goods provided for retail operations, technical training or techniques, instructions on store presentation, operating and procedure manuals, marketing, distribution, Web sites, and service support.

Because of the wide variety of franchise agreements, there is no standard format. Franchising is very common in most every goods and service industry and is particularly prevalent in restaurants (McDonald's, Domino's Pizza, Subway, Quiznos) and service organizations (cleaning, mailbox stores, Fantastic Sams). It is difficult to find an industry without franchising opportunities. Other industries including advertising, auto products and services, business services, child care, cleaning, cosmetics, clothing and other personal goods, computer services, dental, dry cleaning, financial services, health clubs, mobile phones, retail, real estate, restaurants and food, security and protection, and travel agencies.

The franchisor makes money through a variety of methods from the franchisee. Most often, there is an up-front fee (sometimes called "key money") to buy a franchisee. In addition to the up-front fee, there is a revenue share, similar to royalty payments, that the franchisee pays to the franchisor. There might be minimum advertising commitments. The franchisee is often required to buy its goods from the franchisor or send personnel to training under the franchisor's control where the franchisee must pay the franchisor for the training. These goods purchases provide consistency in goods to the end-user, allow the franchisor greater control over franchisees, provides excellent monitoring of franchisee activities, and provides for greater profits to the franchisor, thanks to the selling of the goods to the franchisee.

Franchising can be a very successful tool for franchisors to inexpensively expand operations when they lack capital or they wish to spread the risk of new operations to other individuals. The downside to a franchisor is the lack of complete day-to-day on-site monitoring of franchisees and the ability of franchisees to easily understate revenues and therefore understate royalty expenditures. Further, franchisees have been known to sell unauthorized products in franchisee stores, thereby reducing the image in the eye of the end-user consumers who generally are unaware of stores that are franchised versus company owed.

A franchisee has an incentive to pay the fees and often substantial start-up costs to be a franchisee as the franchisor often holds the hand of the franchisee to help the franchisee establish the business and benefit from consumer recognition/goodwill established by the franchisor. Franchisee businesses often succeed where others fail because procuring a franchisee, such as a Subway restaurant, is often done with a much lower risk of failure than another new business, thanks to recognition from other stores carrying the same name and products and the ability to use proven business plans. Some franchisors even offer financing for the franchisee (up to two-thirds as a general rule), along with in-the-field hand-holding support and training as it is to the benefit of the franchisor that each franchisee succeeds.

Because many franchisors are small (not McDonalds or Subway), it is very important that an attorney be involved to represent the interest of the franchisor and franchisee. The franchisor often looks for a high degree of control over the franchisee and looks to make revenues through various methods from the franchisee, such as start up, selling products, and advertising and other fees. The franchisor wants the agreement to specifically state the costs and fees to be paid to the franchisor and limit the franchisee's ability to obtain these services outside the control of the franchisor. The franchisee, on the other hand, wants to maintain as much business freedom as possible, have freedom to source goods from a variety of suppliers, and secure reduced costs. The document most often used as the base source for franchising contracts is the Uniform Franchise Offering Circular (UFOC). This document seems to be the size of a novel and is filled with so many restrictions that it is often difficult for any franchisee to be expected to follow. Therefore, it is imperative to gain proper legal counsel to argue all the fine points of the franchise agreement.

3.5.2. Key Terms and Conditions That Auditors Care About

Advertising: The auditor will test if advertising to the public, from signs to products, has been properly approved, is not confusing, and conforms to contractual requirements of public notification.

Sample language: "Franchisee shall use signs and other advertising which denote that the Restaurant is named "ABC" and that are approved by the Company in advance. Franchisee shall not develop, create, generate, own, license, lease or use in any manner any computer medium or electronic medium (including, without limitation, any Internet home page, e-mail address, Web site, domain name, bulletin board, newsgroup, or other Internet-related medium) which in any way uses or displays, in whole or in part, the Franchisor's Marks, or any of them, or any words, symbols or terms confusingly similar thereto without Franchisor's express written consent, and then only in such manner and in accordance with such procedures, policies, standards and specifications as Franchisor may establish from time to time. In the event of a breach of this Section, the Company shall have the right to remove any unauthorized material at the expense of Franchisee."

Advertising Fee or Marketing Fee: This fee or fund is either similar to the franchisee royalty that must be paid to the franchisor or is a minimum marketing expenditure to be spent in the franchisee's market on authorized marketing expenditures. The marketing contribution tends to be between 3 percent and 5 percent of net sales and may be capped at a certain dollar amount. It is very common for the franchisee to not make the necessary marketing commitment or claim marketing expenditures that are not authorized as acceptable under the agreement to meet the minimum annual marketing expenditure. The self-monitoring company should 1) ask for the marketing support with the claimed marketing expenditures and 2) compare the marketing payments to the agreement for the contract compliance.

The auditor will look to test the same items as can be reviewed remotely by the franchisor, which is the contribution percentage per the agreement to the payments to the licensor. However, if the franchisee is required to directly spend on advertising and promotion, the support for such expenditures is generally maintained at the licensee's location so the auditor will want to see the actual advertisement to make certain it meets franchisor conditions. The proof of payment and the advertising agreement will need to be reviewed in case there are kickbacks or refunds that allow the franchisee, on a net basis, to underpay the marketing or promotion commitment.

Sample language: "A fee for advertising, public relations and promotion and for the creation and development of advertising, public relations and promotional campaigns in the amount of five percent (6%) of Franchisee's weekly Gross Sales, if the Restaurant is located outside of the designated market area ("DMA"), or four percent (3.5%) of Franchisee's weekly Gross Sales, as defined if the Restaurant is located within the DMA."

Audit/Inspection Rights: Audit and inspection rights for a franchise extend well beyond those of many other third party monitoring agreements because the focus is on financial records as well as the presentation of the franchisee in a manner consistent with other franchisees and franchisor operating requirements. A franchisor maintains a high degree of control over the franchisee and therefore works to control daily operations. As such, the inspection needs to review all franchisee operations.

Sample language: "In order to maintain the high standards of quality necessary for the mutual success of the Franchisor and Franchisee hereunder, the Franchisor and its authorized representatives shall have the right to inspect the Restaurant and the supplies and inventory of franchisee. The Franchisor's personnel and representatives shall have the right to enter the Restaurant at any reasonable time, and from time to time, with or without notice, for the purposes of examination, conferences with Franchisee and personnel of Franchisee, observation and evaluation of the operations being conducted at the Restaurant, and for all other purposes in connection with a determination that the Restaurant is being operated in accordance with the terms of this Agreement, the Specifications and Manual and other applicable laws and regulations.

In the event that any such Inspection Report indicates a deficiency or unsatisfactory condition with respect to any item listed thereon, Franchisee shall promptly commence to correct or repair such deficiency or unsatisfactory condition and thereafter diligently pursue the same to completion. In the event of a failure by Franchisee to comply with the foregoing obligation to correct or repair, the Franchisor, in addition to all other available rights and remedies, including the right to terminate this Agreement, shall have the right, but not the obligation, to forthwith make or cause to be made such correction or repair, and the expenses thereof, including, without limitation, meals, lodging, wages, and transportation for the Franchisor's personnel, if so utilized in the Franchisor's sole discretion, shall be reimbursed by Franchisee. Should any deficiency or unsatisfactory condition be reported more than once within any thirty (30) day period, the Franchisor shall have the right, in addition to all other available rights and remedies, to place a Franchisor representative in charge of the Restaurant for a period of up to thirty (30) days in each such instance, and the wages and expenses of meals, lodging and transportation of said representative, which shall be commensurate with that provided for managers of other Franchisor-owned restaurants, shall promptly be reimbursed by Franchisee. All such expenses incurred by the Franchisor pursuant to this Section shall be set forth in a written invoice delivered to Franchisee by the Franchisor. Franchisee shall reimburse the Franchisor for the invoice amount within seven (7) days after the invoice has been delivered to Franchisee."

Designated Supplier: One of the key ways that a franchisor monitors a franchisee is by being the supplier of food and supplies. By knowing the number of products purchased by the franchisee, the franchisor can very closely monitor the franchisee's reporting of revenues. Generally, anything more than a small variance between goods sold to the franchisee and goods reported and sold to customers will be an instant indication to the franchisor that there is a misreporting. Hence, franchisors are amongst the best at being able to monitor contract compliance of the self-reporting third party. Therefore, it is critical that franchisors use designated suppliers and franchisors make certain franchisees only purchase supplies from designated suppliers. Further, designated suppliers must be required to report directly to the franchisor all sales made to franchisees. Franchisors generally have audit rights of both the franchisee and the supplier to make certain the supplier is properly reporting all sales. Sometimes, the franchisor is also the designated supplier, thereby removing the doubt of the number of units of goods sold to the franchisees.

The auditor will look at purchasing records to make certain supplies only came from properly authorized suppliers. Further, the records of the designated supplier will be compared to the purchase records of the franchisee to make certain the two sets of records agree. This is a method to also monitor the supplier in case the supplier must pay a fee on each good sold to the franchisor.

Sample language: "Franchisee agrees to purchase all ingredients and products exclusively from the Franchisor or, in the Franchisor's sole discretion, from the Franchisor's designated distributor. The right to purchase and use such products is licensed to Franchisee pursuant to this Agreement, and such right is restricted to use in the franchise business at the Restaurant and solely for the term of this Agreement."

Distributorship or Subfranchisees: Some franchisees have a right to sub-distribute the product. The further downstream the final distribution to the end user customer (i.e., going through various middlemen) the greater the chances of misreporting as each subdistributor reporting manipulates the numbers and therefore can miscalculate the numbers. Further, a franchisor often does not have rights or access to subdistributor information, thus making monitoring more difficult. See the section on distributors for more information.

An auditor will want to see all subdistribution or subfranchisee agreements, make certain the subdistributors or subfranchisees are authorized, and will want to see statements from sub-distributors in case the amounts from these sub-distributors role up to the amounts due the franchisor.

Franchise or Key Fee: A company wishing to be a franchisee must purchase the right to be a franchisee from the franchisor. This purchase is called a "franchisee fee." Franchisee fees are generally calculated based on the expected net profits of the franchisee. Having a high franchisee fee helps encourage a franchisee to be more successful as they have "more skin in the game." Some franchisors will finance the franchisee fee.

An auditor will just want to make certain the franchisee fee was paid in a timely manner and may calculate interest in case there was a late payment.

Sample language: "An initial franchise fee of Thirty-five Thousand Dollars ($35,000), payable as follows: (i) Ten Thousand Dollars ($10,000) upon execution of this Agreement (and within 30 days of delivery of execution copies of this Agreement to Franchisee); and (ii) Twenty-five Thousand Dollars ($25,000) on the earlier of (a) forty-eight hours following the commencement of physical construction or remodeling of the Restaurant; or (b) 12 months following Company's execution of this Agreement; provided, however, if the Restaurant is a Turnkey Restaurant the initial franchise fee shall be payable upon execution of this Agreement. All such payments shall be made by cashier's check or other form of payment acceptable to the Company. Franchisee hereby acknowledges and agrees that the grant of this franchise and the agreements of the Company contained in this Agreement constitute the sole and only consideration for the payment of the initial franchise fee and the initial franchise fee shall be fully earned by the Company upon execution of this Agreement. In that regard, upon the payment of any portion of the initial franchise fee, the entire initial franchise fee shall be deemed fully earned and non-refundable in consideration of the administrative and other expenses incurred by the Company in granting this franchise and for the Company's lost or deferred opportunity to franchise to others. Additionally, there is a Grand Opening Fee of Ten Thousand Dollars ($10,000), payable upon payment in full of the Initial Fee."

Insurance: A franchisee should be required to maintain a certain level of general liability insurance. The auditor will make certain that such insurance is in place for the franchise period.

Sample language: "During the term hereof, Franchisee shall obtain and maintain insurance coverage with insurance carriers acceptable to the Company in accordance with the Company's current insurance requirements. The coverage shall commence when the Location is secured by Franchisee by executed deed or lease and shall comply with the requirements of Franchisee's lease, if any, for products liability and broad form contractual liability coverage in the amount of at least five million dollars ($5,000,000.00) combined single limit. Franchisee shall also carry fire and extended coverage insurance with endorsements for vandalism and malicious mischief, covering the building, structures, equipment, improvements and the contents thereof in and at the Restaurant, on a full replacement cost basis, insuring against all risks of direct physical loss except for unusual perils such as nuclear attack, earth movement and war, and business interruption insurance in actual loss sustained form covering the rental of the Location, previous profit margins, maintenance of competent personnel and other fixed expenses. Franchisee shall also carry such worker's compensation insurance as may be required by applicable law. In connection with and prior to commencing any construction, reimage or remodeling of the Restaurant, Franchisee shall maintain Builder's All Risks Insurance and performance and completion bonds in forms and amounts, and written by a carrier or carriers, acceptable to the Company. As proof of such insurance, a certificate of insurance shall be submitted by Franchisee for the Company's approval prior to Franchisee's commencement of any activities or services to be performed under this Agreement. Franchisee shall deliver a complete copy of Franchisee's then-prevailing policies of insurance to the Company within thirty (30) days following the delivery of the certificate of insurance. The Company shall be named as an additional insured on all of such policies referenced to the extent of its interests and shall be provided with certificates of insurance evidencing such coverage prior to the Opening Date and promptly following the date any policy of insurance is renewed, modified or replaced during the term of this Agreement. All coverages shall be placed with an insurer with a rating of A or better from Moody's or S&P or a rating of A-VIII or better from Best's."

Late Payment: Royalty and franchisee fees are due for payment as of a certain date. The timeliness of payment should be monitored with interest on the late payment charged in accordance with the agreement.

Sample language: "Franchisee agrees to pay interest to the Company on any amounts which may become due to the Company from Franchisee, if such are not paid when due, at the rate of 1.5 percent compounded monthly, or the maximum interest rate permitted by law, whichever is less."

Lease Agreement: The franchisee should be required to have certain language in the lease agreement with the landlord to make certain the franchisee can advertise the business as required and to make certain the landlord will notify the licensee of any restrictions or actions against the property. The auditor will read the lease agreement to make certain it contains the contracted requirements with the leaseholder.

Sample language: "Any lease entered into by Franchisee shall include the following terms and conditions:

i. The landlord consents to Franchisee's use of the premises as an Franchisor restaurant and such restaurant may be open for business during the required days and hours set forth in the Manual from time to time;
ii. The landlord agrees to furnish the Company with copies of any and all notices of default, if any, pertaining to the lease and the premises, at the same time that such notices are sent to Franchisee; and
iii. The landlord agrees that, subject to any other applicable provisions in this Agreement, the Company shall have the right, at its sole option and without any obligation whatsoever to do so, to assume Franchisee's occupancy rights under the lease for the remainder of its term upon Franchisee's default or termination under such lease, the termination of this Agreement, or the exercise by the Company of its right of first refusal or right to purchase."

Books, Records, and Net Worth: Many franchisees are required to maintain a certain financial viability in order to stay in business. Franchisees that are performing poorly tend to cut corners and not perform to the licensor's expectations. To monitor the franchisee, the franchisor looks to the statement of income and the franchisee's "net worth." Net worth is simply a balance sheet calculation of total assets minus liabilities. Companies with negative or low net worth can be challenged as to their ability to be a going concern. As these companies could face bankruptcy in the near future, the franchisor may wish to keep a close eye on the franchisee or consider actions to help boost the franchisee back to a successful business model. Net worth should be considered with other financial statement ratios. One must keep in mind that net worth is based on financial statements, which are historical in nature, and therefore might not reflect current activities or values. For example, if a building is purchased for $1,000, it might be later worth $20,000 as of the financial statement date thus boosting value of the company by $19,000; however, the financial statements will not reflect this unrealized gain in the value of the building as the net worth will still be based on the building with a value of $1,000. On the other hand, if the building drops in value, such as to $500, then the building should be devalued in the financial statements and net worth will be a better reflection of the business.

The auditor will ask to see the franchisee's financial statements to review the balance sheet for the financial stability of the entity. If the franchisee is audited by an independent accounting firm, the franchisor's auditor will take an especially close look at the financial auditor's opinion as to if the entity ha a going-concern issue.

Sample language: "Thirty (30) days after the end of each fiscal quarter of the franchise business during the term of this Agreement, Franchisee shall provide to the Franchisor an unaudited profit and loss statement and a balance sheet of the franchise business which shall include such information and data as specified by the Company. Such fiscal year-end financial statements must be signed by Franchisee Owner or Franchisee's chief financial officer and contain a representation that the financial statements present fairly the financial position of Franchisee and the results of operations of the franchise business during the period covered in accordance with generally accepted accounting procedures. Franchisee shall maintain accurate and complete books and records pertaining to the operation and maintenance of the Restaurant as required by the standards, policies and procedures established by the Company in accordance with the Manual. Franchisee shall be solely responsible for performing all record keeping duties, and the cost for all such services shall be borne solely by Franchisee."

Noncompete Clause: A noncompete clause is important to help make certain a former franchisee no longer performs services the franchisor will be selling to perhaps a new franchisee. The applicability of the noncompete clause needs to be evaluated on a state-by-state basis as some states do not enforce noncompete clauses as they can be against public policy or the general benefit of the public.

Operating Manual: One of the most valuable services of a franchisor is to train the franchisee. This training is generally provided by the franchisor to the franchisee, and it contains the basic instruction related to running the business and reporting on the business's operations.

The auditor will compare the operating manual to the franchisee's actual activities with a special emphasis on cash controls, security, human resources, and point of sale operations.

Sample language: "Franchisee acknowledges and agrees that strict and continued adherence by Franchisee to the Company's standards, policies, procedures and requirements, as set forth in this Section, is expressly made a condition of this Agreement, so that failure on the part of Franchisee to so perform will be grounds for termination of this Agreement. Franchisee acknowledges that changes, modifications, deletions and additions to the standards, specifications, procedures and menu items may be necessary and desirable from time to time. The Company may make such modifications, revisions, deletions and additions, including without limitation modifications, revisions, deletions and additions to the Manual and to the menu items required to be offered by Franchisee, which the Company, in good faith and exercising its judgment, believes to be desirable and reasonably necessary. Franchisee agrees to comply with any such modification, revision, deletion or addition as of the date that such modification, revision, deletion or addition becomes effective. Franchisee acknowledges that it shall receive the Manual on loan from the Company and that the Manual shall at all times remain the sole property of the Company. Franchisee understands that the Company has entered into this Agreement in reliance upon Franchisee's representation that it will strictly comply with all the provisions of the Manual. For purposes of this Agreement, the Manual shall be deemed to include all written directions delivered to Franchisee by Company from time to time setting forth standards, specifications and procedures for the operation of Franchisee's restaurant."

Point of Sale Registers: Of extreme importance is making certain that all sales are captured. Franchisees can be very inventive in not reporting sales, and the franchisor must go to great lengths to make certain all sales are captured so the proper royalty can be paid. Franchisees are known to procure products from sources other than the franchisor or approved sources and sell those products off book or not record all sales on a franchisor approved invoice and/or sales register system. An auditor performing a surprise inspection is always first on the lookout for a tick sheet next to the register indicating off-register sales. A quick count of the cash drawer can also indicate off-invoice or register sales if there is more money than expected in the till.

Sample language: "Franchisee shall record all sales and all receipts of revenue on individual machine serial numbered guest checks. Cash registers must validate a receipt which will be presented at the time of sale to each customer. Franchisee shall only use cash registers of a cumulative non-resettable type as designated and approved in writing by the Company and shall provide the Company or its employees with a key to permit readings of the running of such cash registers at any time, at the Company's discretion. If, for any reason, the Restaurant's cash registers must be repaired, replacement cash registers must be used in their absence, with a beginning non-resettable total recorded. The presence of any more than the original non-resettable cash registers must have the Company's prior written approval. During any period of repair of the authorized cash registers in the Restaurant, all business records of Franchisee shall be kept on forms and in accordance with the procedures as prescribed by the Franchisor from time to time in its sole discretion. Notification of the replacement of any cash registers must be made in advance to the Franchisor. The Franchisor may require Franchisee, at Franchisee's expense, to convert to, install and use in the Restaurant a computer-based cash control and restaurant management, or "point of sale," system. The Franchisor must approve the criteria on which Franchisee's system will run and communicate with the Franchisor's system. Franchisee also agrees to procure and install such data processing equipment computer hardware, software, required dedicated telephone, communication and power lines, modems, printers, and other computer-related accessory or peripheral equipment as the Franchisor may require. Franchisee agrees that the Franchisor shall have the free and unfettered right to retrieve any data and information from Franchisee's computers as the Franchisor, in its sole discretion, may deem appropriate, with the telephonic (or similar means of communication) cost of the retrieval to be borne by the Franchisor, including electronically polling the daily sales, menu mix and other data of the Restaurant. Franchisor may require Franchisee to maintain an e-mail account and connect the Franchisee's computer system to a telephone line (or other communications medium specified by the Franchisor) at all times and be capable of accessing the Internet via a designated third-party network. Upon request, Franchisee shall permit the Franchisor to access its computer system in the Restaurant and the files stored therein, with or without prior notice via any means specified by the Franchisor, including electronic polling communications. All of the hardware and software specified to be installed or purchased, shall be at Franchisee's expense. Franchisee must utilize any proprietary software program that the Franchisor may develop in addition to system documentation manuals and other proprietary materials developed by the Franchisor in connection to the operation of the Restaurant. If and when the Franchisor develops proprietary software, the Franchisor may require that Franchisee execute a standard form software license agreement and input and maintain in the Franchisee's computer the software programs, data and information as the Franchisor prescribes. Franchisee must purchase the proprietary software programs, manuals whenever the Franchisor decides to use new or upgraded programs, manuals and/or materials from Franchisor or an approved distributor, if any, and if from an approved distributor, upon terms determined by such distributor; provided, however, that Franchisee shall not be required to replace such system more frequently than once every five (5) years during the term of this Agreement. In such event, Franchisee shall adopt such related procedures as the Franchisor may require to obtain the efficient use of such system."

Royalty: The periodic fee paid, generally as a percent of gross sales, is a royalty. This is different than that of a licensee because a licensee's royalty is generally based on net sales as opposed to gross (however, there might be an allowance for returns against gross revenues). The definition of what constitutes the royalty payment base must be very clear as explained throughout this book. Payments to the franchisor are generally monthly but can stretch to as far as quarterly.

The auditor will focus on the royalty calculation to make certain that gross sales are properly supported based on supplies, point of sale receipts, expectations, and other sources.

Sample language for defining the royalty is, "A weekly royalty fee in the sum of five percent (5%) of Franchisee's weekly Gross Sales."

Sample language for defining gross revenue is, "The term "Gross Sales" as used in this Agreement shall mean the total revenues derived by Franchisee in and from the Restaurant from all sales of food, goods, wares, merchandise and all services made in, upon, or from the Restaurant, whether for cash, check, credit or otherwise, without reserve or deduction for inability or failure to collect the same, including, without limitation, all revenues derived from delivery, catering, and special event sales, such sales and services where the orders therefore originate at and are accepted by Franchisee into the Restaurant but delivery or performance thereof is made from or at any other place, or other similar orders are received or billed at or from the Restaurant, and any sums or receipts derived from the sale of meals to employees of the Restaurant. Gross Sales shall not include rebates or refunds to customers; or the amount of any sales taxes or other similar taxes that Franchisee may be required to and does collect from customers to be paid to any federal, state or local taxing authority."

Sample language to provide for monitoring is, "Franchisee shall deliver to the Company on or before the tenth (10th) calendar day after each week a weekly Gross Sales statement (WGSS), in the form specified by the Company, setting forth the amount of Gross Sales for the preceding week and a calculation of the weekly fees payable on such sales. Weekly fees, including royalty and advertising fees, shall be due and payable on the tenth (10th) day after the close of the sales week, which closing shall be designated by the franchisor. Franchisee shall make all payments due hereunder by one of the following forms of payment (the "Forms of Payment"): check, electronic funds transfer, pre-arranged draft or sweep of Franchisee's bank account. Franchisee will give the Company authorization for direct debits from Franchisee's business bank operating account. If Franchisee is delinquent in any payment of such fees, or if Franchisee has not submitted the WGSS for more than a two-week period, the Company may, in its sole discretion initiate an EFT transfer from Franchisee's business bank account an estimated amount of fees due the Company for such period which shall be based on the average of the immediately preceding three (3) months Gross Sales. If, at any time, the Company determines that Franchisee has under-reported the weekly Gross Sales of the Restaurant, or underpaid the weekly royalty, advertising fees, DMA Advertising Fee, or other amounts due to the Company under this Agreement, or any other agreement, the Company may, in addition to exercising all other rights and remedies available to it under this Agreement, initiate an immediate transfer from the Account in the amount equal to the unpaid fees in accordance with the foregoing procedure, including interest. Any overpayment of fees will be credited to the Account effective as of the first Due Date after the Company and Franchisee determine that such credit is due.

In connection with payment of the weekly royalty fee and advertising fee by EFT, Franchisee shall: (1) comply with procedures specified by the Company relating to EFT transfers; (2) perform those acts and sign and deliver those documents as may be necessary to accomplish payment by EFT as described in this Section 7.2; (3) give the Company an authorization in the form designated by the Company to initiate debit entries and/or credit correction entries to the Account for payments of the weekly royalty and advertising fees, or other amounts due to the Company under this Agreement, or any other agreement, including any interest charges; and (4) make sufficient funds available in the Account for withdrawal by EFT of fees due no later than each Due Date.

In addition to the sales data required to be provided in the WGSS to be delivered, Franchisee shall deliver to the Company on or before the tenth (10th) day after the end of each sales week during the term of this Agreement any other sales and menu mix data reasonably requested by the Company with respect to the preceding sales week, whether specified in the Manual or otherwise."

Territory: A franchisor needs to protect territories. Generally, a franchisor must follow a few commonsense business rules associated with approving retail store or other franchisee locations to make certain there is not market saturation, and the franchisee can be viable. The franchisor must consider both competition and other franchisees before assigning a location or territory to a new franchisee. A franchisee will want to know it owns a specific territory from the franchisor as the franchisee does not want to be competing against another franchisee for the same customers. Territories are often defined by street boundaries, zip codes, or locations such as a mall. Franchisees who attempt to sell out of their territory can face serious consequences as this may be considered a major breach if the franchisee is taking revenues away from another franchisee.

Auditors will look at the territory to which a franchisee is given rights to sell products. While the franchisee might have one store location, the auditor still needs to make certain the franchisee is not expanding that store to more than one location or potentially delivering product or sending marketing materials outside the franchisees authorized territory.

Working Capital: Similar to net worth, a franchisee must maintain a certain ratio of working capital. Working capital means cash liquid assets. It is the amount of money to meet cash flow needs. If a franchisee cannot meet cash flow requirements, even with a lot of net worth, then the franchisee can face serious going concern consequences not to mention human resource issues if cash flow is insufficient to cover payroll and taxes.

The auditor will make certain cash on hand is sufficient to handle ongoing operating needs. The auditor might also look at accounts receivables to assess if the amounts will be collectable or if write-offs are still being monitored in case the franchisor benefits from any reversal of write-offs.

3.5.3. Reporting Areas and Associated Risks

The primary reporting area for a franchisee is gross sales. Franchisor controls help to mitigate these risks by monitoring reported revenues against sales to the franchisee and comparing reported gross sales of other franchisees based on similar supply shipments.

Risks of franchisees underreporting are minimal if the franchisee is required to use a designated supplier, and the franchisor reconciles the supplies purchased to reported sales.

If a franchisee fails to make timely royalty payments, the franchisor can simply cut off the supply of product (if allowed by law) so the franchisee can sell no goods until the franchisor is paid. This gives a great deal of power to the franchisor.

3.5.4. Documents to Consider Requesting in the Contract to Allow for Adequate External Monitoring

Many franchisors rely on constant monitoring of franchisees to quickly identify any potential underreporting. Franchisors might think they don't have the luxury of constant monitoring, such as franchised storage facilities, franchised services, or franchised facilities where there are no designated suppliers; however, with proper planning and controls, just about any franchisor can constantly monitor the franchisees. The forward-thinking franchisor can identify many different ways to constantly monitor franchisees even when one might not think there is a good way. The most prevalent method is through the use of common networks that require franchisees to conduct all business on a computer server hosted by the franchisor. For example, a franchisee storage location would be required to have all lease contracts entered into a computer system controlled by the franchisor so that the franchisor knows as soon as the lease agreement is signed and therefore knows how much money to expect from the storage location. Therefore, by making use of adequate external monitoring, the franchisor, in most cases, need simply establish different control points via a computer network and then make certain all business of a franchisee must pass through that computer network (commonly referred to as the point of sale).

Some franchisees try to have off-computer transactions, such as by having a second cash register not tied into the computer network or using a tick sheet to record off-computer transactions, but a good franchisor will identify when such off-computer network transactions are occurring because expected sales revenues will not be achieved. To catch the franchisee in action, it is therefore important that the franchisor have audit inspection rights that include "surprise audits" where an auditor can drop in at anytime and get immediate access to books and records; failure to fully comply with a surprise inspection can result in contract termination. A sharp royalty auditor can identify a tick sheet or the extra point of sale system (i.e., calculator with a separate tap) and thereby quickly identify misreporting. Franchisee field audits generally occur after a franchisor senses the franchisee is misreporting as such audits can quickly cost more than the value of the actual audit given the small size of most franchisee operations.

3.6. Joint Venture and Partner Contract

3.6.1. Contract Description

A joint venture is when entities work together under a contract to share risk and reward. It is a co-ownership arrangement; however, control over operations is subject to contractual terms such as one of the co-owners controlling all operations, joint venture holders controlling operations through certain designated tasks, joint venture holders controlling by committee, or a new legal entity is created with independent operators who report to the joint venture operators.

Also known as a "JV," a joint venture is commonly started when two or more entities make a capital contribution and share in the rewards and loss in accordance with a contracted formula. A JV can be many different types of entities, such as a partnership, corporation, LLC, or other legal structure.

When I worked for Occidental Petroleum's (Oxy) internal audit department, I was called upon to audit joint venture operations where Oxy had an investment in operations run by another company. As the auditor, I had to determine if net remittances to Oxy were proper and if the joint venture was being operated as required under the agreement. What further complicated the audit was one of the joint venture holders was also a foreign government, so there was a constant need to make certain the JV was acting well above the law and in complete compliance with all contractual provisions as breach of the JV agreement by any party (other than the government) could result in very adverse publicity, lost profits, or even company seizure. Therefore, having a very well-defined JV contract was critical for both government related reasons and of course to make certain the millions of dollars of revenues were properly reported to Oxy.

The JV agreement I audited for Oxy gave almost complete control to the other entity but audit rights allowed for an annual audit of the JV. And because it was a JV in the oil and gas industry, we were concerned with many items that posed potential risks to the JV beyond just counting the revenues correctly such as proper environmental and safety controls, procurement controls (such as bidding), payment controls, and all other facets of the operations where a mistake by the JV could affect the benefits that Oxy could have been receiving.

3.6.2. Key Terms and Conditions That Auditors Care About

1. Profit and Loss Statement and Allocations (aka revenue sharing).
   A company will invest into a JV in hope of an economic return. Most often this return is expressed as the sharing of net revenues as defined by the JV agreement. The calculation of net revenues often provides the

self-reporting company (i.e., the JV operator) the opportunity for significant interpretation of items regarding what should be excluded from revenues and included in expenses. Because of these interpretations, JV statements of revenue sharing are often filled with contract noncompliance issues.

JV contracts attempt to specifically identify all items that can and cannot be included in the calculation of profit and loss and the associated allocation to the joint venture investors. But, as nature would have it, not all economic activities of a JV and its operator can be anticipated, thus providing the self-reporting JV operator the responsibility to interpret how the revenues will be reported and shared. Unfortunately, for the JV investor, these contract interpretations always seem to result in a higher share of net revenues to the JV operator at the expense of the investor.

To help prevent interpretation issues, the profit and loss allocation calculation must generally be described in painstaking detail within the JV contract. This includes a sample profit and loss statement (aka "income statement" when there is a net profit or "statement of operations" when there is a net loss).

All sources of revenues should be clearly identified within the operating description of the joint venture with flexibility to allow unanticipated revenue streams to also be captured within the JV's revenues (such as a geothermal company in a pristine jungle area that leases land for a tourist hotel that was not anticipated when the JV geothermal operations were started). Care must be taken to make certain that all revenues or potential revenues from JV properties shall be properly accounted for by the JV operator at an arm's-length transaction. Further, the decision should also be made as to how these revenues affect the minimum expectation of the JV investor, including the operator's responsibilities and results.

Expenses generally see more reporting issues than revenues due to the various types of expenses that a JV operator may incur, many of which might be unrelated to the JV. For example, executive compensation and perks are often subject to high charges to a joint venture operation at the expense of the investor into the JV, especially when the executive is an owner of the JV operator. Another common expense abuse area is overhead or corporate allocation charges of the parent company of the JV operator. And last, a very common area for abuse is the use of JV operator employees who are working on operations unrelated to the JV but have the full expense of their services charged to the JV.

One area with self-reporting issues is related to expense refunds and kickbacks. JV operators tend to not report expense refunds, especially related to government tax incentives or offsets (particularly true for countries with value-added taxes). For example, joint ventures are very common in movie productions, and it is common for the motion picture production company to pay a large dollar amount for Kodak film (yes, some directors still like old-fashioned film) and at the end of the film production, Kodak will give a rebate to the motion picture production company. It is amazing the number of times this rebate from Kodak will not be reported by the motion picture production company to the JV partners. There can be a variety of reasons for this, including the fact that the rebate can take months to be received after the end of the movie, so production statements are stale, and everyone has forgotten about the need to spread the wealth of the refund.

The profit and loss statement is to have the losses and profits allocated to the JVs (investor). This is generally a simple allocation of the bottom line net revenues (or loss) in accordance with a percentage established in the agreement.

The auditor will spend the most time during an audit examining the income statement. Great care will be taken to make certain that all revenues have been reported in the proper period and that all expenses are properly supported.

Contract language should clearly identify that unsupported expenses will be denied unless such expenses are approved in advance by the JV investor. Approval of a budget is not the same as approving expenses in advance, and this should only occur for emergency or unique situations. New revenue streams caused by significant changes in operations (i.e., building a tourist hotel on geothermal property) should also be subject to advance approval by the JV investor.

Sample language: "'Profits' and 'Losses' means, for each fiscal year or other period, an amount for such year or period determined in the manner prescribed in the United States Internal Revenue Service Code Section XXXX, (i) using the tax accounting methods used for Federal income tax purposes, (ii) adding any tax-exempt income and subtracting any deductions or expenditures described in or treated as expenditures under IRS Code Section XXX not otherwise taken into account, (iii) reflecting the book adjustment of the Capital Accounts as initially reflected in Article X hereof and as prescribed in IRS Code Section XXX, and (iv) taking into account any amounts or items of income or expense specially allocated pursuant to 'Net Income' or 'Net Loss' means, for each fiscal year or other applicable period, an amount equal to the Joint Venture's net income or loss for such year or period as determined for federal income tax purposes by Independent Public Accountants, determined in accordance with IRS Code Section XXX (for this purpose, all items of income, gain, loss, or deduction required to be stated separately pursuant to IRS Code Section shall be included in taxable income or loss), with the following adjustments: (a) by including as an item of gross income any tax-exempt income received by the

Partnership; (b) by treating as a deductible expense any expenditure of the Partnership described in IRS Code Section (including amounts paid or incurred to organize the Partnership (unless an election is made pursuant to IRS Code Section XXX)) or to promote the sale of interests in the Partnership and by treating deductions for any losses incurred in connection with the sale or exchange of Partnership property disallowed pursuant to IRS Code Section XXX expenditures; (c) in lieu of depreciation, depletion, amortization, and other cost recovery deductions taken into account in computing total income or loss, there shall be taken into account depreciation; (d) gain or loss resulting from any disposition of Partnership property with respect to which gain or loss is recognized for federal income tax purposes shall be computed by reference to the Gross Asset Value of such property rather than its adjusted tax basis; (e) in the event of an adjustment of the Gross Asset Value of any Partnership asset which requires that the Capital Accounts of the Partnership be adjusted pursuant to Section XXXX, the amount of such adjustment is to be taken into account as additional Net Income or Net Loss pursuant to Section XX; and (f) excluding any items specially allocated pursuant to Section xx. Once an item of income, gain, loss or deduction has been included in the initial computation of Net Income or Net Loss and is subjected to the special allocation rules in Section XX, Net Income and Net Loss shall be computed without regard to such item."

Sample language for the allocation of net income is, "Net Income. Except as otherwise provided herein, Net Income for any fiscal year or other applicable period shall be allocated in the following order and priority:

i. First, to the Partners, until the cumulative Net Income allocated pursuant to this subparagraph (i) for the current and all prior periods equals the cumulative Net Loss allocated pursuant to subparagraph (ii) hereof for all prior periods, among the Partners in the reverse order that such Net Loss was allocated to the Permitted Partners pursuant to subparagraph (ii) hereof.
ii. Thereafter, the balance of the Net Income, if any, shall be allocated to the Partners in accordance with their respective Percentage Interests."

Sample language for the allocation of net loss is, "Net Loss. Except as otherwise provided herein, Net Loss of the Partnership for each fiscal year or other applicable period shall be allocated to the Partners in accordance with their respective Percentage Interests."

2. Duties of the Joint Venture Operator.
The description of the duties of the joint venture operator should go into great detail about the do's and the don'ts. Laying down expectation

helps to prevent disputes. The description of the obligations should include those instances when the JV operator must either notify, at a minimum, or gain approval of the JV investor. Such occasions requiring notification beyond periodic reports might include a significant litigation, a major catastrophic event (i.e., manufacturing facility fire), government seizure, deviation of a certain percentage from the expected operating results from the annual budget, adverse publicity, or other unexpected events that may have a material impact on the expected profit share to the investor.

The auditor will go down the list of the duties of the joint venture operator and test each restriction and obligation. The JV investor should consider the penalties or breaches and associated remedies should the JV operator falter in their obligations. Obligations and restrictions without penalties are often violated by the JV operator.

3. Insurance.

A JV operator should have certain levels of insurance such as general liability or loss of revenues from operations. The levels of insurance should state a specific dollar amount by a well-rated insurance company.

The auditor will make certain the insurance was in effect for the time period specified by the agreement. If the insurance was not purchased, language can be drafted noting any savings achieved by the JV operator by not procuring the required insurance shall be given to the JV investors at 100 percent as opposed to their proportionate share they may have received and further, that cash flow payment shall not be taken as an expense to reduce the revenues of the JV investor.

4. Books and Records.

The need to retain books and records is critical to support the operating results of the entity. The JV operator should not only be told to maintain books and records but should also be instructed to maintain internal controls over these books and records to make certain they reflect a materially correct account of the JV's results. Further, the back-up and disaster recovery plans should be prescribed in the agreement including the requirements for testing the plan and time in which the JV operator has to restart operations.

The auditor will look into the books and records to support the statements of results. If there are other potential exposures, such as litigation or regulatory compliance, the auditor will also want access to the records of litigation and of any regulatory noncompliance reports. Therefore, the books and records available to the auditor must include financial records in addition to operating records at the discretion of the auditor.

Sample language: "Books and Records. At all times during the continuance of the Partnership, the Managing Partner shall maintain or cause to be maintained full, true, complete and correct books of account in accordance with GAAP, using the calendar year as the fiscal and taxable year of the Partnership."

5. Audit Rights.

Audit rights of a JV investor should be more vast than those of other contract auditors, such as those auditing royalties, primarily due to the more significant exposures of a JV operator as compared to a licensor or other contractor.

These audit rights might allow for an audit at least once a year or whenever there is a significant exposure to the JV operations, such as adverse publicity, major litigation, or a host of other issues that might spark an audit. Audit rights should also clearly identify that all books and records of the joint venture are subject to inspection, including financial and operational. Operational could include maintenance, litigation, legal bills, procurement and bid records, environmental and safety records, notices of violation from regulatory agencies, and human resource records.

The auditor will want access to all records to determine if the JV operator is fulfilling all contracted obligations and to identify any financial loss exposures that the JV investor may be facing.

6. Accounting Treatment.

The JV operator should be instructed on how to maintain the books and records. In the United States, this tends to be in accordance with Generally Accepted Accounting Procedures (GAAP).

Consideration should also be made to require the JV operator to have audited financial statements that are submitted to the investors. Audited financial statements are not a substitute for a JV audit as a financial statement auditor is primarily concerned with "materiality" which means that as long as the financial statements and balance sheets are about 90 percent correct, then the financial statements are deemed to be reliable. However, for the JV investor who shares in a large percentage of the JV, 90 percent accuracy is insufficient, especially if the JV required a significant investment.

The auditor generally does not spend much time reviewing the financial statements. Instead, the JV investor will want to review the financial statements to make certain the company is a "going concern" and to identify any other financial or operational concerns.

Sample language: "All references in this Agreement to "generally accepted accounting principles" or "GAAP" shall mean generally accepted accounting principles in effect in the United States of America at the time of application thereof. Unless otherwise specified herein, all accounting terms used herein shall be interpreted, all determinations with respect to accounting matters hereunder shall be made, and all financial statements and certificates and reports as to financial matters required to be furnished hereunder shall be prepared, in accordance with generally accepted accounting principles, applied on a consistent basis."

7. Capital Outlay.

Each member of the JV is required to make a capital investment. The amount of the capital investment is subject to several variables such as who will be the operator (the operator generally makes a small capital investment as they are they operator and are therefore supplying non-monetary human and operational capital), the return on investment, the size of the JV operation, tax treatment, projected needed cash flows, and ownership percentage.

The JV investor will want to make certain the JV operator has communicated capital funds as required in addition to other capital investments such as human resources. This can all be done through an audit that traces the sources and uses of cash through a Statement of Cash Flows. As such, the agreement should note the financial statements should include not only income statements and balance sheets but also a statement of cash flows.

8. Ability to Contract or Bind the JV.

The JV operator should have JV executive approval to make certain purchases and signed contracts. Procurement approval requirements are often memorialized in a procurement policy approved by the JV's executive committee. Major JV procurements or commitments should be approved by the JV executive committee, and such approval should be well documented. The ramifications of a JV operator making a binding agreement without proper approval should be severe, including have the JV operator cover any losses resulting from violating the procurement policy.

The auditor will want to look at the contracting and procurement policies and then select contracts to make certain they were properly bid and proper contracts were signed with adequate levels of approval as established by the procurement policy.

9. Legal Compliance.

The JV operator is required to comply with a wide variety of laws too numerous to state in an agreement. Areas of particular interest to a JV investor are those that can create adverse publicity, such as human resources (especially sexual harassment, discrimination, and right to work); environmental compliance; safety; privacy (protection of customer confidential information); procurement, etc . . . As such, these are also of particular interest to an auditor. Therefore, any JV agreement should make certain that the auditor has full access to all operational records, including so-called confidential legal department documents. Care will need to be taken when exposing the auditor to confidential legal departments in case there may be issues of attorney work product;

however, such concerns must be considered in advance when the agreement is being written so there are not negotiation issues during the course of any internal review or audit.

JV investors may wish to be notified in advance of any potentially detrimental legal issues, especially before they become public knowledge or quickly after becoming public knowledge. Such communication requirements should be established by the contract. These special communications are in addition to periodic communication requirements.

3.6.3. Documents to Consider Requesting in the Contract to Allow for Adequate External Monitoring

JV operators should provide sufficient periodic reports to allow the investor adequate information in a timely manner to inquire or affect JV operator decisions. Communication protocols are usually established based on the needs of the JV investor and the abilities of the operator. A JV investor who has a larger percentage of ownership will be able to negotiate better access to communications.

The mistake that many investors make is to not establish communication protocols that take into account both normal operating activities and periodic unplanned communication necessities. Basic documents should include monthly or quarterly financial statements and variance analysis against budgets with appropriate footnotes identifying significant changes in operations or management. Other operating information that is helpful includes number of employees, units of product sold, trend analysis, liquidity, debt, and various financial ratio analyses.

Periodic reporting for special events should clearly be established in the agreement such, as reporting on executive management changes, unplanned discounted operations (i.e., a factory fire), strikes, significant adverse publicity, disasters, material financial restatements, takeover offers, or any other significant change that could affect the value of the JV's investment.

3.7. Most-Favored-Nation Contracts

3.7.1. Contract Description

A most-favored-nation clause, also called an "antidiscrimination," or a "most-favored customer," is a promise of best pricing to a customer. It is a guarantee to the buyer he will be treated as the most-favored customer. Because the most-favored-nation clause is generally contracted prior to the supplier knowing future contracting arrangements, it is very easily violated by the supplier. Additionally, the buyer often has very little information to allow it to adequately externally monitor if the supplier is complying with the provision. The buyer often has to speak with competitors to discover if they are not receiving most-favored-nation pricing and, of course, most competitors will not disclose this confidential information. An additional challenge for the buyer to determine if they are receiving most-favored status comes from a complexity of a contract that bases pricing on more than a simple measurable point, such as a straight price. Best pricing often has many variables, such as quantity minimums, shipping costs, quality, timing, and services.

A most-favored-nation clause is generally negotiated by a customer that has significant purchasing power over the supplier. The supplier then can offer a most-favored-nation clause and will have an advantage to secure business at the risk of profits but the benefit of future business, often with minimum purchase guarantees. For the supplier, profit is often achieved on volume as opposed to price.

Auditors try to look at most-favored-nation clauses in verifiable numbers as they see the work as black or white. The subjectivity and ambiguities of a contract create significant difficulties for auditors in assessing compliance. It is common to find that pricing incentives, such as year-end rebates, volume-based discounts, and signing bonuses that have been provided to other customers are not factored into most-favored-nation pricing comparisons.

3.7.2. Key Terms and Conditions That Auditors Care About

When negotiating, it is important to realize that vague wording leads to difficulties in securing best pricing. There are going to be legitimate reasons why the best price is not achieved due to the wide variety of different pricing arrangements. Understanding where errors or misunderstandings may occur, along with your ultimate objectives, are amongst the first steps to take in identifying your terms and conditions that will be successful for both parties.

The most-favored-nation clause should consider variables such as:

- Volume.
- Pricing for the product.
- Quality.
- Ultimate pricing for the product to be delivered including such items as freight, taxes, rebates, kickbacks, incentives, research & development, etc. . . .
- Pricing for government versus companies.
- Time of year or quantities per period.
- Renewal options.

- Rights of first refusal.
- Length of contract period and multiyear discounts.
- Training.
- Warranties.
- Maintenance.
- Customer support.
- Speed of delivery/ delivery times.
- Payment terms (i.e., 30, 60, 90 days).
- Interest on late payments.
- Priority treatment.
- Advance payments.
- Early payment discounts.
- The territory to which the terms apply (i.e., locally, nationally, globally).
- Right-to-audit provision that clearly notes the auditor will not be restricted in the documents they review and specially states the auditor will have complete access to all contracts and purchase agreements regardless if there is a confidentially clause in the agreement. As such, the supplier has the burden to make certain if they sign a confidentiality clause with another vendor, that clause does not prohibit the most-favored-nation audit.
- Audit cost recovery based on the lower of a dollar overcharging or a percentage overcharging in anyone period, such as a quarter.
- Interest on overcharging (such as 1.5 percent compounded monthly).

Consideration must always be made toward codevelopment costs, joint venture operations, strategic relationships, cooperative advertising between the supplier and customer, termination clauses, audit-right clauses, and just about any other area where, in litigation, a party might wish to challenge a somewhat otherwise innocuous provision.

For suppliers in some nations, extreme care must be taken when providing most-favored customer status to government agencies. Some countries impose civil and criminal penalties for failure to provide most-favored-nation pricing to the government as required under a contract.

A strategy for a supplier to minimize most-favored-nation pricing rebate risks is to clearly note contract minimums, maximums, or other parameters for most-favored-nation pricing. A supplier placing many well-defined constraints on pricing or by clearly identifying the measurements for most-favored-nation pricing can work to minimize the risk of buyer rebates due to not providing most-favored-nation pricing. For example, noting the pricing is based for an unusual time period, such as a 17 months commitment between certain months and years, may help avoid a claim for not providing most-favored pricing as the odds of another customer having pricing for the same 17 months period are minimal. Likewise for the buyer, it should be clear that most-favored pricing should not be restricted to time periods, thereby preventing such unscrupulous methods as trying to avoid having to comply with the spirit of a most-favored-nation clause. The buyer may wish to include most-favored language that states it is up to an independent auditor's discretion if most-favored-nation pricing was not provided, and a rebate is due.

3.7.3. Reporting Areas and Associated Risks

The advantage of a most-favored-nation clause can disappear quickly if the vendor does not comply with the agreement.

Noncompliance can occur for many reasons. The most common cause is that the supplier's employees selling the goods are not aware of most-favored-nation clauses with other buyers so they execute better pricing agreements with new customers, thereby sparking the most-favored-nation clause requirement for a rebate. Generally, most companies do not track if better pricing is given to another customer, sparking the need for a rebate to the customer with the most-favored national language. Another major cause of a reporting error is that the supplier will purposely make minor modifications to a contract knowing there exists a most-favored customer contract with another customer and then claim the contracts are too different for the existing most-favored-nation clause to apply. Other causes are ambiguous terms, lack of internal controls, bad faith, clerical errors, complex contracts that allow for rebates, or other benefits that are not easily valued and decentralization. Many most-favored-nation clauses are poorly/vaguely worded, with critical terms such as "comparable products," "comparable periods," and "lesser price" inadequately defined. Terms and conditions of commercial sales vary, and there may be legitimate reasons why the best price is not achieved.

Few customers have the time, resources, or ability to monitor vendors' compliance with these contracts. Ability restrictions are placed by the vendors who do not wish their customers to have access to sensitive financial and competitor information. In fact, many competitor contracts have confidentiality clauses that work to prevent a customer from testing if the supplier is complying with its most-favored-nation requirements. Sensitive financial information that generally must be reviewed in a most-favored-nation contract often includes volumes purchased by competitors and supplier profits. If a customer could access supplier profit, then that would give an unfair advantage to the buyer in future negotiations.

It is also very hard to define what exactly most-favored pricing includes. Because of this, customers often don't receive best pricing. For example, in a most-favored-nation arrangement, a customer might be guaranteed the lowest price per unit for a product at 10 cents. If another customer can buy the same product at 11 cents a unit but that other customer also receives free shipping worth 2 cents a unit, does that mean the most-favored-nation clause has been violated? For an auditor, the answer would be yes as he looks at the total price paid after factoring in all pricing/rebate and nonmonetary considerations. However, for the customer and vendor that are in dispute, these sides will not agree, often stating the contract's most-favored-nation wording did not address all pricing and nonmonetary considerations, just per unit pricing.

3.7.4. Documents to Consider Requesting in the Contract to Allow for Adequate External Monitoring

To conduct a most-favored-nation review generally requires testing by a third party, such as an auditor. Such auditors are usually required to sign a non-disclosure agreement. Therefore, when constructing the "right-to-audit" provision of the contract, it is helpful to note the non-disclosure requirements of any auditor to be selected in the future and that a non-disclosure agreement will not have to be signed by the auditor as the auditor will be restricted by the purchase agreement.

However, if you should be so lucky as to have the ability to negotiate periodic updates from the supplier, it would be beneficial to require reporting on the following (it would also be very helpful to have this information prior to signing the contract):

- Copy of all new contracts the supplier signs, or if not the contract, quarterly notification of contracts that were signed (i.e., a listing of all new business relationships).
- A requirement the supplier provides its quarterly sales ledger or other list from contract administration identifying pricing for the sales.
- List of all locations where the goods are being produced.

It seems the most common method for external monitoring is for the buyer to stay current with the seller's announcements of new business deals and common industry tracking methods to identify situations where the supplier has signed deals that may result in more favorable treatment to another customer.

When contract violations are found, the rewards can be enormous, especially compared with the cost of monitoring. To illustrate, a most-favored-nation audit of a simple pricing clause can generally be conducted in a couple of days, and if it identifies a contract violation, for example, 5 percent on sales of $10 million, the rewards to the buyer are almost immediately recognizable, hard to negotiate away, audit costs recovered, and future benefits received.

3.7.5. Example of Most-Favored-Nations Contract Language

1.0 "Favored-Nation Status: Vendor represents, covenants and warrants the net fees charged in connection with any Service under this Agreement, taking into account all relevant factors, including all minimum spending or volume commitments, credits, discounts, rebates, advances or other payments, bonuses, inducements, adjustments and allowances, length of term, payment terms, the facilities involved and any other term that is, or can be converted into, a form of economic benefit to the Buyer, however, denominated and in whatever form, excluding however, any "Rent" or "Additional Rent" under the Lease Agreement, are currently at the Effective Date and shall be in any Term Year no less favorable to the Buyer than the fees charged to Vendor's most favored customer for any like service, taking into account all discounts, during a comparable period in such Term Year. Within 30 days after the expiration of each Term Year, Vendor shall deliver to Company in accordance with Section XX a certificate ("Most-Favored-Nation Certificate") executed by the Chief Financial Officer (or equivalent senior officer if no Chief Financial Officer exists) of Vendor, confirming Vendor's Compliance with the provisions of this paragraph."

"*1.1 Annual Based Fees Review and Adjustment:* Subject always to the provisions of Paragraph 1.0, the Fees set forth on Exhibit X-X for each service shall be subject to annual review and adjustment in accordance with this paragraph. No later than 30 days prior to the first day of any Post-Opening Term Year (including, for clarity only, during any Extension Period, each as defined below), commencing with the second Post-Opening Year, Vendor shall delivery to Buyer in accordance with Section XX (Notices) a certificate ("Fee Adjustment Certificate") executed by the Chief Financial Officer (or equivalent senior officer if no Chief Financial Officer exists) of Vendor, setting forth, for each Service, the actual base fee (i.e., the actual invoice price for each service) charged to Vendor's most-favored customer for like service at any time during such Post-Opening Term Year. Provided Buyer does not object to a provision of the Fee Adjustment Certificate and subject to Buy's rights of audit as identified in paragraph 1.2, the fee for each Service that is set forth in such Fee Adjustment Certificate shall be deemed the fee for such Service for the immediately following Post-Opening Term Year, unless and until adjusted in accordance with this paragraph, provided, however, that if Buyer objects to a fee set forth in the Fee Adjustment Certificate that exceeds the Fee from the immediately preceding Post-Opening Term Year by more than five (5%), then the increase in the Fee for such Service shall not exceed five percent (5%) unless until otherwise agreed by the parties in writing or the matter is resolved pursuant to an audit as provided for under Paragraph 1.2.

1.2 Books and Records; Audits. [See right to audit provisions in other sections of this book.]

1.3 Audit Disputes. If Vendor contests or disputes any portion or all of the findings, determinations or conclusions of any audit undertaken by Buyer pursuant to Paragraph 1.2, then Buyer and Vendor shall use their reasonable efforts to resolve such dispute (the "Dispute") within thirty (30) calendar days after delivery by Vendor to Buyer in accordance with Section XX (Notices) of written notification of the details of such Dispute. If Buyer and Vendor are unable to resolve such Dispute within such thirty (30) calendar days, such Dispute shall promptly thereafter be submitted by Vendor and Buyer to their independent certified public accountants, and the parties shall use reasonable efforts to cause these public accounting firms to promptly review and assist the parties in resolving the Dispute. Buyer and Vendor shall each be responsible for the fees, costs and expenses of their respective independent certified public accountants. If the independent certified public accountants for Buyer and Vendor are unable to resolve the Dispute within an additional thirty (30) calendar days, then the Dispute shall be resolved by a third independent certified public accountant, other than the Independent Certified Public Accountants, mutually acceptable to the independent certified public accountants of Buyer and Vendor (the "Special Accounting Master"). The parties shall use reasonable efforts to cause the Special Accounting Master to promptly review the Dispute and determine if Vendor was in compliance under this Agreement with the pricing or other obligations of Vendor that were the subject of the Dispute. In making such determination, the Special Accounting Master shall consider only the particular items or amounts in Dispute (and any other items or amounts relating thereto). Such determination shall be made within thirty (30) calendar days after the date on which the Special Accounting Master receives such notice of the Dispute, or as soon thereafter as possible. Such determination by the Special Accounting Master shall be the final resolution of any Dispute and shall be binding on the parties hereto and enforceable in a court of law. The fees, costs, and expenses of the Special Accounting Master in conducting such review shall be paid as follows: (i) by Vendor if the Special Accounting Master determines the Dispute in favor of the Buyer's position; (ii) by Buyer if the Special Accounting Master determines the Dispute in favor of the Vendor's position; or (iii) fifty percent (50%) by Buyer and fifty percent (50%) by Vendor if the Special Accounting Master determines the Dispute by a compromise position. In connection with any proceeding pursuant to this paragraph, Buyer's independent certified public accountant and any Special Accounting Master shall be required to agree in writing with Vendor not to disclose to Buyer or any third party the confidential information of Vendor or Vendor's third party customers that is obtained by said independent certified public accountant or Special Accounting Master, as the case may be, as a result of such proceeding."

3.8. Manufacturing Contracts

3.8.1. Contract Description

Like many agreements of different types, manufacturing contracts vary significantly, so it would take an entire book to discuss the wide variety of challenges associated with monitoring and contracting with manufacturers. Therefore, this book attempts to highlight some of the key areas that should be monitored in accordance with contract requirements that tend to be common among various manufacturing agreements.

Manufacturing contracts addressed in this book are those where a company is ordering goods to be produced, the cost of those goods are variable, and, therefore the buyer needs to monitor the costs, along with other items such as regulatory compliance (i.e., lead in toys), deadlines, employee welfare (i.e., child labor), and quality control. By contracting out manufacturing (aka outsourcing), the buyer can have the manufacturer assume responsibility for many processes the buyer might wish to avoid, such as ordering, supply chain management, inventory control, shipping, labor, and capital investment. Often, the buyer of goods does not have sufficient need for a manufacturing plant to run full-time, so the cost of buying the plant is best left to the manufacturer. Such a manufacturer is often referred to as an original equipment manufacturer or OEM. The OEM produces the goods under the buyer's brand. If the OEM sells the goods to a third party, then a royalty is often due. If the OEM just sells the goods for the buyer, then the OEM is paid the cost of manufacturing plus a profit margin. This chapter deals with monitoring the costs and profit margin of an OEM.

3.8.2. Key Terms and Conditions That Auditors Care About

In the world of manufacturing contract enforcement, auditors focus on cost recovery and risk avoidance. When they read the agreement, these are the main categories for monitoring. With many manufacturing agreements, the prices are set annually, so pricing is often less of an issue as with nonmanufacturing agreements. Only variable pricing deals need close monitoring, and therefore, the contract needs to make certain the tools are in place to facilitate the monitoring.

  1. *Books and Records.*
     Maintaining the financial books and records for a specified time period is required to make certain that monitoring can be accomplished and issues can be challenged. Books and records need to be maintained to a greater degree than the American Institute of Certified Public Accountant (AICPA) standards as AICPA standards only deal with

materiality and don't address many of the records that a buyer may wish to require the OEM to maintain, such as quality control and government inspections. As such, all potential records to be maintained should be specified in the agreement.

Sample language: "OEM shall maintain true and accurate books, records, test and laboratory data, reports and all other information relating to Manufacturing and Packaging under this Agreement, including all information required to be maintained by the Specifications and all Applicable Laws. Such records shall include, without limitation, quarterly inventory records, receiving records, purchase orders, quality control testing records, inspection records by third parties, shipping records, product cost records, and labor records. Such information shall be maintained in forms, notebooks and records for a period of at least three (3) years from the relevant finished Product expiration date or longer if required under Applicable Laws. If such records are recorded electronically, then system extracts in original software form shall be maintained for extract."

2. *Audit Rights.*

As stated, monitoring basically has two requirements: external monitoring via receipt of reports from the self-reporting party and public information, and such monitoring through on-site audit. Many OEM agreements fail to adequately address audit rights, thereby complicating the efforts of the buyer to monitor the OEM. Easy and quick access to OEM operations is essential given how off-specification product can quickly result in significant losses both in reputation and monetarily to a branded buyer.

Sample language: "Upon reasonable prior notice and at reasonable intervals, but not less than four times a year, OEM shall allow Buyer and its representatives to inspect OEM's books and records relating to the manufacture of the Finished Product and permit Buyer to access OEM's facilities used to manufacture the Finished Product for the purposes of (a) making quality assurance audits of the facilities and of the procedures and processes used by OEM in manufacturing, packaging, testing, storing and shipping Finished Product, and (b) confirming OEM's compliance with this Agreement, provided that a OEM representative is present during any such inspection. Buyer, or its representative(s), shall conduct such audit during normal business hours at a time on which the Parties have mutually agreed, and in such a manner that does not unreasonably interfere with OEM's normal business activities."

3. *Rules to be Followed in the Manufactured Product (i.e., FDA).*

Monitoring an OEM is often more about risk control than monetary recovery. Few things cause more grievance to a buyer than an OEM that has violated a regulation in the production of a buyer's branded

products. News of a toy being tainted by lead, slave labor used in clothing manufacturing, and release of toxins in the air and soil are all real
examples where the buyer was not adequately monitoring the OEM,
and each instance cost the buyer material sales and public perception
damage that took years and millions of dollars of advertising to
remedy.

The contract language needs to specify the rules to be followed from
environmental compliance to product sourcing to minimize operational risks. While I am a CPA, like many auditors, I also am also a
Certified Professional Environmental Auditor with designations in
both Health & Safety and Environmental Compliance. These certifications come in handy because as an auditor, my clients want me to focus
on these high-risk audits when I visit OEMs. The following example is
related to environmental and other regulatory compliance.

Sample language: "In carrying out its obligations under this
Agreement, OEM shall comply with all applicable federal, state, and
local environmental and health and safety laws (current or as amended
or added), and shall be solely responsible for determining how to comply
with same in carrying out these obligations. Notwithstanding the foregoing, nothing provided to OEM by Buyer, by way of materials, specifications, processing information or otherwise, is meant to diminish
OEM's responsibility for such compliance. OEM shall obtain and maintain all necessary licenses, permits and governmental approvals (except
for product-related Regulatory Approvals such as NDA's) required to
perform its manufacturing and supply services hereunder, including
licensure and permitting of its manufacturing facilities by the FDA.
OEM shall promptly notify Buyer of any circumstances, including the
receipt of any notice, warning, citation, finding, report or service of process or the occurrence of any release, spill, upset, or discharge of hazard-
ous substances (as may be defined under Applicable Laws) relating to
OEM's compliance with this Section and which relates to the manufacture of Finished Product. Buyer reserves the right to conduct an environmental inspection of the Facility, at reasonable intervals, but not less
than four times a year, during normal business hours and with 1 business day advance notice, for the purpose of determining compliance
with this Section. Such inspection shall not relieve OEM of its obligation
to comply with all applicable environmental and health and safety laws
and does not constitute a waiver of any right otherwise available to
Buyer."

4. *Reporting Periods.*

OEMs are required to periodically report in addition to providing
special notifications. Such periodic reporting often includes quality
control test results, returns, recalls, consumer complaints, labor issues,

on-time delivery performance, inventory levels, out-of-stock issues, senior management changes, and other items that allow the buyer to adequately monitor the self-reporting OEM.

This is a critical area, and the buyer should spend significant time considering what is required to adequately monitor the OEM as well as how often the reports should be provided. Some reports, such as production, can be provided daily, while others, such as inventory turns or other key performance indicators can be provided sporadically, such as quarterly.

The auditor will take the reports provided by the OEM and attempt to compare them and have them agree with supporting documentation when at the OEM. Particular care is taken by an auditor to make certain that all items have been properly reported. Should items not be reported properly, the contract should note how those issues will be remedied. Most often the remedy is not monetary in nature but have a program designed to correct the action, and if the action is not corrected, then this can be grounds for termination, with the OEM paying for any losses due to the termination.

5. *Variable Pricing.*

Pricing for finished goods or other services becomes an issue when the pricing for the products is a variable. This is common in industries where the raw material costs can fluctuate, such as metals. Pricing is a main focus for the buyer to monitor, and therefore, great efforts should be taken to make certain the buyer is paying for the net cost of the finished goods, after all the rebates and special pricing arrangements the OEM may have secured.

The buyer may wish to include access to the OEM's purchase contracts and direct access to the suppliers to make certain that the ultimate price being charged to the buyer is correct without nonpermitted markups.

For products with a stable price, the preference is to state a specific price for each product. This will require little monitoring and auditing.

Auditors will focus on the pricing support and the purchase agreements. They may also wish to see payment support.

Sample language: "'Price' means the price for the manufacture and supply of Finished Product under this Agreement specified in the pricing structure set forth in Schedule A, as may be amended from time to time in accordance with Section X.X of this Agreement."

Or

"'Finished Product Pricing' includes all Raw Materials, manufacturing, packaging, testing and temporary storing costs associated with manufacturing and supplying the Finished Product, and includes the costs of such quality control measures as required by the Specifications and the Quality Agreement. The costs of shipping, handling, insurance and freight will be borne by Buyer and form no part of the Price."

6. *Other Permitted Costs.*

Agreements should clearly note permitted charges and use general language that only specifically approved charges can be included. For example, one commonly preapproved additional cost is for storage of finished goods at the OEM's factory for when the buyer is slow to take delivery. The auditor will check for support for these extra charges.

Sample language: "Buyer may store finished product for a maximum of fifteen (15) days after production, after which buyer shall pay OEM a storage charge of $2 per pallet of Finished Product per day."
Or
"OEM shall be solely responsible for all costs associated with hiring personnel to maintain the Manufacturing Tools necessary to comply with its obligations pursuant to this Agreement."

7. *Delays.*

It is critical the buyer be able to monitor the OEM for production delays so corrective actions can be take in a timely manner. If an OEM cannot produce product to meet order deadlines, then the OEM should be required to notify the buyer as soon as it is reasonable. Penalties for failure to notify can be included in the agreement.

The auditor will check to compare purchase order delivery dates to actual delivery date to identify any unreported delays.

Sample language: "OEM shall timely fill each Purchase Order, subject to the terms and conditions of this Agreement. OEM shall notify Buyer within fifteen (15) days of receipt of any Firm Commitment or Purchase Order if OEM determines that any Manufacturing or Packaging will be delayed or eliminated for any reason, provided however that such notice shall not relieve OEM of any of its obligations, absent written consent of Buyer.

8. *Litigation and Outside Inspection Notification.*

The buyer wants to make certain they are notified in advance of any special events that could affect the production schedule. One common event, especially in the pharmaceutical industry, is a government inspection. An adverse inspection can shut down a facility or put it at risk of closure, so the buyer must pay close attention to such inspections to make certain the OEM is correcting any inspection findings in a timely manner.

The auditor will want to pull all litigation, government inspection, and other third-party inspection reports and search for results or risks that should have been communicated to the OEM. The penalty for failure to communicate should go as far as termination at the discretion of the buyer.

Sample language: "OEM shall immediately advise Buyer if an authorized agent of any Regulatory Authority visits either the Manufacturing Facility or the Packaging Facility if related to the Manufacturing or Packaging of the Product. OEM shall furnish to Buyer a copy of the report by such Regulatory Authority, if any, within ten (10) days of OEM's receipt of such report. Further, on receipt of a Regulatory Authority request to inspect the Facilities or audit OEM's books and records with respect to Manufacturing or packaging under this Agreement, OEM shall immediately notify Buyer, and shall provide Buyer with a copy of any written document received from such Regulatory Authority and OEM shall permit Buyer to have a representative present for any such Facility inspection unless such presence would be unreasonable under the circumstances. Absence of a Buyer representative shall not impede any such inspection, provided OEM has complied with the foregoing. To the extent related to Manufacturing or Packaging hereunder, OEM shall provide to Buyer a copy of any proposed written response to any such inspection prior to its submission and a reasonable opportunity for Buyer to review and approve such response, provided that such approval shall not be unreasonably withheld."

9. *Minimum Orders.*

   A buyer may have obligations to purchase minimum quantities of goods. A buyer needs to plan the timing of purchases to make certain minimums are being met. To help make certain minimums indeed are being met, it is helpful to receive from the OEM a monthly report of procurement's to date versus annual minimum goals, so there are no year-end surprises of having failed to purchase the minimum. If a buyer pays a penalty for failure to purchase the minimum quantity, then the auditor will want to check to make certain the minimum has been correctly calculated.

   Sample language: "During each Contract Year, Buyer shall order the minimum number of units of Product ("Minimum Orders") set forth on Schedule A. If Buyer does not purchase such Minimum Orders during any Contract Year, within thirty (30) days after the end of such Contract Year, Buyer shall pay OEM the difference between (i) the total amount Buyer would have paid to OEM if the Minimum Orders had been fulfilled for the Product (calculated using an average batch price as shown in Schedule A) and (ii) the sum of (a) all purchases from OEM for the Product during the just-concluded Contract Year plus (b) OEM's cost of all Raw Materials for that portion of the Minimum Orders not placed. For clarity, Buyer shall not be obligated to pay for any Product ordered but not delivered by OEM in accordance with this Agreement. OEM shall, within ten days following each month, provide the buyer purchases to date for the year up through the most recent month and remaining purchases to be made in order to fulfill minimum purchase requirements."

10. *Payment.*

The goal of most buyers is to delay payment (for cash flow consideration purposes) and only be responsible to pay for goods that have past a stringent quality control process. Therefore, to delay payment, many agreements note the payment is not due for at least 30 days, and there may be a reserve for defective products or returns, such as 10 percent of the amount due for a rolling period of a year or other defined period.

Sample language: "Buyer shall pay OEM for the Finished Product shipped to Buyer within thirty (30) days of the date of the invoice issued. OEM shall send all invoices by e-mail or facsimile to the e-mail address or facsimile number of the accounts payable personnel designated by Buyer from time to time. All invoices shall be dated as of the date of the email or facsimile as noted in the foregoing sentence, and not any earlier date. OEM's invoice shall reference the Firm Purchase Order number and be sent to the "Bill to" address of Buyer specified on the Firm Purchase Order, and OEM's packing list must reference the Firm Purchase Order number and be sent to the applicable "Ship to" address on the Firm Purchase Order. Buyer may withhold a portion of any invoice that it disputes in good faith pending resolution of such dispute [or alternatively, a reserve can be established for a certain period—the reserve helps maintain relationships]. OEM shall invoice Buyer for all Product as provided in Section X.X, and payment for the undisputed portions of such invoices shall be due within forty-five (45) days after the date of such invoice. In the event payment is not received by OEM on or before the forty-fifth (45th) day after the date of the invoice, then such unpaid amount shall accrue interest each month at the rate of one percent (1%) per month until paid in full."

11. *Recall or Other Special Events.*

Recalls are becoming an ever-increasing threat to a business primarily due to increased consumer advocacy and advanced testing techniques. Children's toys are constantly being recalled for a variety of reasons, from bad design (generally the fault of the buyer) to use of toxic or lead paint (generally the fault of the OEM). The cost of a recall or other similar event should be borne by the responsible part, or if the buyer and OEM are jointly culpable, then there should be a method to allocate fault, generally best done by an independent low-cost third party. Language could be added to identify that both parties need to cooperate to fight a recall or handle adverse publicity.

Sample language: "In the event OEM believes a recall, field alert, Product withdrawal or field correction may be necessary with respect to any Product provided under this Agreement, OEM shall immediately notify Buyer in writing. OEM will not act to initiate a recall, field alert, Product withdrawal or field correction without the express prior written approval of Buyer, unless otherwise required by Applicable Laws. In the event Buyer believes a recall, field alert, Product withdrawal or field correction may be necessary with respect to any Product provided under this Agreement, Buyer shall immediately notify OEM in writing and OEM shall provide all necessary cooperation and assistance to Buyer. The cost of any recall, field alert, Product withdrawal or field correction shall be borne by Buyer except to the extent such recall, field alert, Product withdrawal or field correction is caused by OEM's breach of its warranties, representations or obligations under this Agreement or Applicable Laws or its negligence or willful misconduct, then such cost shall be borne by OEM. For purposes hereof, such cost shall be limited to reasonable, actual and documented Administrative Costs incurred by Buyer for such recall, withdrawal or correction, and replacement of the Defective Product to be recalled. Buyer shall solely control the implementation of any such recall, field alert, withdrawal, or field correction."

12. *Packaging and Labeling.*

Packaging and labeling is extremely important for brand and product protections. Goods shipped to customers and damaged due to bad packaging or the use of inferior package material (i.e., a lower grade cardboard) by a money saving OEM can result in significant damage of reputation, not to mention products, that is typically borne by the buyer. The contract should specify trade marks to be included on all packaging, and required packaging should be approved by the buyer. Restrictions can also be placed on the OEM to make certain the OEM does not associate itself as the owner of the buyer's patent or brand in any marketing material or packaging.

Sample language: "Buyer shall provide or approve, prior to the procurement of applicable components, all artwork, advertising and packaging information necessary to Manufacture or Package the Product. Such artwork, advertising and packaging information is and shall remain the exclusive property of Buyer, and Buyer shall be solely responsible for the content thereof. Such artwork, advertising and packaging information or any reproduction thereof may not be used by OEM following the termination of this Agreement, or during the Term of this Agreement in any manner other than solely for the purpose of performing its obligations hereunder. OEM shall mark all buyer product made hereunder with appropriate patent markings identifying buyer as the owner of the pertinent patents and/or patent applications. The content, form and language used in such markings shall be in accordance with the laws and practices of the country where such markings are used. The buyer's trademark may not be used in direct combination with the trade name, trademark or symbol of OEM or another entity in any manner that suggests a connection or relationship. The validity and exclusive ownership of the trademark by licensor are acknowledged by OEM. The ownership of the trademark shall be indicated whenever used in any manner by OEM as follows: 'XXXX.' The expense of obtaining and maintaining registrations of the trademark shall be borne by buyer."

13. *Raw Materials and Costs.*

Controlling costs is perhaps the main reason to outsource production to an OEM. OEMs spread their fixed asset and other costs amongst many different buyers and are often able to secure materials at a favorable price, thanks to volume discounts as compared to what a buyer may achieve on its own.

The buyer may wish to implement "most-favored-nation" pricing controls to make certain that he is paying the lowest price for all goods. The quality control over raw materials is of fundamental importance, so specifications of the raw materials and perhaps, even the identification of the raw material suppliers helps to control a cost-cutting OEM that will sacrifice a good's quality to improve profits. Buyer research, development and engineering personnel are often needed to write the specification contract requirements of the OEM. Buyer procurement personnel can also assist to make certain the raw material pricing is favorable.

Further, the OEM has a responsibility to ensure that there are adequate raw materials to meet the order needs of the buyer. Order lead times can be established in the agreement, along with costs to be borne by the OEM should the OEM run out of raw materials and not be able to supply finished goods on time. Requiring the OEM to have multiple prequalified suppliers helps reduce risks to the buyer of goods not being available. Some raw material suppliers may take months to be qualified as being able to supply the proper raw materials (common in the chemical and healthcare industries), so this requirement to preapprove vendors is key for some industries in order to control risks. OEMs should be required to notify the buyer if the supply chain may be interrupted so the buyer can notify their customers or seek alternative production sources.

Language should also be included regarding who bears the cost for excess raw material, obsolete raw material, lost raw materials, or damaged raw material under the control of the OEM. The OEM should generally not bear the cost if purchases were made based on buyer forecasts; however, the OEM can bear the cost for most other raw material issues (i.e., damage, shrinkage).

Finally, if there are competing buyers using the raw materials, the buyer will want to prioritize itself in the pecking order of who gets access to the raw materials in case of a shortage.

Sample language: "OEM shall be responsible for procuring, inspecting and releasing adequate Raw Materials as necessary to meet the Firm Commitment, unless otherwise agreed to by the parties in writing. Only authorized suppliers may be used as specified in Exhibit B. If after initial Product qualification Buyer requires a change of any Raw Material supplier for its own benefit (e.g., not due to the failure of a supplier to timely supply Raw Materials to specifications), the specifications shall be amended and if the cost of any such Raw Material is different than OEM's costs for the same raw material of equal quality from other suppliers, OEM shall adjust for the difference between OEM's cost of the Raw Material and Buyer's mandated supplier's cost in the Unit Price of the Product. Buyer will be responsible for all costs associated with qualification of such new Buyer-required supplier of a Raw Material not previously qualified by OEM. Except as provided above, all Raw Material supplier changes must be agreed by the parties by amending the specifications in writing. In the event of a specification change requested by Buyer or OEM for Buyer's benefit and agreed by the parties or to comply with any new requirement of a Regulatory Authority, termination by Buyer without cause or expiration of this Agreement; or unforeseeable obsolescence of any Raw Material, Buyer shall bear the cost of any unused Raw Materials which cannot be otherwise used by OEM nor returned for credit, provided that OEM purchased such Raw Materials in quantities consistent with Buyer's most recent Firm Commitment and the supplier's minimum purchase obligations."

And, as some more alternative language for excess raw material:

"If Raw Materials becomes obsolete or otherwise no longer useable in the manufacturing process for the Finished Product because Buyer deviated from the Forecast, or the specifications have been changed, OEM shall use its commercially reasonable efforts to cover the cost of excess Raw Materials by returning such Raw Materials to the vendor, selling such Raw Materials in an arm's-length transaction, utilizing such Raw Materials in manufacturing products for its other customers to the extent possible at arm's-length pricing, and implementing other measures to mitigate the loss due to such excess Raw Materials. To the extent that OEM is unable to offset such loss fully, Buyer shall reimburse OEM for such Raw Materials and its out-of-pocket expenses but solely to the extent actually incurred by OEM and in no event beyond the limit of liability set forth in Paragraph X.X."

14. Insurance.

Insurance is a key component to any OEM agreement, especially insurance should the finished product cause harm to a user at no fault of the buyer's design (i.e., use of out-of-specification raw materials). The penalty for failure to maintain the insurance should clearly be identified in the agreement as a payment to the buyer for the cost of such insurance from an AAA rated or better insurance company. Further, the OEM should be required to provide a certificate of insurance to the buyer naming the buyer as additionally insured. The OEM should also be required to inform the buyer of any changes of insurance coverage. It is also important that the insurance coverage be for at least three years after the expiration of the manufacturing agreement.

Additional sample insurance language is included in the sample licensing agreement included as an appendix within this book.

Sample language: "Buyer shall, at its own cost and expense, obtain and maintain in full force and effect the following insurance or program of self insurance (provided Buyer maintains a financial condition reasonably sufficient to cover such commitments) during the term of this Agreement: (i) Products and Completed Operations Liability Insurance with per-occurrence and general aggregate limits of not less than $10 million; (ii) Workers' Compensation and Employer's Liability Insurance with statutory limits for Workers' Compensation and Employer's Liability insurance limits of not less than $2 million; (iii) All Risk Property Insurance, including transit coverage, in an amount equal to full replacement value covering Buyer's property while it is at OEM's facility or in transit to or from OEM's facility. In the event that any of the required policies of insurance are written on a claims-made basis, then such policies shall be maintained during the entire term of this Agreement and for a period of not less than three (3) years following the termination or expiration of this Agreement. Buyer shall obtain a waiver from any insurance carrier with whom Buyer carries Workers' Compensation insurance releasing its subrogation rights against OEM. Buyer shall obtain a waiver from any insurance carrier with whom Buyer carries Property Insurance releasing its subrogation rights against OEM. Buyer shall not seek reimbursement for any property claim, or portion thereof, that is not fully recovered from Buyer's Property Insurance policy. OEM and its Subsidiaries and Parent Corporation shall be named as additional insureds under the Products and Completed Operations Liability insurance policies as respects the products and completed operations outlined in this Agreement. Buyer shall furnish certificates of insurance for any policies obtained hereunder and required additional insured status to OEM as soon as practicable after the Effective Date of the Agreement and upon renewal of any such policies. Any insurance policy that is obtained in satisfaction of this Section shall be obtained from an insurance carrier with an A.M. Best rating of at least AAA."

15. *Unit.*

There are basically two components to any purchase: the cost and the number of units. As such, care should be taken to properly define a unit. Depending on the product, a unit may be confusing, such as one computer chip or multiple chips on a circuit board or multiple chips on a spindle of chips. A unit could also be a crate of goods.

Sample language: "One unit is defined as one XXX Finished Products including one cord, one battery, instruction manual, and AC adapter."

16. *Unit Pricing.*

As noted in the "unit" section above, a unit must be properly defined, and the price for each unit needs to be adequately identified. For longer term contracts, the change in price may be tied to actual increases in costs not to exceed an index, such as the Consumer Price Index (an index of retail prices to measure the change of goods and services), the Employers Cost Index (a quarterly report from the U.S. Department of Labor that measures changes in employee compensation), or my favorite, the Producer Price Index (an index from the U.S. Bureau of Labor Statistics that measures changes in wholesale price levels).

Sample language: "Buyer shall pay to OEM the unit pricing set forth in the following Unit Pricing matrix. In the event Buyer requests services other than manufacturing or product packaging, OEM shall provide a written quote of the fee for such additional services at most-favored-nation pricing and Buyer shall advise OEM whether it wishes to have such additional services performed by OEM. For each year after the first, the Unit Pricing shall be increased or decreased based on actual costs, provided such changes are less than or equal to the proportionate change in the Producer Price Index as published by the U.S. Government from June 30 of the second preceding year to June 30 of the immediately preceding year. Price adjustments shall be subject to the following limitations: The Unit Pricing for Product shall include product identified in Schedule A, the cost of packaging materials and OEM's overhead as defined in Schedule B. OEM agrees to provide back-up documentation of labor and/or materials costs for all annual increases and such costs and related documentation shall be auditable in accordance with Section XX, by an independent third party reasonably acceptable to Buyer and OEM whose findings shall be binding."

17. *Key Performance Indicators.*

A key performance indicator (KPI) is a numerical performance measurement tool that helps the buyer monitor if the OEM is operating as required under the agreement. The KPIs are often ratios (i.e., cost divided by units produced) or comparisons to a fixed number, such as downtime in a period. KPIs are some of the most effective tools to monitor the performance of an OEM, and therefore, should be explicitly identified in the agreement. KPIs should be established for financial and nonfinancial/operational performance. Financial KPIs help monitor various costs and savings, such as changes in various costs as compared to the overall costs (i.e., shipping, raw materials, overhead, distribution, logistics, labor). Operating KPIs monitor items, such as complaints per number of items shipped, rework percentages, and on-time deliveries.

Sample language: "For each quarter, OEM shall meet or exceed the key performance indicators ("KPI") established in good faith by OEM and Buyer for each such quarter. The preliminary categories of KPIs in respect of the first quarter following contract execution, the KPIs to be reported are set forth in Schedule A, and the parties mutually agree to refine such KPIs at least annually and as reasonably requested by the Buyer."

3.8.3. Documents to Consider Requesting in the Contract to Allow for Monitoring

The documents to request, as identified in the prior section, are:

1. Books and records sufficient to allow for an audit of the OEM's operations. These would include financial and operational records. Financial records may include cost components and inventory levels to make certain the OEM is not manufacturing unauthorized gray market product. Operational records would include quality control, health, environmental, safety, labor practices, human resource records, security records, scrap records, damage records, product testing records, and any other operational records that could be used to monitor the OEM's performance, including any key performance indicators.
2. Third-party inspection records, such as reports from government (i.e., FDA) inspectors.
3. Manufacturing policies and procedures
4. Safety guidelines and Material Safety Data Sheets.
5. Customer complaints.
6. Reasons for returns and credits.
7. Demurrage and on-time shipping records.
8. Product return records.
9. Product warranty and repair records.
10. Invoice and contract support for all chargeable amounts.
11. Any notices of violation received from government agencies.
12. Supplier agreements and procurement records.
13. Causes for delays and action plans.

14. Shrinkage investigation reports.
15. Certificates of insurance.
16. Litigation records.
17. Most-favored-nation pricing support.
18. Invoicing support.
19. Product and packaging samples.
20. Periodic (up to daily), Key Performance Indicator reports.

3.9. Royalty/Licensing Contracts

3.9.1. Contract Description

This book focuses primarily on royalty or license agreements. The process of licensing is the renting of a legally protected intellectual property (i.e., copyright, trademark, process, item, service, software, name, logo, saying, etc. . .). A royalty or licensing agreement is the agreement "that rents to intellectual property and establishes the conditions for its use and the benefit to be received by the intellectual property owner who is known as the licensor." The user of the intellectual property is the licensee. In return for the licensor allowing the licensee to use the intellectual property, a royalty is generally paid based on a fixed amount or under a revenue sharing arrangement where the licensor shares the benefits with the licensee without sharing the costs or risks of business. A royalty can be a one-time payment, sometimes occurring as a minimum guarantee or advance and/or a series of payments to licensor so the licensor can share in the benefits of the use of the intellectual property at the same time as the licensee. If the royalty is based on when transactions occur by the licensee, the royalty is generally based as a flat amount on the sale of goods, the delivery of services, or under a revenue sharing arrangement such as a percentage of net sales of licensed product. Revenues from unit sales and the associated royalty liability will fluctuate over the life of the license agreement. To help maintain a steady stream of royalty income, license agreements often have minimum guarantee terms, which are minimum royalty payments.

As mentioned, the two key players to a licensing agreement are the licensor and the licensee.

3.9.1.1. The Licensor

There are many reasons why an individual or company will become a licensor, but the primary reason is to allow brand or market extension through unaffiliated companies. Licensed intellectual property is protected under trademark or copyright laws, thereby allowing the licensing process to occur.

The licensor, by licensing the intellectual property, seeks to control the activities of the licensee through the agreement and periodic monitoring of the licensee's activities. The licensing of intellectual property does pose many risks to the licensor such as these ways a licensee can diminish the property's value: making substandard product, selling through undesirable channels (i.e., a label that should be selling at Neiman Marcus is instead sold at Wal-Mart), adverse publicity by the licensee, not presenting the licensed brand in a favorable image or using the wrong image, selling out of territory, flooding the market with merchandise, providing the licensed product free, or selling the licensed product with other unrelated or undesirable products (i.e., selling cigarettes with children's clothing). Additionally, there is the risk the licensee will not pay the licensor the proper royalties or failure to include proper copyright protection on packaging. The licensor also has costs, such as providing the licensee with designs or specifications, enforcing trademark and copyright protection, innovation of the intellectual property, and overall monitoring of the licensee's use of the licensed products. Many licensors license out their intellectual property also to exploit stale intellectual property to new areas, as a method to reach new global markets and to seek cash with minimal risk from their proprietary properties.

3.9.1.2. The Licensee

A licensee rents the intellectual property from the licensor. Generally, the licensee has no ownership interest in the intellectual property but has the authority to use the property and sell the property within guidelines established by the licensor and memorialized in a contract. Licensees are able to benefit from the costs borne by the licensor in establishing the intellectual property and generally from being able to use a proven product. Licensors usually absorb all initial research and development costs, legal costs, initial marketing costs, and other expenses the licensee is able to avoid.

Intellectual property (IP) affects all industries and both tangible and intangible assets. Some industries and their IP include:

- *Aerospace*: Electronic components, new composite materials, high technology, software (such as for measuring, monitoring, and operations).
- *Software*: Preprogrammed microchips, operating system and applications software, games and characters.
- *Entertainment*: Licensing of cartoon characters for use in consumer products, participating and residual payments to talent, video/DVD distribution, theatrical distribution, TV distribution, music, personality images, and sport team names.
- *Computer Hardware*: Components or systems.
- *Healthcare*: Biotechnology, pharmaceutical drugs, and medical devices.

- *Consumer products*: Licensing of systems, manufacturing methods, copyright symbols, images, names, artwork, and designs.
- *Franchising*: Shared revenues from sales such as from hotels and restaurants.

While intentional underreporting of royalty fees may occur, inadvertent underreporting may be the most prevalent. Even the best of systems and procedures may not capture information, or if captured, may be unintentionally mismanaged. Common reasons for underpayment include:

- Failure by licensees to report on licensed product lines, especially new ones.
- Deducting inappropriate items or amounts from gross sales to reach net sales (costs for advertising, operating, taxes, shipping, etc.).
- Inflating deductible costs, especially from related parties.
- Using wrong exchange rates.
- Deducting for cash discounts that are not granted.
- Selling product after agreement termination.
- Sublicensing product without licensor approval.
- Sales to related parties that resell the licensed product at higher costs.
- Wrong royalty rates.
- Missing licensed goods due to shrinkage or undocumented destructions.
- Bundling with other product and inappropriate selling price allocation.

3.9.2. Key Terms and Conditions That Auditors Care About

An auditor generally reviews a license agreement with an eye for what can be monitored and what items should be monitored to provide the highest value to the licensor. There are three major areas for consideration by the auditor:

i. *Financial recovery*. Most monitoring programs work on a basis of financial recovery. If the program cannot more than pay for itself, then it is subject to being discontinued.

A program should be self-funded with an initial budget for year number one and subsequent years paid by recoveries of the first year or first few audit results. As such, the auditor will focus on those areas of the agreement that cannot be monitored should there be a contract violation. The most obvious is the underpayment of royalties. Other areas high on the list are failure to make expenditure commitments, such as advertising and selling out of territory or unlicensed versions of the intellectual property where the finding is generally calculated as equal to the gross margin from the sale.

ii. *Intellectual property protection.* Some licensors might argue that intellectual property audits are required to preserve intellectual property rights, and performing royalty audits is sound business practice and should be as normal to operations as balancing a check book. A royalty auditor will review the agreement and look for how the intellectual property may be exploited. The auditor will also review for copyright or trademark notification requirements to help preserve the value of the intellectual property or the rights of the IP owner.

iii. *Reporting, communications, and document retention.* The auditor will want to know the communication and reporting requirements in the agreement. This is primarily related to the royalty reports. Then the auditor will want to know what documents need to be retained for what time period so the scope of audit can be determined as well as what documents can be expected from the licensee. Many agreements err in not specifying the documents to be retained by the licensee, resulting in limited scope audits that don't provide real value to the licensor.

After these three major areas, there are other items an auditor may consider, but generally those are of lesser importance to the licensor.

Royalty compliance monitoring procedures can vary greatly between licensors and individual licensees. As such, the following areas an auditor might wish to consider are only guidelines. The lawyer should pay careful attention to these areas; however, when drafting the contract to make certain each area has specific details of document retention requirements to allow for the monitoring of the agreement. The astute royalty auditor will develop her own course of actions based on the unique circumstances that change with each engagement.

There are two basic areas that an auditor must concentrate her efforts in order to determine if royalties have been properly paid for items associated with products that have been licensed; these are "inventory" and "sales." A licensee must be able to account for all licensed inventory created and then must be able to account for its final deposition. When the royalty is variable based on units sold or otherwise disposed, the licensee must be able to provide clear, complete, and adequate sales records. It is actually amazing how many license agreements fail to mention the need for the licensee to maintain and report on intellectual property manufactured. More than one audit has been stymied because the royalty is based on net sales, and the right-to-audit provision only states the auditor has a right to review records associated with net sales. Licensees generally believe this means that the auditor cannot review the inventory records. Reviewing the inventory records is essential to determine if all units produced have flowed through the sales records as provided. There are some agreements where the royalty is based on only the number of units manufactured, making the inventory roll forwards essential for properly monitoring a licensee while the sales records take a back seat in the degree of importance.

First, a look at Inventory. The auditor must understand how inventory units of licensed product is acquired, processed, and disbursed. Understanding inventory movement is the foundation or starting point of any royalty compliance where royalties are paid based on the sale of goods. If the licensee cannot account for inventory, then it is hard to place reliance on the sales records and subsequently reported royalties. The license agreement must make it possible for the auditor to have complete access to all inventory records from raw materials through finished goods.

To understand the movement of inventory, the auditor relies on the licensee's creation of the inventory roll forward. The roll forward requires the licensee to explain all sources and uses of inventory. Every licensee should be required by contract to have to prepare an inventory roll forward. Many licensees refuse to provide an inventory roll forward as they say they are not required to under the agreement . . . only to provide existing books and records. As such, it is important the licensee be informed in the agreement that they must provide special reports as required by the auditor including an inventory roll forward. Further, it is best practice to require the licensee to provide an inventory roll forward on at least an aggregated level by contact agreement annually.

There are two types of roll forwards: Raw Materials and Finished Goods. Manufacturers will need to produce both roll forwards or only the finished goods roll forward. Manufacturers who use the intellectual property as a raw material, such as a memory chip in a computer or DVD player, will have to produce both roll forwards, one of the memory chip showing how many where purchased and what happened to them, and then a finished goods roll forward, showing how the memory chips where consumed in the finished end product. Alternatively, some intellectual property is attached or associated with the finished good and does not exist in raw materials, such as a logo or brand name that is silkscreened onto a shirt. In this instance, only a finished goods inventory roll forward makes sense.

It is important to understand all roll forwards are unit quantities by licensed product and are not dollar value based. Inventory roll forwards are an accounting for the number of licensed units. Sales value is captured during the selling of the units.

Unfortunately, many licensees do not maintain adequate records to allow them to complete an inventory roll forward. For example, not all licensees maintain year-end inventory amounts, physical count records or inventory disposal records, so the licensees are unable to identify what has happened to the entire licensed inventory they have produced or purchased. Therefore, it is essential the agreement require that all disposals be adequately supported and failure to identify or have evidence of how the licensed inventory was disposed will result in a royalty payment as if the items as sold. When I perform a royalty audit and I discover missing inventory, there is eventually the conversation of the licensee saying a royalty is not due on the missing inventory because the licensee claims it was not sold and the licensor arguing a royalty is due as there is a presumption the missing inventory was sold and not reported and it is the responsibility of the licensee to maintain adequate records to prove the inventory was sold or not sold. Many agreements cover this issue by stating a royalty is due on all units sold or otherwise disposed with the value of the otherwise disposed at list or some average arm's-length transaction price.

When inventory records are missing, alternative procedures must be designed to identify the total quantity of licensed products produced and sold or otherwise transferred. For such instances, it is helpful to have contract language that allows the licensor to make an estimate and requires the licensee to accept as final the auditors or licensors estimate for underreporting royalties. Along the same lines, if a licensee cannot account for shrinkage, the licensor should make a claim for unpaid royalties based on the understanding that the licensee is responsible for controlling stolen or lost inventory as the goods are now in the marketplace so the licensor has lost their royalty while a customer is enjoying the licensed product. Many licensees argue there is no proof of sale; however, the counterargument is that it is not up to the auditor to prove a sale, it is up to the licensee to prove if the licensed product was sold or not sold. Further, a licensor may wish to argue that any licensed product transferred to the market, regardless if sold, should generate a royalty to the licensor because since the product is on the market and with an end user (consumer), then the end user will not have to purchase the licensed product through normal methods where a royalty is paid. Hence, a licensor may wish to argue that even a theft results in a royalty due to the licensor and this argument is often won or lost based on the definition of a sale in the agreement.

While both inventory roll forwards are important (raw materials and finished goods), the most important is finished goods because the finished goods roll forward includes the number of units sold. The number of units sold per the finished goods roll forward must be compared to the number of units sold per the sales records to access if the sales records are complete. Any discrepancies of more units sold per the inventory roll forward as compared to the sales records results in a finding of underpaid royalties.

The next page provides an example of a finished goods inventory roll forward. The license agreement should require the finished goods inventory roll forward be available for the auditor and perhaps even be sent annually to the licensor. The license agreement should also require all the documents under the "compare to" side to be retained and presented to the auditor.

Finished Goods Inventory Roll Forward

	Unit Quantities	Compare To:
START	Beginning Inventory (1/1/XX)	Quantity to inventory subledger. Subledger value to G/L.
ADD	Purchases	3rd Party Confirmation or procurement records
	Intercompany Transfers	Intercompany transfer records. Should net to zero
	Goods Manufacturered	Production records or key component purchases to 3rd party confirmation. [Often traces in from WIP rollforward]
EQUALS	Goods Available for Sales	
LESS	Net Sales	Quantity to sales subledger. Subledger value to G/L.
	Intercompany Transfers	Intercompany transfer records. Should net to zero
	Free Goods	Evidence that was really free and not combined with other product sales.
	Destructions	Certificate of destruction signed by more than one person.
	Research & Development	Use in R&D and final dispostion.
	Employee Sales	Invoices
	Count Differences	Generally a finding.
	Shrinkage/Other	Generally a finding.
EQUALS	Ending Inventory (12/31/xx)	Quantity to inventory subledger. Subledger value to G/L.

The second major concept of a royalty compliance is Sales. This is because royalties are generally based on the sales. Now, I say generally, because there are many instances, especially related to electronic goods, where the royalty is based on the number of units manufactured and a straight dollar amount per unit, and therefore, sales is somewhat irrelevant to how the royalty is to be calculated. Still; however, it is important to have the sales records for the inventory roll forward as the inventory roll forward should still be tied to the sales records even when the royalty is based on units manufactured and not sold.

An overwhelming majority of royalty compliance findings result from the auditor or the licensor reviewing the computation of net sales. These findings usually fall into one of the following categories, with inappropriate deductions being the most common. It is important that the royalty report require the licensee to report gross sales and a detailed list of all deductions by type from gross to reach net sales when the royalty is based on net sales. It is actually amazing how many license agreements do require the deductions to be separately listed on the royalty reports and how many licensees fail to list the deductions, and yet the licensors do not read the royalty statements or question why gross sales, net sales, and deductions are not listed on the royalty statements even if required by the contract.

Perhaps the number one cause of such findings is inappropriate deductions from gross sales to net sales or deductions that exceed a certain percentage limitation from gross sales, such as 10 percent. My recommendation to make everything simple is to just state that deductions, no matter what, can be taken from the gross sales price (the gross sales price being clearly defined as the list price and not the invoice price) provided the deductions do not exceed a certain percentage, such as 10 percent. I have yet to see an agreement that allows deductions up to a certain percentage no matter what type, but if this is done, it could greatly increase compliance, reduce monitoring costs, and avoid arguments between licensors and licensees as to the definition of a discount (i.e., is it a trade discount, price protection, volume discount, return credit, or some other allowed or prohibited deduction).

Appropriate deductions tend to be limited to trade discounts or volume discounts. Confusion occurs when trade discounts or volume discounts are not defined or limits placed are "reasonable" which means absolutely little in an enforcement program.

A review of sales records often result in findings in one of the following categories:

- Deductions taken to calculate net sales from gross sales. Most royalties are based on net sales. The following are deductions that are often not allowed, are taken by licensees, and result in findings:
    □ Intercompany shipping.
    □ Advertising including cooperative (co-op).
    □ Rebates.
    □ Discounts other than cash discounts issued at the time of sale.
    □ Deducting government fees as taxes. This is more common in third world countries such as Brazil where the government imposes social welfare fees that are not taxes.
    □ Deducting taxes or fees that are reimbursable by the government.
    □ Manufacturing costs.
    □ Price protection
    □ Discounts on related party sales.
    □ Closeout or other excessive discounts.
    □ Discounts to employees.
    □ Free goods (100 percent discounts) on samples or other reasons.
    □ Damaged and defective discounts.

- ◘ Year-end volume discounts.
- ◘ Freight (needs to be allowed under the agreement).
- Returns
  - ◘ Return value exceeds sales value.
  - ◘ Returns are not allowed at all.
  - ◘ Returned item is resold to the same vendor at a lower price, thus masking a discount.
  - ◘ Credits provided while the goods are never actually physically returned.
- Exchange Rates
  - ◘ Sale value not converted to U.S. dollars or other proper reporting currency.
  - ◘ Exchange rate used is the wrong day or wrong period average. Often the exchange rate to be used is the last business day of the quarter, but the licensee uses the daily exchange rate.
  - ◘ Multiple conversions of exchange rates to reach final proper reporting currency. This occurs when a sale occurs in one currency (a division of the licensee) and is then converted to an exchange rate of the licensee's headquarter country, and then the currency of the licensee's headquarter country is converted to the proper reporting currency.
  - ◘ Use of the wrong exchange rate source. Most agreements require the *Wall Street Journal*; however, many licensees use the exchange rate of their bank that can be very different than the exchange rate used in the *Wall Street Journal* or other appropriate source.
  - ◘ Use of buy or sell exchange rate and not end of day or average exchange rate as required by the agreement.
- Missed SKU numbers.
- Unlicensed product sales.

The sales subledger received by the auditor must be tied to the financial statements for completeness. As such, the contract must require the general ledger and financial statements be provided to the auditor. Further, the auditor will want to look at the general ledger for any "other sales" or "other revenue" in case all sales are not reported in the sales ledger. As an example, I was hired by a major university to audit $15,000 of royalties received from a licensee using a technology on flat panel TVs. The university had seen its intellectual property in use so they were certain they were due $50,000. We went and audited the licensee, and the sales records supported about $40,000 of royalties due to the university; however, when I reviewed "other revenue" in the general ledger, I found one entry for $75 million. I read the associated contract for the $75 million of other revenue and it turned out the licensee had sublicensed the technology and the university was due one-third of all sublicensing revenues so the audit finding, from just two days of work, was

$25 million plus interest. Therefore, not all revenue is reported in the sales ledger, and it is essential the auditor have access to the entire general ledger.

Finally, the inventory roll forward needs to be tied into the sales ledger. This is done by comparing the number of units as reported as sold per the inventory roll forward to the number of units sold per the sales ledger. Differences result in a finding. After accounting for all quantities, the auditor will proceed to test individual invoices selected from the sales extract and review how net sales are calculated from gross sales.

Some of the key terms and conditions an auditor will seek to test follow along with the top concern for each area:

1. "Territory": Out-of-territory sales can result in a finding equal to gross sales value, gross margin value, and/or contract breach.
2. "Net Sales": Knowing how net sales are computed generally determines if the royalty rate was paid from the proper basis.
3. "Gross Sales": Gross sales are often not gross sales but instead include a deduction. It is important the contact defines gross sales at a list price or the highest price at which the goods were sold since inception or for a certain period, such as within the prior two quarters.
4. "Royalty Due Dates": The auditor will need to know due dates to pay royalties with late payments often resulting in findings at a certain interest rate. It is essential the agreement mention the interest rate for late payments.
5. "Cost Recovery": Cost recovery provisions help make certain the licensee pays for the cost of the audit for those instances when the licensee has not been following the agreement. Cost recovery is generally the lesser of 5 percent of any reporting period or a dollar amount such as $5000.
6. "License Period": The auditor needs to know when the agreement was started and when it ended, as applicable. Out-of-license period sales can result in findings for the sale of unlicensed goods, and such findings can be based on the gross margin value of the sold goods or even more.
7. "Advance & Minimum Guarantee": The advance is how much of the royalty the licensee had to pay upfront of the agreement or at the start of each reporting period. Future royalty obligations are reduced by the advance.
8. "Royalty Rates": The royalty rate(s) are key to determine the remuneration due the licensor. Royalty rates vary greatly and include a fixed amount or variable amount such as a percentage of the value of goods sold or a fixed price for each unit sold. Some are based on the greater of a percentage of net sales or the minimum price per unit.
   For example:
   - Units sold 0 to 100,000 at the greater of $1.25 or 10 percent of net sales dollars

- Units sold 101,000 to 500,000 at the greater of $1.50 or 12 percent of net sales dollars
- All units sold above 500,000 at the greater of $2.00 or 15 percent of net sales dollars

9. "Licensed Products": Knowing authorized products are essential as many licensees, especially those just using a brand, tend to make unlicensed products.

10. "Audit Rights": Audit rights are generally defined in a period of time, such as the prior three years. Audit rights going back beyond three years are often very difficult to enforce due to the lack of documentation.

11. "Interest": Interest or late fee is generally an interest rate that is added to findings. It is usually around 1.5 percent monthly up to the maximum allowed by law.

12. "Reporting Requirements": These deal with how often the royalty reports are due, such as within 30 days after the end of each reporting period.

13. "Unsold Units at Agreement Termination, Damaged Units, or Excess Units": Many agreements require these units to be destroyed, and the actual destruction event is to be witnessed by an independent party. Alternative language might require the units to be destroyed under inspection of the licensor's auditor at licensee's expense or to be delivered at no charge to the licensor. It is best if it is up to the licensor to decide what to do with the unsold units. Destruction of units not authorized by the licensor should be considered sold and royalties are due.

14. "Intellectual Property Notices (i.e., copyright, trademarks, etc.)": The auditor will want to inspect manuals and product samples to make certain there is proper notification.

15. "Prohibition Against Assignment and Sublicense" The auditor will want to make certain the product has not been sublicensed or a part of the process outsourced unless authorized under the agreement.

3.9.3. Documents to Consider Requesting in the Contract to Allow for Adequate External Monitoring

What an auditor needs is completely different from what a licensor will receive from a licensee to allow for sufficient external monitoring. Each licensor should start with a wish list of items to receive to allow for proper external monitoring. This wish list starts with a review of the agreement and all areas for compliance by the licensee including approval of third-party manufacturers, safety tests of products, sales records, inventory records, annual financial statements, notification of changes in management and accounting systems, changes in royalty calculations, royalty reports, exchange rate sources, annual auditor's report, details of deductions, sales records, design specifications and new product approval sheets, price lists, returns, reasons for returns, and the list goes on and on depending on the creativity of the licensor and the ability of the licensor to processed the received information. However, even if the licensor cannot process all of the received information, it might be good to have it on hand for future reference. After reviewing the agreement for potential items to periodically receive from the licensee, the licensor should consider what a royalty auditor might wish to monitor. The following section can help with this. Then, all items the royalty auditor might need to do his job, including the key inventory roll forward, can be included as one part of the items the licensor receives periodically from the licensee.

At the most basic level, a licensor needs to receive a royalty report that details sales and all information to calculate the royalty due (i.e., if unit-based, number of units sold, and if sales-based, gross sales, deductions, and net sales by product). Additionally, the licensor should always be sending new product requests to the licensor for approval with clear penalties should a new product be produced that has not been approved by the licensor.

The next level of information would be a complete download of the licensee's sales records that includes the sale dates and territories. Additionally, a quarterly or annual inventory roll forward would be helpful, along with a quarterly or annual checklist or certification of compliance with key provisions of the licensing agreement. The checklist is to be completed by a licensee, preferably each quarter, in which the licensee identifies if they have any changes that might affect the royalty payment. Also, it is a chance for the licensee to certify they are still calculating the royalty properly through comments such as they are only deducting what is allowed under the agreement. The licensee can also certify they are not violating any special clauses such as manufacturing and selling for a key competitor.

If the licensee is from a different country than the licensor and the licensee makes a withholding of taxes from the royalty payment, then such withholding, if allowed under the royalty agreement, should be evidenced by a withholding certificate to be sent to the licensor so they can take a tax credit on their tax return.

3.10. Software/End User License Contracts

3.10.1. Contract Description

A software or end user license agreement grants the buyer the right to use the software on a certain number of operating systems/personal computers for a specified time period. There are a vast number of different software license agreements. This book takes a quick look at software license agreements for companies that are installing the software to be used by multiple users, as opposed to the license an individual receives for personal use, such as when buying a home personal computer.

The various different types of software license agreements include:

- Shrink-wrap Agreement
  - By opening the package, you agree to the license terms on the container.
- Clickwrap Agreement
  - By clicking "I agree" on a Web site, resulting in you agreeing to the terms and conditions.
- Volume Agreement
  - License the right to use the software on a specified number of computers. Usually a greater discount with increased volume.
- "All-you-can-eat" Agreement/Enterprise License Agreement
  - Allows unlimited use of software by an enterprise.
- End User License Agreement (EULA)
  - Dictates the terms under which an end user may use the licensed software. May be as simple as the shrink-wrap agreement, identifying a certain number of units (volume agreement) or a franchise agreement.
- International Program License Agreement
- Enterprise License Agreement
  - A license agreement that covers all use of the software in an entity.
- OEM License
  - License for original equipment manufacturer to install software in a personal computer.

And these are based on various types of licensing models:

- CPU or Server Based Licensing
  - The license cost is based on the number of personal computers or servers using the licensed software.
- User Based Licensing
  - The license cost is based on the number of users with access to the licensed software, regardless if they actually used it.
- Tier Based Licensing
  - License cost depends on a defined combination of metrics such as number of personal computers, services, number of users, numbers with access, access hours, etc. . . .
- Value Unit Based Licensing
  - License cost is proportional to value units related to specific hardware and software criteria.
- Client Access Licenses
  - License required for desktop clients to access server-based software.

End User License Agreements (EULAs) can be complicated agreements that generally grant one or a specific number of users within a specified enterprise to operate a certain version(s) of the license software. The EULA will describe what is permitted under the agreement and may include such items as copying, location, servers, and versions.

For example, an EULA might specify that up to 1000 computers at XYZ company may use version 6.0 of Software ABC until December 31, 2010. Should more than 1000 computers have access to the Software ABC, then the company will be in violation of the agreement and may have to face significant licensing penalties (civil and criminal). Underdeployment, or using less than the 1000 authorized units of Software ABC used in the example results in the payment of unproductive licensing fees. It is in the best interest of a company to self-monitor if all uses of software is legally licensed and not over- or underdeployed. Compliance can be difficult for a company as employees are known to procure illegal or unlicensed software and introduce it to their company-owned personal computer. Most unlicensed software is secured through the Internet, through unauthorized copies of licensed software, or through loading software on a network that inappropriately shares the software.

Advanced companies require employees to sign a software policy acknowledging they will not place unlicensed software on their computer. Such signatures may help a company avoid civil and criminal penalties should the unlicensed software be discovered.

The criminal and civil penalties for using unlicensed software can be severe. Each country tends to have its own software protection laws, but penalties for each personal computer without software can be more than $100,000, depending of course, on the country where the violation occurred.

Many software companies hire outside auditors to conduct audits to enforce the EULAs. A large number of these audits start after tips from disgruntled employees. Some software vendors offer rewards to encourage employees to report if their employer is violating a license agreement.

3.10.2. Key Terms and Conditions That Auditors Care About

Software audits can be very quick if the licensee has a sufficient software assessment management system in place. The most basic audit is concerned with numbers of users of the licensed version within a specified time period. Other questions that could come up are as follows:

- Payments against projections?
- Payment due dates and payment histories?
- Exchange rates?
- Agreement expiration dates?
- Variable licensing rates?

- Different products?
- Interest charges on late payments?
- Minimum guarantee payments?
- Advances?
- Product payment gaps when multiple products are licensed under one agreement and a payment is not received in one period for an individually licensed product?
- Other agreement milestones?

3.10.3. Reporting Areas and Associated Risks

Software seems to suffer the most from the unlicensed use of product. That is because of its portability, ease of access through CDs and the Internet, the sometimes high cost of the product, and the lack of enforcement for the intellectual property's theft around the world. In addition to the challenge of unlicensed product use, there continues to be falling prices, intense competition, high development costs, increase regulatory antimonopoly scrutiny, and associated litigation. This pressure on software vendors to recover losses and increase profits leads to increased audits of major using entities. For a relatively low cost, software companies can discover the unlicensed use of software at large companies that are also likely to pay the fines associated with the unlicensed product rather than lose the right to use the software.

Many software licensees are starting to realize the risks associated with deployment of unlicensed software and are taking steps through proactive software asset management programs to compare licensed usage to actual usage. Still, most licensees fail to adequately monitor their compliance with their software license agreements.

Discovering customers with unlicensed software is very common with unlicensed software in excess of 1000 units a very common event at companies with more than 25,000 users. Most noncompliance comes from just poor record management; however, incorrect installation of product and hard to follow license agreements lead to much overdeployment.

The EULA should help guide the licensee in the establishment of effective software deployment monitoring controls and make it clear for the need to monitor the deployment against the license. In fact, requiring a licensee to report quarterly on deployment versus licensed units is a very helpful tool to help make certain the licensee is compliant with the agreement.

Areas that a licensor should consider monitoring, and therefore, make certain adequate information is received from the licensee are:

- Royalty revenues from the licensee by location.
  - Identifying a drop in royalty revenues can be a sign of many different problems such as competition, not reporting on a division, and new versions not properly accounted for in the monitoring systems.

- Understanding how licensees are using the software. This can be done through obtaining authorization to place monitoring tools within the software with the offer that you will provide better solutions to the customer with the data that is extracted. Other benefits include:
  - Knowing the actual number of units deployed and used, to the number of licensed units reflects the customer's needs.
  - Providing opportunities to enhance customer data
  - Increased customer service by identifying issues and solutions in a timely manner.
  - Improved customer service and relations.
  - Decreased risk by increased control over licensor intellectual property.
  - Early identification of noncompliance so customers are informed prior to there being major issues.
  - Early identification of system issues for quick resolution.
  - Identification of system enhancement opportunities and possible business opportunities.
  - Nonadversarial continuous monitoring.
  - Enhanced return on investment.
  - Identification of unauthorized duplication of intellectual property.

3.10.3.1. Causes of Contract Violations

The most common cause of a software license agreement compliance violation is not continuously tracking and comparing deployment rights to the actual number of units deployed. This is because licensees generally do have the knowledge, capability, priority, or concern to track deployed software and even if they did, they may not have the controls in place to quickly react to software overdeployment (those being the authority to limit the number of users or quickly buy additional licenses for overdeployed software.)

- Not tracking deployment of licensed software.
- Deployment of unlicensed software.
- Not updating license agreements after company mergers or sales.
- Deployment of software upgrades that have not been properly licensed.
- Not comparing deployed licensed software to authorized number of copies.
- Royalty-free evaluation software used for nonevaluation purposes or outside the allowed scope of the free usage.
- Not tracking license agreement/version expiration dates.
- Not tracking maintenance agreement expiration dates.
- Unauthorized redeployment of software such as to overseas locations.

- Not removing old versions of the software, even if no longer being used.
- IP transfers without removing the source license.
- Excessive use of the software on machines where there are more CPUs than the number authorized under the license agreement.
- Licensee employees in charge of installations are not aware of licensing terms and/or do not track current license usage.
- Multiple license keys deployed when only one is required and licensed.
- Software used outside of production, such as being quality or comparability tested, used in sales, demonstrations, or duplicated on personal (nonbusiness) PCs not licensed.

3.10.3.2. Problem Areas

- Contractual Interpretation.
- What is actually defined?
- What are the allowed usage types?
- Vendor standard policies vs. actual contractual terms.
- Multiplexing.
- Who/What are the ultimate end users? How are these audited?
- Is this defined in the contract?
- Disaster Recovery
- What are the license or support requirements?
- Hot/Warm/Cold Standby requirements.
- Metric changes.
- CPU partitioning.
- Dual-core technology.
- Hyperthreading.
- Lack of SAM system.
- Lack of discovery tools.
- Poor records.

3.10.3.3. Documents to Consider Requesting in the Contract to Allow for Adequate External Monitoring

At the end of the day, because external monitoring is difficult, it is best to require the licensee to maintain a program to self-monitor using commercially available tools such as:

- nmap
- Network Inspector
- LanGuard
- PingSweep

- DNS Audit
- SamSpade

As an alternative, licensors may wish to deploy proprietary software for the licensees to use to monitor their software deployment, thus providing consistency. This should be clearly provided for in the license agreement.

CHAPTER
4

Roles in Third-Party Monitoring

4.1. Establishing Roles   140

4.2. Key Decision-Makers   141

4.3. Influencers   141

    4.3.1. Step #1: Who's Job Is It to Run the
    Monitoring Program?   142

        4.3.1.1. From a Licensor's Perspective   142

    4.3.2. Step #2: Questions to Ask to Determine the Level
    of Effort in Monitoring the Licensees   144

    4.3.3. Determining the Roles in Monitoring
    Third-Party Licensees   146

        4.3.3.1. Questions   146

    4.3.4. In-House Lawyer's Role   152

    4.3.5. Program Coordination Licensor's Role in an Audit   153

    4.3.6. Licensee's Role in an Audit   153

4.1. Establishing Roles

Establishing a contract monitoring program with a large company is generally very difficult due to the many conflicting interests within an organization. The battle lines are almost always known before the start of the program. Those for a monitoring program include in-house counsel, auditors, and the finance department. Those opposed to a monitoring program include sales, marketing, and operations. Those neutral or swing votes include the CFO, owner, COO, and president. Getting everyone to first support a program and then to establish it is often very difficult.

Who's against it? Sales, marketing, and operations personnel tend to oppose third-party monitoring programs because these individuals are fearful of messing up the relationship caused by the monitors finding a difference with the contract's compliance requirements. Sales or new business development personnel work to sign a contractual relationship and certainly don't want some finance person calling the third party to question a minor detail that may disrupt the hard-to-establish relationship. The bigger or more important the self-reporting party to the overall financial value of the monitoring company, the greater the chance there will not be monitoring due to fear of harming the relationship. These fears are generally groundless; however, a finance person making a call to the self-reporting company or an inexperienced auditor reporting on potential findings may cause tensions to rise, resulting in a loss of business—so, of course, all communications must be well thought-out.

Who's for a contract monitoring program? The auditor, without saying, is for an in-house and external audit program of the licensees for obvious reasons. The finance department is generally responsible with the collection side of revenues or disbursement of funds under a third-party relationship, so the finance department, as part of its cash flow internal control structure, usually favor a strong third-party monitoring program. Finally, lawyers tend to want to make certain the contracts they have written are being complied by the self-reporting third party for obvious reasons.

Who's neutral? The CFO or in-house counsel are generally in charge of the third-party monitoring program. These individuals tend to offer a neutral perspective that balances financial internal control compliance needs and operational and business development needs. The CFO typically needs to be sold on the idea to use resources to conduct third-party monitoring, and it is usually the role of the person in charge of monitoring the contract who leads the pursuit. The other neutral parties as to if there should be a monitoring program are other executives who have a dual role that includes maximizing financial results and developing new business or controlling costs through the use of a third party, the main executive being the president and/or chief operating officer.

It is obvious the neutral parties need to determine first the level of third-party monitoring that is to occur (i.e., remote/desktop versus on-site inspections) and then the roles the different individuals in the organization must play during this monitoring process. Often, a committee is established to provide guidance as to the roles to be taken within the organization for third-party monitoring. Members of that decision-making committee generally includes sales/new business development, operations, legal, and finance management.

4.2. Key Decision-Makers

Understanding the roles of individuals within a third-party monitoring program helps to identify who will need to participate and to what degree. This starts at the top with the key decision-makers. These individuals and they roles they play are as follows:

1. President: Provides overall blessing.
2. CFO: Identifies the need to the executive branch of the organization and understands roles, operational risks, legal rights, and fiscal costs and recoveries. Generally, she is the ultimate decision-maker regarding if a third-party monitoring will occur and who will be involved.
3. Head of Operations: Understands the business needs of the organization.

4.3. Influencers

The influencers provide guidance to the president, CFO, and head of operations. These people and the roles they play are:

1. Legal counsel: Can discuss the right to audit provisions, legal challenges the organization may face to monitor and enforce the contract, and legal consequences of attempting to enforce and not attempting to enforce the agreement.
2. Vice President of Internal Audit or Controller: Will present the viewpoint of the need for strong internal controls and the ability of the company to monitor the third party by just reviewing statements and other source documents received from the third party versus the benefit of on-site visits.
3. Outside financial auditors: The financial auditors are concerned with any receivables due from the third party (have they been overstated?) or liabilities with the third party (have they been understated?). The financial auditors prefer monitoring programs that provide stronger levels of

assurance to the financial auditors before they opine on the financial statements. If the company is a Securities and Exchange Commission registrant, then there may also be Sarbanes-Oxley compliance requirements that include the need to monitor third parties.

4. VP—Licensing (or other third-party position that controls the contract): This person is responsible for ultimately making certain there are current contracts, and they are being adequately monitored. This person is often one of the most important stakeholders.

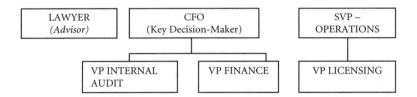

4.3.1. Step #1: Who's Job Is It to Run the Monitoring Program?

4.3.1.1. From a Licensor's Perspective

Tens of billions of dollars in royalties are paid annually to licensors; however, few licensors have enacted programs to actively monitor their royalty streams resulting in hundreds of millions, if not billions, of dollars in lost revenues. I have found that, on average, every dollar spent on royalty auditing results in a ten-fold return and the average licensee underreports from five percent in pharmaceutical to over 100 percent in software and apparel, so there is a need for licensors to monitor licensees. Much of the misreporting doesn't require a royalty audit and can simply be discovered by comparing royalty statements to contract provisions. Some calculations may be required, but it is worth the effort. Given the ease to discover misreporting by licensors, there is the question of why aren't licensors doing more to monitor their licensees?

Many licensors consider licensing income icing on the cake, while for others it may be their primary source of income. Regardless, it is amazing how many licensors rely on blind trust and in licensees to properly self-report and comply with all of the contractual provisions. Companies fail to realize that significant additional income is often overlooked through passive or minimal monitoring and enforcement of the licensee agreement. Licensors tend not to delegate roles for monitoring licensees. Roles of finding licensees and negotiation agreements are clearly defined, while an accounting department is just given the role to collect the royalties and generally, for the most part, just to make certain the royalties are received in a timely manner. These accounting departments rarely see themselves in the position of generating income though active monitoring. Instead, personnel see themselves as just reporting the numbers accurately. Further, if there is potential misreporting identified by the accounting department, the procedures to investigate the underreporting has not been clearly established. Generally, it is a matter of lack of personal benefit for accounting personnel to monitor if royalties are being properly reported so company oversight is lax in monitoring the licensees.

The overall duty to make certain there is adequate monitoring of licensees generally rests with one of three areas: 1) Business Development, 2) Operations, 3) Legal, or 4) Finance/Accounting (and sometimes, internal audit). Each of these areas operates independently, hence the primary reason why there is a lack of monitoring. When I make calls to sell royalty auditing services, it can take a lot of time before finding the right department, if any, that is in charge of monitoring the third party as there are so many different stakeholders, and the company has not clearly defined the lead stakeholder.

Business development sells the deal, so they generally walk away after the agreement is signed other than to stay in touch with the licensee to provide updates and see if everything is OK. Business development generally just tells accounting to start looking for the royalty revenues. Operations benefits from the additional royalty revenue stream but then turns again to accounting to monitor the agreement. Legal helps business development close the deal and makes itself available to accounting or operations should there be a problem with the licensee or the agreement but generally has a "we will respond when you call us" client service mentality. And accounting merely follows orders it receives, which is just to cash the check. Overall, I would suggest the monitoring of licensees is best done as a chief financial officer responsibility based on guidelines established by the business development and the legal department. Further, accounting needs to be told what they should be monitoring to determine contractual compliance and when they should be consulting with the CFO, operations, and the legal department, based on different actions or reporting irregularities by the licensee. Operations should also be monitoring with accounting to make certain expected royalties are being received based on market conditions.

But before a company decides who should be monitoring what and the extent of such monitoring, the company first has to perform a risk/benefit assessment of creating a monitoring program. The more financially material the royalty streams are to a company, the greater the level of effort required to monitor licensees. If the royalty streams are material, then the level of effort further needs to be categorized based on a variety factors starting with key terms in the agreement and the likelihood they may be violated by each individual licensee. The legal department plays a key role in identifying the contract terms that should be monitored. Then, operations and business development should provide counsel on the chances of the licensee misreporting. I have plenty of licensors tell me that they are working with people they don't trust. The accounting department receives information from legal, business development, and operations and then, based on materiality as defined by the accounting departments, establishes a risk ranking of licensees and royalty statements for monitoring and the associated procedures for monitoring each licensee (or sets of licensees if there are many licensees).

4.3.2. Step #2: Questions to Ask to Determine the Level of Effort in Monitoring the Licensees

To determine the extent of the need to monitor your licensees, consider the following:

- *Have you risk ranked your licensees to determine categories of high, moderate, and low risk? This risk ranking is best done by creating a risk ranking matrix*
- *Do you create a budget of expected royalties?*
- *Do you compare royalty revenues to market conditions?*
- *How many licensees to you have?*
- *Do licensing revenues exceed $200,000 per year?* The risk of the cost of the audit must be worth the potential reward. Depending on the industry, the typical licensees underreport from 10 percent to 50 percent. So, if over two years a licensor has received $400,000 in royalties, it would be more usual than unusual to have recoveries in excess of $40,000 in addition to the recovery of audit costs.
- *Has your company's internal monitoring indicated the licensee may be underpaying, or does your company have sufficient information to monitor the licensee?* Most companies monitor their licensees by knowing the growth of the industry and using their marketing personnel to report on the licensee's activities. This internal monitoring is usually very imprecise and cannot reliably detect the underreporting of royalties based on licensee sales or improper bundling of product.
- *Has the licensee nearly met or exceeded the minimum guarantee?* If the licensee is at least 25 percent below paying their minimum guarantee, then the cost of the audit probably will not be worth the potential reward.
- *Is your right to audit period near expiration?* To get the most "bang for your buck," try auditing as many periods as possible under the agreement, prior to the expiration of your right-to-audit period. Generally, you should audit at least every two years as records prior to this period are often hard to find, and employee turnover can result in unanswered questions.

- *Is a license agreement up for renewal?* The audit should be completed prior to the start of the new contract negotiations. There are three primary reasons: underreporting royalties are often negotiated within the terms of the next contact if the licensee is unable to pay, unclear financial terms identified during the royalty audit can be corrected prior to the next contract, and trust in the licensee can be measured prior to signing a new agreement.
- *Is the licensee changing their accounting system?* Changed accounting systems often present significant challenges to the royalty auditor as archived financial records often become irretrievable or special system reports cannot be generated.
- *Has the licensee been experiencing financial uncertainties or paying late?* Often the licensor is the first to be underpaid if a licensee is experiencing financial uncertainties. The licensee can underpay the licensor because the licensor has limited exposure to the amount due, or the licensee will underpay in current periods with the expectation to make up the payments in later periods. Unfortunately, the delayed payments often don't occur.
- *Does the licensee have unsophisticated accounting controls, or is the licensee located outside of a "first world" country?* Unsophisticated accounting controls often mean accounting clerks unfamiliar with the terms of the contract are calculating the royalties to be paid to the licensee. This occurs at both small and large licensees.
- *Is the licensed product subject prone to underreporting?* Certain industries almost always underreport royalties. Most underreported royalties are found in software, apparel, and entertainment.
- *Do you have any business needs to investigate your licensee's operations such as to determine copyright violations or find contract violations to sever a contract?* If you want out of your contract, try sending in the auditors to find contact violations that might allow for dissolution of the agreement.
- *Are the sales several companies away from the licensee actual paying the royalties?* It is common in the software industry for a license to be granted to a software developer who in turn licensees out the end product to another software developer or an OEM. The end result is the opportunity for underreporting by either the primary licensors or a third-party licensee.

Unfortunately, too many licensors fear upsetting the relationship and therefore do not execute their rights to audit. This is a real risk if using an inexperienced auditor to perform the royalty audit. Financial auditors have a history of seeing items in black and white and not understanding the business relationships that go beyond and often exceed the importance of monetary findings. It is therefore important to use a seasoned royalty auditor to perform the audit who knows how to preserve and can even enhance the relationship while using the skills to find the most money for their clients.

A second prohibiting factor to performing license audits is the cost; however, this obstacle can easily be overcome by using an auditor on a contingency basis. It is an especially easy cost to cover if audit costs can be recovered under the terms of the agreement. Contracts that allow a recovery of audit costs when there is underreporting in any period in excess of 5 percent almost always result in the recovery of audit costs when an experienced royalty auditor conducts the audit. Over the last year, more than 95 percent of the royalty audits that I have conducted resulted in audit findings that at least covered the cost of the audit, and more than 90 percent result in reaching the cost recovery provision.

An experienced royalty auditor can reap significant bottom line income for a licensor while also enhancing the licensee relationship and strengthening controls to ensure that all revenues due are paid.

4.3.3. Determining the Roles in Monitoring Third-Party Licensees

To determine roles to be play by individuals in an organization, the company can go through these questions to make certain the monitoring responsibilities have been defined and roles established. These questions and answers are viewed from the legal perspective.

4.3.3.1. Questions

1. What is the licensor's organizational structure?
   a. Organizational structure is required to be known to identify who is the chief decision-maker. Will it be a company owner, president, or divisional leader? Knowing who might be designated to lead the program is an important first step.
2. Who negotiates the licenses, and what is the approval process?
   a. Generally counsel, working with business development, will negotiate the agreement. Keep in mind the important role that finance should plan to help establish the money side of the agreement. Often, this part is overlooked as people work to close the deal and forget about the money. I have always found that to be strange, but I find on almost every royalty audit that the royalty obligations have not been well defined.
3. Who maintains the signed agreements?
   a. Generally, the executed agreement should be maintained by the legal department with one copy to business development and one to accounting (if accounting is responsible for monitoring).
   - Who is responsible for monitoring the agreements?

a. Generally, accounting for in-house monitoring along with sales or business development.

- Who performs the cash collection activities?
  a. Generally, accounting will collect the cash in coordination with Treasury for electronic deposits.
- To whom do you have third-party relationships?
  a. This is one of the hardest steps. Companies starting a monitoring program often don't have one database or record of all third-party agreements that should be monitored. I once visited a global Fortune 50 transportation company with multiple divisions, and each division was independently signing licensing deals, all of which used different contracts, often to the same licensees, and not a single division could provide a list of all their licensing deals or even when cash payments were due. With turnover, it took over two years to identify all the license agreements. The company was receiving checks from licensees and didn't even know what the money was for, they just deposited the checks. The list of third-party relationships should generally be maintained by business development and/or accounting. It helps to have accounting monitoring the list as they can have the role of making certain minimum payments, royalty statements, and periodic payments are received, and they can also alert operations and business development to expiring contracts.
- How many products, patents, copyrights, trademarks, technology, or other intellectual properties are currently being licensed, and how many variable payment plan agreements does the company have with third-party vendors?
  a. Surveys of operations often need to be taken to create the list of third-party monitoring needs.
- Do the license agreements include a "right-to-audit" provision?
  a. A company needs to know what rights they have under each agreement to determine the extent of monitoring that can be performed. This is a key factor in determining the scope of the program and therefore the level of personnel and time of personnel required to run the monitoring program.
- What is the right-to-audit period, or when does it expire?
  a. Companies that fail to monitor when right-to-audit provisions expire often find themselves unable to easily discover violations. More often than not, companies do not pay attention to their right-to-audit time periods.
- What royalty compliance engagements have been conducted, when were they conducted, what were the results, and who conducted the reviews?

- a. Knowing the history of past monitoring activities, especially results, helps guide future activities.
- What is the current level of monitoring, and do personnel consider it adequate?
  - a. There are many different levels of monitoring, including active and passive. That is what this books addresses, so it is obviously too much to discuss in this limited space.
- How have you decided which agreements to review in the past?
  - a. Management often starts a monitoring program for reactionary reasons. Such high-target third parties have often already been decided.
- How do you know your population of license agreements is complete?
  - a. Getting your hand around all the agreements is often difficult. Just asking divisions or people to fill out a list usually does not work as it is a low priority. An investment in time and resources must be planned to create a comprehensive list of third-party contracted companies that need to be monitored.
- Are there other departments that might have license agreements that you should be aware of or controlling, or do the other departments monitor their own agreements?
  - a. As mentioned, companies with multiple divisions or departments often have scattered records that may require third-party monitoring.
- What is the system to monitor licensee agreement compliance? Is it manual or software based?
  - a. Knowing systems in place helps to identify what needs to be done to have a well-oiled monitoring system.
- How often is the monitoring system compared to the actual agreements for accuracy?
  - a. Periodic self audits are necessary to make certain the system is working.
- How do you know the monitoring system is properly updated for amendments?
  - a. There must be tested procedures/internal controls in place to make certain the list of agreements to be monitored is accurate and up to date.
- Do you know if there are side agreements or other amendments that have not been forwarded to your department?
  - a. The procedure to make certain all executed agreements and amendments are forwarded to the legal department is extremely important.
- Does the monitoring program take into consideration:
  - Payments against projections?
  - Payment due dates and payment histories?
  - Exchange rates?
  - Agreement expiration dates?

- ▫ Variable royalty rates?
- ▫ Different products?
- ▫ Interest charges on late payments?
- ▫ Minimum guarantee payments?
- ▫ Advances?
- ▫ Product payment gaps when multiple products are licensed under one agreement and a payment is not received in one period for an individually licensed product?
- ▫ Other agreement milestones?
- Does the licensor prepare royalty revenue projections and investigate shortcomings?
  a. This is an in-house function that should have predetermined variance responses, including when consultation with the legal department is required.
- Does the licensor monitor and react to exceptions?
  a. The legal department should be involved to help identify what exceptions should be reported to legal so appropriate actions can be taken such as how the company will react should royalty statements or payments be late.
- Does the licensor consider itself aggressive, passive, or somewhere in between in monitoring and enforcing its license agreements.
  a. Knowing the aggressiveness of management will help legal and other departments in their reaction to licensee contract exceptions.
- Does the license require the licensee to submit royalty statements that break down how the royalty was calculated by product type, country, period, rates, gross sales, deductions, and net sales?
  a. For existing license agreements, this is a good place to start to determine if monitoring can occur. Licensors should amend agreements that don't provide for sufficient adequate monitoring as waiting for a royalty audit to point out weaknesses is generally too late in the game for meaningful adjustments. This is covered in more detail in other sections of this book.
- Does the licensor know who to contact should there be questions regarding the royalty statements and if there are questions, how accurately and quickly are the questions answered?
  a. Clear lines of authority should be established in an organization. Typically, the legal department, working with business development, works to interpret agreements and the accounting department or licensing monitoring department should work to provide statistical information from the royalty statements.
- Are royalty payments compared to industry sales trends, licensee public financial statements, or other information sources?
  a. Legal should make certain accounting is doing its job and accounting should know when to contact legal and business development/

sales when reported royalties are not meeting expectations, and there is an indication a letter from the licensor to the licensee may be warranted.

- Does the licensor provide any components to the licensee such as microchips? If yes, is the licensor the only provider of these components? If yes, also, does the licensor compare the number of units shipped to the licensee to the number of units the licensee has reported as were sold per the royalty statements?

  a. Better license agreements for the manufacturing of licensed product require raw material supplies to come from approved vendors that can have their sales to the licensee to be monitored to help make certain all licensee created licensed goods are accounted for. So shipments from vendors, per vendor records, should be reconciled to what the licensee claimed they received and therefore what they will be accountable for.

- Does the licensor require the licensee to provide an annual inventory roll forward for all licensed products, and if yes, are unexplained events such as missing inventory researched and explained?

  a. The accounting or licensing group should be reviewing inventory roll forwards under license agreements that call for the manufacturing of products. Legal needs to make certain the license agreement includes the requirements to provide inventory roll forwards with sufficient detail, along with penalties should the roll forwards not be provided in time as required under the agreement.

- Does the licensor require the licensee to make royalty payments on unaccounted for or missing inventory?

  a. Unaccounted licensed inventory should generally be considered as sales as it is the responsibility of the licensee to account for all inventory. "Otherwise disposed of" inventory should be valued at a price defined in the agreement. Some agreements allow a certain percentage of inventory shrinkage.

- Has the licensor compared deductions reported as taken by the licensee to those allowed by the license agreement?

  a. Making certain the monitor of the royalty statements understands the license agreement is a role often overlooked by the legal department and new business development. Legal should work closely with the monitor of the royalty agreements or other statements to make certain they understand the controlling contractual language.

- Does the licensor receive sales ledger detail from the licensee related to the sales or other detailed information beyond just the royalty statement?

  a. Having the detailed sales ledger (or other subsidiary records, such as cost records for cost reimbursement contracts) helps significantly in the remote monitoring of the contractee/licensee. Legal needs to make certain that this language to provide subsidiary or cost/sales detail along with the reporting statements is included in the agreement.

- Is all information required by the agreement included on the submitted royalty statements?
  a. Legal should inquire with the monitor of the statements from the contractee if the statements are meeting the contractual requirements. If not, the legal group should ensure compliance by the reporting party.
- Does someone reconcile the contractee statements to the agreements and compare such items as royalty rates, countries, periods, etc. . . . ?
  a. As stated, Legal should make certain they are informed of contractual noncompliance by the monitor early in the process so remedies can be undertaken in a timely manner.
- Are the reporting statements received in a timely manner, and do they contain current information?
  a. As stated, if statements are not being received timely, Legal should take quick action to make certain the statements are being sent as required by the agreement.
- Does the licensor have a list of the licensees' licensed products?
  a. The agreement should require all licensee products to be approved, and the licensor should maintain a system to approve new licensed products and formal letters to accept or reject new products being proposed by a licensee.
- Is there a requirement to have all new products that are going to use the IP to be preapproved?
  a. As a critical part of protecting IP, the licensor should preapprove all uses of the IP. Care to make certain that approval or rejection is made in a timely manner is very important, often to both the licensor and the licensee.
- Does the licensor review the licensee's sales catalogs and Web sites for unlicensed product or product that is not included in the royalty statements?
  a. Legal can help designate a party to be responsible for this task.
- If the license agreements require royalty rate changes based on units sold, how does the licensor monitor reaching these milestones and rate changes?
  a. Legal needs to make certain the agreements allow for proper monitoring of any rate or cost changes.
- How often does the licensor visit the contractee's location(s)?
  a. The legal department can help advise any contractor visitor to the contractee regarding items to examine. It is also important the legal department make certain the visitor does not sign a non-disclosure agreement without the legal department's approval.

- Has the licensor discussed the calculation of the royalty with the licensee?
    a. An initial discussion of reporting responsibilities, attended by a representative of the legal department or using guidelines approved by the legal department, can help make certain the reporting will be accurate and include sufficient information. Legal should make clear the consequences of noncompliance.
- Does the licensor monitor when the licensee has changes in management or changes in the person performing the royalty calculation so extra care can be taken in reviewing the royalty statements?
- Are there other business relationships with the contractee?
    a. The legal department should be aware of all agreements with the contractee prior to signing any new agreements as violations with other agreements should be considered with new agreements.
- Have there been any reorganizations at the contractee's company that could have affected the monitoring of the contractee's contractual agreements?
    a. The legal department should make certain the monitor of the contractee is informing the legal department of any major reorganization of the self-reporting party, such as if the company is taken over or might not be able to fulfill contractual requirements due to changes. If changes could affect contractual compliance, Legal should take proactive steps to make certain the obligations of the contractee are understood.

4.3.4. In-House Lawyer's Role

The in-house lawyer's role in third-party monitoring tends to be compliance focused and, of course, varies by organization. At a minimum, the in-house lawyer is involved in what one would expect: advising management regarding acceptable licensing agreement terms and conditions, coordinating efforts with outside counsel, writing demand letters, and licensing agreement interpretation. Additional areas of responsibilities that counsel may take includes:

1. Controlling the third-party audit program.
2. Defining and investigating conflicts of interest.
3. Investigation and background checks of third parties.
4. Negotiations with third parties. including contract initiation, amendments, demand letters, and settlements.
5. Litigation coordination.
6. Counseling to auditors conducting third-party investigations from what to communicate to the third party to contract interpretation and finding verification.

7. Approval of auditor invoices.
8. Auditor evaluation.
9. Custodian of contract documents, third-party communications, and database management.
10. Supplying the auditor with contract briefs, agreements, amendments, demand letters, and prior audit reports.
11. Establishing goals of the royalty audit and of a third-party monitoring program.
12. Approval of non-disclosure agreements requested by the third party, prior to execution by auditors representing the company.
13. Working to obtain third-party cooperation.

4.3.5. Program Coordination Licensor's Role in an Audit

1. Program coordination.
2. Receives and evaluates royalty reports from the third party.
3. Identifies individuals' roles during the audit from licensee notification to the actual auditors. Selects the company to be audited.
4. Determines the level of audit to be conducted, from desktop to full-blown audit.
5. Sends out the notification letter to the review candidate.
6. Advises the auditor during the audit.
7. Receives a copy of the report.
8. Settles findings.

4.3.6. Licensee's Role in an Audit

1. Coordinates with auditors on the timing of field analysis and preparation of information/document request.
2. Arrange interviews with personnel involved with the contract compliance process such as:
   - Product planning and development
   - Manufacturing/Reproduction/Distribution
   - Sales and marketing
   - Information systems
   - Reporting
3. Supply information to auditor as requested.
4. Discuss findings with the auditor.
5. Work with licensor to resolve findings from field analysis.

CHAPTER

5

Justification and Implementation of a Contract Monitoring Program (CMP)

5.1. Introduction   157

    5.1.1 Create a CMP   158

    5.1.2. CMP Justification   158

    5.1.3. CMP Scope   161

    5.1.4. CMP Objectives   161

    5.1.5. CMP Policy Statement   163

    5.1.6. CMP Board Resolution   163

    5.1.7. Running the CMP Program—Legal or Finance?   165

    5.1.8. Overcoming Objections to Monitoring Third Parties   165

    5.1.9. Selection of the Third Party for Monitoring
        and/or Audit   166

        5.1.9.1. Frequency of Inspections   168

        5.1.9.2. Depth of Monitoring of Each Third Party   168

        5.1.9.3. Number of Licensees to be Evaluated
            Each Period   169

    5.1.10. Selection and Contracting with the Auditor   170

        5.1.10.1. Contracting with the Auditor   171

            5.1.10.1.1. Objectives   172

            5.1.10.1.2. Scope of Work   172

            5.1.10.1.3. Approach   172

            5.1.10.1.4. Deliverables   174

            5.1.10.1.5. Conflict Check   174

            5.1.10.1.6. Engagement Team   175

            5.1.10.1.7. Engagement Fees   175

            5.1.10.1.8. Use of Deliverables   176

            5.1.10.1.9. Other Auditor Responsibilities   177

    5.1.11. Notification Letters to Third Parties of the CMP   178

5.1.12. Notification Letter to the Third Party of an
Impending Audit   179

5.1.13. Red Flag Indicators of Underreporting and Reacting to
Those Indicators   180

5.1.14. Information to the Auditor   184

5.1.15. The Lawyer's Role in Third-Party Audits   184

    5.1.15.1. Contract Auditing—In-House or Outsource?   185

5.1.16. What to Do with the Audit Report   187

5.1.17. Reporting to Management on the Program's
Success and Evaluation—The Contract
Monitoring Program (CMP)   189

5.1.18. Annual Reminder of CMP to the Self-Reporting Party   189

This chapter takes a high-level look at taking these first steps to implement a Contract Monitoring Program (CMP). The champion of such a program can vary widely but is usually either the legal/compliance department or the finance department. It is rarely operations as they often have conflicts of interest (i.e., they don't want to be embarrassed by striking a bad deal with a third party, or they often fear monitoring as it might "upset" a relationship).

I will describe the steps as if the justification and implementation will be handled by the legal department. In summary, the following are the steps that generally must occur. These can change in order, but chances are that all of them will need to be completed. These steps are discussed in more detail in this chapter:

1. Create a CMP
2. CMP Justification
3. CMP Scope
4. CMP Objectives
5. CMP Policy Statement
6. CMP Board Resolution
7. Running the CMP Program—Legal or Finance?
8. Overcoming Objections to Monitoring Third Parties
9. Selection of the Third Party for Monitoring and/or Audit
10. Selection and Contracting with the Auditor
11. Notification Letter to the Third Party of the CMP
12. Notification Letter to the Third Party of an Impending Audit
13. Indicators of Underreporting and Reacting to Those Indicators.
14. Information to the Auditor
15. The Lawyer's Role in Third-Party Audits
16. What to do with the Royalty Audit Report
17. Delinquent Payments—When to get the Lawyers Involved
18. Reporting to Management on the Program Success and Evaluation of the Program
19. Annual Reminder of CMP to the Self-Reporting Party

5.1. Introduction

While the importance and benefits of a Contract Monitoring Program (CMP) may be obvious to the champion of the cause, the many different main and peripheral players within the program will naturally have different levels of commitment and enthusiasm. This is especially true as employee roles continually become more complex and demanding. Contract monitoring can be seen by the neophyte as a necessary evil or internal control that can easily be overlooked because the monitoring of third parties is not considered central to many employees' daily activities or their measurement of success by management.

Should a third party fail to fulfill its obligation, it is simple for an employee to place the blame on the third party. And the perceived risk of upsetting the third-party relationship may exceed any benefit that an employee may personally identify in the success of effectively monitoring a third party and identifying a contract violation. Because employees' individual goals are often different than bigger or wiser company goals, obtaining various employee buy-ins for a CMP can be a challenge to even the most determined champion of the cause.

The following portions of this chapter provide an overview of a CMP, and parts can be copied to communicate a CMP to employees to obtain their support.

5.1.1. Create a CMP

The initial sale to an organization of the need of a CMP is the first step and generally the hardest one. Most people like to do things the way they always have and have an opinion that if it is not broken, then why try to fix it. However, it is important to understand that most reports received from a self reporting third party are only partially correct, so by the nature of self-reporting, it is broken and needs fixing despite what people may want to believe.

Generally, it is not best to focus initially on the monetary benefits of a program when communicating it to skeptical or resistant fellow personnel. Rather, concentrating the overview and justification in terms of business relationship enhancement, creating mutual trust, and increasing awareness and cooperating is the best way to sell a program with an "oh yea, you can make/save a lot of money by properly monitoring the third party." In the following Program Overview and Justification example of such a communication, seeking monetary recovery is not mentioned.

SAMPLE COMMUNICATING THE "PROGRAM OVERVIEW
AND JUSTIFICATION"

*"**Our global Contract Monitoring Program (CMP)** program is designed to increase our contractees' knowledge of, and their compliance with, the terms and conditions of our mutual agreements. By raising our contractees' awareness of their compliance obligations and the importance of being compliant with their contracts, we hope to increase contract compliance. Through the execution of CMP, we ensure that our contractees have the infrastructure and processes in place to administer their contractual obligations accurately and, consequently, that our company is properly benefiting from its relationship with the contractee."*

5.1.2. CMP Justification

Justification of a monitoring program is generally a cost/benefit analysis. A cost benefit analysis can be created by the legal or the finance department.

One way to do this is to create a matrix or spreadsheet through a program like Microsoft Excel and list all contracts where reliance is placed on a third party to report revenues or expenses and then create column headings where each contract's pertinent information is entered that might help justify the program such as (1) audit rights, (2) revenues or expenses during the right-to-audit period, (3) key terms or conditions that should be monitored, (4) terms and conditions likely to be violated, (5) cost recovery provisions, and (6) information about the third party making it a risk. Then, with the knowledge that it is common for expenses to be overreported by 5 percent or more and revenues underreported by 10 percent or more (both depending on the industry), then a calculation can be made to demonstrate the financial impact from potential lost revenues or overpaid expenses. Then by comparing the costs to perform third-party monitoring, both through in-house employee time and third-party audits, a determination can be made if the program would be cost beneficial. On top of the straight cost versus benefit analysis, additional notes are often made that audit costs can also be recovered, intellectual property can be protected, third-party agreements can be improved, and communications can be improved—along with all of the other benefits of a monitoring program expressed throughout this book.

SAMPLE "WHY A COMPLIANCE PROGRAM JUSTIFICATION"

"Organizations increasingly struggle to establish and maintain effective processes and systems to manage their compliance with our contracts. For example, most organizations have rapidly grown their IT environments or distributed applications to their customers without developing the processes or systematic solutions to track and accurately report contractual compliance. IT systems are often created to meet the in-house needs of our third-party contractees but not the needs in order to comply with the contractual agreements. IT systems are generally created to make certain organizations comply with established American Institute of Certified Public Accountants or Security & Exchange Commission rules and regulations; however, these rules and regulations are often different than our needs to monitor contractual compliance as our contracts often have reporting requirements that are different than those of regulatory standards. When third parties report to us, the accuracy of the reporting is often given a low priority, reporting and contract interpretation is generally to the benefit of the self-reporting third party, and management often perceives the reporting is accurate; however, due to the complexity and unique needs we place on the third parties to report accurately, there is often a high degree of misconception by the self-reporting third party that we would like to proactively correct. Our experience has taught us that self-reporting companies attempting to comply with our contracts inappropriately believe the following:

- *The risk of misreporting revenue streams (i.e., sales) and deductions, especially those allowed for under the contract, is extremely low (In actuality, we have found many sales of our products are not properly captured and nonpermitted* deductions or permitted deductions from sales to reach net reportable sales are taken in excess of contact limitations).

- As a well-respected company, including one that must comply with various Sarbanes-Oxley and accounting regulations, the odds of misreporting is low as employees have a good understanding of contractual reporting limitations and requirements. Further, employees read the agreement and have established controls to ensure compliance. (In reality, contractual compliance is often delegated to employees without adequate training and/or reliance is placed on systems not capable of monitoring contract requirements resulting in a multitude of contract violations. These are not necessarily intentional violations but tend to come more from system limitations, misinterpretation of the contract, or simple negligence. Employees are uninformed about contract compliance issues and the organization's agreement with our company).

- Many people have difficulty with the concept that transferring intellectual property to users without reporting those transfers is theft and, in the end, costs us money and ruins relationships built on a certain degree of trust that we work hard to create. [This sentence is easily changed for nonintellectual property contracts, such as "Many people have difficulty with the concept that over-reporting expenses for the benefit of their company is theft, and, in the end, costs us money and ruins relationships built on trust that we work hard to create."]

- Some employees think they are doing their companies a favor by not complying with the contract as it increases their company's revenues or reduces their company's costs at little risk to the employer. (In reality, when we find these contact violations, while we try to work to the benefit of maintaining a mutual beneficial relationship, if we discover significant contact violations, these often lead to dismissal of employees, penalties, unplanned expenses by the third party, a general breakdown of trust, and even potential contract termination and litigation. We prefer to have a well-established monitoring system in order to maintain long-term relationships with our contract partners so that issues, when they do arise, can be handled in a professional business manner at the least cost and disruption to business to ourselves and the self-reporting company with have contacted with.)

Our current third-party contracting programs rely on the contractee [i.e.; licensees] to accurately report their revenues, expenses, and actions as provided for under the contract. Our CMP is designed to educate the self-reporting third party about the terms and conditions of their agreements and to provide guidance regarding compliance management techniques. This education should help reduce noncompliance due to negligence or oversight. In addition, the presence of an active compliance program will help to increase the awareness and associated risk relating to our third-party agreements where the third party must report to us on their activities. Consequently, CMP is designed to keep the importance and issue of contract compliance in the minds the third-party self-reporting company."

5.1.3. CMP Scope

The purpose of the scope is to identify those third-party contractees that are self-reporting that will be subject to some level of monitoring. That monitoring may be simple in-house monitoring to intensive and extensive use of in the field audits. Initial scope programs start with limited scope reviews and then express the need or plan for periodic review of the scope of the program based on results. For example, a scope program may rely on quarterly meetings that plan out the scope of field audits for the following six months, taking into account past results, current risk indicators, budgeting, and right-to-audit contract expirations, amongst other items identified in the risk-ranking section of this book.

SAMPLE COMMUNICATING "PROGRAM SCOPES"

"Regular Contractee Evaluations will allow our Company to:

- *Further develop business relationships with Contractees.*
- *Incentivize Contractees to report and pay royalties and/or license fees on time [or accurately report expense, or other key monetary considerations from the contract].*
- *Increase communications, including better reporting, from the third party allowing better ongoing monitoring of Contract compliance by in-house personnel.*
- *Secure a broad overview of royalty reporting and payment processing and identify, on an early warning basis, problems that may be developing.*
- *Develop resolution plans with the Contractees for any problems identified.*
- *Ascertain if a comprehensive field analysis or other compliance activity is warranted.*

It is our Company's goal to conduct a Contractee Evaluation on each Contractee every two years. (Contractee Evaluations should be conducted more frequently for Contractees who demonstrate lack of improvement in royalty and license reporting). Contractees whose evaluations indicate that material underreporting may be present are candidates for a field analysis to be performed by independent auditors."

5.1.4. CMP Objectives

As with prior sections, it is best to focus objectives on overall compliance as opposed to what is often considered the most important aspects by many people, identifying unreported revenues or overstated expenses. By talking about the overall benefits to be derived through greater contract compliance, resistance to a properly constructed monitoring program will be reduced.

Further, it is possible the third party being monitored will obtain a copy of the CMP objectives, so care should be taken that such language will not upset the relationship. We have not completely ignored the goal to increase revenues in listing the program objectives; we have just included them as a subcategory within overall contract compliance requirements. You will also note the first objective is to benefit the third party, as opposed to benefiting the company that is creating the monitoring program.

Strategy development or objectives should not be taken lightly. Knowledge of the implications of a compliance program should be considered. No company should be viewed as "singling" out individual third parties for audit. I have had a licensor get into legal problems as they were accused in litigation of singling out a certain licensee and therefore not interpreting contracts with the same degree of rigor or interpretation. Overall, the goals of any program should be cash and value.

SAMPLE COMMUNICATING "PROGRAM OBJECTIVES"

"Beyond the issue of historical compliance, one of the primary benefits for our Compliance Monitoring Program (CMP" is the long-lasting impression made on the Contractee about our Company's commitment to our intellectual assets [or contract compliance/monitoring]. For example, while a procedure to track intellectual property usage is considered an essential aspect of a strong intellectual property management program, that procedure is considered the responsibility of the Contractee. If the Contractee is not already conducting periodic agreement compliance reviews and tracking intellectual property usage, they will be encouraged to do so through the CMP process. This encouragement to strengthen intellectual property management practices at the Contractee Company will yield economic benefits to our Company and even the Contractee/self- reporting party in the long run.

CMP has three main objectives:

i. Increase Licensing Awareness
Increase overall awareness of the Contractee's contractual requirements, terms and conditions, while expanding our Company's awareness of the challenges encountered by the Contractee in management of the program.

ii. Assess Compliance of the Terms and Conditions of the Agreements
Help to ensure that proper systems and processes are in place to manage accurately and efficiently our Company's licensed intellectual property used by the Contractee. Additionally, ascertain if the royalties paid to our Company are in accordance with the agreement terms.

iii. Increase the Education Level on Licensing and Share Best Practices
Educate and share best practices with the Contractee's organization to help it become more efficient in managing its intellectual property assets."

5.1.5. CMP Policy Statement

A program policy statement should be a short and to-the-point statement of why the organization is conducting third-party monitoring. These reasons vary by organization and are mentioned multiple times in this chapter and throughout the book. Always keep in mind this may eventually be shared, intentionally or unintentionally, with the third parties to be monitored so the language should be delicately written as to not create issues with third-party ongoing positive business relationships.

SAMPLE "PROGRAM POLICY STATEMENT"

"Due to the complex nature of licensing [or other] contracts and the reliance on Licensees to report and pay royalties accurately without substantiating backup documentation, the only way our Company can verify that royalties are correct and can ensure contract compliance is to establish a proactive contract monitoring program with its Licensees. In the past, there has been no formal program to accomplish this. Because the potential additional revenue from uncovering under-reported royalties and license fees is much greater than the cost of the program, we have decided to implement a systematic license compliance program that will include regular Licensee evaluations conducted by our Company employees along with focused assistance of visits to the Licensees under the Right-to-Audit provisions by the use of experienced outside royalty auditors."

5.1.6. CMP Board Resolution

A SAMPLE "BOARD RESOLUTION"

"ADOPTING LICENSE COMPLIANCE PROGRAM

WHEREAS, Company has, from its beginning, been committed to maximizing shareholder value through the continued expansion of licensing agreements and other types of self-reporting type mechanisms;

WHEREAS, Company has been assessing and enhancing its efforts to ensure compliance with the terms and conditions of the licensing agreements, and wishes to consolidate these efforts into one program;

NOW, THEREFORE, BE IT RESOLVED, that this Board hereby endorses those efforts and adopts as the highest policy of this Company, in the United States and abroad, a diligent corporate License Compliance Program, under the direction of a Chief Licensing Manager to be appointed by this Board; and

BE IT FURTHER RESOLVED, that the Board hereby delegates to the Audit Committee of this Board, responsibility of oversight of the License Compliance

Program, including participation in the annual evaluation of, and setting of goals and objectives for, the Chief Licensing Manager; and that, in this regard, the Audit Committee shall give a detailed annual report to the Board on the progress of the License Compliance Program and plans for its future activities; and

BE IT FURTHER RESOLVED, that _____ is hereby appointed as the Chief Licensing Manager for Company, to serve in that position until a successor is appointed by this Board. The Chief Licensing Manager shall have the authority and responsibility to take all appropriate steps deemed reasonably necessary for the establishment and cooperation of the License Compliance Program, including:

a. Working with all members of the Company to establish a program that is diligent, meets or exceeds industry practice, fosters the highest ethical standards, is effective in preventing and detecting violations of the contract, and meets or exceeds the standards set by the Audit Committee of this Board including those set forth as follows.

b. Establish compliance standards and procedures reasonably capable of reducing the prospect of noncompliance with the contract.

c. Appoint specific, high-level individual(s) with overall responsibility to oversee compliance with such standards and procedures.

d. Take steps to communicate effectively the compliance standards and procedures to all licensees and agents by, for example, licensee training sessions or the dissemination of best practices information.

e. Take reasonable steps to achieve compliance by, for example, utilizing monitoring and auditing systems, and by publicizing a reporting system whereby licensees and agents can report the required information in the format the Company expects.

f. Consistently enforce its standards through appropriate mechanisms, including, as appropriate, discipline of licensees for failure to detect noncompliance.

g. Take responsible steps to respond appropriately to noncompliance after detection and to prevent recurrence, which may require modifications to the License Compliance Program.

h. Delegating to others in the organization responsibility for assisting in implementing the License Compliance Program.

i. Providing a detailed report on the License Compliance Program at each meeting of the Audit Committee, including:
   a. training
   b. discipline
   c. development of standards and procedures
   d. compliance auditing and monitoring
   e. changes in licensing personnel
   f. reports of misconduct received through the reporting system"

5.1.7. Running the CMP Program—Legal or Finance?

There is often the struggle of who should be in charge of the CMP, Legal or Finance. Certainly both organizations must work together to make the program a success, but there can only be one chief. I have witnessed both Legal and Finance run the monitoring programs, and there are benefits and shortcomings to both.

The strength of the legal groups tends to be knowledge of the contracts, immediate contract interpretation, ability to handle conflicts (such as scope limitations placed by the third-party licensee), finding collections, improvement of future contract terms, and confidence. The weakness of the legal groups tend to be they are overwhelmed with work, so they don't have the time to work with the third-party monitors, are sensitive or too personal with the contract language to take criticism, don't understand that the financial ramifications of the contracts, and are not sufficiently sensitive to the business issues, as decisions are often too cut-and-dry, based solely on the contract language as opposed to the ongoing business relationship.

The strength of the finance group is operational experience (sometimes), understanding of the financial/royalty reports, information manipulation, experience working with third-party auditors, working with the legal and operation groups, and understanding risk factors associated with not monitoring agreements. The weakness of the finance group are the legal group's strengths—namely, unable to interpret the contract, conflict avoidance instead of addressing the issue with the third party, and finding negotiations.

So in the end, who is best to run a monitoring program? For larger organizations, it is a person specially assigned to third-party monitoring who understands finance, reporting controls, and can read a contract and work with lawyers to understand how contracts are to be interpreted, as opposed to how contracts have necessarily been written.

5.1.8. Overcoming Objections to Monitoring Third Parties

Eventually, there is almost always someone who will oppose a third-party monitoring program. This resistance is generally directed by finance personnel who don't understand or appreciate the cost benefit or operations/sales personnel who are concerned that monitoring programs where the third party being monitored is aware of the program will result in lost contracts, souring relationships, and overall loss of business (and commissions).

I have seen many different approaches to overcoming objections but there are generally two paths:

1. Identify early in the process who may object and bring that group in to help create the program. I believe this is the least effective method.

2. Identify a high level champion of the program, such as the Chief Operating Officer or the Audit Committee of the Board of Directors, and have them champion the program as a key advocate. This is generally the best way to kick off a program as few people are willing to challenge the "wisdom" of the COO or the Board of Directors.

At the end of the day, if you can work with the program justification and scope sections of this chapter, most reasonable people will support a monitoring program.

5.1.9. Selection of the Third Party for Monitoring and/or Audit

Typically, very early on in the process and as the first step, the company will have an idea of one or two third parties that will be subject to monitoring up to and including the audit. Most companies stop at these first couple of targets and never perform an overall risk assessment of all potential targets primarily because there are just a couple of large targets in one category (such as licensees), and the politics of the organization prevent a full company assessment. A full assessment of third-party relationships (licensees, joint ventures, time and material, utility, telecom, etc. . . . .) that includes a risk ranking by review of contracts will help an organization prioritize the limited sources to maximize returns. It is often wise to start with in-house monitoring prior to starting to outsource to make certain that your risk benefit assessment for a full audit will result in the maximum return on investment based on a focused approach.

Risk ranking of the third party is the proper way to select companies for audit. Risk ranking can be valued, based on a variety of factors. However, always keep in mind the right-to-audit expiration dates as I often have lawyers call me asking for a third-party audit, and it is too late under the agreement for the audit so the company is dead in the water without litigation or a strong negotiating position to force an audit, even if not within the scope period.

For a risk ranking matrix that can be used, see Appendix VI.

In a smaller organization, one preferred method to selecting a third-party contractee for audit is to ask management who they would like to audit based on their knowledge of operations. If the management has selected a third party for audit, it is good to challenge the reasoning as often management is unaware of the right-to-audit provision and auditable provisions, so management's expectations for results and what should be audited might not be allowed for or significant under the contract. If the management has not yet selected the third party for review, then the previously mentioned risk matrix should be used. The following should be considered when selecting the third party for audit:

- Not previously reviewed.
  - ◻ A licensee that has never had a royalty compliance audit almost always underreports.
- Licensor does not have an aggressive royalty compliance or licensee monitoring program, especially related to overseas licensee operations
- Licensee accounting system changes.
  - ◻ System changes often result in the inability to review prior periods or new calculation methods.
- Licensee people change.
  - ◻ Management changes can result in different contract interpretations, and changes in personnel associated with the royalty calculation can result in miscalculations.
- Licensor/licensee relationship.
  - ◻ A poor relationship can indicate the licensee is aggressively under-reporting payments.
- Geographical location.
  - ◻ Certain countries, such as Japan, Korea, and China have a historic pattern of underreporting due to difficulties in understanding English language agreements to management structures where clerks are given responsibility to perform the calculations with minimal supervision.
  - ◻ Foreign country sales often result in foreign exchange rate issues or improper tax deductions.
- Licensee personnel assigned to calculate the royalties are too junior.
  - ◻ Companies often have newer employees perform the royalty calculation, often with less than a year's experience, resulting in significant errors.
- Multiple locations.
  - ◻ Many licensees are located in more than one country, resulting in communication difficulties where calculation and information gathering requirements related to the license agreement have not been properly communicated to each country.
- Complex agreement.
  - ◻ The more complex the agreement, the more chances for error.
- Multiple sublicensees or third parties performing manufacturing.
  - ◻ Each subunit represents another opportunity for errors and individuals who are not aware of the royalty agreement requirements.
- Understand client/licensee relationship.
- Contract up for renewal.
- Contract complexity.

5.1.9.1. Frequency of Inspections

As part of the CMP strategy, different compliance activities may be taken depending on the third party's revenue stream or significance of costs, size, and potential for underreporting of revenues and/or overreporting of costs. To help manage the third-party portfolio more efficiently, the contracting company should systematically categorize the third parties to be monitored into groups with common evaluation criteria. For example, a company may implement the following licensee categories, based on the licensee life cycle:

- Preshipment (research and development stage)
- Growing/early
- Mature/stable
- Shrinking (End-of-life)
- Lost to competitor

5.1.9.2. Depth of Monitoring of Each Third Party

Monitoring needs to be customized for each company as one size does not fit all. Given the variety of revenue loss risks, overcharges of expenses, and other contract violations, and all the number of red flags indicating a possible contract violation, preplanned steps should be taken on how the company should react based on the risks to the monitoring company. The legal department should be involved in setting up the response levels as low risks or isolated items might just require a phone call to straighten out while major violations, such as discovering gray market activity by the third party, may require strong legal action.

An example of setting up the depth of monitoring for licensees is as follows:

The Company A has designed three compliance reaction levels to implement the CMP. Each degree of response is escalated in accordance with established risk rankings. These reactions should be considered in the context of potential for material underreporting at each licensee, and consist of:

- *Low-level response*: Phone call and/or letter to the licensee; informal inquiry
- *Mid-level* response: Formal letter to the licensee, and/or site visit by Company A personnel
- *High-level response*: Full field audit

The following matrix helps to tie in the level of response based on risk criteria as established either by the legal department or jointing by the legal and finance departments.

Not all compliance responses are appropriate for every licensee. For example, a brand new licensee that has not yet shipped product is likely a poor candidate for a full field audit whose aim is to identify and quantify material underreporting. The CMP strategy uses the following matrix as guidance for which activities may be appropriate to each licensee category.

	Low-level	*Mid-level*	*High-level*
Preshipment	√		
Growing/early	√	√	
Mature/stable	√	√	√
Shrinking (EOL)	√	√	√
Lost to competition	√	√	√

5.1.9.3. Number of Licensees to be Evaluated Each Period

Companies with multiple third parties for inspection should attempt to budget for a certain number of inspections each quarter. In reality, the monitors of the third parties rarely commit to a schedule or keep to a schedule of third-party inspections even if such inspections are monetarily successfully because other priorities often govern employees who are not judged by the number of third-party audits that are completed. Further, each third-party audit requires time to monitor, time that many employees don't have. Employees usually find it easy to not take care of third-party monitoring due to the low risk in their performance evaluations associated with not monitoring third parties.

The following is an example for a company that actually has its act together by budgeting and scheduling third parties for monitoring.

> *The CMP will be based on a calendar quarterly cycle. The Company will evaluate at least XX licensees (nn percent of the portfolio) each quarter. Thus, over a two-year period, each licensee will be evaluated at least once.*

SAMPLE CRITERIA FOR SELECTING LICENSEES FOR EVALUATION

"All licensees will be evaluated at least once every two years. However, it is probable that some licensees should be evaluated more frequently based on a variety of preestablished risk factors (such as a one year right to audit clause). In addition, some licensees should be considered in more depth than others. The following indicators are useful in determining whether a licensee should be scheduled for more frequent or more in-depth evaluation:

- *Attempts to get the Licensee to provide complete information when reporting royalties and/or license fees have been unsuccessful (e.g., late reporting, slow cash payment, incomplete or frequently revised reports, missing or incomplete list of new products).*

- *Licensee has inadequate reporting resources (systems and/or personnel) to properly report royalties and/or license fees.*
- *There has been a large increase or decrease in reported units or a change in product mix or other underlying fundamental business factor.*
- *Licensee has changed sales or accounting systems or accounting personnel.*
- *Market information indicates that unit sales are greater than the Licensee has reported through the royalty or license reports.*
- *Licensing Executive has requested an analysis or evaluation based on one or more of the above indicators."*

5.1.10. Selection and Contracting with the Auditor

The rule is simple: experience, experience, and experience. There is no "certificate" to be a third-party auditor, such as a Certified Public Accountant. Just about anyone can say they are qualified to conduct third-party audits, and often I see just that. Being a Certified Public Accountant, Certified Fraud Examiner, Internal Auditor, or lawyer does not qualify one to be a good contract auditor.

People often ask me how much experience is required to be a good forensic, business development relationship person, and overall highly skilled third-party auditor; and my answer is always the same; "at least six years of royalty auditing."

Most royalty auditors start out as financial statement auditors so they have a good understanding of the basics of bookkeeping. The challenges experienced by financial statement auditors are that they are out to prove the numbers are correct, while the royalty auditor is out to prove the numbers are incorrect. It is harder to find unreported revenue as opposed to showing reported revenue is too high. Financial statement auditors work in a world of materiality while royalty auditors work in a world of cost/benefit assessments to determine the quality of work to be conducted. Financial statement auditors are used to working as "independent accountants" while most third-party monitoring agreements don't require the auditor to be independent; so a good royalty auditor becomes a finder of facts or even an advocate for his client.

When selecting an auditor, keep in mind that you only get one shot at the audit. There is generally no redo. Also keep in mind that you don't know what the auditor doesn't tell you about; so an auditor may come back with small findings or no findings, but they have completely missed the boat. For example, even as I write this book, just last week I visited a well-known global company that shifts revenue income from the use of licensed intellectual property (the IP is digitally stored and distributed to customers) from one database to another after the license agreement period expires. The licensee tells me they believe after the license agreement expires, they are free to use the formally licensed IP as they wish, and they don't need to pay a royalty. The licensee also tells me no other royalty auditor has ever inquired as to what the licensee has been doing with the IP after the agreement has expired, and therefore the licensee has always assumed, incorrectly, that they own the IP and can do with it what they wish. This company has been audited dozens of times by auditors from national and global CPA firms. The findings from this audit will be in the millions of dollars, and I know other IP owners have lost this income because an incompetent or not-so-experienced royalty auditor keeps being used, and of course, the IP owner has not been aware of this lost income because as I said, what the IP owner doesn't know is what the royalty auditor fails to find.

There was another instance when auditors from a Big 4 accounting firm failed to make findings. The licensee stated this was acceptance of the under-payment by the licensor. This went to trial and I had to testify whether the auditors' failure to make the monetary findings was not acceptance but just lack of experience. The only way the licensor found out about these missed findings was a subsequent audit that revealed what the first set of auditors missed.

The bottom line rule is to check references, check knowledge, know the audit teams that will be in the field, and make certain the lead auditor has at least six years of specific third-party contract audit experience. No two audits are the same. Work plans are meant to be changed. Financial auditors don't do well with the lack of structure associated with a third-party audit.

5.1.10.1. Contracting with the Auditor

When contracting with the auditor, there are some unique key provisions that should be considered beyond the boilerplate terms and conditions. This language is for work being conducted by a Certified Public Accountant under the looser "Consulting Standards." I recommend that third-party audits be conducted under consulting standards as opposed to the more strict Attestation Standards for a number of reasons, including the auditor does not need to be independent, the procedures do not need to be agreed to, and the auditor will have the flexibility to perform work as required by the always changing situation. I have not included wording required under an Attestation Standards engagement letter as these letters are strict in their terms and conditions and could be changed by the American Institute of Certified Public Accountants, such as the language requiring management to take responsibility for the sufficiency and adequacy of the procedures.

The following is recommended to be in a consulting engagement letter:

5.1.10.1.1. Objectives

The objectives should state the minimum expectations of the work to be performed by the auditor. Sample wording is:
"The objectives of the royalty engagement is to:

- Assess Licensee's compliance with the terms and conditions of the related royalty agreement(s) between Company and Licensee as it relates to sales, deductions, timeliness of payments, and resultant royalty obligations;
- Assess the accuracy and completeness of royalty statements related to net royalty revenues remitted to Company;
- Assess the accuracy and completeness of controls over licensed inventory;
- Quantify any findings of misreported royalty revenues related to the agreement(s); and,
- Assess contract compliance of other select key contract terms and conditions, such as trademarks, advertising, disposals, quality control, returns, allowances, samples, and other areas as applicable."

5.1.10.1.2. Scope of Work

The scope of work should clearly state two important items: namely, the agreement(s) to be reviewed and the time period of the assessment. Also, if there are multiple locations or products under the agreement, any scope or location descriptions should be specified.

Additionally, it would be good to identify the start date of the work. It is difficult to estimate completion dates as so much is dependent on the cooperation of the third-party audited.

5.1.10.1.3. Approach

The approach should identify the work steps the auditor will be performing. It would be a good test of the auditor's experience to ask the auditor to clearly provide his work plan and/or approach up front so you can see if he appears to have an awareness of the work that needs to be performed for a third-party audit. The wording example in this book is very generic but covers basic expectations of an auditor. The actual work plan of the auditor should be significantly more detailed. The example language is:

"The engagements will consist of the following stages: Planning, Fieldwork, and Reporting.

Prepare for Fieldwork

The primary objectives in this phase are to understand the key compliance issues contained in the existing agreements, perform data analysis, and prepare engagement team for fieldwork.

On receiving confirmation from Company that Licensee has been notified of the compliance engagement, Auditor will contact Licensee prior to beginning fieldwork to introduce our team and approach, provide a document request list, determine data availability, identify key personnel for fieldwork interviews, and schedule fieldwork.

Activities in preparing for fieldwork include but are not limited to:

- *Obtaining and analyzing agreement(s), royalty reports, inventory records, and other available documentation.*
- *Discussing with Company personnel to gain an understanding of the contract relationship with Licensee and current reporting procedures.*
- *Performing Data Analyses, as appropriate, prior to visiting Licensee.*
- *Coordination with Company in developing our analysis work plan and testing methodology specific to Licensee, if applicable.*
- *Sending notification to Licensee to coordinate the fieldwork timing, personnel requirements for interviews, data, and documentation required for analysis.*

Fieldwork

Once on-site at Licensee, Auditor will perform procedures to test the accuracy and completeness of the provided royalty reports. The primary objectives in this phase are to commence and complete fieldwork procedures. Fieldwork may include but is not limited to:

- *Examination of agreement(s) with Licensee for relevant provisions.*
- *Agreement of royalty statements to sales ledgers and financial statements.*
- *Recalculation of the royalty obligation based on the contract's terms and conditions and the information provided by Licensee.*
- *Assessment of inventory records and controls from production/order through disposition.*
- *Examination of a judgmental selection of invoices to assess accuracy as compared to the sales ledgers and for unauthorized other deductions, bundling, or other information of interest.*
- *Examination of sales ledgers for related party sales and unauthorized deductions.*
- *Interviews of key personnel regarding controls in place over Licensee's compliance with the agreement.*

- *Examination of financial records for revenues from licensed product that does not flow through the sales ledger.*
- *Conducting an exit meeting in which you hereby authorize us to review with Licensee our preliminary analysis that includes the factual information obtained from Licensee and Company. This approach helps to minimize subsequent disputes and misunderstandings relative to any noncompliance or misreporting identified."*

5.1.10.1.4. Deliverables

It is wise to review a sample report of the auditor prior to selecting the auditor. The audit report should be very clear as to monetary findings and in providing support for those findings. Other items that might be included in a report included nonmonetary findings and suggestions for improving internal controls. The report should state the standards (i.e., consulting) followed in performing the work and the scope of work performed along with any scope restrictions. Example of deliverable wording is:

"Auditor will provide Company with a deliverable shortly after receipt of final information from Licensee. This deliverable will describe our work and summarize the information gathered on Licensee's contract compliance and/or operational efficiencies within the tested areas. If there are no findings, then such information will be communicated in a closure letter identifying the scope of work performed.

Should there be findings, the major sections of our deliverable will include: overview, scope, procedures and approach, summary of findings and recommendations, if applicable. We will include in our deliverable the findings and quantify and note instances of noncompliance and incorrect compliance, as well as weaknesses that impact the agreement compliance environment, if any, that came to our attention during the course of our work. Draft deliverables will be provided to Company's project sponsor for review and comment prior to final delivery.

The engagement will be conducted under American Institute of Certified Public Accountants (AICPA) consulting standards."

5.1.10.1.5. Conflict Check

As is standard with any work, a conflict check needs to be conducted and assurances should be received from the auditor on if there is a conflict. Unfortunately, auditors self check if there is a conflict and there appears, at least in my opinion, no clear definition of conflict for the accounting industry. Auditors are more than happy to perform inspections of their own clients, including tax, financial audit and advisory clients, and declare there is no conflict in the inspection of these clients. Some auditors go so far to say that unless they computed the royalty statements, then there is no conflict. Therefore, it is important to define with the auditor what a conflict is or at least, at a minimum, any business the auditor has conducted with the party to be inspected in the prior two years to be disclosed.

If there is any potential litigation that may occur from the royalty audit, it is helpful to make certain the auditor could eventually be hired as an expert witness. A royalty or other inspection auditor cannot be both an expert witness and the financial statement auditor, so it is generally not wise to use the financial statement auditor as your royalty auditor. Again, in pursuit of the all-mighty sale, many financial statement auditors attempt to persuade their clients they can also perform the third-party inspection audits for their client, but, in such instances, the auditor cannot be an advocate for the company for which they are conducting the inspection. The following is sample wording for a conflict check:

"Auditor has performed an internal search for any potential conflicts with Licensee and none have been identified. As part of this conflict check, we identified that we have been retained for work by the Licensee in the prior two years nor are we involved in any disputes with the Licensee. We are engaged by new clients on a daily basis. As a result, we cannot guarantee that, subsequent to the date of this letter, an engagement with a Licensee or its affiliates will not be accepted elsewhere in our firm. Should any new information come to our attention, Auditor will advise you immediately."

5.1.10.1.6. Engagement Team

The engagement team should be listed, including their roles, so there is no bait and switch in the sale of the audit team. Further, the roles of the team members should be identified, including who will be conducting the fieldwork. Any changes to the engagement team should be subject to the approval of the client.

5.1.10.1.7. Engagement Fees

The following are some potential pricing structures:

- Hourly rates. It is best if the professional fees include a range or a cap on fees subject to client approval.
- Fixed fee or percent of hourly rates per engagement plus an established contingency percentage [contingencies are not permissible under agreed-upon-procedure engagements (work done under attestation standards) and for financial statement assurance clients].
- Fixed fee or percent of hourly rates per engagement plus a value fee billing.
- Fixed fee or percent of hourly rates for multiple predefined phases of each engagement.
- Pure contingency or value billing.

Engagement fees can be complicated if there is a contingency or value billing provision. Of course, if there is a contingency provision, this will affect the ability of the auditor to eventually act as an expert or factual witness should there be litigation.

I recommend against fixed fees because the auditor should perform the necessary level of work to properly test the contract, keeping in mind the return on investment. The only time that fixed fees make sense are instances of a lot of repetitive audits, such as software vendor audits where the procedures are almost always the same, as well as the time commitment. It is bad if an auditor stops working when more money can be found just so he can make a profit on his fixed fee. Also, there is an incentive for an auditor to not do all the work required; the less they do, the bigger the profit under a fixed fee arrangement.

If the engagement will be contingency or value-based, it is important to have the Company review the agreements to be audited prior to signing the engagement letter for auditor fee restrictions because the third-party agreement may restrict the fees paid to the auditor to an hourly basis.

Additionally, certain states or territories may not permit contingency pricing arrangements, such as Washington, DC; Hawaii; Idaho; Mississippi; and Puerto Rico. Additionally, Vermont and Wisconsin have specific reporting restrictions that should be considered. The contingency decision is based on the home state of the Company and not the auditor.

Contingency and value fee arrangements are often complicated and can lead to disputes between the client and the Auditor and as such, are often less desirable than standard hourly rate or fixed fee arrangements. Contingency and value fee arrangements should be based on recoveries and not findings as auditors can pump up findings.

5.1.10.1.8. Use of Deliverables

Many auditors will want to place a restriction on the use of the report as no auditor wants to be sued or held liable based on the report findings. The auditor should not guarantee that he will find all contract violations nor be held responsible for not finding contact violations. The client may need to agree to indemnify the auditor in order to have the report released to the third party being inspected. Therefore, it is very important the use of the report be clearly identified as what is the purpose of an audit if the client cannot use the results of the audit to make a claim against the third party being inspected? You could ask the licensee to sign a release not to sue the auditor in order to receive a copy of the report; however, this is generally impractical.

I have resolved this issue of not having to seek a release from the Licensee by just sharing with the party I am inspecting the monetary findings of the report as opposed to the entire report. By sharing just the monetary findings, which are merely a manipulation of the information the third party already has, the third party has access to all the data in my decision-making and can challenge the findings prior to the report's issuance. I also make certain the Licensee may respond in the report itself to express any differences with the findings. Some clients don't like the findings shared with the audited company in advance; so in these situations, the client generally writes a cover letter to the findings, and the findings are issued by the client as opposed to the auditor.

The following is sample wording:

"Because of the special nature of the engagement, our deliverables are not suited for any purpose other than to assist you in your evaluation of your contract with Licensee and you agree such deliverables will be used by you for that purpose only.

Company acknowledges and agrees that any advice, recommendations, information or work product provided to Company by Auditor in connection with this engagement is for the sole use of Company and may not be relied upon by any third party. Company agrees that if it makes such advice, recommendations, information or work product available to any third party other than as expressly permitted by this Engagement Letter, then Company agrees to indemnify, defend and hold harmless Auditor from and against any and all Liabilities incurred or suffered by or asserted against Auditor in connection with a third-party claim to the extent resulting from such party's use or possession of or reliance upon Auditor's advice, recommendations, information or work product as a result of Company' disclosure of such advice, recommendations, information or work product. The proceeding sentence shall not apply should Company provide a written notice to the third party, which Notice shall be acknowledged in writing by such third party and returned to Company. Upon request, Company shall provide Auditor with a copy of the foregoing Notice and acknowledgement and any notice and acknowledgement sent to Company by such third party as contemplated by the Notice. Notwithstanding the foregoing, (i) in the event of a disclosure made by Company that is required by law or that is made to a regulatory authority having jurisdiction over Company, no acknowledgement of the Notice shall be required and (ii) no Notice or acknowledgement shall be required with respect to disclosures expressly authorized by the Engagement Letter."

5.1.10.1.9. Other Auditor Responsibilities

It helps to have some general clarification of what roles the auditor will and will not be playing such as:

- *"Auditor will not make commitments on behalf of the Company.*
- *Auditor will not act as a member of management or as an employee in decision-making.*
- *Auditor may provide observations regarding Company and Licensee during the engagement and provide comments.*

- *Auditor may assess the terms and conditions of the contract and compare them to practices used by other companies.*
- *Management is responsible to evaluate the adequacy of the controls in place over contract compliance for the adequacy and sufficiency of the Company.*
- *Management is responsible for determining what changes or improvements the Company should implement based on the Auditor's recommendations.*
- *Management is responsible for the resolution and negotiation of findings and issues identified at Licensee.*
- *Auditor is not a part of the Company's internal control structure relating to Licensee's compliance.*
- *The responsibility for establishing and maintaining adequacy of the controls in place over Licensee's contract compliance, and directing activities related to the assessment of business processes and controls rests with management of Company.*
- *Company is responsible for:*
  - *Determining the objectives, scope, and extent of Auditor's services.*
  - *Designating a management-level individual who will have responsibility to oversee the project progress and address issues as they arise.*
  - *Evaluating the adequacy of the procedures performed including findings, observations, and recommendations resulting from the performance of those procedures.*
  - *Negotiating the resolution of any findings with Licensee.*
  - *Implementing any changes to Company internal control over contract compliance of Licensee that Company determines to be appropriate under the circumstances*
  - *The services are not intended to be an audit, examination, attestation, special deliverable, or agreed-upon procedures engagement as those services are defined in American Institute of Certified Public Accountants literature applicable to such engagements conducted by independent auditors. Accordingly, these services will not result in the issuance of a written communication to third parties by Auditor directly reporting on financial data or internal control or expressing a conclusion or any other form of assurance about the adequacy of internal control over Licensee contract compliance."*

5.1.11. Notification Letters to Third Parties of the CMP

One strategy often used by a company that is starting a third-party inspection program is to send a letter to all third parties of the impending program. This letter serves a few different purposes: (1) it identifies to all third parties that they may be subject to an inspection; (2) it helps show that no single third party is being "singled out," a common compliant of a third party being inspected; (3) it helps remind third parties to maintain adequate controls and comply with the contract; and (4) it can result in increased reporting of royalties or likewise decreased costs.

A sample audit notification letter of a third party audit program is located in Appendix VII.

5.1.12. Notification Letter to the Third Party of an Impending Audit

The audit notification letter is an extremely important letter that should be sent out as soon as an audit is planned in order to preserve audit rights. Often, the notification letter is sent out prior to selecting the auditor or can be sent out even without knowing if there will be audit but only to preserve audit rights while a decision is made if an audit will be conducted. Failure to send out the notification letter to preserve audit rights generally results in significant complications or concessions to get an audit of expired right-to-audit periods. A significant complication may be up to and including litigation to audit prior years.

The timing of the audit notification letter is also very important. While many agreements state that audits only require a certain number of days of notice or reasonable notice, in reality, most third parties need many days, if not weeks of notice. In extreme cases where third parties are constantly subject to audit, such as movie studios, it can be months before an audit can begin so getting on the audit schedule can be complicated. Just because a certain number of days' notice is required, such as 48 hours notice, the odds of a third party opening its doors in such a short time period is slim to none, and there is little that can be done about it.

The notification letter should, at a minimum, identify the purpose of the letter to notify the party to be inspected that the right to audit is being preserved, and the third party will be contacted in the future by the auditors to arrange the audit. This acts as a document preservation notice to the third party to be audited.

One risk that many companies are afraid of is that any advance notice of an audit will result in document destruction or alternation, and they will want to do a surprise inspection. For most industries, especially royalty audits, a surprise audit will not work. The licensee, for example, will not open their books and records. The licensee's accounting staff usually can't stop everything and support an audit. The only situations that I am aware of where a surprise inspection will work is one where advance preparation for the auditors is not required, such as a safety inspection of ongoing operations or an inspection of a food restaurant to count inventory. If documents need to be prepared, such as financial statements or inventory records, then advance notice is generally required despite the wording of the contract. If surprise inspections are expected, then the contract should clearly document the steps to be taken during a surprise inspection and the consequences for noncompliance. Just stating a surprise inspection shall be allowed will have little effect unless it is accompanied by a penalty for noncompliance of allowing the surprise audit, such as a doubling of value of all findings that are discovered during the actual audit when it begins.

A sample audit notification letter is located in Appendix VIII.

5.1.13. Red Flag Indicators of Underreporting and Reacting to Those Indicators

Risk ranking licensees includes the identification of underreporting indicators. The risk ranking matrix in Appendix VI and mentioned in this chapter in the section "Selection of the Third Party for Monitoring and/or Audit" addresses these risk factors or indicators in detail. This section goes into more detail, outlining those indicators that should be monitored on a continuous basis along with some other underreporting indicators.

The first question you should ask is, *"Does the company have internal monitoring indicators sufficient to identity potential contract violations and a response plan to those indicators?"* Accompanying this questions is, *"Does the company have sufficient information to monitor the third parties?"* Most companies monitor their licensees by knowing the growth of the industry and using their marketing personnel to report on the licensee's activities. This internal monitoring is usually very imprecise and cannot reliably detect the underreporting of royalties based on licensee sales or improper bundling of product. It also does not allow for the monitoring of nonmonetary contract terms and conditions.

The following are generic items that could be monitored to indicate underreporting by a third party:

- *Has the third party nearly met or just exceed a royalty minimum guarantee?* A third party that just meets or barely exceeds the minimum guarantee in payments is an indication that the licensee is just reporting what is required to show that they are meeting the basic royalty payment requirements of the agreement. In reality, very few licensees accurately predict annual sales that will result in almost exactly meeting royalty minimum guarantee requirements. Licensees just meeting the minimum guarantee requirement rank high on the list of companies to be selected for audit. When an audit is not warranted due to costs or the level of royalties, a letter to the licensee reminding them they are not to just pay minimum guarantees but a percent of sales (or however the royalty is calculated), can result in a licensee discovering they have just been paying the minimum guarantee without regard to following the percentage of sales or other requirement associated to trigger the royalty.

- *Is the licensee changing or have they changed their accounting system, and in association with those changes, has there been a fluctuation in expected reported royalties of more than 10 percent?*

Changed accounting systems often present significant challenges to the licensee in reporting royalties as new systems don't always have the tools necessary to ensure compliance with the reporting requirements of an agreement. For example, in a recent royalty audit of a shoe company that I performed, the shoe company received a new accounting system one-half of the way through the license agreement period, and the new system, based on inventory as opposed to sales as with the old system, was unable to track sales deductions to reach the resulting net sales calculations, so it was nearly impossible to test if deductions to reach net sales were appropriate. All sales were reported at net, and the detail behind the deductions was not retained by the inventory focused accounting system. All the licensee could state was that the system was garbage, but it was the best they had. Because the system could not properly support the paid royalties, we had to estimate inappropriate deductions based on licensee activity in prior periods where deductions were properly being tracked by type. It is best to conduct royalty compliance examination prior to any major system changes; however, if the audit is conducted after the system change, then it should be as soon as possible as companies often purge the software required to gather accounting records from old systems, and the individuals trained to operate old accounting systems are often no longer around due to normal employee turnover.

The monitoring of system changes should be conducted through at least semiannual questionnaires to the licensee asking if there have been or will be any accounting system changes.

- *Has the licensee been experiencing financial uncertainties or paying late?*

Often the licensor is the first to be underpaid if a licensee is experience financial uncertainties. The licensee can underpay the licensor because the licensor has limited exposure to the amount due, or the licensee will underpay in current periods with the expectations to make up the payments in later periods. Unfortunately, the delayed payment makeups often don't occur.

The reaction to a late payment is often governed by the agreement. Some agreements state a late payment of more than a certain number of days is grounds for contract termination. Quick action should be taken for late paying third parties including letters from the company that late payments will not be tolerated and can lead to termination.

- *Has the licensee expanded operations outside of a "first world" country?*
  Unsophisticated accounting controls often means accounting clerks unfamiliar with the terms of the contract are calculating the royalties to be paid to the licensor. This occurs in both small and large licensees. Large multinational companies underpay royalties just as much, if not more than, smaller companies. If a licensee expands to new territories, there is often insufficient communications between remote locations and the person who calculates the royalties so vital information for the calculation of the royalty is not received by the person calculating the royalty. My royalty audits often reveal significant differences between what happens in a remote country versus what is consolidated by the corporate headquarters. Licensees should be required to report on expanded operations to new territories and this is done by having sales reported on a by territory basis.

  Self-reporting companies should be required to report on all new production operations at least semiannually and should also be required to report on each statement any new production locations or at least production/operations by location that may affect the reporting.

- *Have there been any reports of non-monetary contract violations, such as copyright violation, or excessive grey market activity?*
  Increased grey market or black market activity of licensed products is an indicator of potential violations by the self-reporting third party as often the source of IP in the grey market is a licensed company. This is what is sometimes called "operating the factory at night." Many licensees don't report sales to the licensor of discontinued products, substandard product, and excess inventory product because they are selling these items often at a loss or such a small margin that paying a royalty would result in a monetary loss to the licensee. Grey market products are often hard to identify but often are found when IP goes through unauthorized distribution channels or ends up in unauthorized territories. The reaction should be an audit and perhaps a review of customs shipping records.

- *Are there sublicensees, and are the sublicenses having financial challenges, legal, or other challenges?*
  Sublicensees or subcontractors facing financial or other duress tend to pass those problems upward to the self-reporting entity. The self-reporting entity, in turn, tends to hide those unfavorable circumstances from the entity they are supposed to be reporting to either following the rational that it is a problem of the sublicense, and not the licensee, or what the licensor doesn't know will not hurt them, as long as minimum royalties are being paid.

  A problem sublicensee or subcontractor becomes a problem to the actual self-reporting entity and the interrelationship/dependency of all parties is generally so closely connected that a problem in such a subordinate should trigger a letter of inquire or, when there is a great deal of reliance, an audit.

- *Have there been any changes in management or a management reorganization related to the calculation and payment of royalties? Or, has there been turnover in the personnel calculating the self-reported statements.* Changes in management or in personnel who are responsible for contract compliance create an environment ripe for underreporting. Before such underreporting occurs, the monitoring company can take steps to reach out to the new management to stress the importance of properly calculating and reporting under the agreement and even offer to help the third party understand the reporting requirements. Company reorganizations often fail to address reporting requirements to third parties when designing the new structure and responsibilities so a proactive approach to help prevent misreporting is often warranted.

The following are additional items to monitor for that could be indicators for additional detailed inquiries:

- *Have there been unexpected changes in what is being reported?*
- *Are there missing support statements or reports?*
- *Are items missing from within the reports (i.e., dates, invoice detail, country, rates, executive sign-off, deduction detail, net sales support)?*
- *Do payments or expenses have a significant variance from budgeted or projected amounts?*
- *Have wrong exchange rates been used?*
- *Have payments been late?*
- *Have incorrect royalty rates been used in the calculation?*
- *Are various milestones within the agreement being met in a timely manner?*
- *Are there variances from expectations based on industry trends or reported financial statements information?*
- *Are there variances between raw materials supplied and units produced (i.e., difference between microchips shipped to a supplier and the number of goods produced that use those microchips)?*
- *Is there significant missing inventory from an inventory roll forward?*
- *Are unallowable deductions being declared on the statements, or are there any other unusual expenses?*
- *Is there anything on the third party's Web site indicating a deviation from the agreement, such as performing work for a prohibited competitor or products not licensed?*
- *Is the reporting company undergoing a reorganization, merger, or a takeover?*

5.1.14. Information to the Auditor

If it is time to proceed to the audit, then there are some basic documents and information you should expect the auditor to request in order to perform a complete job. It is not uncommon, and it can create a large waste of time if this information is not provided up-front, especially all agreements or side agreements created via e-mail or other methods, including orally. This information is:

1. Key contact information of the third party.
2. Copy of the notification letter of the audit sent to the third party.
3. Copy of the agreement and all amendments, e-mails, or other explanations of the agreement.
4. All statements received during the audit scope period.
5. Interviews of key personnel to understand the needs of the retaining company.
6. If technical in nature, training to the auditors.
7. Contact names at the retaining company during the course of the engagement for contract interpretation and other information.
8. Trademark notification requirements.
9. Approve schematics or formularies for pharmaceuticals and chemicals.

5.1.15. The Lawyer's Role in Third-Party Audits

This book has identified many roles of the lawyer, especially related to the negotiation of the license agreement related to financial terms. But after the contract is executed, the lawyer's role does not end. The lawyer should be aware of issues arising from the self-reporting parties and how these issues can best be rectified through discussions, letters, contract amendments, future contract improvements, termination, or litigation.

The legal department should maintain a supervisory role in the monitoring of third parties. Finance, which is generally responsible for the monitoring, can identify reporting red flags, such as late payments, but it is up to counsel to step forward and make certain that actions are taken in a timely manner to preserve the rights and reduce the risks of loss to the monitoring company. Further, Legal should work to make certain the "right" parties are involved in leading the monitoring effort, including working to help avoid conflicts of interest that most often occur when sales or business development groups attempt to control the monitoring as these groups are most often more concerned about losing established business than legal risks. If fact, operations, sales, and business development often step forward and stop self-reporting monitoring because of the concern of "upsetting the relationship," a concern that I have never seen to be realistic and a destroyer of business.

5.1.15.1. Contract Auditing—In-House or Outsource?

Monitoring companies often struggle with the question of whether to perform the contract audits by using internal personnel or outsource the function. With a high degree of prejudice, as I make my living performing outsourced audits, I have found that it is best to outsource the contract audit function for a number of reasons as follows:

- Most self-reporting parties being audited do not want the internal auditors or other personnel of the monitoring company having access to "confidential" internal documents, especially if that access is to financial statements that could allow the monitoring company to have an unfair advantage during contract negotiations. Further, many companies with contracts are also competitors and are very sensitive about the information being audited, so an outside auditor is required, generally a CPA who is also required to sign a non-disclosure agreement.
- Many companies do not have an appreciation of the level of expertise required to properly perform the forensic investigation specific to contract auditing. Contract auditing is not a "core competency" of the monitoring company, and therefore the function should be outsourced to an "expert" in contract auditing (which does not mean a financial statement auditor or internal auditor as these are completely different types of audits from royalty audits).
- If it comes to the point of litigation and an "expert" is needed to testify, the expert cannot of course be an employee of the licensor. When selecting the outside auditor, consideration should be given to using the auditor eventually as an expert. If he can't eventually qualify as an expert contract auditor, then consideration should be made to using a different more qualified expert for the royalty audit. As an expert witness for contract auditing, I have seen multiple other so-called accounting experts be retained from the other side, and these auditors are merely financial auditors and they are consistently humiliated on the witness stand, causing the side that did not retain me to lose their financial testimony arguments in the cases where the position differs from mine. Also, be mindful that your financial statement auditor cannot also be retained as your expert witness, so this generally causes most monitoring companies to avoid using even qualified contract auditors from their financial statement audit firm.

A FLOW CHART OF IN-HOUSE COUNSEL'S ROLE DURING
A ROYALTY AUDIT

Advise management on need for third-party monitoring program and determine who will lead the program (i.e., finance, legal, internal audit, or special role)

⇩

Identify contracts with self-reporting requirements

⇩

Review decision methodology to select self-reporting parties for monitoring and depth of monitoring based on risk factors identified by legal and finance

⇩

Negotiate agreement with contract auditor (if role is outsourced)

⇩

Send audit notification letter to self-reporting party and to contract auditor or review letter sent to self-reporting party with questions from desk audit

⇩

For third party to be audited, send agreement and amendments to finance for forwarding with reports to contract auditor

⇩

Identify specific items to investigate or other concerns to contract auditor

⇩

Provide contract interpretation during the audit to the contract audit team

⇩

Handle disputes with party being audited (i.e., scope limitations) during audit

⇩

Review final report and approve demand letter. Control termination/litigation

⇩

Evaluate success of program. Enhance contracts based on audit findings

5.1.16. What to Do with the Audit Report

I always find it amazing the number of times a royalty audit report is issued, and no one knows what to do with it, usually due to the shock of the size of the findings. Internal staff may feel a sense of embarrassment or fear of being accused of not properly performing their duties or of not adequately monitoring the royalty statements and therefore push to bury the report. Because of this, legal counsel may wish to make certain they are in the loop regarding the status of all audit activity, generally through a monthly status report that also is circulated to top management that identifies the status of each audit project, including field work dates, findings to date, report issuance date; and settlement stage, including final settlement amount, or other actions to be taken.

Early on in the monitoring process, the company should have a general idea of how they plan to respond to reports including who should be in charge of the responding process (often lead by finance under counsel of legal). A response plan can generally only be created after some level of experience of acting on prior reports. Some companies respond by going after every possible dollar discovered in a report, while other ones go through painstaking negotiation processes that often reveal a weakness in the company's commitment to recovery.

Generally speaking, a company that receives a report goes through the following steps:

a. The auditor walks the report recipient(s) through the findings, making certain there is adequate understanding and support.

b. The monitoring company decides to what extent each finding is to be pursued.

c. The audit report is prepared for issuance to the self-reporting party. This means removing everything except just the monetary findings and internal control recommendations related to the self-reporting party. This report is often issued with a cover letter from the monitoring company demanding payment in accordance with the applicable section of the contract. Other items that might be in the cover letter include a reminder that interest or penalties accrue until payment date; termination may occur if payment is not immediately received (as adjusted for the specific wording of the agreement); a contact phone number; and, if appropriate, an invitation for a phone call to discuss the report with the monitoring company and the auditor.

d. A phone call by the monitoring company is scheduled with the audited company to walk the audited company through the report and make a verbal demand for payment in support of the prior cover letter. This call is generally led by counsel, or at minimum, counsel participates, as contract interpretation issues tend to govern the success of adequately rectifying reporting errors.

It is rare that an audited company will pay what is demanded in the audit report. Therefore, negotiations usually take place between the involved companies. Rarely, these will result in termination and/or litigation. The party that was audited generally seeks to make payments of pennies on the dollar when they admit a contract violation and work hard to dismiss amounts due if there is any sort of contract ambiguity. Therefore, the monitoring company that conducted the audit must be prepared for the audited company to be aggressive in fighting every finding in the report, especially if the agreement being audited has weaknesses, and of course, most every agreement has large weaknesses, especially when it comes to defining the financial obligations.

Few companies actually go to litigation from an audit report. That is due to the costs of litigation even though chances of success tend to favor the monitoring company.

As the goal is a decent settlement (plus, many times, termination), like any negotiation, it is best to know what you are willing to give up to reach the settlement and get your money. Most of my clients settle very quickly because they are so busy, and they view the money as icing on the cake. Others are aggressive and don't settle quickly, therefore spending a great deal of employee resources in many negotiation phone calls and letters. Finding the balance is important to maximize recoveries in a short negotiation period. I have seen the quickest and most success with monitoring companies that start a negotiation by stating everything is due and then very quickly thereafter offering a compromise settlement before every finding is discussed in great deal and the parties get into a heated debate.

A successful negotiation also often considers more than just the agreement in question. If the findings are large and future work with the third party is anticipated, the best way to gain a recovery may be to adjust future contracts with higher royalty rates or lower allowable costs, therefore the self-reporting company's personnel are often able to demonstrate to their senior management that very little was paid as a result of the findings from the audit; yet the findings and payments are actually buried in future higher royalty payments. This type of negotiation strategy is very helpful in dealing with cultures where it is important to "save face." The findings from the audit are spread amongst future payments, and employees from the self-reporting company will appreciate the opportunity they have been given to not make an unbudgeted expenditure as the result of an audit. The downside of negotiating for future benefits is that the future is unknown, and it might not create a sufficient lesson for the self-reporting party to start reporting properly, and senior management may be unaware of the errors made by the staff. Further, many monitoring companies like to monitor the success of their audit program and waiting for future benefits might make the evaluation of the current activity of the program difficult.

After the report is settled and the releases, if so demanded, are signed (which I recommend against as subsequent audits often find missed items from prior audits), significant findings can show that it may be very beneficial to make certain that monitoring is increased for the problem areas identified in the audit report, including a quick follow-up/re-audit of the self-reporting company focused on the prior findings. Even with big audit findings, it is amazing how many companies never actually fix their violations, especially if they were able to settle for pennies on the dollar. Such a limited scope follow-up audit is often negotiated during the settlement stage so as to not have the follow-up audit count as one of the periodically allowed audits in the agreement. In fact, some companies state a follow-up audit will be allowed on prior findings, even at the cost of the self-reporting company, if the findings exceed a certain threshold, such as cost recovery.

5.1.17. Reporting to Management on the Program's Success and Evaluation—The Contract Monitoring Program (CMP)

As part of CMP, the retaining company, often with assistance of the auditor, should monitor the results of the implementation of the CMP on an ongoing basis. For this to be done, key performance indicators (KPIs) need to be identified.

These KPIS's are return on investment, complaints against the audit, identification of nonfinancial findings (i.e., poor management) number of reviews conducted, time from end of fieldwork to issuance of final report, settlement costs, lack of control over intellectual property, increases in self-reported royalties, dollars recovered, improvement in compliance with license reporting requirements, administrative cost reductions, and increased benefit to the third party being monitored such as increased level of sophistication in intellectual property management at a licensee.

Each audit should be measured on its own in addition to the overall CMP to assess the effectiveness of the CMP effort and aid in the selection of future third parties for evaluation.

5.1.18. Annual Reminder of CMP to the Self-Reporting Party

Self-reporting parties should receive at least annually, and, if practical, semi-annually, a letter reminding them of their contractual obligations. The letter should be friendly and advisory in nature but still be strong enough to indicate the consequences of noncompliance.

Items that can be mentioned in the annual reminder letter include:

- The Company has enacted a CMP that may include inquiry letters and field audits. (this helps reduce acquisitions of singling out a particular self-reporting party).

- Interest, as applicable, will be charged on late payments and findings.
- A summary of audit findings in the prior periods so the self-reporting party can take efforts to remediate prior to an audit.
- A list of the most common contraction violations and how to avoid them.
- Specific reporting requirements.
- Contact information for questions about the contract.
- Any specific shortcomings identified in the reports provided by the self-reporting party that need to be corrected, such as not reporting all items as required by the contract.
- Comments of the letter that help advise the self-reporting party of its obligations, and the letter helps a self-reporting party avoid noncompliance that can lead to audit cost recovery, penalties, and contract termination.
- A recommendation to self audit and self-report to avoid penalties.

CHAPTER
6

Writing the Contract
Financial Terms and Conditions

6.1. Advertising: External Expenditure Commitments   194

6.2. Advertising: As a Payment to the Licensors   196

6.3. Closeouts   197

6.4. Counterfeiting Protection   199

6.5. Cost Recovery   201

6.6. Deduction and Discount Limitations   204

6.7. Exchange Rates   208

6.8. Granting the Right   209

6.9. Gross Sales   212

6.10. Insurance   215

6.11. Interest (Late Fees) Penalties   216

6.12. Inventory   219

6.13. Minimum Guarantees   222

6.14. Most-Favored-Nation   224

6.15. Net Sales   226

6.16. Non-Disclosure Agreements   229

6.17. Price Controls   230

6.18. Record Keeping   230

6.19. Related Party Sales   235

6.20. Reporting   237

6.21. Returns   241

6.22. Right to Audit   242

6.23. Royalty Calculations   245

6.24. Royalty Payment   249

6.25. Territory   251

6.26. Termination   253

6.27. Posttermination Rights   255
  6.27.1. Effect of Termination   258

6.28. Tax Deductions—On Royalty Payments   260

6.29. Tax Deductions—As a Reduction From Gross Sales   260

6.30. Unauthorized Use of Licensed Product   261

As written about in prior chapters, I have never seen a well-written license agreement because so few take into account "what can go wrong, will go wrong" and either don't have remedies for the contract violations or go right to termination when both sides know termination is not a reasonable option. The sample language in this chapter is focused on these provisions where there tends to be the most common contract violations identified through third-party monitoring activity, specifically audits. This chapter explains the pitfalls of weak language versus stronger language. Further, the reader will find some language that is often missing from agreements. Some of this language is original to this book so has not yet been tested in practice, and there are going to be lawyers who will believe some of the language won't hold up in court, so *buyer beware!*

There is also a complete license agreement in Appendix I. The language in this chapter is from different sources than language in the appendix, so both the samples in this chapter and the language in the appendix should be considered when looking for an example. Due to the length of today's license agreements, it is often impractical to include all the language suggested in this chapter; however, when the language is not used, management should be fully informed of the consequences by legal counsel.

Like most of this book, the language is mostly geared toward a royalty/license agreement; however, much of the language can easily be adopted for other agreements.

I believe one of the greatest causes for litigation disputes under executed contracts is due to poorly written contract language. The general rule of thumb is that lawyers do a good job of writing the boilerplate standard terms and conditions and do a poor job indentifying the financial remedies should there be a contract violation. Some of the most important language in any contract controls the transactions contemplated under the agreement; however, the typical contract does not address the many different variables that often occur in the real business world. Further, when there are contract violations, many agreement go right to "termination," while in the real world, remedies and not termination are the real solutions. The general rule of thumb for writing good contract language is to mention specific real number limitations and real number damages should the limitations not be met. For example, instead of using "deductions are limited to customary trade discounts," use "deductions are limited to 10 percent of gross sales of the specified transaction." Or, for another example, instead of just listing the licensed territories, also stated should be the penalty if such goods are to be sold out of the licensed territory, such as the penalty shall be the gross margin (of which gross margin will need to be defined in intricate detail including (1) It is gross margin on the entire product or the value of the IP and (2) What constitutes costs to reduce revenues to calculate the gross margin?).

Top 10 Errors in Writing IP License Agreements

1. Defining gross sales as the "invoice price."
2. Not limiting deductions to a percentage of gross sales.
3. Not defining deductions.
4. Not having monetary penalties instead of termination.
5. Not listing records to be retained for an audit.
6. Not including interest on late payments.
7. Not including an audit cost recovery provision based on reporting periods.
8. Not providing a sample royalty audit statement with all the information the licensor will need to know to monitor the licensee.
9. Not stating the penalty for unlicensed sales.
10. Not having unspent adverising commitments paid to the licensor.

6.1. Advertising: External Expenditure Commitments

Overview:

Royalty agreements often require the licensee to spend a certain percentage of net sales or gross revenues on advertising. Advertising is one area with one of the highest risks of reporting errors or noncompliance, primarily due to the subjectivity of what constitutes acceptable advertising expenditures. Further, may contracts will not require revenues from closeout sales, sales to the licensor, or related party sales to count toward the minimum advertising revenue expenditures.

The simplest method to require minimum advertising expenditures is just to state an annual amount that must be spent as opposed to requiring the expenditure to be based on a percentage of sales. Also, when advertising expenditures are based on a percentage of sales, when the royalty audit finds the inevitable underreporting of sales, this also correlates to an underreporting of advertising expenditures.

It is important that if advertising sales are based on a percentage of sales or net sales, that such percentage be consistent with how the royalties are paid (i.e., based on sales or net sales). This consistency helps to ensure licensee compliance with the proper base on which to calculate the minimum advertising expenditure.

If the licensee is required to spend the advertising money (as opposed to paying a percentage for advertising to the Licensor, which is covered in the next section), critical language to include in the contract is that if the licensee does not spend the money on authorized advertising, then the unspent amount must be paid to the licensor in coordination with the royalty statement for the relevant period (generally 30 to 45 days after the end of the advertising commitment expenditure period).

An annual advertising plan that must be preapproved is an important tool to make certain that expenditures that occur are within the goals of the licensor. Such an advertising plan should be submitted at least thirty days prior to the start of the advertising period (i.e., the new year). It is also important to note that if the advertising expenditure is not approved by the licensor, the minimum 10 percent commitment is not waived.

Identifying acceptable and nonacceptable advertising expenditures in the agreement can be helpful such as identifying if trade show and booth expenditures are acceptable and also noting that sales commissions and free samples are not acceptable. Other items to note are if advertising payments to the licensor count toward the minimum advertising commitment expenditures.

Some areas where I have seen advertising expenditures that were rejected by the licensor include (1) uniforms for factory employees with the name of the licensor on the uniform; (2) advertising for children's cartoon characters painted on the side of a truck that also advertised cigarettes; (3) in-house employee advertising costs at rates similar to much higher third-party advertising agencies (the licensee was only allowed to deduct the employee's wages plus overhead); and (4) co-op advertising where the licensor's product accounted for approximately 5 percent of the advertisement, but the licensor was charged for 50 percent of the contribution.

Weak Language:

A. "Licensee shall submit to Licensor for Licensor's approval, its proposed advertising program with respect to each License Year, but in no case shall the annual advertising spend be less than ten percent of revenue generated by Licensee."

   [It failed to identify when the proposal is due, what happens if it is not approved, and the contract speaks in terms of net sales and not revenue so there was inconsistency in the language.]

B. "All Articles and any related packaging and advertising must be approved by Licensor in writing before distribution or sale by Licensee. Such approvals or disapprovals are within Licensor's sole and absolute discretion, and any submission not approved in writing is deemed disapproved."

   [It needs to note that failure to spend money as approved will not count toward any annual advertising obligations, and failure to spend the advertising money will result in a payment to the Licensor of the same amount not properly spent.]

Stronger Language:

A. "Quarterly, Licensee shall spend three percent (3%) of Net Invoiced Billing on Advertising. *Advertising* means any communication of any kind or nature, whether now existing or developed in the future, by Licensee through any medium (including without limitation electronic and computer-based systems) directed to the trade or the public, including trade and public directory listings, store window displays, posters, point of sale materials, broadcasts, radio, brochures, pamphlets, business cards, trade shows, and billboards. Advertising shall not include free licensed product distributions, parties, employee events, and the like. Any underexpenditure on advertising acceptable to the Licensor at the sole discretion of the Licensor shall be paid quarterly to the Licensor as an additional royalty payment at the same time all other royalty payments are due."

6.2. Advertising: As a Payment to the Licensors

Overview:
The royalty agreement may require the licensee to pay a certain percentage of sales to the licensor so the licensor may use this money for advertising expenditures. The simplest calculation is based on the same base sales number as for standard royalty payments; however, often there are exclusions from the advertising commitment, such as closeout sales.

Weak language for calculating the payment to the licensor tends to be more complicated. This is one area where simple is better as it is less subject to error.

It is not unusual for the licensor, by contract, to have to spend at least a minimum amount of the advertising payments received from the Licensee for marketing, advertising, or promoting the licensed products as part of a larger license campaign. If such language is in the contract, the licensor should strive to not have to spend more than a certain percentage of the advertising payments on advertising, such as 50 percent.

Weak Language:

A. "Licensee shall make a promotional commitment payment equal to 3 percent of revenues each year."
    [It is weak because the contract does not defined revenues, and the penalty for not making the payment is not specified within the language of the contract.]

Stronger Language:

A. "Marketing Fees" are defined as, "During the Term, Licensee will pay to Licensor a sum equal to three percent (3%) of the greater of Net Sales or Minimum Net Sales . . ."

B. "In addition to the royalty payments, an additional 3% shall be paid to the licensor on net sales for advertising expenditures. Such expenditure shall be made at the same time as the quarterly royalty payments and any under payment shall be treated as a late royalty payment with interest due until paid."

C. "In addition to the Royalty payments provided herby, Licensee shall pay to Licensor during each Annual Period of the Term hereof, except as otherwise expressly provided in paragraph A [see below], a payment on account of advertising expenditures incurred by Licensor (the "Advertising Payment") equal to the greater of three (3%) percent, of minimum sales goals or three 3 percent of Licensee's actual Net Sales in such Annual Period. The Advertisement Payments shall be made on a quarterly basis, within twenty (20) days following the end of each calendar quarter during the Term, at the same time Royalty payments are made." Paragraph A- "The Advertising Payment for the Initial Term will be Ten Thousand ($10,000) Dollars, payable quarterly, for which the initial payment is due on December 31, 2008 and the three (3) subsequent quarterly payments are payable with the Royalty payments on the dates specified hereof. For each calendar quarter following the Initial Term, Licensee shall pay to Licensor the Advertising Payment otherwise due. Licensee shall make regular Advertising Payments for the remainder of the Annual Period, if any is due, based on Net Sales."

6.3. Closeouts

Overview:
Closeout sale price limitations are amongst the worst written as they often rely on vague contract language that limits discounting to customary trade practices or prohibit closeout sales without specific percentage limitations. The best controls clearly state the maximum discount percentage that can be provided to a closeout retailer, and that discount percentage must be based on the higher of the approved wholesale list price or the highest price that similar goods were actually sold for. It is important to have both the wholesale list price and the highest price similar goods were sold for because it is common that the licensor does not have wholesale list pricing, and there needs to be a base for the calculation of the discount.

Further, many agreements limit to whom the closeout products may be sold (i.e., allowed on sales to Ross Dress for Less, but not allowed to Target), but the penalty should the closeout be made to an unauthorized discounter is not specified so there is little the licensor can do other than terminate the agreement or write a decease letter. The optimal control to discourage the improper selling of closeouts to unauthorized retailers is to clearly note the penalty to be paid, such as a royalty rate double the standard rate on all such sales.

Weak Language:

A. "Distributor in exercising the rights and licenses granted hereunder shall use its commercially reasonable best efforts, consistent with sound business policy, in distributing and exploiting Video Devices so as to (i) maximize Gross Receipts and Net Receipts . . ." "None of the following shall be made by Distributor without Studios' prior written consent: . . . (ii) distribution of Video Devices at pricing less than that standard in the industry (e.g., cut-offs or close-outs) . . ."

   [This language is weak as it establishes the discount cannot be more than "industry standard." The challenge is establishing "industry standard," and given the large number of video devices with many different features and with changing technologies, identifying of the industry standard is basically impractical making this provision nearly impossible to enforce. Just about any monetary finding is certain to be challenged due to the vagueness of this language.]

B. "All sales by Licensee of any Licensed Products for a price ("Closeout Price") less than sixty-five percent (65%) of the *established sales price* (but excluding make-up orders, sales by Licensee to the Licensor, cancellations and sales of physically defective Licensed Products) shall be deemed a 'Close-Out Sale.' Make-up orders, sales by Licensee to the Licensor, cancellations and sales of physically defective Licensed Products shall not counts as Closeout Sales hereunder event if sold at less than sixty-five (65%) *of the established sales price.* The royalty rate on Close-Out Sales shall be the Off Price Royalty Rate set forth in Section XX above and may only be distributed or *sold to the Off Price Channels of Distribution set forth on Schedule A-1* attached hereto; provided, however, that the Off Price Royalty Rate shall only apply to Close-Out Sales in any Annual Period that comprise up to seven and one half percent (7.5%) of the total aggregate Net Sales in such Annual Period." "Nowithstanding the foregoing, Licensee shall not sell any Licensed Products for a price less than fifty percent (50%) of the established sales price without the prior written consent of Licensor, which consent may be withheld in Licensor's sole discretion."

   [It is weak because the limit is placed on the "established sales price," which is subject to interpretation and argument. It is also weak because the penalty for the sale to companies not listed in Schedule A-1 is not clearly identified. With a few minor changes, this can be strong language, as noted below with the underlined sections.]

Stronger Language:

A. "All sales *or other distributions* by Licensee of any Licensed Products for a price ("Closeout Price") less than sixty-five percent (65%) of the 'established sales price' (*the established sales price shall be defined as the greater of the wholesale list price or highest selling price similar units were sold at any time*) (but excluding make-up orders, sales by Licensee to the Licensor, cancellations, and sales of physically defective Licensed Products) shall be deemed a 'Closeout Sale.' Make-up orders, sales by Licensee to the Licensor, cancellations, and sales of physically defective Licensed Products shall not counts as Closeout Sales hereunder event if sold at less than sixty-five (65%) of the established sales price. The royalty rate on Closeout Sales shall be the Off Price Royalty Rate set forth in Section XX above and may only be distributed or sold to the Off Price Channels of Distribution set forth on Schedule A-1 attached hereto; provided, however, that the Off Price Royalty Rate shall only apply to Closeout Sales in any Annual Period that comprise up to seven and one half percent (7.5%) of the total aggregate Net Sales in such Annual Period and shall only *apply on sales through retailers listed in Schedule A-1.*" "Nowithstanding the foregoing, Licensee shall not sell any Licensed Products for a price less than fifty percent (50%) of the established sales price without the prior written consent of Licensor, which consent may be withheld in Licensor's sole discretion."

B. "Notwithstanding anything contained herein, Licensee may not manufacture Licensed Products specifically for closeout, off-price, and/or discount accounts of any kind, nor may it sell less than first-quality Licensed Products to such accounts. Any closeout, off-price, discount, or similar account which may be approved by Licensor (for the limited purpose of Licensee's sales of Closeouts) may only be sold Licensed Products which are actually Closeouts, namely, discontinued merchandise. Each Closeout Licensed Product must retain the original, separate and individual SKU, and the original, separate and individual MSRP (with the applicable discount shown separately in Licensee's records and reports) as each were submitted to Licensor on the Licensed Product."

6.4. Counterfeiting Protection

Overview:
Counterfeiting and grey market activity runs rampant with almost all intellectual property. Licensees, knowingly or not, often support counterfeiting activity.

And licensees certainly are commonly involved in grey market activity, especially for factories located in certain parts of the world, like China, where counterfeiting and grey market activity is the norm as opposed to the exception.

Well-constructed contracts place controls, when appropriate, over licensees to help prevent counterfeiting and grey market activity. Obviously, the strength of the counterfeiting controls needs to be based on the value of the licensed property and ease of counterfeiting.

Microsoft helps identify computers with illegally loaded software by use of numerous control measures. The most visible to the customer is the "Certificate of Authenticity." Most any Personal Computer today is preloaded with Microsoft software, and each computer has the Microsoft Certificate of Authenticity placed on the PC's chassis. Each certificate is individually traceable to the unique manufacturer (check your own PC for the sticker). Personal computer manufacturers with excess inventory have been known to sell their Microsoft sticker to unlicensed manufacturers (OEMs) to make a profit on the sticker. Unfortunately for the selling company, if caught by Microsoft, they still must pay the full royalty on the certificate sticker as a royalty is due on all certificate stickers unaccounted for.

Microsoft literature describes their Certificates of Authenticity (COA) as follows:

"The Certificate of Authenticity is only a visual identifier that helps determine whether Microsoft software is genuine. It should never be distributed by itself without the software it authenticates. The COA label is contained within the OEM System Builder software pack for Windows software. System builders are required to affix the Windows COA label to the side of the PC on which the software is being preinstalled. Licenses must also be distributed with hologram media, documentation, and the EULA."

"The COA assists you [the OEM] and your customers to determine whether the Microsoft software and components are genuine. The COA is included with each CD Pack and authenticates only the software components with which it is legally distributed. Note: The COA is not the license. However, since the end user cannot be legally licensed unless the software is genuine, the COA is used as part of the process to determine whether an end user has genuine software that is legally licensed." "The COA included with each OEM software unit authenticates only the software components with which it is legally distributed. With Windows software, it is important that you adhere the Windows COA label included in the original software pack to the computer system you distribute to the end user. The end user is responsible for keeping track of the software and applicable materials distributed with each computer (for all software programs). The COA, product key in the center of the COA, and the original software are essential for determining license rights and installation."

Apparel licensors, such as the NFL, are also known to use anticounterfeiting stickers that mention the product is officially licensed. These stickers are not prenumbered and therefore are more likely to be copied by the counterfeiter. Therefore, the stickers provided a lower level of control than the prenumbered Microsoft certificate stickers.

Sample Language:
"Licensee shall comply with and adhere to Licensor's mandatory 'Official Licensed Product' identification system or such other shipment tracking, identification and anticounterfeiting systems, tags, and labels that Licensor may establish from time to time, which may include the obligation, at Licensee's sole cost and expense, to use product authentication hang tags or stickers which must at all times comply with specific criteria determined by Licensor or to purchase such hang tags or stickers from a third party designated by Licensor from time to time, and to affix such hang tags or stickers on each Article before sale or distribution. Licensee shall at all times conduct all aspects of its business in compliance with all shipment tracking, identification, and anticounterfeiting systems, tags, and labeling requirements that Licensor may establish from time to time. Licensee shall use commercially reasonable efforts to ensure that all retailers and authorized distributors purchasing Articles comply with Licensor's anticounterfeiting systems, tags and labeling requirements established from time to time."

6.5. Cost Recovery

Overview:
Leading practice is to include a provision in the right-of-inspection clause that requires the licensee to pay for the inspection's costs if the findings exceed within any reporting period the lesser of a certain percentage (e.g., 1 percent to 3 percent) of royalties paid or a base dollar amount (e.g., $10,000). Costs are often defined as the reasonable cost to hire the independent accountant and licensor administrative costs (licensor administrative costs often are set at a fixed amount (e.g., $25,000 so that the chances of disputes in calculating this amount in specific instances of license inspections are lessened). As an alternative to using a recovery based on a percentage, the limit for cost recovery can be based on an amount not to exceed recoveries.

An important aspect of which almost all contracts err is that cost recovery is only based on underpayment of royalties. Contracts should allow for cost recovery for the underexpenditure of any commitments, such as advertising dollars, or for other major contract violations, such as if more than $5000 of goods are sold outside of the authorized license period (in addition to other damages), out of territory sales (even if the royalty is paid), or if the licensee violates a noncompete clause. The lawyer needs to be a bit inventive to make certain there can be cost recovery with just about any major violation of the contract that could cause harm to the contractor or at least any provision violation that could lead to termination.

Many contracts also err in stating that cost recovery will only occur if the underreporting of other contract violations that spark cost recovery are based on an activity that occurred during the entire period of the audit, such as stating an underpayment of 5 percent for the audit period. It is recommended that a cost recovery provision require the licensee to pay for all inspection costs if the underreporting in any *single period* exceeds the established threshold.

Costs that can be recovered should also be clearly identified in the agreement. For example, this includes reasonable costs of an accountant at her standard hourly rates plus out-of-pocket expenditures. Also, the licensor often incurs costs to manage the audit, and these costs should be recoverable. The best method to allow for the recovery of these costs is to provide for a flat administration fee cost to be recovered, such as $25,000, in addition to any collection and attorneys' fees.

Weak Language:

A. "If such inspection . . . (ii) reveals that for the period covered by such inspection or examination there is an error of five percent (5%) or more in the Earned Royalties previously reported on the Statement(s) as being due from Licensee, all expenses involved in conducting of such inspection or examination shall be borne by Licensee."

   [Weak because based on period, underinspection as opposed to underreporting in any one period/royalty report. Also requires crossing the 5 percent minimum for royalties paid and does not take into account other contract violations that could spark cost recovery.]

B. "If Licensor's duly authorized representative discovers a deficiency in the License Fees paid to Licensor for any period under audit (an 'Audit Deficiency'), Licensee shall promptly pay such Audit Deficiency to Licensor and, if such Audit Deficiency is three percent (3%) or more of the Licensee Fees paid to Licensor for such audit period, Licensee shall also reimburse Licensor for all reasonable third-party costs and expenses incurred by Licensor in connection with such audit. Licensee shall also reimburse Licensor for all out-of-pocket costs and expenses incurred by Licensor in connection with such audit. If such Audit Deficiency is twenty percent (20%) or more of the Royalties paid to Licensor for such audit period, then in addition to the above, Licensor may, at its sole option, immediately terminate the Agreement upon notice to Licensee, even if Licensee tenders the Audit Deficiency and associated costs and expenses to Licensor."

   [This is weak for the same reasons as "A"; however, strong in that it notes recovery of the Licensor's costs.]

Stronger Language:

A. "In the event that such inspection reveals a discrepancy in the amount of Royalties or other amounts owed to Licensor under this Agreement from what was actually paid, Licensee shall pay such discrepancy, plus interest, calculated at the rate of the greater of the highest amount allowed by law or one and one-half percent (1.5%) per month, no later than thirty (30) Days after the earlier of receipt of notice or knowledge thereof by Licensee. In the event that such underpayment discrepancy is in excess of twenty percent (20%) in any License Year, then Licensor may elect to treat such occurrence as an incurable default under this Agreement. In the event that such inspection reveals or Licensor or Licensee otherwise discovers an overpayment of Royalties or other amounts paid to Licensor, the amount of such overpayment shall be credited against future payment of any or all of the Guaranteed Royalties and Earned Royalties or, in the event of the expiration or termination of this Agreement and there is no such future payment, such amount shall be paid by Licensor to Licensee no later than thirty (30) Days after the discovery thereof by Licensor or Licensee, subject to Licensor's rights of setoff, recoupment, and counterclaim. In the event that such inspection reveals that for any License Quarter covered by such inspection there is a discrepancy of five percent (5%) or more in the amount of Royalties or other amounts owed Licensor under this Agreement from what was actually paid, Licensee shall reimburse Licensor for the cost and expenses of such inspection, including any accounting and/or attorney fees and expenses incurred in connection therewith, and shall pay to Licensor a nonrefundable Ten Thousand Dollar ($10,000) audit administration fee, which shall be payable by Licensee to Licensor no later than ten (10) Days following Licensee's receipt of notice of such discrepancy from Licensor. If such discrepancy is less than five percent (5%), such expenses shall be borne by Licensor."

B. "If any inspection or audit carried out demonstrates that any monies are owing to the Licensor, the Licensee shall insure that such monies are received by the licensor within thirty (30) days of notice of the monies owed, together with interest due on such amounts. Where any such inspection or audit is made necessary by the failure of the Licensee to supply reports or information as required by the Licensor, OR, in the event that there is a shortfall in excess of three (3%) percent or more in any Royalty Statement, OR, in the event there is an underexpenditure of any commitments required in this Agreement of three (3%) or more in any Royalty Statement period, OR, if there is any sales of product outside the licensed period, OR, if there is any material breach of the contract that under any provision identified with the contract that would allow for termination of the agreement due to noncompliance of the agreement, THEN, the Licensee shall also reimburse Licensor for the reasonable cost of such inspection including any reasonable attorney's fees. If the records kept by the Licensee are insufficient to enable the Licensor to establish the amount of Royalties due from the Licensee to the Licensor under this Agreement, the Licensor shall, in its sole discretion, make a reasonable estimate of such Royalties, based upon such information as is readily available in relation to the relevant market and the Licensee's business, and such estimate shall be binding upon the Licensee."

C. "If any inspection or audit carried out pursuant to Clause X.X or certificate provided pursuant to Clause X.X demonstrates that any monies are owing to the Licensor, the Licensee shall insure that such monies are received by the Licensor within thirty (30) days of notice of the monies owed, together with interest due on such amounts in accordance with Clause X.X. Where any such inspection or audit is made necessary by the failure of the Licensee to supply reports or information as required by the Licensor or in the event that there is a shortfall in excess of five percent (5%) or more *in any Royalty statement*, Licensee shall also reimburse Licensor for the reasonable cost of such inspection including any reasonable attorneys' fees, licensor's internal costs not to exceed $10,000, and the cost of auditors incurred in connection therewith. If the records kept by the Licensee are insufficient to enable the Licensor to establish the amount of Royalties due from the Licensee to the Licensor under this Agreement, the Licensor shall, in its sole discretion, make a reasonable estimate of such Royalties, based upon such information as is readily available in relation to the relevant market and the Licensee's business, and such estimate shall be binding upon the Licensee."

D. "If such inspection and examination show that Licensee owes Licensor additional royalties, Licensee shall, in addition to paying such additional royalties, reimburse Licensor for the cost of such inspection and examination, but such reimbursement shall not exceed such additional royalties.

6.6. Deduction and Discount Limitations

Overview:

Deduction limitations are perhaps the one area with the greatest number of contract violations by licensees. Deductions are a key component in the calculation of net sales, and therefore, great effort must be taken to define all deductions including a definition of the deduction and a specific limitation to the amount that may be taken. Further, the contract should state that only the specified deductions can be taken, and it is up to the sole discretion of the licensor to decide if the deduction should be allowed.

In regard to deductions, many limitations are based on the gross selling price. The problem is that the gross selling price to each side of the contract is often not calculated in the same manner. Hence, from the start, many contracts have weak deduction limitations because the gross amount is not adequately defined. In fact, most contracts don't even define "gross sales."

"Gross sales" need to be defined as the greater of the licensor approved wholesale list price (it is important it be approved by the licensor or the wholesale price can fluctuate meaning embedded discounts) or the actual highest price similar goods were sold for. Many licensees will not have generated a whole list price, and even if they do, they rarely get it approved by the licensor, even if required by the agreement. *It is important that the gross sales price not be the invoice price!!!* This is one of the biggest mistakes made in licensing contracts as it allows the licensee to discount the goods sales price prior to listing it on the invoice, thereby burying the deduction within the sales price.

After defining "gross sales," the next step is to establish the allowable deductions. There are two approaches to this; namely, the easy one is to state deductions and returns from gross sales cannot exceed a certain percentage of annual sales without advanced approval, such as 10 percent. Under this easy method, you can avoid the problems associated with defining deductions, though it would be good to define deductions as any reduction from gross sales to calculate net sales, such as but not all inclusive, returns, defects, make-goods, write-offs, taxes, etc. . . . Basically, the licensee is stating they don't wish to monitor these deductions and is accepting that deductions will happen, including write-offs, which most licensees don't allow.

The preferred method of limiting deductions is to state the specific deductions that are allowable. These deductions are generally taxes (only when paid and a tax certificate that can be used to reduced the licensor's taxes is provided within sixty days), returns actually received, and customary trade discounts. Customary trade discounts must be defined as there are many different types of discounts, only some of which should be allowed. Further, deductions should generally only be allowed if listed on the invoice and are not allowed after sale, such as price protection, breakage, and write-offs. When defining allowable trade discounts, it is important to state exactly what the discount is; for example, if you are limiting it to volume discounts, then the volume should be defined so such discounts are not provided on the sales of just a few items. Or, for another example, if the deduction is for goods damaged in shipping, the contract should state a requirement that a claim be filed with the shipping company for the deduction to be allowed.

Also, deduction limitations are often separately stated for returns. Limitations can be placed on returns to help prevent the licensee from flooding the market with goods. The devaluation of the licensed goods can be seen when a licensee receives a lot of returns or has too much inventory, and that inventory must be sold at bargain basement prices to closeout retailers like Ross Dress for Less. Some licensors attempt to control excessive inventory production by not allowing returns to be credited against sales to reduce the royalties due. It is important to state that returns are not allowed to reduce net sales because just avoiding the language regarding that returns are not allowed often leads to disagreements.

After establishing allowable deductions and the gross sales price, you can begin to place discount limitations from the gross sales price. Such limitations are generally placed on a per invoice basis or on an annual basis. Those limitations established on a per invoice basis are the strongest and least likely to be violated by the licensee; however, can also be a bit strict to allow the licensee to adjust individual sale pricing for market conditions. Annual discount limitations are more likely to be violated as licensees have a difficult time monitoring if the annualized discounts have exceeded established annual maximums.

When writing the deduction limitation language, it is extremely important the licensee be required to maintain sufficient records, usually in the sales journal, showing the full approved wholesale price and listing each deduction separately to get to net sales. Then, the royalty statements should also clearly have a column labeled "approved wholesale price" and then a column for each allowable deduction for the licensee to insert the amounts. If there is no column for a deduction the licensee wants to take in calculating net sales on the royalty statement, then the licensee will get a hint that the deduction is not allowed (though that will not keep the licensee from recategorizing the deduction). When monitoring the royalty statements, it is important the licensor examine the deductions taken in each column. Some licensors completely ignore amounts being placed in each column. A good clue that all is not kosher on a royalty statement is when there are no amounts listed in the deduction columns as that indicates the licensee's reported gross sales are really net sales.

Weak Language:

A. Paragraph 2d(ii) "Statements and Payments" states, "As used in this Agreement, the term "Net Sales" means the invoice price charged by Licensee for Products shipped by Licensee less (x) refunds, credits and allowances actually made or allowed to customers for returned Products, (y) customary trade discounts (including anticipations) afforded to and actually taken by customers against payment for the Products and (z) sales, use or value added tax assess on sales (only where applicable and specially excluding any franchise, remittance, gross receipts or income taxes)."

[This language is weak because limiting trade discounts to "customary" without specifically stating a limit can lead to confusion between the licensor and licensee over what is a customary discount. To help avoid this confusion, a specific discount limitation is often given and specific discounts are listed, such as volume discounts. Related to taxes, most licensees receive a refund on credit on various taxes, such as on Value Added Taxes that are not reflected on the invoice. It is helpful to note the "net" value added tax actually paid shall be deductible, after consideration of all credits. Further, the language does not require the tax certificate to be sent to the licensor for the tax credit to be allowed.]

Stronger Language:

A. "'Trade Discounts' shall mean all reductions in the wholesale list price that are customary in the trade and are given by Licensee in writing prior to the delivery and invoice of specific Licensed Products and indicated on the original invoice of such Licensed Products. Licensee shall be allowed to give such Trade Discounts, as long as such Trade Discounts do not exceed ten percent (10%) of gross sales per Contract Year. No other deductions, whether for unpaid or uncollectible accounts, late shipment charges, warehousing violations, chargebacks, or other discounts given or costs incurred by Licensee shall be taken. . . ."

B. "It is understood that credit against sales will be allowed only for actual returns of damaged goods, and that no credit against sales will be allowed on the basis of an accrual or reserve system. No other deductions shall be taken from Net Sales including, without limitation, deductions for cash or other discounts or uncollectible accounts . . ."

C. "'Trade Discounts' shall mean all reductions in the wholesale list price that are customary in the trade and are given by Licensee in writing prior to the delivery and invoice of specific Licensed Products and indicated on the original invoice of such Licensed Products. Licensee shall be allowed to give such Trade Discounts, as long as such Trade Discounts do not exceed ten percent (10%) of gross sales per Contract Year. This does not include Trade Discounts given to any approved off-price retailers listed in Exhibit D."

D. "Allowable Deductions" means:
   a. invoiced charges for shipment or delivery of Licensed Products which are identified separately on the sales invoice; and (b) net taxes paid adjusted for estimated year-end credits(including, if applicable, net value added tax and any equivalent or similar tax); (c) volume discounts, and other trade discounts from the invoice price (or post-invoice credits) unilaterally imposed in the regular course of business by Licensee's customers as reflected on the face of any invoice, so long as Licensee documents such discounts (or credits) to Licensor's satisfaction. In the event a documented unilateral

discount (or credit) is taken with respect to combined sales of Licensed Products and other products not licensed by Licensor, and Licensee cannot document the portion of the discount (or credit) applicable to the Licensed Products, Licensee may apply only a *pro rata* portion of the discount (or credit) to the Licensed Products. Unilateral discounts or· credits are never deductible if they represent items listed below in subparagraph (d). The following are not Allowable Deductions: all other discounts and allowances including, but not limited to, cash discounts granted as terms of payment; early payment discounts; allowances or discounts relating to advertising (unless unilaterally imposed); markdown allowances; new store allowances; defective goods allowances or allowances taken by customers in lieu of returning goods; costs incurred in manufacturing, importing, selling or advertising Licensed Products; freight costs incorporated in the sale price; and unpaid accounts unless otherwise expressly agreed to and permitted by Licensor . . ."

6.7. Exchange Rates

Overview:
Exchange rate usage is one of those areas where there are often errors primarily due to using the wrong source for the exchange rate or using the exchange rate from the wrong date. Therefore, it is very important the source of the exchange rate be a reputable source and one that is expected to last for the life of the contract. Such commonly used reliable sources include the Wall Street Journal and internet exchange rates, such as www.xe.com or www.oanda. com. It can be helpful to list both a first source and a secondary source for exchange rates in case the original source ceases to exist. Unreliable exchange rate sources are banks as they are often subject to merger, name change, or bankruptcy.

The selection of the date for the exchange rate should be very clearly identified in the contract as of the date the transaction is due or the last day of the reporting period and should not be the date the payment is actually made. Further, the agreement should clearly note that should there be a drop in currency value due to a delay in payment, then the exchange rate to be used should be that as of the date of the transactions or the date the payment was due, whichever results in a higher net payment to the recipient.

Finally, it is helpful to note that money transfer fees, conversion fees, or any other bank fees are not deductible from the amount due.

The best way around any exchange rate controversy is to require that all invoices and sales be in United States dollars. This is a very common requirement.

Weak Language:

"In the event that Licensee is paid Contract Sums in a currency other than United States dollars, Licensor shall pay the reasonable charges of converting said foreign currency to United States dollars to the extent of the amount of royalties to be paid hereunder. The date for calculation of the conversion rate to United States dollars shall be set by Licensee on a date within seven (7) days following the date upon which Licensee receives each Contract Sums payment made in foreign currency (the "Conversion Date"). The rate of conversion to United States dollars shall be the rate to be established on the Conversion Date for commercial transactions by the Bank of America, Los Angeles, California."

[This language is weaker because it cites the "Bank of America, Los Angeles rate, a rate that might not be available during the life of the agreement. Further, it allows the licensee the flexibility to choose a rate within a seven day period as opposed to specifying the exact date. Finally, it allows the deduction of "reasonable charges." Argumentation can always occur under the work "reasonable" and therefore a specific dollar limit would be better, such as a reasonable charge not to exceed .05% of the cash received"]

Stronger Language:

"All amounts due from the Licensee to the Licensor under this Agreement shall be paid in United States dollars by wire transfer or check drawn on a U.S. bank to a bank account or by such other means as may be designated from time to time by the Licensor. Any conversions required to United States dollars shall be calculated at the open middle market spot rate of exchange quoted in *The Wall Street Journal* on the last working day (Monday to Friday) of the relevant Quarter."

6.8. Granting the Right

Overview:

Licensees are granted a right to use a trademark or other intellectual property. Such granting of the right rarely identifies the remedy should the licensee not use the granted right properly. Such catch-all language with a remedy can be very important.

Here is an example of a multimillion dollar auditing experience. A licensee was granted the right to use a technology in a DVD player that bore the licensee's name. Instead, all DVD players made by the licensee, who was an Original Equipment Manufacturer (OEM) for other third-party companies, were made for third party companies resulting in none of the more than one million DVD players bearing the name of the licensee, and instead, bore the name of the third party. Unfortunately for the breach, other than termination, there was no language identifying the penalty to be paid. The licensee had paid royalties on all these sales; however, the royalty was for products made in breach of the agreement. A good solution might have been to include in the contract, language that stipulated a remedy for the unlicensed use of the intellectual property, such as one of these three: (1) Net revenues (a bit harsh); (2) Gross margin (a good midpoint but requires extensive definition as to how gross margin shall be calculated and if it is gross margin on the entire product or just the intellectual property via apportionment); or (3) a multiplier of the royalty due, such as a triple the royalty to be paid. In this case, the licensor had attempted to prevent the licensee from becoming an unauthorized OEM by using the following language, which actually was a step beyond the norm; however, it did not include the needed penalty/remediation provision:

> "In the interests of technical standardization, equipment or signal source interchangeability and product identification, Licensee shall not sell or lease Licensed Products which it manufactures to any Other-Trademark Purchaser (any customer of Licensee who, with Licensee's knowledge, intends to resell, use or lease Licensed Products under a trademark other than the Licensee's trade name and trademarks) which does not hold a license from the Licensor. Licensee will refer prospective Other-Trademark Purchasers to the Licensor for a license."

Weak Language:

A. "Licensor hereby grants to Licensee, and Licensee hereby accepts, the right and license to utilize during the Term the Proprietary Subject Matter on or in connection with the manufacture and sale of Articles in the Territory, subject to the terms and conditions hereunder. Licensee shall be entitled to sell Articles solely in the Channels of Distribution set forth in Paragraph XX of the Underlying Agreement. No such sales shall be on an approval, consignment, guaranteed sale, or return basis. Licensee agrees that it will not make or authorize any use, direct or indirect, of the Articles outside the Territory or outside the Channels of Distribution and that it will not intentionally sell Articles to persons who intend or are likely to resell them outside the Territory or outside the Channels of Distribution."

[These terms do not address the remedy should a violation occur of the many restrictions, such as selling outside the Territory.]

Stronger Language:

A. "Subject to the terms and conditions of this Agreement, the Licensor hereby grants to the Licensee the nonexclusive right and license in the Territory and during the Term:
  - To reproduce the Designs on or in connection with the Products;
  - To use the Trademarks on or in connection with the Products;

- To manufacture, distribute for sale, and sell the Products under the Trademarks; and
- To reproduce the Designs and use the Trademarks on packaging for and on sales, marketing, and advertising material related to the Licensed Products.
- The Licensee shall not be entitled to sublicense any of the rights granted in this Clause except as expressly provided by this Agreement. Moreover, this license grant specifically excludes all premiums, promotional product and entertainment rights or any other rights that are not specifically granted herein which are expressly reserved by the Licensor.
- If the parties agree to add any additional Brands and/or Products to this Agreement, the parties shall complete and sign a further version of Schedule 1 for each new Brand and/or Product. The terms of such Schedule and this Agreement shall apply to the design, manufacture, sale and distribution of such additional Product.

Any distribution of Branded Products in violation of the rights granted herein shall be cause for termination of this agreement, and the Licensee shall pay to Licensor the Gross margin from the sale of such products." "Gross margin is defined as net revenues less direct and indirect costs of production, distribution and proportionally allocated overhead."

B. 1.1: The Licensee shall actively exercise the rights granted to the Licensee under this Agreement and shall actively and aggressively market, promote, sell, and distribute the Licensed Products in the Territory. The Licensee shall be entitled to describe itself as the Licensor's "Authorized Licensee" of Licensed Products but shall not disclose any further information about its relationship with the Licensor, nor hold itself out as the Licensor's agent or as being entitled to bind the Licensor in any way.

1.2: Subject to the provisions of this Agreement, the Licensee shall sell the Licensed Products only to the Authorized Customers and within the Channels of Distribution listed in the applicable part of Schedule 1, or as notified by the Licensor from time to time, and to the Licensor and its Affiliates. The Licensor shall appoint, and the Licensee may request that the Licensor appoints, additional customers and/or classes of customer to the list of Authorized Customers provided that such additional customers and/or classes of customer satisfy the objective criteria for such customers identified by the Licensor for the purposes of protecting the reputation and value of the Brand(s). These objective criteria shall be made available to the Licensee on request.

1.3: The Licensee may not sell the Licensed Products by direct marketing methods, including without limitation computer online selling, direct mail, home shopping television programs or door-to-door solicitation, or through mail order catalogs, unless the Licensor or its nominee gives its prior written approval, which shall not be unreasonably withheld, on a case by case basis. The Licensor or its nominee shall give its approval if such direct marketing methods meet the objective criteria identified by the Licensor or its nominee in relation to direct marketing for the protection of the reputation and value of the Brand(s). These objective criteria shall be made available to the Licensee on request. The Licensee shall not supply Licensed Products for use in promotions, giveaways, free prize drawings, competitions, fund raisers or sweepstakes, or for charitable causes without the prior written approval, which shall not be unreasonably withheld, of the Licensor or its nominee.

1.4 The Licensee shall use its best efforts to promote sales of the Licensed Products throughout the Territory and to satisfy market demand for the Licensed Products in the Territory. The licensee shall maintain such inventory of the Licensed Products as may be necessary to meet its customers' requirements. The Licensee will comply with the Promotion Commitment, if any, specified in any part of Schedule 1.

1.5 Any distribution of Branded Products in violation of the rights granted herein shall be causes for termination of this agreement and the Licensee shall pay to Licensor the Gross margin from the sale of such products." "Gross margin is defined as net revenues less direct and indirect costs of production, distribution and proportionally allocated overhead."

6.9. Gross Sales

Overview:
"Gross Sales" is generally meant to be the list selling price of an item before any deductions. In practicality, gross sales is more often than not inadequately defined so the self-reporting party has several deductions prior to reaching gross sales.

The most common mistake is to identify gross sales as the invoice price. The problem with this approach is there are often multiple deductions taken from the list price prior to reaching the invoice price. What makes this scenario even harder to monitor is that when the contract states that gross sales is the invoice price, it often does not then define the gross sales price as an approved list price (or alternatively, the highest price the goods were sold for in the prior periods). Deductions hidden within the starting price on the invoice are often difficult to discover. When they are discovered and the contract is poorly worded, there are often disputes as to what the contract says versus what the parties intended in the identification of the list price.

In many contracts, gross sales is not defined at all but rather just net sales. Net sales is usually defined as the price a good is sold on the invoice less deductions. This reliance again on the invoice price tends to lead to disputes when the monitoring party discovers that deductions have been taken prior to reaching the invoice price. It is important to clearly define gross sales as the approved list price, and then this is followed by allowable deductions to reach net sales, as opposed to skipping the definition of gross sales.

The other area of large disputes is when gross sales is based only on invoiced disbursement of goods. There have been instances when goods are never invoiced, such as free distributions, or sold not on an invoice but by another document, such as a contract. If you say a royalty is only due on invoiced sales, then there will be argumentation because these distributions were not made by invoice. And, I have never seen a contract that states ALL distributions must be evidenced by an invoice. After all, the licensee would argue that shrinkage goods cannot be invoiced.

To further complicate matters, it is not uncommon for goods to be bulk priced for closeouts so that individual units are not separately listed on the invoice; so knowing the real gross sale price prior to deductions is hard to identify. For that reason, the contract should state each product type must be individually priced out on the invoice.

The bottom line is that the only approach that really seems to work is to state the net sales calculations for all sales and other distributions, and the gross sales price shall be defined as the greater of the approved standard list price or the highest price the goods sold for in the period.

Weak Language:

1. "*Gross Sales*" means the invoice price charged by Licensee for Products shipped by Licensee.
2. "*Gross Sales*" shall mean the gross invoice or contract price charged for Licensed Products by Licensee.
3. For purposes of this Agreement, "*Gross Sales*" shall mean Licensee's gross sales (the gross invoice amount billed) of Articles sold or otherwise distributed during the Term pursuant to this agreement.
   [The problems with this weak language is that gross Sales is defined, based on the invoice price, which is subject to manipulation and fails to take into account distributions not recorded on an invoice.]

Stronger Language:

1. "'*Gross Sales*' shall mean the greater of the authorized Wholesale List Price or price the product sold for in the prior 12 months. Gross Sales must be clearly identified in the sales journal. 'Sold,' 'Sale,' 'Sell' means sold, leased, put into use, or otherwise transferred; and a sale of

Subscriber Units shall be deemed to have occurred upon the initial shipment, the initial invoicing, or the initial use, whichever shall first occur."

2. "*Gross Sales*" means Licensee's sales or distributions of Licensed Product units invoiced, shipped, paid for, or otherwise distributed, whichever occurs first, multiplied by the respective licensor approved Listed Wholesale Price of such Licensed Product. '*Listed Wholesale Price*' means the price of a Licensed Product as calculated using the MSRP (defined below) minus the any discounts granted to customers or distributors. '*Manufactured Suggested Retail Price*' (MSRP) means the price of a Licensed Product stated on the applicable Licensed Product Approval Forms submitted to Licensor pursuant to Section X.X."

This gross sales price flowed into the royalty language of "Royalty Rate: The Licensee shall pay to Licensor the greater of:

- Ten Percent (10%) of Licensee's Net Invoiced Billings of the Licensed Article(s) (as defined in Paragraph xxxx of the Standard Terms and Condition attached hereto); or

The minimum per article royalty (MPAR) as set forth in Attachment X on all Licensed Article(s) sold by the Licensee."

[This language requires the approval of a List Price. Such List Price, in a licensing arrangement, is best if it requires approval by the Licensor. This also keeps the Licensor abreast of products being offered by the Licensee. It is important the contract clearly states goods that are sold for a price that has not been approved represent unlicensed sales and the total net revenues of those sales are to be paid to the licensor. As with all contract terms, it is important to spell out the damages in advance for all areas where there can be potential noncompliance.]

Litigation Tips: Royalty audit findings are common where there are discounts prior to the invoice price.

Defending litigator: Will note the contract means as written, the invoice price is the starting point, despite prior discounts. Further, only sold goods must be reported for royalties and it is up to the plaintiff to prove the other distributions were sold. As the other distributions were not sold, the defense received no benefit and therefore no royalty is due.

Plaintiff litigator: The only authorized discounts are those specified in the agreement. Discounts that are not authorized, even if prior to the invoice price, are not allowable. Further, it is not the responsibility of the auditor to identify if missing goods were actually sold as it is the responsibility of the custodian of the records to account for all goods. Any missing units are considered sold. Even if they have not been sold, the fact they have been distributed reduces the end users' need to by the product, and therefore a sale has occurred that is subject to the contract's discount and other limitations, even if the sale was not invoiced.

6.10. Insurance

Overview:
Insurance requirements are very standard in agreements. These can be specific for product liability or be more focused on general liability insurance. The most basic requirement is for the licensor (or other party, as the case may be), is to be named additionally insured within the policy.

The licensor should also require the licensee provide current insurance certificates to the licensor.

The most common weakness is the lack of a penalty should the licensee not maintain adequate insurance and not name the licensee as additionally insured. For failure to cover the required insurance, the generally recommend penalty provision is the licensee must pay to the licensor an amount equal to the cost of the required insurance for the period the licensee did not have insurance plus interest on the underpayment amount.

Weak Language:
"Prior to entering into any contract for licensed services and throughout the term thereof, Licensee shall provide and keep in force:

   i. Comprehensive general liability insurance (including product liability and broad form contractual coverage) having a combined single limit of not less than $100,000,000 per occurrence in respect to any and all loss or liability resulting from personal injury, death or property damage arising directly or indirectly from or out of the design, manufacture, construction, sale, lease, operation, maintenance, expansion, alteration and/or repair of, the performance of consulting or other services with respect to or the furnishing of any parts or other components for the Licensed Products by Licensee and / or any negligent act or omission or Licensee; and

  ii. Such other insurance and in such amounts as may from time to time be required under Licensee's contracts for the Licensed services.

     Such liability insurance, and any and all other liability insurance maintained by Licensee in excess of or in addition to that required hereunder that pertains to this Agreement, shall include protection for and name Licensor, its related, affiliated and subsidiary companies and the officers, directors, agents, employees and assigns of each as insureds thereunder as Licensor's interest shall appear. Before the end of the first term of six years hereunder, at Licensor's request, Licensee shall review with Licensor the limits of its liability insurance and, at that time, shall agree upon any limits to be adjusted, as needed, in view of reasonable exposure antici- pated over the next ensuing six years; provided; however, that in no event shall such limits be adjusted lower than the limits stated above. All such policies shall required thirty days written notice to Licensor prior to any cancellation of change affecting coverage thereafter. Licensee shall deliv- ery to Licensor a certificate or certificates as evidence of coverage."

[This overly long language does not include a penalty provision should the Licensee not maintain adequate insurance (such as payment of the value of the premium to the Licensor, plus interest), does not provide for the Licensee to remediate not having insurance within a specific time period, and does not state the quality of the insurance carrier—after all, what good is it to have a $100,000,000 policy if the insurance company can't pay such an amount?]

Stronger Language:
"Licensee shall at all times while this Agreement is in effect and for three (3) years thereafter, obtain and maintain at its own expense, from a qualified insurance carrier with a Best rating of at least "B," insurance, including, with- out limitation, products, personal injury, advertising, and contractual liabil- ity coverage, that includes as additional insured Licensor and their respective parents, subsidiaries, affiliates, officers, directors, employees, representatives and agents. The amount of coverage shall be not less than the amount speci- fied in Paragraph 15 combined single limit (with no deductible amount) for each single occurrence. The policy shall provide for thirty (30) days written notice to Licensor from the insurer by registered or certified mail, return receipt requested, in the event of any modification, cancellation or termina- tion. Upon execution of this Agreement, Licensee shall furnish Licensor with a certificate of insurance issued by the carrier evidencing the same. In no event shall Licensee manufacture, advertise, distribute or sell any Articles prior to Licensor's receipt of such certificate of insurance. Should the licensee not maintain insurance as required by this policy, the cost to purchase the required insurance for the period as prescribed by this agreement shall be determined by the Licensor and that amount shall be paid, plus interest, to the Licensor."

6.11. Interest (Late Fees) Penalties

Overview:
There are two methods that are generally used to calculate interest on late payments: namely, a fixed rate or a floating rate above a prime rate.

The benefit of the fixed rate is ease of calculation of interest on findings. The deterrent is that it does not adjust based on market conditions. A typical, or industry standard, interest rate is 1.5 percent compounded monthly. There is constant argument this rate could be usury so it is important to note the rate to be charged shall be up to 1.5 percent per month or the highest amount allowed by law. As of this book, industry standard is 1.5 percent per month. Certain states, including California, have laws that make it important to call this interest on late payment and not liquidated damages. If called liquidated damages, there are certain rules that must be applied, on a state by state basis, as applicable, in the contract language. Having a high interest rate listed as liquidated damages can be beneficial to help avoid running afoul of usury laws.

The benefit of a floating interest rate, such as 2 percent over prime, is that it adjusts based on market conditions. The deterrents are the complexity of calculating interest on findings and the risk that the base for the calculation will not be available when the interest needs to be calculated. For example, if the contract states interest will be calculated at 4 percent over the Washington Mutual Bank prime rate, what interest should be used when Washington Mutual Bank goes out of business, as it did in late 2008? Further, it is possible a bank will no longer offer the prime rate described in the agreement, even if the bank is still in business as of the time of the agreement.

It is important the interest be due on all late payments, other obligations, or other monetary amounts identified as findings and not just royalty underpayments. There is a common mistake to state the interest is only due on late royalty payments.

Weak Language:

A. "Each sum, including, but not limited to, Guaranteed Royalties and Earned Royalties, that shall not be paid on the due date by Licensee shall bear interest from such due date until the date on which such sum is paid in full at an amount equal to two percent (2%) over the prime rate of interest as established by Bank of America applicable to ninety (90) day commercial loans on the date such sum should have been paid. This subparagraph (iii) shall also apply to shortfalls found on audit."

   [This is weak as it cites a specific bank that could go out of business, and further, the low interest over the prime rate is not much of an incentive to keep the licensee from cheating on the royalty statements.]

B. " 'Royalty Payments and Statements,' of the Agreement requires interest on late payments to the Licensor to be paid at 2 percent above the prime rate."

   [Fluctuating interest rates and bank mergers often make this calculation complex.]

C. Royalties, Advances, Guarantees, and any other payments received after the date due shall bear interest at the maximum rate permissible by law."

[This is weak language as it requires a determination of the maximum rate permissible by law, which might not be easy to identify. Further, it only refers to royalties, advances, and guarantees and ignores interest that should be charged on other amount due, such as selling licensed goods after the agreement has expired, perhaps resulting in an obligation to pay the licensor the total selling price from the sale of the unlicensed goods as opposed to just the royalty on the sale of the unlicensed goods.]

D. Such interest shall accrue from the due date until the date of payment and shall be payable at the rate of prime (at Bank of America) plus one and one half (1.5) points."

[This is weak language as it is a floating interest rate for a bank that may be out of business in the future, it does not identify the prime rate to be used in case Bank of America has more than one prime rate category (i.e., one for businesses and one for individuals), and the 1.5 percent over the prime rate is insufficient to use the interest as an incentive for the third party to report properly.]

E. Prejudiced to any other rights of Licensor hereunder, time is of the essence regarding all payments due hereunder and Licensee shall pay interest on any Audit Deficiency, as well as on all delinquent Royalty payments hereunder, at two percent plus the "published reference rate" established by the Bank of America in San Francisco, compounded annually at the rate from time to time in effect and calculated from the date on which such payment was due."

Stronger Language:

A. For each royalty or other obligation or fee not received by Licensor when due, or for any other remedies due to the Licensor under this agreement, Licensee must pay to Licensor a simple interest charge of 10 percent per annum to be calculated from the date payment was due until it was actually received by The Licensor.

B. Any amount due Licensor hereunder that is not paid will thereafter bear interest until paid at a rate of interest equal to the lesser of eighteen percent (18%) per annum or the maximum interest rate allowed by applicable law.

C. As time is of the essence with respect to all payments under this Agreement, interest at the rate of one and one-half percent (1-1/2%) per month or three (3) percentage points over prime (whichever is greater but in no event more than the maximum amount permitted by law, in which case the maximum amount permitted under law shall apply) shall accrue on any amount due from Licensee to Licensor, from three (3) days after the date upon which the payment is due until the date of payment.

    i. [While this includes an interest rate based on prime, it is only a back-up interest rate should we reach a period of high inflation and the 1.5% monthly interest (18%) is no longer an incentive for the licensee to pay on time due to inflation. Such a time occurred during the Carter Administration when interest on certificates of deposit exceeded, at one point, more than 20%. The challenge with this language is to identify "prime." As banks go out of business or change their names, the use of a bank's name for prime is not always a viable solution. A better alternative benchmark could be short term U.S. Treasury obligations, with a higher percentage points above the benchmark.]

D. "If Licensee fails to make to Licensor any payment under this Agreement when due in full, (i) Licensee will pay interest on any unpaid balance from and including the date the payment becomes due until the date of payment at a rate equal to one and a half (1 ½%) percent per month . . ."

E. The Licensee shall ensure that all Royalties due under Clause 6 shall be received by Licensor within thirty (30) days of the last day of each Quarter in respect of the total Net Invoiced Sales in such Quarter." Paragraph 7.4 states, "The Licensee shall supply to the Licensor with sixty (60) days of the end of each Contract Year a certificate in writing by its auditors certifying the aggregated Net Sales Value of the Licensed Products sold or otherwise disposed of by the Licensee in such Contract Year and the amount of Royalties due to the Licensor in respect thereof." Paragraph 7.7 states, "Without prejudice to any other remedy of the Licensor, the Licensor shall be entitled to charge interest on any payment due from the Licensee but not paid on the due date, from the due date until payment is made, at the rate of ONE AND ONE-HALF PERCENT (1.5%) per month calculated from the date such payments were due and owing or the highest rate allowable by law.

6.12. Inventory

Overview:
For licensing and other agreements that are dependent on the movement or purchase of inventory, the agreement should specify the requirements of the third party to maintain inventory records at a certain level and the requirements for periodic inventory counts.

Further, for license agreements where inventory is involved, the licensee should be required to track inventory, at least annually, and be required to submit an inventory roll forward annually along with the inventory subledger detailing the quantities by SKU number of all licensed manufactured goods and raw materials, if applicable. The contract must specify that historical records, such as quarterly subledger be maintained as many licensees do not have systems in place that allow for historical records (i.e., inventory as of a certain date) to be re-created.

The contract should specify the extent of the inventory subledger records to be maintained and when the records are to be saved for future review (generally quarterly but not less than annually, in coincidence with the year end of the contract, as opposed to the licensee's year end). The inventory subledgers should be required to maintain the following information for raw materials, if it is the licensed property, and finished goods for not only the licensed product, but all products within the same subsidiary ledger (and the contract should specify the complete records be available for the auditor or the licensor for inspection not just the licensed IP's inventory records): description, location, quantity, cost per unit, SKU or tracking number, total value, and date of the records.

Generally, if there are many licensed products, it is best that there be a requirement that the licensee maintain a separate code for the licensed products.

The licensee should also be required to maintain physical inventory count records along with destruction records. The physical inventory count records and the destruction records to be maintained should be signed by at least two individuals who conducted the count, and it is best if the count is conducted by an independent accountant. Consideration should be made, if the licensed IP is small, such as microchips, that the items set for destruction should be returned to the licensor or the destruction be witnessed by the auditor.

The contract must specify that any unaccounted-for licensed property shall be considered as sold and a royalty be paid (generally referred to in the definition of net sales as "sold or otherwise disposed"). This includes any inventory where the licensee received an insurance payment for the lost inventory. Also, inventory dumping restrictions can be placed into the contract; however, it is important that "dumping" be clearly defined, such as a percentage of inventory not to be sold below a certain reduction of price ("closeout sales").

As mentioned, the licensee should be required to submit an inventory roll forward for the licensed products. The roll forward is a quantity document, not a value document. The purpose of the inventory roll forward is to provide a complete accounting for the movement of all licensed goods from purchase or manufacturing through net sales, other disposal, and inventory. This roll forward should be each licensed raw material part (i.e., chips) and for each licensed finished product (if there are a low number of finished goods/licensed products). If there are a lot of licensed products, then the inventory roll forward should be constructed at an aggregate level. A description of the inventory roll forward should be placed as an appendix to the license agreement. An inventory roll forward is constructed as follows:

Beginning Inventory (XX/1/xx)

Plus: Purchased Goods
Plus: Manufactured Goods
Plus: Internal transfers in

Equals: Goods available for Sale

Less: Net Sales to third parties
Less: Net Sales to related parties
Less: Internal transfers out
Less: Transfers to R&D
Less: Samples
Less: Employee sales
Less: Free Goods
Less: Internal Usage
Less: Disposals
Less: Inventory Adjustments
Less: Unknown

Equals: Ending Inventory (XX/31/xx)

Weak Language:

A. "Throughout the Term and any sell-off period, Licensee agrees to refrain from "dumping" the Articles in the market place. "Dumping" shall mean the distribution of Articles at volume levels significantly above Licensee's above sales practices with respect to the Articles, and at price levels so far below prior sales practices with respect to the Articles as to disparage the Articles . . ."

   [This language is virtually unenforceable as it is missing distinctly measureable limitations, instead relying on general comments such as "prior sales practices" that can vary widely.]

B. "Inventory upon Termination. No more than thirty (30) after Termination of this Agreement, LICENSEE shall provide LICENSOR with a statement indicating the number and description of Licensed Products bearing the Marks which LICENSEE had on hand or was in the process of manufacturing or having manufactured as of the date of the expiration or termination (the "Inventory"). The LICENSOR shall have the option, at LICENSOR's own cost, of conducting a physical inventory in order to ascertain or verify such Inventory. In the event that the LICENSEE refuses to permit the LICENSOR to conduct such physical inventory, the LICENSEE shall forfeit its rights hereunder to dispose of such inventory.

[If a licensee is to maintain inventory records, it is helpful to identify the exact inventory information to be maintained in the records and that such records be maintained electronically as opposed to just hard copy. Information to be included in the inventory records might include descriptions, values, location and quantities.]"

Stronger Language:
"During the last six (6) months of the Picture Term for each Picture, Distributor will not manufacture Video Devices in excess of that number thereof that is reasonably anticipated to meet normal customer requirements and in no event in excess of the number manufactured during the same six (6) month period in the previous calendar year."

"Licensee shall keep true and accurate books and records of all transactions relating to the manufacture, distribution, and exploitation of Licensed Articles hereunder which shall include but not be limited to the following minimum requirements:

    i. Inventory records showing receipt, dispatch, return and balance of Licensed Articles stocked by Licensee.
    ii. Billing records that are capable of being traced to the inventory records.
    iii. An overall reconciliation showing the total number of Licensed Articles received and/or manufactured in connection with the exploitation of Licensee's rights hereunder and showing their actual disposition, i.e., whether with customers, damaged, destroyed, lost, or in stock."

6.13. Minimum Guarantees

Overview:
My experience is there are few findings related to minimum guarantees as they are closely monitored by licensees and licensors. Though, when I worked for a company performing royalty audits, I had a licensee state they never paid the minimum guarantees (which amounted to several million dollars) because the licensee had not been invoiced. The licensor did not have the controls in place to monitor if the minimum guarantees were being paid timely and the licensee was taking advantage of the lack of these controls. The excuse of waiting for an invoice (there was no such invoicing requirement in the contract) was short-lived, and the guarantees were paid.

When writing minimum guarantee language, it is important to clarify any surplus of royalty payments in one period cannot be applied to the minimum guarantee payment in another period.

Minimum guarantees serve two very important purposes: (1) they help make certain the licensee is actually selling the licensed goods, which is essential under an exclusive licensing deal; and (2) a high minimum guarantee can help relieve the risks of licensees who have poor record keeping, that is, if the royalty minimum guarantee is so high the licensor doesn't think the licensee will make enough sales to cover the guarantee, the licensor can focus energies elsewhere and spend precious audit dollars on those other licensees where the licensor expected more royalties than were actually received. I have seen more than one instance, including a six-year intellectual property litigation, where the licensee was given an exclusive licensing deal with no minimum guarantee in the agreement, and the licensee did not attempt to sell the licensed goods. The only language controlling the licensee in this instance was a requirement for the licensee to use best efforts to sell the licensed goods . . . a provision of the agreement the two sides never litigated over, due to its vagueness.

Weak Language:

A. "Licensee shall pay Licensor a nonrefundable Guarantee against Royalties in the amount(s) and at the time(s) specified in Paragraph 9, provided, however, that should Licensee fail to make any of the scheduled payments within forty-five (45) days of the applicable due date, Licensor, in its sole discretion, may demand full payment of the balance of the Guarantee. Licensee shall be entitled to apply the Guarantee against Royalties due Licensor hereunder during the Term."
B. Any language requiring the licensee to use best efforts as opposed to having to pay a specific monetary amount.

Stronger Language:

A. "The Guaranteed Minimum Royalty paid in any Contract Year under any one of Exhibit I-1, I-2, or I-3 may only be applied to offset the Royalty payable under Article 7.1 with respect to sales in the Territory in that Contract Year for the particular Licensed Product Category specified in such Exhibit. No offset or credit of any Guaranteed Minimum Royalty amount from any period or for any Licensed Product Category other than that paid a Contract Year for the particular Licensed Product Category shall be applied to any Royalty payable under Article 7.1 above."
B. "'Guarantee' means the sum(s) specified in Schedule 1 which the Licensee guarantees to pay in accordance with Clause 6.2 as minimum Royalties on the sale of Licensed Products and over the period specified in Schedule 1." Clause 6.1 states, "Where any part of Schedule 1 indicates that an Advance is payable by the Licensee, the Licensee shall pay

such Advance on account of Royalties in accordance with the terms of Schedule 1. No part of any such Advance shall be repayable by the Licensor to the Licensee under any circumstances. The Licensee shall be entitled to retain and set off against such Advance as a credit against any Royalties due to the Licensor up to the amount of the Advance provided that the following shall not be set off against the Advance: 6.1.1 Royalties due in respect of any extension of the Term agreed by the parties; 6.1.2 Sales of Licensed Products to the Licensor or any of its Affiliates; 6.1.3 Sales of Licensed Products after termination of expiration of the Term; or 6.1.4 Sales of Licensed Products through unlicensed distribution channels or outside the licensed territory. Clause 6.2 states, "Where a Guarantee is specified in Schedule 1, the Licensee guarantees and shall pay to the Licensor any shortfall between such Guarantee and the actual Royalties paid by the Licensee to the Licensor over the relevant Guarantee Period. The Licensee shall ensure that such shortfall is received by the Licensor thirty days following the end of the Guarantee Period. Where the Royalties in respect of any Guarantee Period exceed the Guarantee, such excess shall not be taken into account in calculating the shortfall in any subsequent Guarantee Period."

6.14. Most-Favored-Nation

Overview:
Most-favored customer clauses provide both customers and vendors with competitive advantages. By guaranteeing that a customer receives the lowest possible price for a vendor's services, these types of clauses can help vendors reduce costs and increase competitiveness, while assuring the vendor of repeat business with the buyer.

Of course, these advantages can disappear quickly if vendors don't comply fully with the agreements. Noncompliance can occur for many reasons, including clerical errors, ambiguous agreement clauses, lack of process controls, or even bad faith on the part of vendors. One problem is that few customers have the time or resources to determine if their vendors are in full compliance with these contracts. And even if they did, vendors usually prevent customer personnel from accessing sensitive pricing information and customer lists for competitive reasons.

Audit professionals use a combination of industry knowledge and in-depth understanding of contract terms and conditions to conduct MFN clause reviews on behalf of customers to help verify the customer is actually receiving the most favorable pricing on agreed-upon services. Nondisclosure statements help vendors recognize that we respect their confidential information. Audit professionals review the MFN sections of an agreement to identify risk areas and potential problems. This is often necessary because many MFN clauses can be vaguely worded, with critical terms such as "comparable products," "comparable periods," and "lesser price" inadequately defined. As a result, it's common to find that pricing incentives, such as year-end rebates, volume-based discounts, and signing bonuses that have been provided to other customers aren't factored into MFN pricing comparisons.

Weak language requires products be sold to the licensor at a percentage discount off of the list price. Because the list price may be artificially high or because many customers may received percentage discount greater than that provided to the Licensor, any language basing the discount as percentage off of list prices will generally not result in Most-Favored-Nation pricing to the Licensor.

Rather, discounts to the Licensor should be based on the lower amount of a) the lowest actual selling prices of the product or b) a discount off of the list price (this second part is required in case the style is only sold to the Licensor).

Weak Language:

A. "Licensee agrees to sell to Licensor such quantities of Licensed Products requested by Licensor for sales in stores operated by Licensor or its Affiliates for prices equal to Licensee's Landed Costs therefore, plus (20%) percent. Such sales shall be subject to Licensee's availability as reasonably determined and shall not constitute Net Sales hereunder for purposes of paying a Royalty, nor shall they be calculated in Net Sales for purposes of computing Minimum Net Sales."

   [This language is weak because) identifying "landed costs," which need to be separately defined, can be extremely difficult; and (2) landed costs plus 20% might not be the best pricing.]

B. "Licensee agrees to sell to Licensor such quantities of Licensed Products, from time to time, as requested by Licensor for promotional purposes and for sale in stores and Web sites operated by Licensor or its Affiliates for prices equal to twenty percent (20%) percent below Licensee's normal wholesale selling prices at the time of any such sale. Such sales shall constitute Net Sales for purposes of for purposes of computing Minimum Net Sales.

   [Suggesting a price be based on the "normal" wholesale price can be a challenge as there might not be a normal wholesale price, especially if prices on each invoice fluctuate. Further, it is uncertain if the normal price is gross or net of various discounts, including volume discounts to the licensee's best customers. Should the licensor be entitled to volume discounts? Certainly the licensee would argue no and therefore the licensor is only entitled to buy the goods at a price reflected of other "normal" customers, whatever that is. Defining normal will almost be an impossible conversation.]

Stronger Language:

A. "Licensee shall sell to Licensor such quantities of the Articles as Licensor shall request. All sales by Licensee to Licensor of Articles from the Licensee shall be at a price never to exceed the lowest price offered to any customer of the Licensee and on such terms at least as good as the most favorable terms given by Licensee to any of its customers. Royalties shall be payable on all such sales."

B. "Licensee agrees to sell to Licensor such quantities of Licensed Products, from time to time, as requested by Licensor for promotional purposes and for sale in stores and websites operated by Licensor or its Affiliates, licensees and/or subcontractors for prices equal to the lesser of thirty (30%) below Licensee's normal wholesale selling prices at the time of any such sale, or the lowest price charged by Licensee to any of its customers. Such sales shall constitute Net Sales for purposes of computing Minimum Net Sales."

6.15. Net Sales

Overview:

Net Sales is one of the areas of greatest importance in a license agreement and yet often has the most poorly drafted language that does not take into account the various different methods by which a company can calculate net sales. Often, companies will define Net Sales without regards to defining Gross Sales (see the Gross Sales section along with this section for a better understanding), resulting in Net Sales being based on a Gross Sales amount that is not reflective of the true desires of the licensor. Net Sales is the product of Gross Sales less Deductions. Net Sales will only be what the licensor wants if Gross Sales and Deductions are properly defined.

One of the greatest errors is not to define Net Sales as all distributions of the licensed intellectual property but instead to limit sales to those items that appear on invoices. Therefore, sales need to be defined more broadly as all distributions of the licensed product as there are many methods by which a licensee can distribute products outside of the sales ledger (i.e., some of these go out via free products, other revenues, unaccounted-for theft, research and distribution, and employee or owner distributions).

Deductions need to be narrowly defined, and language needs to note only the authorized deductions that can be taken. When defining deductions (see the deduction section), be very explicit and try not define deductions as industry average or normal trade discounts as this will lead to disagreements. Instead, define allowable deductions such as volume discounts as preestablished in purchased orders or annual agreements, destruction allowances, price protection, etc. . . . It is always best to assign a percentage limitation to all of the discounts or possible deductions from gross sales to reach net sales. Such limitations generally are between 7 percent and 10 percent of annual sales.

The starting point for all products should be the list price. Therefore, free products are valued based on the list price, and deductions are limited based on the list price. The general idea is that free products in the hand of the end user result in an end user that no longer needs to buy the licensed products and therefore the licensor looses out on the sales and the associated royalty. Therefore, a royalty is due on all distributions.

Returns, if allowed, need to be identified as allowed. Returns are often limited to a percent or only to damaged goods. Also, it should be clear if the returned items must be physically returned.

Also, consideration should be given to how to assign income if the units are sold in combination with other nonlicensed items, such as licensed games sold with plush toys. To help overcome this issue, it can be helpful to note the sales price shall not be less than the price if the items was sold individually or the contract can simply state items shall not be sold in combination with other nonlicensed products. Basing the price off of the list price helps to eliminate this concern.

Weak Language:

A. "As used in this Agreement, the term "Net Sales" means the invoice price charged by Licensee for Products shipped by Licensee less (x) refunds, credits and allowances actually made or allowed to customers for returned Products, (y) customary trade discounts (including anticipations) afforded to and actually taken by customers against payment for the Products and (z) sales, use or value added tax assess on sales (only where applicable and specially excluding any franchise, remittance, gross receipts, or income taxes)."

[This is weak because there is no percent limit to the deductions and because it starts with "invoice price" which means the intellectual property can have any discount from list prices prior to being placed on the invoice. In other words, basing the start price on the invoice basically gives free reign for the licensee to have any deductions they want without regard to discount limitations! Further, this only addresses items distributed via an invoice and does not take in account the dozens of other methods a product may be distributed off-invoice.]

B. "Net Sales as the total amount received by Licensee or any Affiliate from the sale or distribution of Licensed Products, less the sum of the following deductions when applicable and separately invoiced: cash, trade, or quantity discounts; sales, use, tariff, import/export duties or other excise taxes imposed upon particular sales; transportation charges; and rebates, allowances, or credits to customers because of rejections, recalls or returns. Calculation of Net Sales of Licensed Products combined with other products that are not Licensed Products (SLM Products) shall be modified by reduction of the Net Sales by the cost of the SLM Products."

[This does not take into account that other distributions might be for an "amount" less than list price. As such, the language should be changed from amount received to list price. Further, this is confusing, as the "amount received" will always be after the deductions so this is what could be call by an Excel program, a circular reference since you can't allow the deductions from the amount received.]

C. "The price of any Licensed Product used for the calculation of Net Sales shall not be discounted by more than fifty percent (50%) from Licensee's usual selling price, even if such products are sold for less than such amount at close-out or on liquidation."

[This is weak because it relies on "usual selling price." The problem is defining what is "usual." Instead of using terms that can't be clearly defined such as "usual" and "customary," the language should use specific language such as "from Licensee's list price or the highest price goods were sold for.]"

D. "'Net Invoiced Billings' shall mean actual invoiced billings . . . for Articles sold and all other receivables of any kind whatsoever received in payment for the Articles . . ., less volume discounts and other customary discounts separately identified by Article on the sales invoices. Customary discounts shall not include cash discounts granted as terms of payments, early payment discounts, year-end rebates and allowances, or discounts relating to advertising, mark down allowances, or new store allowances . . ."

[This is weak for reasons already cited for other language; namely, based on "invoiced billings" as opposed to list prices, no percentage limits on deductions, and reliance on "customary discounts" which allows for too much discretion. Even with the listed discounts that will not be allowed, the inventive licensee will come up with new deductions that will allow for a bending of the rules. Never doubt the creativity of the licensee.]

E. "Licensee shall pay to Licensor royalties equal to ten percent (10%) of the Net Sales Revenue realized on each Unit (as defined herein) of the Adapted Game(s) sold by Licensee or any distributor (related or unrelated) . . ."

[It does not have a provision for other distributions where "revenue" is not involved, such as barter sales or combination sales, common with games.]

Stronger Language:

A. "Net Sales shall mean Licensee's gross sales . . . less deductions for trade and quantity discounts actually taken (provided, however, that such trade in quantity discount shall not exceed ten percent (10%) of gross sales), returns for damaged goods actually credited (and supported by credit memoranda actually issued to the customers) and sales tax (if applicable). It is understood that a credit against sales will be allowed only for actual returns for damaged goods (provided, however, that such returns shall not exceed ten percent (10%) of gross sales), and that no credit against sales will be allowed on the basis of an accrual or reserve system. No other deduction shall be taken from net sales including, without limitation, deductions for cash or other discounts or uncollectible accounts . . ."

B. " 'Net Selling Price' means, with respect to any Subscriber Unit Sold, the greater of (a) the selling price which a seller would realize from an un-Affiliated buyer in an arm's length sale of an identical product in the same quantity and at the same time and place as such sale, or (b) the selling price actually obtained for such product in the form in which it is Sold, whether or not assembled and without excluding therefrom any components or subassemblies thereof except as expressly permitted under Section 6. In determining the "selling price" of a Subscriber Unit, only the following shall be excluded to the extent actually included in the price obtained for such products: (i) usual trade discounts actually allowed to un-Affiliated persons or entities; (ii) packing costs; (iii) costs of insurance and transportation; and (iv) import, export, excise, sales and value added taxes and custom duties. For the avoidance of doubt, if a Subscriber Unit is Sold in a package containing, e.g., the Subscriber value of the Subscriber Unit shall be used for determining the selling price."

6.16. Non-Disclosure Agreements

Overview:
It is not uncommon that at the start of an audit, especially when at the field, that a licensee will pull a fast one and refuse to cooperate until the auditor signs a Non-Disclosure Agreement. To help avoid this, leading practice is to state the inspecting auditor is not required to sign a non-disclosure agreement or any other statements of confidentiality in order to have access to the licensee's records but must work within the provisions of confidentiality specified in the license agreement.

I recommend a statement to the effect that the accountant is not required to sign a non-disclosure agreement be added to the Agreement. This is generally placed within the right-to audit-provision.

Sample Language:

A. "The Licensor's auditors shall not be required to sign a non-disclosure agreement, as the auditors shall be bound by the confidentiality provisions of this Agreement."

6.17. Price Controls

Overview:
Price controls help the licensor protect the value of the licensed goods in the market. It is important to have such controls, especially as a contract gets closer to termination and the licensee might wish to start dumping product, which, in turn, will hurt future license agreements for the same products.

Weak Language:

A. If Licensee sells Licensed Products at a price lower than that customarily charged to an unrelated third party, the royalties paid to the licensor will be based on the Net Sales of Licensed Products by the Affiliate or Sublicensee to their Customers."

   [Customary is not defined so it is hard to say what customary is, especially if there are a range of prices. Efforts should be made to avoid words such as "reasonable" and "customary" when defined definitions, such as percentage limitations, can be use instead as this will place a limitation for measurement.]

Stronger Language:

A. " . . . (b) unless Licensor provides prior written consent to the contrary, during the last year of the Term, the price for all products must be maintained at no less than the average price charged by Distributor in the previous year of the Term."

6.18. Record Keeping

Overview:
It is common for the third party being monitored to not retain or maintain documents to a level to allow proper third-party monitoring. The needs of the

contractor to monitor are often different than the needs of the contractee. Therefore, it is essential the documents to be maintained are clearly specified in the agreement.

Leading practice is to list all books, records, and other items to be retained for inspection (e.g., annual sales records, inventory records, stock movement records, licensed technology procurement records, shipping records, invoices, operations manuals used with licensed product, licensed product examples, destruction records, and all other licensed product distribution records). Additionally specific provisions often extend to allowing interviews of relevant licensee personnel and inspection of manufacturing operations.

Separately, it is recommend that specific lists are made of minimum records the licensee is required to maintain and that there be a monetary penalty provision should such records not be maintained, such as a dollar amount or a percentage (i.e., 25 percent) of royalties owed during the period the records are missing.

Leading practice is to require books and records to be maintained for three years from the year such sales or disposals occurred and identify that on receipt of an inspection notification letter, the books and records must be retained for the three years from the date the notification letter was received as opposed to when the audit commences. Additionally, leading practice is to require the books and records to be maintained for three years following the expiration of the agreement as opposed to when the related statement was submitted.

It is also beneficial to require books and records to be maintained based on calendar years and, upon engagement letter notification of an inspection, all records for the prior three years to the date of the notification letter must be retained at least until the conclusion of the engagement by the accountant and any settlement of findings.

The contract should state the specific books and records to be maintained (electronically in a data sortable format such as excel), including, but not limited to raw material, work in progress, and finished goods year-end inventories, inventory count records, sales records, disposal records, inventory count records, shipping records, manufacturing records, return records, refurbishment records, other usage records, invoices, credit memos, etc. . . .

Weak Language:

A. Licensee shall maintain in good order and condition all such books and records for a period of two (2) years after the expiration or termination of the License and this Agreement. . . ."

[This language does not specify the books and records, allowing disagreement as what is meant. It is not uncommon for a licensee to state, for example, the royalty is based on net sales and therefore only net sales records are maintained even though the inspector would require access to records such as inventory and the general ledger.]

B. "The Licensee shall keep complete, accurate, and detailed books and records in relation to all of its obligations hereunder including manufacturing inventory and sales records involving the Licensed Products which shall be sufficient to enable the Licensor to check the accuracy of the information contained in the statements submitted under Clause X.x. The Licensor or its authorized representative shall be entitled to inspect and audit such books and records on 72 hours notice during business hours during the Term and for a period of two years following termination or expiration of this Agreement and to take copies of or extracts from such books and records. Licensee shall fully cooperate with the Licensor or its representative in connection with such inspection. All books and records relative to Licensee's obligations hereunder shall be maintained and kept accessible and available to Licensor for inspection for at least three (3) years after termination of this Agreement."

[There is no penalty for failure to maintain books, no requirement for special reports to be created, no definition of the books and records, and it only allows inspection related to the royalty statements but does not permit other inspection of books and records for other potential contract obligations that are not included on the statements, such as no requirement for electronic records to be maintained or provided in a suitable electronic native format for data sorting by the inspector.]

C. "Licensee shall keep and maintain accurate books of account and records covering all transactions relating to this Agreement. Licensor or its designee shall be entitled to (i) audit and inspect such books and records at any time or times during or after the Term of the Agreement during reasonable business hours and upon five (5) days prior written notice to Licensee, and (ii) make copies and summaries of such books and records. All such books of account and records shall be retained by Licensee for a minimum of three (3) years after expiration or termination of this Agreement."

[It does not specify copies of books and records but includes electronic media and only includes books and records covering transactions but excludes records that are necessary to verify other obligations, such as manufacturing records of the IP that are not part of sales transactions. There is no penalty for failure to maintain records and no requirement to provide records in a soft copy, data sortable format.]

D. "Paragraph X.1, 'Books and Records,' states, 'Licensee shall keep complete books and records of all manufacture, sales, leases, uses or other disposals by Licensee of Licensed Product. Paragraph X.2, "Right to Inspect Books and Records," states, "Licensor shall have the right, at Licensor's expense, to inspect, examine and make abstracts of Licensee's books and records insofar as may be necessary to verify the accuracy of the same and of the statements provided for herein, but such inspection and examination shall be made during normal business hours upon reasonable notice and not more often than twice per calendar year."

E. "The Licensee will establish books and accounting records in accordance with good accounting practice and undertake to keep such books and records (including all supporting documentation related to the importation, manufacturing, storage, distribution, and sale of the Licensed Products and in general, all activities related to the rights and obligations conferred by this Agreement) for the four (4) years following the end of the calendar year to which those documents pertain. The supporting documentation must include perpetual inventory records for the Licensed Products and that the books and records must be structured so that the quantities of the Licensed Products can easily be identified for all transactions related to the Licensed Products."

[Establishing records in accordance with "good accounting practice" does not adequately define any specific rules, such as in accordance with Generally Accepted Accounting Principles, or to support all transactions from production through disbursement of goods and books and records related to compliance of all provisions of the agreement. Further, this does not require the records to be maintained in an electronic format for future retrieval and data manipulation. Also, there is no penalty for failure to maintain books.

Stronger Language:

A. "*Books and Records*: Distributor shall keep true and accurate books and records (in a form meeting GAAP standards) of all transactions relating to the manufacture, distribution and exploitation of Rights hereunder which shall include, but not be limited to, the following minimum requirements:
   i. Inventory records showing the receipt, dispatch, return, and balance of Devices stocked by Distributor.
   ii. Billing records that are capable of being traced to the above inventory records.
   iii. An overall reconciliation showing the total number of Devices received and/or manufactured in connection with the exploitation of Distributor's rights hereunder and showing their actual disposition (*i.e.*, whether with customers, damaged, destroyed, erased, reduplicated, lost, or in stock).
   iv. Sales registers for licensed and unlicensed products and original invoices indicating gross sales price and all discounts to reach net sales price.
   v. Sales analysis reports.

     vi. Accounting general ledgers.

    vii. Sublicense and distributor agreements.

   viii. Price lists, catalogs, and marketing materials.

    ix. Audited financial statements and/or income tax returns.

     x. Sales tax returns.

    xi. Shipping documents.

   xii. Sales agreements.

    The records will be available in electronic native format. Further, reasonable special reports requested by the auditor shall be provided, including, but not limited to, inventory roll forwards by licensed product identification number. Failure to maintain records as required under this provision will result in a doubling of the royalty rate for those periods when the records are not provided and will result in cost recovery of the audit in accordance with paragraph X.X."

B. "A*vailability of Records.* Licensee agrees that it will be keep accurate and complete books and records of account (including, without limitation, utilization of consecutively numbered invoices which reconcile to each Royalty Statement and Licensee's general lender) covering all transactions relating to or arising out of this Agreement in accordance with Generally Accepted Accounting Principles. Such books and records shall be maintained separately from Licensee's documentation relating to other items manufactured or sold by Licensee and shall include manufacturing records, purchase records, and any electronics database, sales, inventory, and all other documents and materials in the possession of or under the control of Licensee or any of its Affiliates with respect to the subject matter of this Agreement. Licensee will obtain and maintain such accounting, information, communication, and operating systems and capabilities as Licensor may require from time to time, including systems or processes that will allow its records to be exportable to Excel to assist Licensor's auditors. At all times during the Term of this Agreement and any time following its termination or expiration, Licensor or Licensor's auditors shall have the right at all reasonable times during normal business hours and on reasonable notice to Licensee to inspect and make copies of Licensee's books and records at the place or places where such records are normally retained by Licensee or any of its Affiliates. The Licensor's auditors shall not be required to sign a nondisclosure agreement, as the auditors shall be bound by the confidentiality provisions of this Agreement. Receipt or acceptance by Licensor of any Royalty Statement furnished pursuant hereto or any sums paid by Licensee hereunder shall not preclude Licensor from questioning the correctness thereof at any time, and if one or more inconsistencies or mistakes are discovered by Licensor in such Statement, it or they shall be rectified in an amended Royalty Statement received by Licensor no later than ten (10) Days after the date of receipt by Licensee of notice of that which should be rectified. Licensee shall also provide special reports as reasonably requested by Licensor's auditors to properly complete their audit obligations, including, but not limited to, reports showing inventory roll forwards, sales by SKU number and discounts by customer. If the records kept by the Licensee are insufficient to enable the Licensor to establish the amount of Royalties due from the Licensee to the Licensor under this Agreement, the Licensor shall, in its sole discretion, make a reasonable estimate of such Royalties, based upon such information as its readily available in relation to the relevant market and the Licensee's business, and such estimate shall be binding upon the Licensee."

6.19. Related Party Sales

Overview:
Many agreements have related party sale limitations, and they often have the same couple of flaws: a). a failure to properly or adequately identify what creates a related party and/or b). the requirement that the sales price for identification of gross sales is based on the ultimate selling price of the product to a third party.

The related third party should be defined as any company under control or under common ownership. Contracts that define related parties as those only under control of the licensee miss out on multiple different sales that should be related party. One method to identify a related party is to use Generally Accepted Accountant Standards that state a "related party transactions include transactions between (a) a parent company and its subsidiaries; (b) subsidiaries of a common parent; (c) an enterprise and trusts for the benefit of employees, such as pension and profit-sharing trusts that are managed by or under the trusteeship of the enterprise's management; (d) an enterprise and its principal owners, management, or members of their immediate families; and (e) affiliates."

Requiring the selling price be based on the related party's ultimate selling price to a nonrelated party is flawed if the related party never sells the licensed goods to a third party or if the sale to the ultimate third party has excessive discounts. For example, if the goods are sold or provided at no cost to the company owner and given to his family or as mass giveaways to employees, it could be argued these are all related party transactions and a royalty is not due on these disbursed goods to the detriment of the licensor. Or take the case of a related party selling the goods to a third party at an excessive discount beyond than what is provided for in the license agreement. If the agreement states the royalty is based on the ultimate selling price to the third party by the related party, this allows the related party to use a loophole in the agreement that allows the related party to sell the goods without any restrictions experienced by the licensee, such as restrictions on discounts, provided the royalty is paid on the ultimate selling price of the related third party.

Therefore, sales to related parties should be subject to the same pricing as original arm's-length transitions by the original licensor to third parties, and such pricing should be defined such as weighted average pricing, highest selling price, or not to be less than the lowest price sold to a third party for the same or similar product.

Weak Language:

A. " . . . Net Sales shall further include an amount based on Licensee's usual selling price where: . . . (c) the Licensed Products sold by Licensee to an Affiliated Company."

   [Usual selling price is too difficult to define, especially if there are a variety of prices, or a variety of discounts, to reach the net selling price.]

B. "If Licensee sells or otherwise transfers any Licensed Products to any Affiliated Entity at an invoice price that is less than the price that Licensee charges to nonaffiliated full-priced retailers, then the invoice price to the Affiliated Entities, for purposes of calculating Net Sales, shall be deemed to be the current invoice price charged to nonaffiliated full-priced retailers. . . ."

   [Like the prior weak language, this requires the use of "current" invoice price that may be subject to change by invoice or customer.]

C. "If Licensee sells or otherwise transfers any Licensed Products to any Affiliated Entity at an invoice price that is less than the price that Licensee charges to nonaffiliated full-priced retailers, then the invoice price to the Affiliated Entities, for purposes of calculating Net Sales, shall be deemed to be the current invoice price charged to nonaffiliated full-priced retailers. . . ."

D. "In the event of sales by Licensee of Licensed Products to a marketing organization or any individual or company in whole or in part controlled by Licensee, or to one or more distributors for ultimate sale or a retailer, or in any transaction other than an arm's-length transaction, the invoice price used to determine Net Sales hereunder shall be the invoice price at which the Licensed Products are resold by any such entity to an unrelated retail customer in an arm's-length transaction. Licensed Products shall be deemed sold when shipped, distributed, billed, sold, or paid for, whichever comes first."

   [This is weak because it relies on the goods to be resold by the related party and fails to take into account in the related party consumes the licensed product.]

Stronger Language:

A. " 'Affiliate means in relation to either party, any legal entity which: (a) is directly or indirectly owned and/or controlled by that party; (b) directly or indirectly owns and or controls that party; (c) is directly or indirectly owned and/or controlled by the licensor; or (d) shares the same ownership. In the case of legal entities having stock, member unit and/or shares through the direct or indirect ownership and/or control of more than fifty percent (50S%) of the voting shares. In the case of any other legal entity, ownership and/or control shall exist through the ability to directly or indirectly control the management and /or business of the legal entity." "The sums paid to Licensor as Royalties on any sales to Licensee's Affiliates shall be no less than the sums paid on sales to customers not affiliated with Licensee."

6.20. Reporting

Overview:

Reporting is one of the most important parts of the contract yet is often one of the worst written sections. The objective of the writer should be to ask for as much information as possible so remote detailed monitoring of the self-reporting party can be successfully performed. With adequate external monitoring, the chances of misreporting and the need for an onsite auditing is greatly reduced; however, on-site inspection cannot be replaced by external monitoring alone. Ensuring proper and adequate reporting provides for the early identification of problems for remediation of potential concerns especially from contract misinterpretation.

Prior to executing a contract, an organization should have identified how it will monitor the agreement including setting measurement milestones and red flag warning signs of when to react to specific reported information that does not fall within guidelines. After the organization knows what it intends to monitor from the self-reporting third party (i.e., gross sales, deductions, territories, sublicenses, changes in personnel or systems, services to competitors, exchange rates, etc . . .), the contract can be designed to make certain the reporting meets the needs of the monitor.

A key to making certain that reporting is adequate is to attach to the contract a template the self-reporting party must complete when reporting. Such a template is included in Appendix III of this book.

In addition to the standard royalty or expense reporting reports, the self-reporting entity should be required to report whenever this is a major event contemplated or occurring that could affect the ability to monitor the self-reporting entity such as a change in ownership, bankruptcy, change in accounting systems or a change in reporting. While the self-reporting entity may be required to report these events when they occur or when they are first known, chances are it will not be reported timely, and therefore an excellent reminder is to have the self-reporting entity complete a quick survey with each royalty report that is signed by an executive acknowledging, under oath, the survey and royalty report is accurate. The survey can ask key yes or no questions, along with an explanation section for any affirmative answers, that are important to the monitor. For example, the survey may ask the following questions:

- Have you changed your accounting system?
- Have you had any losses of licensed products, and if yes, describe the loss and if an insurance claim was filed?
- Have you changed the method by which you calculate royalties or other reportable items?
- Has there been a change in accounting personnel who handle the reporting?
- Is your company troubled or declared bankruptcy?
- Has there been any litigation threatened involving the licensed intellectual property?
- Are any of the reported amounts estimates?
- Have there been any related party sales, and if so, please list separately?
- Have there been any noncash or barter transactions involving the property?
- Has there been any actual or threatened product recalls involving the property?
- Has the product or your company been in any adverse media or made any adverse announcements?
- Has your company been issued a "going concern" statement by your auditors?
- Have you changed auditors? Why?
- Have any members of management been arrested, or are there any SEC investigations ongoing of your company?
- Do you have any cash flow issues where you might be unable to pay your commitments?
- Have you signed any subcontractors?
- Is your company for sale, or are you considering any mergers?

Consideration as to what should be reported should be made through input of the various departments that may have to rely on the reported information and generally best includes input from senior management, legal, sales, business affairs, finance, internal audit, and external royalty audit.

The bottom line is if companies could obtain adequate reporting, then much of this book would be unnecessary, and litigation could be greatly reduced.

Weak Language:

A. The Licensee shall deliver to the Licensor a statement, as provided for in Exhibit A setting out (i) the amount of the Net Sales made by the Licensee during the relevant quarter; (ii) the amount of the Net Sales made by the Sublicensees—if any—during the relevant quarter; and iii) the amount of the Royalty and the amount of the Royalty accrued in respect of each quarter, as follows:
—10th May for the first calendar quarter;
—10th August for the second calendar quarter;
—10th November for the third calendar quarter; and
—10th February for the fourth calendar quarter
[This most basic language does not cover key items to be reported such as the number of units sold, gross sales, deductions, territories of sales, names of products sold, and other information to allow for adequate monitoring.]

Stronger Language:

A. "On the form provided by Licensor or on such other form as Licensor may from time to time provide to Licensee, Licensee shall (i) render royalty reports ("Royalty Reports") on an Article-by-Article (i.e., SKU-by-SKU) basis to Licensor quarterly within thirty (30) days after the close of each calendar quarter during the Term hereof, whether or not any payment is shown to be due to Licensor thereunder, and (ii) remit payments due Licensor, if any, along with such Royalty Reports. If the Territory covers more than one country, Royalty Reports shall be prepared on a country-by-country basis. Royalties may be computed in the currency of the country where earned and paid to the Licensor in U.S. Dollars at the exchange rate received by Licensee at the time of conversion. Licensee shall be solely responsible for all costs of any conversion to U.S. Dollars, and such costs shall not reduce the amounts due to Licensor hereunder. Acceptance of Royalties or Royalty Reports by Licensor shall not preclude Licensor from questioning the correctness of same at any time. All Royalty payments shall be made without set-off or deduction for costs or other expenses whatsoever (including bank fees, if any), whether based upon any claimed debt or liability of Licensor to Licensee. Unless otherwise instructed by Licensor, all Royalty and other payments due hereunder shall be sent to the lock box address set forth in Paragraph 1 and all Royalty Reports shall be sent to the street address set forth in Paragraph 1, attention Accounting."

B. "The Licensee shall ensure that all Royalties due under Clause 6 shall be received by the Licensor within thirty (30) days of the last day of each Quarter in respect of the total Net Invoiced Sales in such Quarter. The Licensor may require the Licensee at the Licensor's sole discretion and upon six (6) months notice in writing to pay royalties and provide statements pursuant to this Agreement on a monthly basis. The Licensee shall forward a Royalty statement to the Licensor with the payments made under Clause X.X giving particulars of invoiced supplies of each type of Licensed Products during the relevant Quarter and showing the quantity of each type of Licensed Products supplied, the price charged therefore and itemizing any Allowable Deductions in respect thereof, the Net Invoiced Sales therefore and the Royalty due thereon, any Advance against which such Royalties are set off, the amount of any Guarantee applicable to the relevant period and any shortfall payable to the Licensor pursuant to Clause X.X. The Licensee shall present the information in such format and together with such other information as the Licensor may reasonably require from time to time. The Licensor's current standard reporting form is attached as Schedule 2. The Royalty statement shall be due whether or not any Royalties are due for the applicable period. The Licensee shall supply to the Licensor within sixty (60) days of the end of each Contract Year a certificate in writing by its auditors certifying the aggregated Net Sales Value of the Licensed Products sold or otherwise disposed of by the Licensee in such Contract Year and the amount of Royalties due to the Licensor in respect thereof."

C. "**Reporting**. Licensee will make available to the Licensor Remote Tools for reporting as described in Section x.x. The Licensor will be able to produce electronic and hard copies of standard reports in numerical or chart formats. LICENSEE's standard reports as of the Effective Date, which will be made available to the Licensor in accordance with this Agreement, are listed on *Exhibit "E"* attached hereto. Additionally, LICENSEE will use commercially reasonable efforts to provide the Licensor with Customized Reports at the reasonable request of the Licensor. Any Customized Reports that LICENSEE agrees to provide would be provided as an Additional Service. For purposes hereof, a "Customized Report" shall mean any report not required to be delivered hereunder that is provided by LICENSEE for the Licensor upon the Licensor's prior written request, other than reports generated by the Licensor with Remote Tools or reports made generally available to the Persons for which LICENSEE operates the Other LICENSEE Web Sites. To the extent that, prior to the Phase One Launch Date, there are Orders placed through the Licensor 800 Number Store and/or sales of Merchandise through the Other LICENSEE Web Sites, LICENSEE shall make available to Licensor all information contained in *Exhibit "E"* related to such Orders upon Licensor's reasonable request."

6.21. Returns

Overview:

Limits over returns for licensing is generally considered important for a few reasons: (1) it helps prevent a licensee from flooding the market with goods and therefore driving down the value of the licensed goods (the old rule of supply and demand), (2) it provides an incentive for the licensee to make quality products that are not likely to be returned, and (3) it helps prevent closeout sales. When returns are permitted under an agreement, they should generally be limited to a certain percentage of gross sales on an annual basis, such as 5 percent. Further, depending on the nature of the product, returns are sometimes limited for goods actually returned, as opposed to allowances where there is no evidence required of the return.

Some companies permit a return allowance (sometimes called a damage and defective allowance) as the cost to return the goods is not worth the shipping. The contract should specify if goods must be physically returned in ordered for the return to be credited against gross sales in calculating net sales.

Agreements should also specify that a return reserve is not allowed. While a return reserve is generally only permitted if so stated in the agreement, it can help avoid confusion by specifically noting a reserve is not allowed.

One method to help avoid returns is for a company to allow for price protection. Price protection works as a credit back to a retailer as an incentive for the retailer not to return the goods to the seller. This is, in effect, a lowering of the selling price to help ensure the retailers profit margin. Price protection should only be allowed as a deduction from gross sales to calculate net sales for royalty reporting purposes if specially provided for in the agreement.

Weak Language:

A. "As used in this Agreement, the term 'Net Sales' means the invoice price charged by Licensee for Products shipped by Licensee less returns, credit and allowances actually made or allowed to customers for returned products. In the event the percentage of returns of Products in any License Year exceeds twenty percent (20%) of Net Sales for such License Year, then Licensor may elect to treat such an occurrence as an incurable default by Licensee under this Agreement."

[This language is weak as it goes right to termination instead of just stating returns may not exceed a certain percentage. It would be better to state returns may not exceed a certain percentage, such as 5 percent.]

Stronger Language:

A. " 'Net Sales' shall mean License's gross sales less returns for damaged goods actually credited (and supported by credit memoranda actually issued to customers). . . . It is understood that credit against sales will be allowed only for actual returns of damaged goods, and that no credit against sales will be allowed on the basis or an accrual or reserve system. In any Annual Period in no event shall returns exceed three (3%) of sales of Licensed Products in such Annual Period. In computing Net Sales, no costs incurred in the distribution or return of the Licensed Products shall be deducted."

6.22. Right to Audit

Overview:
It is always amazing how many contracts fail to include a right to audit, or when it is included, the language is so weak that enforcing the audit rights is met with considerable challenges, mostly where the company being audited limits the scope of the engagement thereby preventing a reasonable chance of determining contract compliance.

Audit rights must be well constructed to note the following, as a minimum:

- How often the audit can occur. (Generally, it is annually with more frequent visits if findings spark the cost recovery provision).
- Advance notification requirements. (Generally, it is with one week's notice. Use of "reasonable" notice should be avoided as reasonable is subject to interpretation.)
- Who may conduct the audit. (Typically, it is an outside auditor as most companies don't want the monitoring company to send their own personnel due to competition and/or confidentiality concerns).
- The records that must be provided to the auditors. (See the "record" section of this chapter).
- Cost recovery. (See the "cost recovery" section of this chapter).
- Record retention. (This is usually either three years after the royalty report, or better yet, three years after contract expiration).
- Auditor shall have the right to make copies and extracts and take with them. (It happens a lot where the party being inspected says you can look, but you can't take any notes or copies . . . now this is a hard way to build a report and support work).
- Licensee pays for all costs to produce the documents for the audit and for licensee employee time associated with supporting the audit. The licensee shall not bill the licensor for any costs to support the audit.

It is also helpful to note the auditors are not required to sign a Non-Disclosure Agreement in order to conduct the audit.

Weak Language:

A. "Licensor will, upon reasonable advance notice to Licensee, have customary audit rights with respect to all monies (including royalties) payable hereunder by Licensee to Licensor. "

[This was about the worst language I had seen, and my client paid the price. My client wanted me to start the audit as soon as possible, but the licensee insisted I wait at least two months as that was when they could first accommodate me and therefore to the licensee, two months was reasonable notice. When requesting documents, the licensee refused permission to examine inventory records as royalties were calculated on net sales, and my explanation that the licensee had to account for all licensed intellectual property produced fell on deaf ears. Further, the licensee stated no copies of any confidential information could be taken, making it difficult to support findings and allowed the licensee to change documents after inspection. Then there were challenges as to what "customary audit rights" are, since there really is no such thing as customary audit rights. The client spent more money on legal fees and time arguing over what the audit included as opposed to auditing.]

B. "Licensor shall have the right, upon at least five days written notice and no more than once per calendar year, to inspect Licensee's books and records and all other documents and material in the possession of or under the control of Licensee with respect to the subject matter of this Agreement at the place or places where such records are normally retained by Licensee. Licensor may similarly inspect the books and records of sublicensees."

[This is more typical weak language. Because specific documents that may be inspected are not included, this audit was foiled by the licensee who stated inventory records are not subject to audit as the licensee defined the subject matter as net sales. As far as the licensee was concerned, if it is not part of the net sale calculation, then I could not look at the records, and this also included free products, shrinkage, gifts, and any other goods disposed that were not recorded in the sales ledgers. Further, it was insightful to identify that I had the right to inspect the sublicensee records; the only problem was the licensor had no contract with the sublicensees so the sublicensees did not cooperate and allow an inspection of their books. The licensor forgot to require all sublicensees to be preapproved and sign an agreement allowing the sublicensees to be audited by the licensor. Eventually, the two sides negotiated a settlement, and the audit never occurred due to the weak language.]

C. "Licensee shall keep and maintain accurate books of account and records covering all transactions relating to this Agreement. Licensor or its designee shall be entitled to (i) audit and inspect such books and records at any time or times during or after the Term of the Agreement during reasonable business hours and upon five (5) days prior written notice to Licensee, and (ii) make copies and summaries of such books and records. All such books of account and records shall be retained by Licensee for a minimum of three (3) years after expiration or termination of this Agreement. If Licensor's duly authorized representative discovers a deficiency in the Royalties paid to Licensor for any period under audit (an "Audit Deficiency"), Licensee shall promptly pay such Audit Deficiency and any interest thereon to Licensor and, if such Audit Deficiency is three percent (3%) or more of the Royalties paid to Licensor for any accounting quarter in such audit period, Licensee shall also reimburse Licensor for all out-of-pocket costs and expenses incurred by Licensor in connection with such audit. If such Audit Deficiency is twenty percent (20%) or more of the Royalties paid to Licensor for such audit period, then in addition to the above, Licensor may, at its sold option, immediately terminate the Agreement upon notice to Licensee, even if Licensee tenders the Audit Deficiency and associated costs and expenses to Licensor."

[This seems good on initial inspection, but in this audit, the licensee decided "transactions" meant only sales transactions and therefore allowed access to any records not related to sales.]

Stronger Language:
"Audits and Inspections

  a. During the term of this Agreement and for three (3) years thereafter, licensee agrees to keep all usual and proper records and books of account and all usual and proper entries relating to each Product licensed sufficient to substantiate the number of copies of Product acquired, manufactured, distributed, or otherwise disposed of by or for Company, and the number of Customer Systems distributed by or for licensee. Licensee shall maintain on licensee's premises such records for itself and for each licensee subsidiary which exercises rights under this Agreement.

  b. In order to verify statements issued by licensee and licensee's compliance with the terms of this Agreement, Licensor may cause (i) an audit to be made of licensee's and/or licensee's Subsidiaries facilities and procedures. Any audit and/or inspection shall be conducted during regular business hours at licensee's and/or licensee's Subsidiaries facilities, with or without notice. Any audit shall be conducted by an independent certified public accountant selected by licensor. There shall be no requirements for the independent certified public accounting firm selected by licensor to perform the audit to sign a letter of confidentiality prior to accessing licensee's records.

c. Licensee agrees to provide licensor's designated audit or inspection team access to relevant licensee's and/or licensee's Subsidiaries records and facilities at the auditor or inspection teams discretion.

d. Prompt adjustment shall be made to compensate for any errors or omissions disclosed by such audit. Any such audit shall be paid for by licensor unless material discrepancies are disclosed. "Material" shall mean the lesser of Ten Thousand Dollars ($10,000.00) or five percent (5%) of the amount that was reported in any given quarterly reporting period or in aggregate for the period under audit. If material discrepancies are disclosed, licensee agrees to pay licensor for the costs associated with the audit. If the audit is conducted on a contingency basis, the cost of the audit shall be calculated as the public accounting firm's 100 percent chargeable rates plus any other charges from the firm such as administrative charges. Further, licensee shall pay licensor an additional royalty of twenty-five (25%) of the applicable royalty on for each sale dollar licensee failed to report and shall pay interest on the underreported principal at the greater of 18 percent or the Prime Rate plus 5 percent as listed in the *Wall Street Journal* as of the date such underpayment is discovered to the date the claim is settled. Interest is to be compounded monthly. If, at any time, licensor becomes aware of any distribution of Product in violation of this Agreement or if licensee cannot properly account for any units of Product acquired by licensee, then without limiting licensor's remedies, licensee shall pay licensor the highest royalty applicable to such product and licensor may charge licensee for each such unit of Product, an additional royalty equal to 30 percent of the highest royalty for the Product plus interest.

e. In the event that licensee's monthly report is not received by licensor within the specified 60 day period, a 5 percent late reporting charge shall be added to licensee's invoice for the month.

f. Interest is due on underreported principal to licensor at the greater of 18 percent or the Prime Rate plus 5 percent as listed in the *Wall Street Journal* as of the date such underpayment is discovered to the date the claim is settled. Interest is to be compounded monthly.

g. In the event licensee fails to accrue any royalties due licensor under this Agreement, prior to termination or expiration, licensor may charge licensee an administrative charge in the amount of $10,000."

6.23. Royalty Calculations

Overview:

It is beneficial to note that the royalty is owed on all inventory sold or otherwise disposed. This is important for instances of missing inventory or inventory that is provided as free samples or distributed in a basis otherwise than sold. The sales value of the otherwise disposed inventory should be at the listed wholesale price. Some contracts clearly state a royalty must be paid on free products and employee or related party disbursements to help avoid any confusion.

It is beneficial to note that a royalty is due on all forms of income from the sale or disposal of licensed products. For example, a licensee I audited charged a restocking fee of 20 percent for first quality refused/returned goods so the licensee received a benefit from the return of goods, a benefit that was not shared with the licensor.

The primary mistake made by contract writers is to try to simplify the royalty calculation. Unfortunately, simplified calculations generally lead to contact misinterpretations. Care should be taken to build royalty calculations that properly take into account the risks and rewards associated with sales and clearly take into account sales price allocations, bundling with nonlicensed products, minimum unit pricing, moment of sales (i.e., invoice date, shipping date, cash receipt date, etc. . . .), if freight and other indirect revenues are to be included in the royalty base (as licensees have been none to charge high amounts for freight to offset lower prices on the licensed IP), most-favored-nation pricing, etc. . . .

The worst mistake seen over and over is to base the royalty due just on "net sales" as there are many different transactions that may occur that don't appear in "net sales" in the sales ledger, such as internal consumption, missing units, promotional giveaways, etc. . . .

Bundling becomes a big issue if licensed goods are sold with unlicensed goods, and there is almost always an argument over what value is to be assigned to the licensed goods. The licensee will tend to allocate the sales price on cost or equally amongst all products regardless of each item's fair market value if sold separately. The licensor will generally attempt to allocate, at a minimum, the sales price of the product if the product was sold separately or the entire value of the sale stating the bundled nonlicensed items was worthless without the licensor's product.

Sharing the risk can affect the royalty calculation. As sales increase and fixed costs are covered, many licensors like to increase the royalty rate after certain milestones are reached. This is particularly common in DVD sales, such as by charging a royalty of $1 for the first 100,000 units sold and $2 for all units sold above 100,000 units. This stratified royalty rate system rewards both parties with the increase in sales.

Weak Language:

A. "Earned Royalties are "Ten percent (10%) of "Net Sales"
   [In this case, there is no definition of net sales, so about anything goes. This wording was used on a pharmaceutical contract with annual royalty

payments in excess of $500 million. The litigation associated with this contract was well into the tens of millions of dollars. Also, one straight royalty rate does not take into the account different types of sales such as FOB or related party sales. FOB sales generally should have a higher royalty rate because the licensed product does not flow through the licensee's control, thereby reducing risks to the licensee. Instead, the product goes directly from the third-party manufacturer to the retailer/buyer.]

B. "Licensee reserves the right to source and pay a royalty of 3.5 percent of net wholesale invoiced billing (less 15 percent withholding allowance in anticipation of returns) for the nonexclusive right to manufacture, or have manufactured, distribute and sell through its wholly-owned subsidiaries product for sale in the fund raising channel of distribution only. Notwithstanding the foregoing, licensee reserves the right to source and pay a royalty of 1.75 percent of the actual retail selling price (less returns and other discounts and/or deductions as standard in the industry) for the nonexclusive right to manufacture or have manufactured, distribute and sell in the United States and Canada."

[It's hard to say exactly what is a fundraising channel, and of course, knowing what standard deductions are for the industry is anyone's guess or the licensee's selection.]

Stronger Language:

- These terms and conditions share the risk and reward. For each unit, the greater to be paid is a dollar amount or percentage of the gross sales dollars such as the greater of $1.25 or 10 percent of the gross sale amount for each unit, whichever is greater. The dollar amount and percentage often increase based on the number of units sold, for instance:
  - "Units sold 0 to 100,000 at the greater of $1.25 or 10 percent of net sales dollars
  - Units sold 101,000 to 500,000 at the greater of $1.50 or 12 percent of net sales dollars
  - All units sold above 500,000 at the greater of $2.00 or 15% percent of net sales dollars"
- "A royalty at a rate of twenty percent (20%) of Wholesale Price (as used herein, 'Wholesale Price' shall mean fifty percent (50%) of retail price) will be paid for Budget Video Devices sold, paid for and not returned. 'Budget Video Devices' are those Video Devices that sell for nine dollars and ninety-nine cents ($9.99) or less for DVD and for five dollars and ninety-nine cents ($5.99) or less for VHS.

  A royalty at a rate of twenty five percent (25%) of Wholesale Price will be paid for Mid-Price Video Devices sold, paid for and not returned. Mid-Price Video Devices are those Video Devices that sell for ten dollars ($10.00) or more for DVD and for six dollars ($6.00) or more for VHS.

A royalty rate of twenty five percent (25%) for all Box Sets. 'Box Sets' are defined herein as single sale units containing two or more Video Devices."

- "Licensee shall pay Licensor Royalties at the Royalty Rate specified in Paragraph 8. Royalties shall be paid on all units of Articles (i) sold by Licensee or (ii) distributed by Licensee on a "no charge" basis for promotional, marketing, or goodwill purposes in excess of one-half percent (1/2%) of total sales. For purposes of this Agreement, 'Net Sales' shall mean Licensee's gross sales (the gross invoice amount billed customers) of Articles sold or otherwise distributed during the Term pursuant to this Agreement, less deductions for trade and quantity discounts actually taken (provided, however, that such trade and quantity discounts shall not exceed ten percent (10%) of gross sales), returns for damaged goods actually credited (and supported by credit memoranda actually issued to the customers), and sales taxes (if included in gross sales, collected from customers and remitted to the proper government authority). It is understood that credit against sales will be allowed only for actual returns of damaged goods and that no credit against sales will be allowed on the basis of an accrual or reserve system. No other deductions shall be taken from Net Sales, including, without limitation, deductions for cash or other discounts or uncollectible accounts. No costs incurred in the manufacture, sale, distribution, or promotion of Articles shall be deducted from any Royalties payable to Licensor. Licensee shall pay, and hold Licensor forever harmless from, all taxes, customs, duties, levies, import or any other charges now or hereafter imposed or based upon the manufacture, delivery, license, sale, possession, or use hereunder to or by Licensee of the Articles (including, but not limited to sales, use, inventory, income, and value added taxes on sales of Articles), which charges shall not be deducted from Licensor's Royalties, the Advance, or the Guarantee. In addition, Royalties shall be paid by the Licensee based on Licensee's usual sales price where (a) articles are distributed by Licensee on a 'no charge' basis for promotional marketing or goodwill purposes; (b) the billed price for the Articles is less than the usual sales price, and the Licensee receives other compensation attributable to the distribution of the Articles separate from the price which appears on the respective invoice; or (c) the Articles are sold by Licensee to an affiliate. Unless otherwise expressly provided herein, Licensee shall not, without the express prior written consent of Licensor, permit the distribution or other marketing of any Articles on an F.O.B. or L.C. basis (as those terms are commonly understood in the international merchandising business). All Articles distributed or marketed (and subject to Licensor's prior written approval) on an F.O.B. or L.C. basis will be subject to Royalties based on the greater of (a) a royalty rate computed on the same basis as if such Articles had been shipped directly to Licensee, or (b) a royalty rate equal to one-half of the Royalty Rate specified in Paragraph 8 but based on the suggested retail sales price of Articles sold by Licensee's customers. All royalties due Licensor as set forth in Paragraphs 19.2 and 19.3 shall be collectively referred to as 'Royalties.' Royalties hereunder shall accrue when the Articles are sold, shipped, distributed, billed and/or paid for, whichever occurs first."

6.24. Royalty Payment

Overview:

Royalty payments are generally payable after 30 or 45 days after the end of each reporting period. Most reporting periods are either monthly or quarterly. It is important to note if the reporting periods are calendar or fiscal, and some agreements go so far as to list the end date of each quarter. It is generally best to avoid fiscal quarter ends, but some licensees may need to report based on their fiscal quarter if they don't coincide with the calendar quarter ends. Some agreements refer to the last business day of each quarter; however this is not recommended as business days change by country, making it hard to track the actual due date.

For international sales, it is important to note the currency in which royalties will be due; if the licensee is allowed to deduct bank and conversion charges; and the exchange rate to be used, including the date of the exchange rate to be used, generally the same rate as the actual due date of the royalty.

It is also good to encourage electronic payment of royalties to help avoid checks getting lost in the mail. Larger licensors have Web sites for the reporting of royalty obligations, including statements, so when such Web sites are used, it is important to note the requirement to use the Web site in the license agreement.

Sample Language:

A. "Licensee will pay License Fees owed to Licensor within thirty (30) calendar days following the end of the calendar month in which the Royalty Bearing Product was sold, leased, transferred to, or placed with a third party. If Licensee fails to make timely payment of Royalties when due or fails to make timely submission of Royalty Reports when due. However, in the event Licensee has previously been given notification and time to cure a prior breach relating to Licensee's failure to remit a Royalty payment (including Advances or Guarantees) and/or Royalty Report when due, then Licensor may terminate this Agreement immediately upon notice to

Licensee and no further time to cure need be given to Licensee by Licensor regardless of whether or not Licensee cured any prior failure or breach."

B. "Where a Guarantee is specified in Schedule 1, the Licensee guarantees and shall pay to the Licensor any shortfall between such Guarantee and the actual Royalties paid by the Licensee to the Licensor over the relevant Guarantee Period. The Licensee shall ensure that such shortfall is received by the Licensor thirty (30) days following the end of the Guarantee Period. Where the Royalties in respect of any Guarantee Period exceed the Guarantee, such excess shall not be taken into account in calculating the shortfall in any subsequent Guarantee Period."

C. "i. Royalty Period. The Percentage Royalty owed to Licensor in excess of the Guaranteed Minimum Royalties shall be calculated on a quarterly calendar basis (the "Royalty Period") and shall be payable no later than thirty (30) days after the termination of the preceding full calendar quarter, i.e., commencing on the first (1st) day of January, April, July, and October. Thus, the Percentage Royalties are payable on January 30, April 30, July 30, and October 30 for the immediate preceding quarter of sales less the Guaranteed Minimum Royalty payments for such period.

ii. Accrual of Percentage Royalty. A Percentage Royalty obligation shall accrue when Licensed Products are sold or otherwise distributed regardless of the time of collection by Licensee. For purposes of Licensee's Percentage Royalty obligations, Licensed Products shall be considered "sold" upon the date of billing, invoicing, shipping or payment, whichever event occurs first.

a. Royalty Statement. With each Percentage Royalty payment, Licensee shall provide Licensor with a written royalty statement in substantially the form attached hereto as Schedule A for the Actual Royalty payable under Section X.X and Schedule B for the Actual Royalty payable under Section X.X). In the event an Actual Royalty is owed under Section X.X, the royalty statement shall provide a level of detail similar to Schedules A and B. Such royalty statements shall be certified as accurate by a duly authorized officer of Licensee. The receipt or acceptance by Licensor of any royalty statement, or the receipt or acceptance of any royalty payment made, shall not prevent Licensor from challenging the validity or accuracy of such statement or payment within three years of the expiration of the agreement.

b. Survival of Obligations. Licensee's obligations for the payment of the Percentage Royalty shall survive the termination of this Agreement, and will continue for so long as Licensee continues to manufacture, sell, distribute, market or promote the Licensed Products. The Minimum Guarantee shall not be payable during any Sell-Off Period (as defined below).

c. Manner of Payment. All payments due hereunder shall be made in United States currency drawn on a United States bank, unless otherwise specified by the parties.

d. Interest on Late Payments. Late payments shall incur interest at the rate of 1.5 percent (1.5%) per month from the date such payments were originally due until payment is made.

e. Late Payment. In the event any royalty payment has not been received by Licensor by the third business day after its due date, Licensor may serve a notice to cure on Licensee in the manner specified in Section XX. If Licensee fails to cure by making payment within three (3) business days of Licensee's receipt of such notice, Licensor may commence an arbitration which shall be administered by JAMS pursuant to the JAMS Streamlined Arbitration Rules & Procedures then in effect. The decision by the arbitrator shall be final and binding, may be confirmed by a court of competent jurisdiction and judgment shall be entered thereon."

6.25. Territory

Overview:

Territory is usually straightforward and is generally offered on a by country or global basis. Some agreements will also specify global licensing except those countries where the United States government has prohibited sales, such as countries listed as sponsoring terrorist or where the propriety technology, such as software, has not been approved for experts due to national security reasons. Territory is generally not done by state.

Additionally, stating if the agreement is exclusive or nonexclusive commonly accompanies territory language.

The most prominent weakness with territory language is that agreements do not specify the penalty should a licensee sell outside its authorized territory. This can be very important if a licensee is selling in an unauthorized territory and that unauthorized territory is an exclusive area for a competing licensee selling the same product. The licensor should take measures to protect themselves should they be sued by a licensee because another licensee has sold into an unlicensed exclusive territory.

Generally, there are three methods of penalties to list for selling in an unauthorized territory beyond breach:

1. A penalty equal to a percentage increase in the base royalty, such as a tripling of the royalty rate.
2. A penalty equal to the estimated gross margin defined as the aggregate net selling price less the cost of goods sold. This does not allow the

licensee to deduct overhead costs that are not included in the cost of goods sold, and language should specify the cost of goods sold as estimated by the licensor's auditors.
3. A penalty equal to all net revenues from goods sold in the unauthorized territory.

Additionally, to whatever penalty is listed, the contract should also identify that interest shall be due on the penalty and any sales to an unauthorized territory shall result in audit cost recovery. This moves unlicensed out of territory sales to the same level as the failure to report royalties.

Weak Language:

A. "Territory means the countries, regions, or other geographic destinations specified in Schedule A. The licensee shall use its best efforts to promote sales of Licensed Products throughout the Territory and to satisfy market demand for the Licensed Products in the Territory. The Licensor shall be entitled to terminate this agreement if the licensee delivers Licensed Products outside the Territory or knowingly sells Licensed Products to a third party for delivery outside the Territory."

[This language is weak as it only refers to termination and does not refer to third-party distributors who may attempt to sell the licensed products in an unauthorized territory.]

B. "Exclusivity. Licensee shall not sell, have sold, distribute, have distributed, advertising, have advertised, or promote and have promoted the Licensed Products in any country outside the Territory and will not knowingly sell the Licensed Products to any person who Licensee has knowledge intends or is likely to resell them in any country outside the Territory. Licensor acknowledges and agrees that the grant of rights to Licensee under this Section is exclusive to Licensee, and Licensor shall not itself exploit or grant to any third party the right to exploit any such rights in the Territory, including but not limited to the right to use the Marks in connection with the manufacture, sale, distribution, advertising and promotion of goods and/or services. For the avoidance of doubt, Licensee and sublicensees may have Licensed Products manufactured outside of the Territory. Licensee shall be responsible for making sure that all manufacturers who supply goods to Licensee or its customers comply with the terms of this Agreement, in particular, Licensor's exclusive rights outside of the territory. Licensee shall have the affirmative obligation to cease doing business with any supplier who Licensee knows is manufacturing and/or distributing Licensed Products outside of the Territory."

[This is weak as there are no penalty provisions, including the basic termination.]

Stronger Language:

C. " 'Territory' shall mean the United States, its territories, and possessions
    (including Puerto Rico), and all United States military exchanges where-
    soever located and additional territories listed on Schedule A. Except for
    the rights to use the Property in connection with the manufacture and
    sale of the Licensed Products in the Territory through the Licensed
    Channels of Distribution expressly provided for herein, Licensor reserves
    all rights to use the Trademarks and the Property which in no way will
    conflict with Licensee's rights hereunder. The licensee hereby granted
    shall be used for the manufacturing, marketing, sale, and distribution of
    Licensed Products only in the Territory through the Licensed Channels of
    Distribution as described herein. Except as provided herein, the Licensee
    shall not make use of or authorize the use of the Property outside the
    Territory nor will it sell any Licensed Products to anyone for resale out-
    side the Territory, or to anyone that Licensee has reason to believe will sell
    same outside the Territory. Notwithstanding the foregoing, Licensee may
    manufacture or cause Licensed Products that bear reference to the
    Property in any form to be manufactured outside the Territory solely for
    sale and distribution within the Territory through the Licensed Channels
    of Distribution. In connection therewith, Licensee may develop, manu-
    facture and produce Packaging, advertising or promotional material
    bearing reference to the Property outside the Territory solely for sale and
    distribution of the Licensed Products within the Territory through the
    Licensed Channels of Distribution. Any Manufacturer performing work
    of Licensee hereunder must execute and deliver to Licensor a
    Manufacturer's Agreement identifying they will only product goods for
    sale to the Licensee and only for distribution in the Territory. Licensee
    shall pay to licensor, plus interest at 1.5 percent compounded monthly
    from the date of sale, any gross margin the licensee receives from the sale
    of Licensed Products outside the Territory. Gross margin for this section
    is defined as net sales less cost of goods sold as reasonable estimated by
    the Licensor's auditors and whose decision shall be final."

6.26. Termination

Overview:

Throughout this book, we note the overuse of termination and the lack of use
of remediation or penalties. When termination is warranted under the agreement, the reasons for termination should be clearly identified. License
Agreements with simple breaches may not rise to the point of termination if
causes for it have not been clearly identified in the agreement, thereby

resulting in extensive litigation over a breach if the licensor is seeking termination. No doubt these are some of the most expensive, unproductive, and time-consuming litigations when the causes for breach and termination are not clearly identified in the agreement.

A major mistake of licensors is to also not note that, when there are multiple contracts with the same licensee, that a terminable violation of any one contract can cause all contracts to be terminated. Many licensors have experienced the pain of doing business with a licensee under one contract that has not been terminated, when another contract has been terminated for cause.

It can also be beneficial to note that any sales after termination shall result in the gross or net revenues being paid, plus interest, to the licensor. It is also helpful to note that any inventory not sold during an authorized sell-off period (with its own restrictions to prevent the dumping of product) shall revert at no cost to the licensor.

Weak Language:

A. "Upon the expiration or termination of this Agreement, Licensee will promptly return to the Licensor all Licensor-Furnished Merchandise then in Licensee's possession "freight collect" to a location designated by the Licensor. Upon the expiration or earlier termination of this Agreement, Licensee will return all Licensor-Furnished Items to the Licensor, and Licensee will have no further rights thereto. "Upon the expiration or earlier termination of this Agreement, each Party in receipt, possession or control of the other Party's intellectual or proprietary property, information, and materials or Confidential Information pursuant to this Agreement must return to the other Party (or at the other Party's written request, destroy) such property, information and materials. Sections X and XX (together with all other provisions that reasonably may be interpreted as surviving the expiration or earlier termination of this Agreement) will survive any such expiration or termination. Notwithstanding the foregoing, the expiration or earlier termination of this Agreement will not relieve either Party from its obligation to pay any monies due to the other Party for any period prior to the effective date of such expiration or termination."

   [This relies on "provisions that reasonably may be interpreted" which is always a bad idea. If you want a provision to survive the agreement, then the extra effort should be taken to list it. Further, this agreement never mentions the causes for termination, only the dates of the agreement. This agreement did identify that a royalty still needs to be paid in Section X; however, there was no penalty associated for selling after termination, such a dramatic increase in the royalty rate.]

B. "Survival of Obligations. Licensee's obligations for the payment of the Percentage Royalty shall survive the termination of this Agreement, and will continue for so long as Licensee continues to manufacture, sell, distribute, market or promote the Licensed Products. The Minimum Guarantee shall not be payable during any Sell-Off Period (as defined below). This Agreement is not terminable by Licensor except as provided in Section x.x. No claim of breach of this Agreement, whether characterized as 'material' "total" or otherwise, shall entitle Licensor to terminate this Agreement."

Stronger Language:

A. "TERMINATION:
   a. Licensee shall have the right to terminate this Agreement at any time on sixty (60) days written notice to Licensor. Unless Licensor breaches Section X hereof and such breach is not cured within fifteen days, upon the effective date of the termination by Licensee, all monies paid to Licensor shall be deemed non-refundable and Licensee's obligation to pay any guaranteed moneys, including the Guaranteed Minimum Royalty, shall be accelerated and any yet unpaid guaranteed moneys shall become immediately due and payable. If Licensor has not timely cured a breach of Section X hereof, the Guaranteed Minimum Royalty shall not be owed by Licensee for any period following the effective date of Licensee's termination.
   b. Mutual Agreement. The Agreement may also be terminated if Licensor and Licensee mutually agree in writing that the Agreement shall be terminated."

6.27. Posttermination Rights

A. "Inventory upon Termination. No more than thirty (30) days after Termination of this Agreement, Licensee shall provide Licensor with a statement indicating the number and description of Licensed Products bearing the Marks which Licensee had on hand or was in the process of manufacturing or having manufactured as of the date of the expiration or termination (the "Inventory"). The Licensor shall have the option, at Licensor's own cost, of conducting a physical inventory in order to ascertain or verify such Inventory. In the event that the Licensee refuses to permit the Licensor to conduct such physical inventory, the Licensee shall forfeit its rights hereunder to dispose of such inventory."
   a. Sell-Off Period. Upon termination of this Agreement, Licensee shall be entitled, for an additional period of one (1) year and on a nonexclusive basis, to continue to sell Inventory (Sell-Off Period). Such sales shall be made subject to all of the provisions of this Agreement

and to an accounting for and the payment of a Percentage Royalty thereon. Such accounting and payment shall be due and paid within thirty (30) days after the close of the said one (1) year period. At the end of the Sell-Off Period, Licensor may require that Licensee either destroy any Licensed Products bearing the Marks still on hand or alternatively, sell them to Licensor at cost.

   b. Freedom to License. After termination of this Agreement, except as otherwise provided in this Agreement, all rights granted herein shall revert to Licensor who may use, or license others to use the Marks in any way whatsoever. Subject to the Sell-Off Period, Licensee shall thereafter refrain from all further use of the Marks, and turn over to the Licensor all materials relating to the Marks and the Licensed Products, including, but not limited to, all artwork, color separations, prototypes, and the like, as well as any market studies or other tests or studies conducted by Licensee at no cost whatsoever to Licensor.

   c. Disposition of Licensed Products. Subject to the Sell-Off Period, upon termination of this Agreement, Licensee agrees to immediately return to Licensor all material relating to the Licensed Products in Licensee's possession, owned by Licensor or bearing the Marks at no cost whatsoever to Licensor."

B. "a. In addition to any and all other remedies available to it hereunder, Licensor shall have the right to immediately terminate this Agreement upon written notice to Licensee upon the occurrence of any of the following:

   i. Licensee makes, sells, uses, or distributes any Article without having the prior written approval of Licensor as specified in Paragraph X or continues to make, sell, offer for sale, use, or distribute any Article after receipt of notice from Licensor withdrawing approval of same.

   ii. Licensee becomes subject to any voluntary or involuntary order of any government agency involving the recall of any of the Articles because of safety, health or other hazards or risks to the public.

   iii. In addition to any and all other remedies available to it hereunder, on ten (10) days prior written notice to Licensee, Licensor may terminate this Agreement (in which case such termination shall be effective immediately upon expiration of the ten (10) day notice period), upon the occurrence of any of the following circumstances, provided that during such ten (10) day period, Licensee fails to cure the breach to Licensor's satisfaction.

   iv. Licensee fails to immediately discontinue the advertising, distribution, or sale of Articles which do not contain the appropriate legal legend or notice.

    v. Licensee breaches any of the provisions of this Agreement relating to the unauthorized assertion of rights in the Proprietary Subject Matter.

    vi. Licensee fails to make timely payment of Royalties when due or fails to make timely submission of Royalty Reports when due. However, in the event Licensee has previously been given notification and time to cure a prior breach relating to Licensee's failure to remit a Royalty payment (including Advances or Guarantees) and/or Royalty Report when due, then Licensor may terminate this Agreement immediately upon notice to Licensee and no further time to cure need be given to Licensee by Licensor regardless of whether or not Licensee cured any prior failure or breach.

    vii. Licensee intentionally sells or authorizes the sales of Articles outside the Territory or outside the Channels of Distribution or sells the Articles to persons who intend or are likely to resell them outside the Territory or outside the Channels of Distribution.

    viii. In addition to any and all other remedies available to it hereunder, on thirty (30) days prior written notice to Licensee, Licensor may terminate this Agreement (in which case such termination shall be effective immediately upon expiration of the thirty (30) day notice period), upon the occurrence of any of the following circumstances, provided that during such thirty (30) day period, Licensee fails to cure the breach to Licensor's satisfaction.

    ix. Licensee fails to obtain or maintain insurance as required under Paragraph X hereof.

    x. If Licensee fails to satisfy Paragraph X or, during any calendar quarter of the Term, Paragraph X, Licensor may terminate this Agreement as to such Article(s) in any country in the Territory or in whole, by written notice to Licensee.

    xi. Licensee fails to timely submit Prototype and/or Preliminary Artwork for approval by Licensor as provided in Paragraph X.

    xii. If, in Licensor's opinion, Licensee's ability to perform under this Agreement is or will be impaired due to Licensee's financial inability to comply with its anticipated obligations under this Agreement; a petition in bankruptcy is filed by or against Licensee; Licensee is adjudicated bankrupt or insolvent, or makes an assignment for the benefit of creditors or an arrangement pursuant to any bankruptcy law; Licensee discontinues its business; or a receiver is appointed for Licensee or Licensee's business and such receiver is not discharged within thirty (30) days.

    xiii. Licensee or any of its controlling shareholders, officers, directors, or employees take any actions in connection with the manufacture, sale, distribution, or advertising of the Articles or takes any other actions which damages or reflects adversely upon the Licensor, the Property, and/or the Proprietary Subject Matter.

xiv. If a substantial portion of assets or controlling stock or ownership in Licensee's business is sold or transferred, or if there is a substantial change in Licensee's management, or if Licensee's property is expropriated, confiscated, or nationalized by any government, or if any government assumes *de facto* control of Licensee's business, in whole or in part.

xv. Licensee breaches any material term of any other license agreement between Licensee and Licensor, and such license agreement is terminated for cause.

xvi. Licensee fails to obtain Licensor's consent or fails to provide Licensor with a Manufacturer's Agreement as required under Paragraph X.

xvii. Licensee violates any of its other obligations or breaches any of its covenants, agreements, representations, or warranties hereunder.

6.27.1. Effect of Termination

a. On expiration or termination of this Agreement, all Royalties (including unpaid portions of the Guarantee, if any) shall be immediately due and payable without set-off of any kind, and no Advance or Guarantee paid to Licensor shall be refunded to Licensee. Termination of this Agreement, or any portions thereof, by Licensor pursuant to Paragraph X shall in no way reduce, proportionally or otherwise, the Guarantee required to be paid to Licensor hereunder. Upon expiration of the Term, and in the event of its sooner termination, ten (10) business days after receipt of notice of termination, a statement showing the number and description of Articles on hand or in process shall be furnished by Licensee to Licensor. Licensor shall have the right to take a physical inventory to ascertain or verify such inventory and statement. Refusal by Licensee to submit to such physical inventory by Licensor and/or failure by Licensee to render the final statement as and when required by this provision, shall result in a forfeiture by Licensee of Licensee's right to dispose of its inventory (as provided by Paragraph X hereof), Licensor retaining all other legal and equitable rights Licensor may have in the circumstances.

b. On expiration of this Agreement only (as compared to an early termination pursuant to Paragraph X), Licensee shall have a period of ninety (90) days commencing with the expiration date, in which to sell-off (on a nonexclusive basis) Articles which are on hand or in process as of the expiration date; provided, however: (i) Licensee complies with all the terms and conditions of this Agreement, including, but not limited to, Licensee's obligation to pay Royalties on and to account to Licensor for such sales (such accounting to be provided to Licensor within fifteen (15) days after the expiration of the sell-off period); (ii) Licensee has not manufactured Articles solely or principally for sale during the sell-off period; and (iii) Licensee has given Licensor the opportunity to purchase such Articles at Licensee's cost of manufacture thereof, which purchase may be of some or all such units, in Licensor's sole discretion. Royalties earned during the sell-off period may not be applied to any Guarantee shortfall. Licensee shall not be authorized to dispose of the excess inventory in the sell-off period to the extent that it exceeds ten percent (10%) of the total number of Articles sold during the Term, without Licensor's prior written consent. During the sell-off period, Licensor may use or license the use of the Proprietary Subject Matter in any manner, at anytime, anywhere in the world.

c. On expiration or termination of this Agreement, except as noted in Paragraph X above, Licensee shall have no further right to exercise the rights licensed hereunder or otherwise acquired in relation to this Agreement and such rights shall forthwith revert to Licensor. All Artwork and other materials supplied to Licensee by Licensor hereunder shall be immediately returned to Licensor at Licensee's expense. All remaining Collateral Materials and Articles and component parts thereof shall be destroyed within five (5) business days. Licensee shall within five (5) business days after such destruction deliver to Licensor a certificate of destruction evidencing same. Licensee agrees that (i) its failure to cease the manufacture, sale and/or distribution of Articles upon the expiration or termination of this Agreement will result in immediate and irreparable damage to Licensor; (ii) there is no adequate remedy at law for such failure; and (iii) in the event of such failure, Licensor shall be entitled to injunctive relief.

d. Upon expiration or termination of this Agreement, (i) if the Underlying Agreement specifies that the license granted hereunder is an exclusive license, Licensor shall be free to license others to use the Proprietary Subject Matter in connection with the manufacture, sale, distribution, and promotion of the Articles in the Territory (it being acknowledged that Licensor has the full and complete right so to do during the Term if the license granted is a nonexclusive License); and (ii) Licensee shall refrain from further use of the Proprietary Subject Matter or any further reference, direct or indirect, thereto or to anything deemed by Licensor to be similar to the Proprietary Subject Matter, in connection with the manufacture, sale, distribution or promotion of Licensee's products except as permitted in Paragraph X above. It shall not be a violation of any right of Licensee if Licensor should at any time during the Term enter into negotiations with another to license use of the Proprietary Subject Matter in respect to the Articles within the Territory provided that, in the event that the license granted to Licensee hereunder is an exclusive license, it is contemplated that such prospective license shall commence after termination of the Agreement."

6.28. Tax Deductions—On Royalty Payments

Overview:

Some countries require a tax on royalty payments that leave the country of origin. For example, Hong Kong charges a 5.25 percent royalty tax on any payments from a Hong Kong licensee to a licensor outside of Hong Kong. This royalty tax, or reduction of royalty payments, can often be offset in the receiving companies' tax obligations within their own country. When such tax payments are made and royalty payments are reduced, the payor should receive a tax certificate to evidence the payment was made and for domestic tax credit application purposes. Therefore, contract language should clearly indicate that if a company is to reduce payments for taxes, then the reduction is only authorized if it is evidenced by a tax certificate.

Sample Language:

A. "If withholding taxes based on Licensor's direct net income are required, Licensee may deduct the required amount from Royalties prior to remitting same to Licensor, provided Licensee provides Licensor with a copy of such withholding tax payment prior to such deduction and provides Licensor with the appropriate tax credit forms within sixty (60) days of payment of such withholding tax and affords all necessary cooperation and support to Licensor in order to get reimbursed and/or credited. In the event Licensee does not provide the appropriate tax credit form within sixty (60) days of payment of withholding taxes, Licensee shall be liable to and shall reimburse Licensor for the amounts deducted from Royalties for withholding taxes in the immediately following Royalty Report, plus interest."

6.29. Tax Deductions—As a Reduction From Gross Sales

Overview:

Value Added Taxes (VAT) are charged by countries that require a tax payment each time a good increases in value and changes ownership, including payment of the tax by the manufacturer, licensee, and eventually the end user. These value added taxes can be very high, with amounts approaching 20 percent not unusual. Many agreements allow for the deduction of VAT; however, few of these agreements take into account the company taking the deduction can often receive a year-end or periodic credit for the deduction, thus the deductions reported to the monitoring third party are often overstated as they fail to take into account the periodic offsets. Offsets to the declared value added tax occurs because the tax is only to be charged, in most instances, on the value increase to the properly when in the hands of the payor, so the payor can take a credit against the cost of the products; the problem is, the payor never seems to remember to declare that credit as an offset to their deduction.

As an example, this is what I have seen when performing royalty audits in Brazil. A licensee will manufacturer a good, let's say a shirt, and on sale to a retailer, and take an 18 percent deduction for the VAT paid on the sale of the shirt, thereby reducing gross sales to reach net sales on which the royalty is paid as a percentage of net sales. However, what the licensees always fail to do is report the VAT tax credit they received on the purchase of the raw materials to make the shirt. To put numbers behind the example, if the raw materials cost $10 and the shirt sold for $15, the net VAT that was really paid was 18 percent on $5 ($15–$10), and not the $15 as it appears on the sales invoice.

Contract language should clearly note that only "net value added taxes actually paid" should be deducted when such deductions are allowed, and the payor will need to provide proof of payment to the third-party monitor.

Weak Language:

A. "Net Sales as the total amount received by Licensee or any Affiliate from the sale or distribution of Licensed Products, less the sum of the following deductions when applicable and separately invoiced: cash, trade or quantity discounts, sales, use, tariff, import/export duties, or value added taxes imposed upon particular sales."

   [This language is weak as it allows a deduction of VAT on invoices; however, the credit or reduction of the VAT is never on an invoice rather, it is generally recorded separately in a tax ledger. The language should clearly note the deduction is limited to net taxes actually paid as evidenced by the amounts on the invoices and offsetting tax credits.]

Stronger Language:
It is ny language that refers to net taxes paid supported by tax certificates, tax returns, and tax remittances.

6.30. Unauthorized Use of Licensed Product

Overview:
The unauthorized use of licensed product is very common by licensees, and it is more common for license agreements to not address the ramifications should a licensee manufacturer, distribute, or otherwise sell the licensed product in a manner that is not allowed for in the agreement. Generally, it is known that it would be a breach of the contract should unauthorized distributions occur or a royalty is owed on the unauthorized distribution, at a

minimum; however, neither of these results tend to influence a licensee to only distribute products through an authorized channel. Few licensors wish to terminate an agreement due to an unauthorized distribution of licensed product. Therefore, steps should be taken to clearly identify the penalty for the unauthorized use or distribution of the product by a licensee. Such penalty is generally gross revenues, gross margin, or net profit. Defining in the agreement how each of these potential penalties is to be computed is important as any of these amounts are subject to manipulation. As a basic rule, it is good to cite how the gross revenue, margin, or profit should be calculated in accordance with AICPA accrual accounting standards. Noting the use of accrual standards, as opposed to cash standards, helps prevent cash flow manipulation and, therefore, penalty manipulation.

Examples of unauthorized distribution of licensed products include distribution prior to the effective date or after the termination date of the contract. Other examples include distribution through unauthorized channels (i.e., the contract limits the sale of goods to department stores, yet the goods are sold to gift stores), unauthorized countries, or third-party distributors.

Weak Language:
It is any language that has no remedy penalty for the unauthorized distribution of licensed goods, including language that just calls for termination of the agreement.

Stronger Language:

A. "You agree that you will not use the Licensed Material or the Trademarks or any other material owned by us in any way other than as herein authorized (or as is authorized in such other written contract signed by both of us as may be in effect between us). In addition to any other remedy we may have, you agree that the profits from any use thereof on 11products other than the Articles (unless authorized by us in writing), and all gross revenues from the use of any other trademarks or copyrighted material of ours without written authorization, shall be payable to us."

B. "Licensee shall not use either the Licensed Material or Artwork on any other material, the copyright or trademark to which is owned or controlled by Licensor, in any way other than as herein authorized (or as authorized in such other written contract addition by both Licensee and Licensor in effect). In addition to any other remedy Licensor may have, Licensee agrees that the total revenue to Licensee from any use of such material on products other than the Licensee Articles (unless authorized by Licensor in writing), and total revenues to Licensee from the use of any other copyright or registered material of Licensor's without written authorization, shall be payable to Licensor."

CHAPTER

7

Best Practices for a Licensee

7.1. Some Top Best Practices for a Licensee   264

7.2. Why Licensees Underreport Royalties   269

7.3. IP Inventory Monitoring   272

7.4. Preparing for the Royalty Audit   273

7.5. Non-Disclosure Agreement (NDA)   276

7.6. Communications with the Licensor   276

7.7. Creating the Control Environment   276

7.8. How to Avoid Being Audited   277

7.1. Some Top Best Practices for a Licensee

1. In preparation of the first royalty statement, financial management, independent from the royalty statement creator, should compare the royalty statement to the agreement and supporting documentation prior to the royalty statement's issuance.
   a. Senior financial management should make certain all requested information, but only what is requested, is included in the royalty report.
   b. Care should be taken to compare the gross sales reported to the actual sales ledger.
   c. A review should be made as to what is being deducted from gross sales to get to net sales to see if the deduction is authorized.
   d. A calculation should be made that deductions do not exceed limitations.
   e. A review should be made to make certain all IP has been picked up in the royalty report.
   f. A practical review of the royalty statement, contract requirements, and available information should be made to determine if the agreement or reporting requirements need to be adjusted to reflect the actual ability of the company to report and comply with the agreement.
   g. An assessment of the reasonableness of any minimum guarantee should be made versus actual sales to determine if the minimum guarantee is too high and should be adjusted down, based on a better understanding of market conditions. Addressing disappointing sales and the inability to reach the minimum guarantee early in the life of an agreement may allow management to work with the licensor to identify a better solution to royalty that falls short of minimum guarantee requirements.
2. After the first royalty statement is issued, discuss the statement with the licensor to make certain that all the information is correctly presented.
   a. Getting the licensor involved early is a great method to make certain that issues do not arise in the future. If such issues do arise in the future based on items early on that were approved by the licensor, even if not in the contract, can be helpful to remedy future issues.
3. Request An early on royalty audit where any findings will not result in cost recovery or interest but rather to make certain the information was properly accumulated in the eyes of the licensor's auditor.
   a. Eagerly showing a desire to work with the licensor to make certain royalty statements are correct does a couple of things: (1) it helps make certain the royalty statements are correct, and (2).it reduces the likelihood of a royalty audit in the future. Licensors tend to audit high-risk companies so placing yourself as a low risk company is an important deterrent to a royalty audit.

    b. Having a royalty audit helps establish a baseline of acceptable reporting so any future breach may be rebutted by noting acceptance by earlier audits.

4. Maintain historical records to support royalty statements, such as quarter-end inventory records and annual sales records.

    a. Many licensees fail to maintain the reports to support royalty statements and then incur significant employee resources to recreate supporting documents, and if such records cannot be re-created, find themselves with money royalty audit findings from extrapolations from periods where records were available. The least expensive alternative is to retain documents so they don't have to be re-created in the distant future, especially after systems or employees change.

5. Maintain IP destruction records with all destructions witnessed by at least two employees or an independent outside auditor. If the IP is small, such as microchips, consider not destroying the microchips but instead storing them until the destruction can be witnessed by the licensor's auditor. For clothing, consider cutting out the label still sewed to the licensed product instead of the entire piece of apparel. As an alternative, ship all microchips to the licensor, and let the licensor destroy the microchips.

    a. Licensees need to provide support for the disbursement of all licensed IP. Unaccounted-for licensed product often results in findings. Just stating that licensed IP was disposed of is generally not considered sufficient to avoid a liability. There must be hard evidence of the disposal, and such hard evidence generally includes a statement by at least two employees stating they witnessed the destruction.

    b. It is helpful to ask the licensor how to handle goods that are to be destroyed.

6. Maintain a file for all e-mail and other side letters to provide evidence of contract amendments that are not through a more formalized amendment process.

    a. It never ceases to amaze me that a number of side agreements occur that are not through an amendment and then the number of disputes as to what side agreements were actually made. It is not unusual for a licensor to be unaware of a side agreement, such as allowing a licensee to pay late without penalty or to violate certain parts of the agreement without a breach. These side agreements, generally by e-mail or made verbally, are often made by sales personnel of the licensor and outside the formal contracting process—and often in violation of the amendment notification requirements of the actual agreement. Such side agreements can provide substantial relief to a licensee, so it is critical that the licensee have controls over side agreements that are often missed by the licensor.

7. If there are multiple licensors to a licensee, consider a license agreement monitoring software.
   a. Trademark licensees often have many different license agreements requiring compliance. A master schedule should be maintained in a software as simple as Excel to identify all license agreements requiring compliance and the major parts of each agreement, such as royalty payment due dates, minimum guarantee dates, advertising expenditure commitments, royalty rates, and other aspects of the agreement that require reporting.
   b. There are various license agreement monitoring software packages that a licensee can use to track compliance. Most software will need to be customized, and this can be expensive, so it only makes sense if the licensee has many compliance requirements, such as thirty or more license agreements, or, as I have seen, one agreement with thirty different formulas for license compliance.
8. For end user agreements (i.e., software in multiple work stations), have internal information technology personnel periodically, at least quarterly, compare the number of licensees to the number of instances the software is in use). See the BSA Web site for more information at www.bsa.org.
   a. There is over-the-counter software that can be used to help monitor if there exists adequate licenses for the number of instances that software is in use.
9. For licensees using third-party manufacturers, be certain to secure rights to audit the third party's records and implement strong controls to help prevent the third-party manufacturer from producing licensed goods and not reporting them. For example, a clothing licensee should have controls to make certain their product is not going to the grey market by the third-party manufacturer who is making licensed products by day and unlicensed products by night (as the old saying goes).
   a. It is bad for both the licensor and the licensee if the third-party manufacturer is making unlicensed goods and flooding the market. The licensee must maintain strong controls over the third-party manufacturer, especially if the company is located in a country known for producing counterfeit products, such as China.
10. Make certain personnel completing the royalty statement have a copy of the license agreement and have been instructed to read all provisions.
    a. It is amazing how many errors are made by the licensee for the simple fact that the person who calculates the royalty due has never read the license agreement. I often ask for a copy of the agreement by the clerk calculating the royalty payment and find out that she does not have a copy.

11. Create a contract brief for all license agreements.
    a. This contract brief should be available for anyone who has anything to do with contract compliance, including legal, accounting, sales, manufacturing, and inventory personnel.
12. If there are minimum advertising expenditure requirements, obtain from the licensor, in writing, what qualifies as an acceptable advertising expenditure.
    a. For example, should a tradeshow booth qualify as an advertising expenditure, and if so, how much of the expenditure if more than one licensed product is included in the booth..Is the expenditure allocated by sales volume or percentage of the booth dedicated to the licensed product?
13. Have controls in place to make certain royalties are paid in a timely manner.
    a. At least two employees should have a schedule of when payments are due, the person calculating the royalty and the person reviewing the calculation.
14. If there are many license agreements, try to have each royalty report due at different month ends so personnel calculating the royalties are not overwhelmed.
    a. This requires coordination between the accounting group controlling the calculations and the business affairs group or sales groups negotiating the new agreements.
15. Consideration should be made to having vague wording in the agreements, such as "reasonable trade discounts" as such wording is hard for a licensor to enforce.
    a. Licensors should strive to have very strictly defined license terms that can easily be tested without question for compliance. Licensees like to have vague terms subject to interpretation, which, of course, they always interpret to their favor.
16. Read each agreement and determine what could go wrong, and then make certain controls are in place to make sure that each part of each agreement is properly controlled.
    a. The people to determine what could go wrong should be both legal and accounting personnel. Consideration can also be made to having a royalty auditor take a look at the agreement and explain what would be typical misreportings under the agreement.
17. Put into writing the guidelines for calculating the royalties so the information can be passed onto new employees who take over the agreements.
    a. This should be written as guidelines, as opposed to strict procedures.

18. If the license agreement covers multiple countries and each country reports separately, such as common in pharmaceuticals, make certain there are controls over all the countries to ensure consistent and proper reporting.
    a. Individual country personnel should talk with each other to make certain they are calculating the royalties on a consistent basis. My experience has been that rarely do individual country personnel talk to each other to establish best practices, and further, headquarter personnel consolidating the information rarely speak to the individual countries to make certain the information they are getting is correct. Often, the licensees just pull system information remotely that is not always consistently recorded in the financial records.

19. Attempt to negotiate low interest on late payments to no interest and the removal of any recovery of audit costs (the argument is usually, "don't you trust me?"), and be very specific as to what the auditor may examine during an audit, using wording such as, "only the sales ledgers can be audited." Of course, this is counter to my advice to the licensors because to them I recommend the whole world of records, financial or otherwise, be open to audit.

20. Require at least thirty days notification prior to the start of an audit so there is adequate time for preparation.
    a. After the audit notification letter is received, immediate action should be taken to prepare for the audit, including a self audit under the direction of in-house counsel to help make certain work is done as attorney work product and is therefore privileged.

21. Insist all audit requests be in writing and submitted at least two days in advance.
    a. Requiring audit requests to be in writing accomplishes several things:
        i. Frustrates the auditors.
        ii. Helps make certain incorrect information is not provided.
        iii. Delays the completion of the audit, and if the auditors are traveling, might keep the auditors from completing all steps they intended.
        iv. Provides information as to what the auditor may be trying to accomplish so the licensee can be better prepared for issues.
        v. Allows the licensee to pre-audit the information prior to providing it to the auditor.

22. Negotiate hard on audit findings. Settling for pennies on the dollar is a realistic expectation.

23. Perform a periodic self-assessment of contract compliance. Consider engaging a royalty auditor to perform an internal audit of controls over proper royalty reporting.

24. If a notice of a royalty audit is received, conduct a self-examination of potential contract violations, and be prepared how to handle the errors in advance if discovered by the auditor.

    a. Just paying any self-identified amounts due to the licensor often results in a report finding and does not reduce the cost recovery or interest due to the licensor. A strategy might be taken that just allows the licensee to pay a fraction of the amount due, even if discovered by the auditor, through the report settlement negotiation process.

7.2. Why Licensees Underreport Royalties

As stated earlier in this book, my experience has been that all licensees underreport royalties. Of course, there will be the exception; I just have not found it in twenty years. Now if I were to estimate unscientifically, I would guess one-half of all licensees insist they have properly reported royalties prior to any on-site inspection, and I think at least one-half of those really believe they have properly reported royalties. So, by conjecture, I would say one-quarter of all licensees *believe* they have totally and honestly followed the license agreement. So, why do even the most honest of licensees underreport? The reasons for underreporting vary but generally fall into one of these categories:

1. The #1 reason in my opinion—poorly written license agreements where the licensee interprets the agreement completely different from the licensor. Of course, there is a direct tie-in with my opinion that I have never read a well-written license agreement to control royalty reporting, so you can't expect a licensee to report properly when license agreements have so many flaws.

2. The #2 reason in my opinion—there is no incentive for the licensee to properly report, so they purposely underreport. Incentives to properly report include remediation provisions listing reasonable monetary penalties for all types of potential contract violations, interest on late payments and on other financial obligations, and audit cost recovery provisions with low thresholds (i.e., 3 percent) to spark cost recovery. Of course, the self-reporting party also has to believe the agreement will be enforced, and the licensor or other party receiving the information has the will to seek litigation or restitution through other channels should the contract violations be discovered.

3. Companies use of accounting clerks who do not have a copy of the agreement or adequate training on how to calculate royalty liabilities and

therefore make assumptions or use estimates. This is often complicated by the fact that royalty agreements have many different terms and conditions, and the accountant preparing the royalty statement is only concerned with the calculation of the royalty due and is therefore not monitoring the other provisions of the agreement that may lead to contract breaches or other obligations, such as trademark, copyright, or patent notification; or sales restrictions, such as territorial or on discounts.

4. Salespeople or other individuals committing the self-reporting entity (i.e., licensee) are not aware of the agreement's restrictions and therefore are not taking actions to comply with the agreement. For example, an agreement might state that sales through certain distribution channels are not allowed (i.e., a high-end designer like Coach would not want its products being sold through a discount retailer such as Wal-Mart); however, the sales personnel are not aware of this restriction and therefore sell the licensed product through the unauthorized channel. Further, the accountant preparing the royalty report is not reviewing who the customers were who purchased the goods, so there is no internal control environment that has been established to capture contract violations.

5. The individuals who negotiate the agreement are not responsible for the calculations and compliance under the agreement. Generally, the individual negotiating the agreement is a business affairs attorney and/or company executive. After the agreement is executed, it is handed to the royalty accountant who must guess the intention of the agreement. Further, because the royalty accountant is not involved in the contract negotiation, it might not be possible for the self-reporting entity to report as required under the agreement.

6. There are too many agreements and not sufficient resources, so all reporting obligations are reported under similar assumptions by the accountant.

7. There are annual restrictions on the agreement that cannot be monitored in day-to-day operations, and the violation is only identified after it is too late to correct. For example, an agreement might state that discounts are limited to 10 percent per year in the calculation of net sales; however, the year must be concluded before the limit is fully tested, and by time the year is over, it is too late for the self-reporting entity to correct its actions and not breach the agreement.

For licensees that purposely underreport royalties, the question is why they do it, other than the obvious desire to maximize income by reducing royalty expenses. The answer is simply that the cost for noncompliance is small compared to the benefit of reducing the royalty expense. Even companies that are audited all the time, such as entertainment studios, have a reputation for underpayment of royalties as the cost for litigation and settlement are small compared to the higher cost of compliance. In more detail, licensees purposely underreport because:

8. *The risk of being audited is very low.* Less than 5 percent of licensors conduct royalty audits. Licensees that pay over $300,000 annually in royalties have a much greater chance of being audited while licensees with annual royalty obligations of less than $50,000 have almost no chance of being audited as the cost of an audit would most likely exceed any potential findings. Even with cost recovery provisions, it would seem a bit absurd to pay a royalty auditor $15,000 to audit $50,000 in royalties, discover an underreporting of $2500 to spark the cost recovery provision, and then charge the licensee $15,000 for the audit costs. Leading practice for a licensor, therefore, is to charge a high enough minimum guarantee that a royalty audit is not necessary. Such a minimum guarantee should be great enough that the licensor is basically saying that if you pay me this amount, I will be satisfied and if you pay me more, lucky me because I was not expecting it.

9. *Most people conducting royalty audits don't have the skills to find the hidden contract violations.* For some reason, licensors hire financial auditors, internal auditors, or use in-house auditors to conduct royalty audits. These neophytes generally will not be able to understand the nuances of royalty underreporting and other contract violations by the sophisticated licensee, and therefore the potential breeches go undetected.

10. *The chance of finding the misreporting can be low if the licensee manipulates the records.* Many licensees are proud of their ability to hide data. The simplest method is not providing the requested information for the auditor by stating the system is unable to retrieve the data. The next method is just refusing to provide the data even if it is available. This most often occurs when the right-to-audit provision refers to the right to audit both sales and royalties, and therefore the licensee says only the sales ledgers can be reviewed and no other records may be examined, even if they are required to verify sales, such as inventory records and shipping records. Then, there are the multiple sets of books (given in such countries as China, Russia, and Brazil), complex related party sales that are conveniently hidden away as regular sales, the so-called after-hour manufacturing (in grey-market activity, we seem to find the company making the reported licensed products is also making all the nonreported licensed products, especially when a third-party manufacturer is used), and rebates, kickbacks, nonreturned products, and just about every other inventive method to hide sales and production.

11. *The agreements are vaguely written, so collection is futile.* The forward-thinking licensee purposely has vague language in the agreement.

This vague language is often not enforceable though nonlitigation strategies, and the cost of litigation might not make it worth the effort to define what was meant by the language. Therefore, the licensee will look at the language and always interpret the language to their benefit.

12. *There is settlement for pennies on the dollar.* It almost always seems to happen the licensee will argue just about every point of an auditor's finding. It is not that the licensee personally believes the findings are wrong, but if they argue even the most obvious findings, they know the licensor will most often be happy to avoid the pain of litigation and settle for amounts well less than even the most basic amounts due under the royalty agreement. Because of the licensee's knowledge that licensors tend to settle for a fraction of findings, many licensors encourage the auditor to make every finding in the world, in addition to identifying expensive penalties for noncompliance because the licensor knows it will be necessary to negotiate away much of the findings to get payment. Licensees also like to play the fear card with the licensors threatening to go elsewhere for the same IP; however, these threats are generally saber rattling guises that hold little real value as the licensees generally need the IP more than the licensor, especially if the licensee has made significant investments to support the IP.

A licensee that truly wants to report properly should work with the licensor to make certain there is a strong contract that adequately defines the licensee's obligations. These include full definitions of all restrictions and calculations by example. The strong contract starts with the licensor and licensee having the desire to not negotiate away provisions that allow for the monitoring of the agreements.

In the real world, the licensor often is most concerned about closing the deal and therefore readily negotiates away audit right provisions, interest rates, and other remedies to close the deal. If such actions are taken, the licensor then needs to realize they are probably also negotiating away 50 percent or more of potential royalties due, as only the licensee that plans to underreport would insist these basic monitoring tools be negotiated out of the agreement. The licensee may think it is wise to have vague terms and conditions and to negotiate away audit rights; however, this can easily backfire on the licensee as costs are quickly accelerated if the licensor must litigate and undertake discovery as opposed to the less expensive alternative of an audit to seek discovery.

7.3. IP Inventory Monitoring

If the intellectual property is a physical inventory unit, such as a shirt or DVD, or software under end user license agreements, then the licensee must install proper inventory controls to avoid findings associated with unaccounted-for intellectual property. Trademark licensees concentrate on sales and often forget they must also appropriately account for all the licensed intellectual property, not just what has been sold.

For trademark licensed products, licensees get in trouble because they don't adequately monitor the disposition of all intellectual property, such as units shipped for free, research and development, and scrap. What licensees don't always realize is that if they can't account for these units that are not sold, then the licensees often owe a royalty as the assumption is made the units were sold.

For software downloads under end user agreements, licensees must install systems that allow them to periodically monitor the installations. Any company with more than 1000 installations of a software will certainly be audited. Plus, employees can get a reward from licensors for turning in companies that don't properly license all of their software in use.

7.4. Preparing for the Royalty Audit

A licensee should be formally notified of a royalty audit by a notification letter. The notification letter typically will identify the agreement(s) to be audited, the scope period of the audit, who will be conducting the audit, contact information, and next steps. On receiving the notification letter, the licensee should consider the team to manage the audit if such a team has not been previously identified. Building a team is important as there are many different challenges that may be encountered during a royalty audit, including document retrieval from both information systems and hard copy format, contract interpretation, inventory counts, production and manufacturing inspections, and sales. The team may include participants from departments such as accounting, legal, finance, executive management, and production.

After the team is established, the licensee should establish a lead person to whom all communications should be focused so that a consistent message is sent to the auditor. This person should make certain that all requests are written and all responses answer the questions posed.

The licensee should begin to prepare by reading the agreement, identify all auditable areas, and performing a self-assessment, generally under attorney-client privilege/attorney work product to identify any potential exposures. After that work is completed, the licensee can decide if they will report any discovered adjustments to the reported royalty statements. Some licensees find it best to immediately pay additional royalties due in hopes of avoid interest payments and sparking an audit cost recovery provision; however, the typical auditor will still calculate interest and have a finding for audit cost recovery.

The licensee should insist the auditor define all areas to where the auditor desires to test so that any out-of-scope questions may be addressed early on, and the auditor is instructed of any restrictions.

The following steps will help make certain that you are adequately preparing for the royalty audit:

1. Review the contract to understand the audit rights with an emphasis on the period that can be audited and what can be audited under the audit rights.

   - **Audit Rights:** First, make certain there are audit rights. If there are, then check the time period allowed under the audit rights, such as two years from the date of the notification letter. Many auditors will attempt to go beyond those two years allowed under the agreement. The acceptable period can be identified in a non-disclosure period the auditors sign so that they resist testing unauthorized areas.

     The audit rights also often talk about what is auditable, such as "sales." If there are limitations you may wish to clarify with the auditors, they are only able to audit what is provided for under the agreement (hence the reason for the licensor to include language that allows auditing just not sales or royalty records).

     Read the terms and conditions to establish whether the software publisher indeed has the right to audit the business in the first place. Understand the terms and conditions of noncompliance.

   - **Audit Cost Recovery:** Understanding the threshold for audit cost recovery often drives the level of effort a company may wish to take to help admitting fault. Of course, also understanding or capping audit costs is helpful. Early on, the licensee should check if the royalty auditor is being paid on a contingency basis, and therefore any cost recovery is based on reasonable hourly rates and not the contingency if the contingency exceeds the hourly rates. Of course, if the contingency is less than the hourly rates that would be charged not under a contingency arrangement, then efforts should be made to make certain the audit costs paid, if payable, are what the auditor has actually been paid.

   - **Understand Interest Rates for Late Payments and Other Noncompliance:** Understand if interest can be charged only on late royalty payments or underpayments,or if it can be charged on any penalties resulting from noncompliance. Then, make certain the interest rate is allowable by law (not usury).

   - **Determine What Can be Audited so You Can Prepare:** Many companies mistakenly believe the auditor will just be interested in financial terms such as costs or revenues, but auditors will go through an agreement and often try to audit anything auditable—that is if there is a restriction or requirement, the auditor will test to see if there is compliance, such as territories for sale, copyright notification, design approval, advertising expenditures, or other items. If the auditor is attempting to audit different areas, the auditee should first make certain it is permissible under the agreement and then know the exposure or risks for noncompliance, so proper planning and support can be provided to the auditor.

2. **Consider How You Would Like Your Company Presented to the Auditor and the Contractor:** Actions should be taken to make certain you are shown in the most favorable light. You can control this by clearly understanding the documents that are requested and providing only the most basic information required to comply with the contracts audit compliance requirements. It is helpful to obtain a draft of the report style the auditor will plan to deliver to the contractor during the non-disclosure approval (NDA) process, so the report can be reviewed and an assessment made if the report will include any undesirable areas. If so, action can be taken to help manipulate how the auditor is allowed to present the information and the information that may be presented to the contractor. Often, the NDA can be used to clarify the report and may only include confidential information that directly relates to a contract violation.

3. **Establish Communication Protocols:** The auditor should be required to make all requests in writing and send periodic open item lists.

4. **Establish Field Dates the Auditor Will be Allowed to Work:** This helps prevent a run-on audit with the auditor coming and going and disrupting your company's operations. The auditor should work within an agreed number of days.

5. **Identify Internal Resources to Support the Audit and Restrict or Control Auditor Communications Through a Point Person.**

6. **Perform a Self-Audit**: This can vary by the type of audit. For example, if it is a software vendor audit, check that software and hardware inventory is up-to-date and licensed; the software is being used only as licensed; there are sufficient numbers of licenses to cover all users; software inventory titles reports can be generated for all machines and the information is accurate; proof of purchases and license agreements are ready for inspection; paperwork is in order, including invoices showing payment for license agreements and proper certificates of license are available; there are adequate records in place to demonstrate an understanding of where all licensed software is located, including user names and machines; and license types are understood in conjunction with the computing environment. Additionally, for a software license audit, the licensee's right monitor, generally the IT department, must provide evidence that upgrades are monitored and licensed. Having a well-documented enterprise-wide Software Asset Management (SAM) system in place will help reduce the exposure to financial liabilities from

the licensor as any misreporting can be shown to be unintentional, and actions have been taken to help prevent misreporting. As the self-audit is performed, if there are instances of unlicensed product, it is best to acknowledge the underlicensed products or work out a settlement with the licensor prior to the start of the audit and pay the license fee as just removing the overdeployed software will be discovered by the auditor who will examine historic deployment records, and this also increases the likelihood of interest and audit cost penalties being added if the underreporting is found by the auditor as opposed to self-reported.

7.5. Non-Disclosure Agreement (NDA)

A licensee should require the execution of a non-disclosure agreement by the auditor. To help avoid delays in the audit, the NDA should be forwarded to the auditor after initial disclosure of the royalty audit to help prevent negotiation delays. A sample NDA is included in Appendix V.

The NDA needs to be adjusted to allow the auditor to maintain confidential documents required to support her work as this is required by American Institute of Certified Public Accountant standards. Auditors should maintain the confidentiality of these documents at the same standard as their own personal confidential documents.

7.6. Communications with the Licensor

The licensee should maintain excellent communications with the licensor. This sounds logical, but many licensors and licensees find themselves in disputes, especially when sales don't meet projected goals. Further, as management changes, disputes arise when changes to agreements are not memorialized and communication protocols have not been established.

Licensees should proactively partner with the licensors to make certain all activities, internal controls, marketing, confidentiality, security and other items will meet the demands of the licensor.

7.7. Creating the Control Environment

For the honest licensee, perhaps one of the top reasons for underreporting or other contract breaches is the lack of proper internal controls. As a new license agreement is implemented, the licensee should make certain a properly trained financially trained individual with the assistance of legal personnel, draft a contract summary of all points for compliance and then designs controls to make certain the contract is not breached.

A licensor can take the first step in supporting the licensee's compliance with the contract by dictating the minimum standards for the licensee to maintain for a proper internal control environment. This is often, at a minimum, defined in the royalty statement by identifying the items that must be reported.

There are two types of internal controls, "preventive" and "detective." The best internal controls are "preventive," meaning the noncompliance is prevented from occurring in the first place. Licensees should focus on establishing preventive internal controls. Detective internal controls only work to capture the breach after it might have occurred. As examples, assume a contract limits deductions from list price to 10 percent. A preventive internal control is one that will not allow an invoice to be created with a discount greater than 10 percent such as a system control that limits this 10 percent discount; however, a detective internal control would be one where the system allows any discount percentage to be entered, and hopefully someone will catch a discount in the review process that is was granted greater than 10 percent.

As mentioned earlier in the book, an SEC reporting entity may need to comply with Sarbanes-Oxley reporting requirements. If royalties are material to the organization, this will include establishing an internal control environment that includes the proper reporting of royalties. Therefore, a licensee must bear in mind not only the license agreement requirements to properly report royalties but also the legal requirements under SEC regulations.

7.8. How to Avoid Being Audited

Licensees generally have a series of criteria to identify licensees to be audited that go beyond gut instinct. Therefore, if a licensee is aware of these items, they can take steps to help avoid being audited.

The #1 reason for selecting a licensee for audit is dollars reported. The higher the royalties reported (or anticipated to have been reported), the greater the chance of being audited for the simple reason that findings will help cover the costs of the audit and result in additional revenues to the licensee.

To help avoid being audited, the licensee should make certain that royalty reports are always on time with the proper payments being made on time, also. Further, periodic conversations with licensor personnel help ensure the licensor that communications are strong, and therefore, royalties are accurate (even if it is a false sense of security.

The following are additional reasons why licensees are generally selected for audit. By helping to control these factors, a licensee can help avoid an audit:

b. Not previously audited or no audit within the last three years.
c. Significant findings from the last audit.
d. Licensee is late on royalty payments.
e. Licensee does not make royalty payments as projected.
f. Licensee royalty payments just meet minimum guarantees.
g. Licensee has underreported royalties to another licensor, and licensors talk to each other to find out who is underreporting (or licensor employees go from company to company through normal job transitions and bring the knowledge of underreporting with them).
h. Licensee is facing financial difficulties.
i. Licensee is not responding to e-mails and other communications.
j. Licensee reported sales do not match public announcements of sales.
k. Licensee is not provided requested information in royalty statements.
l. Sales personnel "hear" the licensee is underreporting.
m. The licensee is in a country known for high underreporting such as Brazil, China, Korea, and Japan.
n. IP is being dumped on the market.
o. There is a lot of grey market activity.
p. Contract is up for renewal
q. Royalties are not increasing as expected in an expanding market, or royalties are decreasing faster than expected.
r. Licensee begins to market competitive IP.
s. Confusing side agreements to amendments to the original agreement.
t. Licensee is involved in litigation with other licensors.
u. Royalties have fluctuated more than expected on a quarterly basis.
v. A high number of returns.
w. Licensee is not answering questions.

After the notification is received, many licensees seem to believe a delay tactic will cause the auditor to disappear to more important or easier jobs. Unfortunately for the licensee, such delay tactics generally cause the auditor to want to inspect the licensee even more as the auditor questions what is being hidden and why the delays. Therefore, from what I have seen, the best method to ward off an announced audit is for the licensee to contact the licensor and question why the audit is occurring and working to make the audit of a very limited scope.

APPENDIX

|

Sample License Agreement

I.1. Trademark License Agreement   280

I.2. Exhibit A—Licensed Product Approval Form   323

I.3. Schedule to Trademark License Agreement   324

I.1. Trademark License Agreement

THIS TRADEMARK LICENSE AGREEMENT (this *"Agreement"*) is made effective as of _____, 20__ (the *"Effective Date"*), by and between _____, a _____Corporation with its principal place of business at _____ (*"Licensor"*), and _____, a _____ with its principal place of business at _____(*"Licensee"*).

Recitals

WHEREAS, _____ (the *"Master Licensor"*) is the sole owner of the registered trademarks "_____," "_____" and "_____" (such trademarks, together with all registrations and any and all common-law rights pertaining thereto, are referred to collectively as the *"Licensed Marks"*) and has granted to Licensor the exclusive right and license (the *"Master License"*) to design, manufacture, advertise, promote, sell, distribute, and license to others the right to design, manufacture, advertise, promote, sell and distribute, high quality _____ and various other products bearing the Licensed Marks and to use the artwork and designs provided by _____ (the *"Master Licensor Properties"*); and

WHEREAS, Licensee desires to obtain the right to use the Licensed Marks and Master Licensor Properties on and in connection with the design, manufacture, advertisement, promotion, sale and distribution of Licensed Products (as defined below) bearing, incorporating or otherwise utilizing the Licensed Marks and the Master Licensor Properties in the Territory (as defined below); and

WHEREAS, Licensor has agreed to grant to Licensee such license under and subject to the terms and conditions hereinafter set forth.

Agreement

NOW, THEREFORE, for and in consideration of the premises and the mutual promises and conditions contained herein, the parties hereby agree as follows:

1. Definitions

As used in this Agreement, the following terms shall have the meanings set forth below:

1.1 *"LBMG"* has the meaning set forth in Section 15.1 hereof.

1.2 *"Affiliate"* means, with respect to any party, its officers, directors, shareholders, members, partners, parents corporations, subsidiary corporations, partnerships, joint ventures or other entities that are under common ownership with such party (whether incorporated or not), and any other entity that, directly or indirectly, controls, is controlled by or is under common control with, that entity; provided, however, that in each case any such other entity shall be considered to be an Affiliate only during the time period during which such control exists. For purposes of this definition, "control" (including, with correlative meaning, the terms "controlled by" and "under common control with"), as used with respect to any entity, shall mean the possession, directly or indirectly, of the power to direct and/or cause the direction of the management and policies of such entity, whether through the ownership of voting securities, by contract or otherwise.

1.3 *"Advertising"* means any communication of any kind or nature, whether now existing or developed in the future, by Licensee through any medium (including without limitation electronic and computer-based systems) directed to the trade or the public, including trade and public directory listings, store window displays, posters, point of sale materials, broadcasts, radio, brochures, pamphlets, business cards, trade shows and billboards. Advertising shall not include free licensed product distributions, parties, employee events, and the like.

1.4 *"Allowances"* means any written credits actually given after sale by Licensee to its customers for any purpose, other than Returns, Payment Terms Discounts and Closeout Discounts and freight expenses.

1.5 *"Closeouts"* mean out of season, discontinued and end of season Licensed Products that remain merchantable and are sold (i) at a reduction of more than ten percent (10%) from the respective Listed Wholesale Price and/or (ii) to a Licensor approved liquidator.

1.6 *"Closeout Discounts"* means all discounts of more than ten percent (10%) from the Listed Wholesale Prices of Licensed Products that are discontinued and end of season and that are actually given by Licensee to its customers.

1.7 *"COA" has the meaning set forth in Section 6.1.15 hereof.*

1.8 *"Days"* means calendar days unless specifically referred to as "business days."

1.9 *"Distributor Contract"* has the meaning set forth in Section 6.2.2 hereof.

1.10 *"Earned Royalties"* means royalties in an amount equal to **[ten percent (10%) for F.O.B. In Sales or twelve (12%) for F.O.B. Out Sales]** of Net Sales of all Licensed Products for the applicable License Year, but only to the extent that such calculated amount exceeds the Guaranteed Royalty for the applicable License Year.

1.11 *"Effective Date "* has the meaning set forth in the introductory paragraph of this Agreement.

1.12 *"Employee Discounts"* has the meaning set forth in Section 4.3.3 hereof.

1.13 *"Expiration Date"* means _____, 20__.

1.14 *"F.O.B. In Sales"* means those sales that occur when Licensed Products are shipped by or on behalf of Licensee form a location within or outside the Territory for delivery to a customer located in the Territory.

1.15 *"F.O.B. Out Sales"* means Sales of Licensed Products by the License where the customer takes title and/or risk in such Licensed Products at the place of manufacturer.

1.16 *"Guaranteed Royalties"* means the following aggregate minimum guaranteed royalties for each License Year:

License Year	Amount
Year 1 period ending _____, 20__	$
Year 2 period ending _____, 20__	$
Year 3 period ending _____, 20__	$
Year 4 period ending _____, 20__	$
Year 5 period ending _____, 20__	$

1.17 *"Gross Sales"* means Licensee's sales of Licensed Product units invoiced, shipped or paid for, whichever occurs first, multiplied by the respective Listed Wholesale Price of such Licensed Product.

1.18 *"Initial Term"* has the meaning set forth in Section 3.1 hereof.

1.19 *"Inventory"* has the meaning set forth in Section 12.2 hereof.

1.20 *"Inventory Statement"* has the meaning set forth in Section 12.2 hereof.

1.21 *"Key Money"* means the meaning set forth in Section 4.1.1 hereof.

1.22 *"License"* means the exclusive, nonassignable right to use the Licensed Marks and Master Licensor Properties in connection with the design, manufacture, advertising, promotion, sale and distribution of the Licensed Products in the Territory.

1.23 *"License Quarter"* means calendar quarters, i.e., each of the three-month periods during each License Year from (i) January through March, (ii) April through June, (iii) July through September, and (iv) October through December, provided, that the first quarter shall be the period commencing as of the Effective Date and continuing through the end of the calendar quarter in which the Effective Date falls; and provided further, that if the expiration or termination of this Agreement is effective other than at the end of a License Year, then the final period of less than three (3) months ending on the effective date of such expiration or termination shall be deemed to be a License Quarter.

Quarter	Period	Royalty Statement Due
First Quarter	January 1 Through March 31	April 30
Second Quarter	April 1 Through June 30	July 31
Third Quarter	July 1 Through September 30	October 31
Fourth Quarter	October 1 Through December 31	January 31

1.24 *"License Year"* with respect to any License Year other than Year 1, means the period commencing as of the date of expiration of the previous License Year and shall continue for twelve (12) successive calendar months, with the First License Year ending **[eighteen (18) months/fifteen (15) months/twelve (12) months]** from the Effective Date.

1.25 *"Licensed Marks"* means only those trademarks as specified in the Recitals set forth above. Other Master Licensor trademarks may be added upon mutual written agreement of the parties, in which case, all such trademarks shall be deemed Licensed Marks for all purposes hereunder. This Agreement does not grant to Licensee any right to any variation of the Licensed Marks. Licensor shall have the sole right to determine the manner and use each of the Licensed Marks and Master Licensor Properties in connection with each particular Licensed Product.

1.26 *"Licensed Products"* means those products listed in the Schedule to this Agreement attached hereto and made a part hereof, and all bearing the Licensed Marks and Master Licensor Properties. From time to time Licensor may authorize Licensee to manufacture and distribute products bearing the Licensed Marks and Master Licensor Properties not expressly listed in the Schedule to this Agreement, in which case, such products shall be deemed Licensed Products for all purposes hereunder. Absent the mutual written agreement of Licensor and Licensee with respect to such products, all such products shall not be deemed Licensed Products for all purposes hereunder.

1.27 *"Licensor"* means _____, a corporation organized under the laws of _ _____.

1.28 *"Licensee"* means _____, a corporation organized under the laws of _____.

1.29 *"Listed Wholesale Price"* means the price of a Licensed Product as calculated using the MSRP (defined below) minus the any discounts granted to customers or distributors.

1.30 *"Manufactured Suggested Retail Price"* ("MSRP") means the price of a Licensed Product stated on the applicable Licensed Product Approval Forms submitted to Licensor pursuant to Section 7.3.

1.31 *"Master License"* has the meaning set forth in the Recitals above.

1.32 *"Master Licensor"* has the meaning set forth in the Recitals above.

1.33 *"Master Licensor Properties"* has the meaning set forth in the Recitals above and means all intellectual and industrial property interests now or hereafter owned by Master Licensor, other than the Trademarks, whether or not copyrightable or patentable, including, without limitation, manufacturing formulas, concepts, designs, trade dress and similar materials in and to any Licensed Products or components thereof and to any prints, package designs, containers, bottles, tubes or other packaging and form thereof (including the shape and graphic design), tooling, molds, sketches, artwork, labels, Advertising and any promotional materials using or used in conjunction with any of the Trademarks or the Licensed Products or components thereof, whether created by or on behalf of Master Licensor or Licensee and embodied in any form whatsoever (including without limitation, electronic media, computer discs and hard drives).

1.34 *"Materials"* has the meaning set forth in Section 7.3.1 hereof.

1.35 *"Manufacturers"* means the manufacturers appointed by the Licensee to manufacture and/or assemble the licensed products, components of Licensed Products, labels, hang tags, packaging and/or any other item related to the Licensed Products and any further manufacturers appointed by such manufacturers, including without limitation factories, suppliers and facilities.

1.36 *"Minimum Net Sales"* means the minimum amount of Net Sales of Licensed Products that Licensee is required to achieve for each License Year, as set forth in the following schedule:

License Year		Amount
Year 1 period ending _____, 20__	$
Year 2 period ending _____, 20__	$
Year 3 period ending _____, 20__	$
Year 4 period ending _____, 20__	$
Year 5 period ending _____, 20__	$

1.37 *"Net Sales"* means the Gross Sales at which Licensee bills its customers for Licensed Products less only (i) credits to customers for Returns, Payment Terms Discounts, Closeout Discounts and Allowances, as specifically permitted by this Agreement, and (ii) sales, use or value added tax assessed on sales (only where applicable, actually paid and not reimbursed through tax credits or other offsets, and specifically excluding any franchise, remittance, gross receipts or income taxes). No other deductions, whether for unpaid or uncollectible accounts, bad debts, late shipment charges, warehousing violations, chargebacks or other discounts given or costs incurred by Licensee shall be taken.

1.38 *"Other Agreements"* has the meaning set forth in Section 11.5 hereof.

1.39 *"Payment Terms Discounts"* means all discounts from the Listed Wholesale Price actually given by Licensee to its customers for timely payment, that are customary in the trade and the terms of which are specified on the face of such customer's invoice.

1.40 *"Product Samples"* has the meaning set forth in Section 7.3.1 hereof.

1.41 *"Renewal Term"* has the meaning set forth in Section 3.2 hereof.

1.41 *"Returns"* means Licensed Products actually returned to Licensee by its customers multiplied by the unit prices actually credited to the customers for such Licensed Products.

1.42 *"Royalties"* shall mean, collectively, the Guaranteed Royalties, the Earned Royalties and any other royalties due to Licensor or its designee hereunder.

1.42 *"Rules"* has the meaning set forth in Section 22.1 hereof.

1.43 *"Sell-Off Period"* has the meaning set forth in Section 12.1 hereof.

1.44 *"Term"* has the meaning set forth in Section 3.2 hereof.

1.45 *"Territory"* means _____. Licensee understands and agrees that Licensor may itself manufacture, authorize third parties to manufacture, and/or license to third party in the Territory, the Licensed Products for ultimate sale outside of the Territory in accordance with the terms and conditions hereof.

2. Grant Of License

2.1 *License*

2.1.1 Licensor hereby grants to Licensee an exclusive, nonassignable, nontransferable license, during the Term of this Agreement (and any Sell-Off Period, if applicable), and subject to all the terms and conditions contained in this Agreement, to use, manufacture, sell, have used, have manufactured and have sold, Licensed Products utilizing the Licensed Marks and the Master Licensor Properties, including, without limitation, on or in association with the design, manufacture, distribution at wholesale, sale, marketing, promotion and Advertising of the Licensed Products, as well as on the packaging, promotional and Advertising material associated therewith, in the Territory, provided, however, that Licensor and its Affiliates may also Advertise and otherwise promote the Licensed Products.

2.1.2 Licensee hereby recognizes and acknowledges that Licensor also licenses other products (other than the Licensed Products) to other licensees and that evolving changes make it difficult to define with absolute specificity the various products covered by the different licenses granted by Licensor. Licensor and Licensee agree to use their best efforts to avoid any conflicts between Licensed Products and products covered by other licenses granted by Licensor. In the event of conflict between this Agreement and other license agreements to which Licensor is or becomes a party, Licensor reserves the right to resolve such conflicts in its absolute discretion, taking into account the intent of this Agreement with respect to the license granted to Licensee for Licensed Products and the protection of the Licensed Marks and Master Licensor Properties. Licensor's decisions in resolving any conflicts shall be final and binding.

2.2 *Rights Not Granted*. It is understood and agreed that this license shall pertain only to the Licensed Products and does not extend to any other products or services. All rights not specifically granted herein are hereby expressly reserved by Licensor, including, but not limited to, the following:

2.2.1 Nothing contained in this Agreement shall prohibit Licensor (on behalf of itself or its Affiliates) from selling any services or goods other than the Licensed Products in any or all area(s) of the world, including the Territory.

2.2.2 Licensor and its Affiliates shall be authorized to sell the Licensed Products to Licensor retail stores, Licensor licensed stores, and to any retail stores of an Affiliate of Licensor.

2.2.3. This Agreement is not an assignment or grant to Licensee of any right, title or interest in or to the Licensed Marks or Master Licensor Properties, or any of Master Licensor's other trademarks, other than the grant of rights to use the Licensed Marks and Master Licensor Properties subject to the terms and conditions of this Agreement. Licensor expressly does not grant to Licensee the right to use any variation of the Licensed Marks that now exist or hereafter are developed by Master Licensor, Licensee or any other person.

2.3 *Minimum Net Sales*. Notwithstanding anything in this Agreement to the contrary, if Licensee's Net Sales in any License Year are less than the required minimum for such License Year, then Licensor shall have the right, at its sole election, to either: (i) terminate this Agreement by deeming the failure to be an incurable default under this Agreement; or (ii) declare Licensee to be in default of this Agreement, in which case, Licensee shall have the right to cure such default. Such termination or declaration shall be immediately effective upon the receipt by Licensee of written notice from Licensor, which shall be sent no later than forty-five (45) Days after Licensor's receipt of the Royalty Statement for the end of such License Year and which evidences such shortfall. If Licensor elects to terminate this Agreement pursuant to this Section 2.3, Licensee shall pay to Licensor no later than ten (10) Days after the effective date of such termination all Earned Royalties and any other amounts due hereunder through the effective date of termination pursuant to Section 12.4 hereunder.

2.4 *Outside the Territory*. Licensee shall not authorize any use, advertisement, promotion, distribution or sale, direct or indirect, of the Licensed Products in any geographic region outside the Territory and will not knowingly sell or supply the Licensed Products to distributors, other subcontractors or other persons who intend or are likely to export in any geographic region outside the Territory. If Licensee learns that any distributor, other subcontractor or other person to whom/which Licensee has sold Licensed Products has exported Licensed Products from the Territory, it shall cease selling or supplying Licensed Products to such person or entity, or buying from such person or entity. Nothing herein shall be deemed to preclude Licensee from purchasing from subcontractors, including manufacturers, located outside of the Territory for distribution solely within the Territory.

2.5 *Additional Restrictions*. Notwithstanding anything to the contrary contained in this Agreement, Licensee shall have no right to open or operate, directly or indirectly, a free-standing retail store, or department within a retail store, using the Licensed Products or the Master Licensor Properties or copyrighted material on or in connection with such store or the signage for such store.

2.6 *Sales in United States Dollars*. All sales by Licensee shall be invoiced in United States dollars, and Licensed Products shall be invoiced separately from products which are not Licensed Products.

3. Term Of Agreement

3.1 *Initial Term*. This Agreement, the License granted hereunder and the provisions hereof, except as otherwise provided, shall be in full force and effect on and as of the Effective Date, and shall continue for a period ending on the Expiration Date (the "*Initial Term*"), unless sooner terminated as provided herein.

3.2 *Renewal Term*. On the condition that Licensee has met the Minimum Net Sales requirements for the final License Year of the Initial Term, and on the condition that Licensee is in full compliance with all other material terms and conditions of this Agreement, including the timely payment of all amounts required to be paid under this Agreement, at Licensor's sole election, the parties shall enter into good faith negotiations for the renewal of this Agreement for an additional period of **[five (5) years]** (a "*Renewal Term*" and together with the Initial Term, the "*Term*"), on the same terms and conditions set forth herein, provided, however, that Licensee and Licensor shall mutually agree upon revised Guaranteed Royalties, Earned Royalties and Minimum Net Sales for each License Year of such Renewal Term, and provided further, that additional Key Money, in an amount to be determined by Licensor, shall be required. Licensee shall forfeit such Key Money, and Licensor shall not be required to refund such Key Money to Licensee, in the event that the Initial Term or any other Term terminates early or this Agreement is not ultimately in fact renewed despite Licensee's payment of Key Money for purposes of renewal, regardless of the reason therefore. Licensee shall deliver written notice to Licensor of its desire to renew this Agreement at any time during the Initial Term or Renewal Term but no less than sixty (60) Days prior to expiration of the Initial Term or Renewal Term. Notwithstanding the foregoing, if the Master License terminates for any reason prior to the expiration of the Term (including the Initial Term and Renewal Term), this Agreement shall automatically terminate upon termination of the Master License. Expiration or termination of this Agreement shall not affect any obligation of Licensee to make payments hereunder accruing prior to, or after, such expiration or termination, as applicable.

4. Compensation

4.1 *Royalties*. In consideration of the rights granted to Licensee pursuant to this Agreement, Licensee shall pay to Licensor the following:

4.1.1 *License Fee*. Licensee shall pay to Licensor or its designee a non-refundable, non-recoupable fee of _____ Dollars ($_____,____) ("*Key Money*") immediately upon execution of this Agreement.

4.1.2 *Guaranteed Royalties*. Licensee shall pay to Licensor or its designee the required minimum Guaranteed Royalties for each License Year. Guaranteed Royalties for License Year 1 shall be payable immediately upon execution of this Agreement. Guaranteed Royalties for subsequent License Years shall be payable in four (4) equal quarterly installments, each equal to twenty-five percent (25%) of the Guaranteed Royalties for the License Year in question, payable on the first day of each License Quarter.

4.1.3 *Earned Royalties*. In addition to the Guaranteed Royalties, Licensee shall pay to Licensor or its designee Earned Royalties for each License Year. Such Earned Royalties shall be remitted to Licensor or its designee along with Licensee's delivery of its Royalty Statement for the fourth quarter of the applicable License Year pursuant to Section 4.2 below.

4.2 *Royalty Statements*. By the last day of the month following the completion of a License Quarter as set forth in Section 1.19, and, if applicable, within twenty (20) Days after the conclusion of the Sell-Off Period, Licensee shall furnish to Licensor or its designee, in the same manner as required for notices under Section 17 hereof, an itemized statement certified to be true and correct by the Chief Financial Officer, Chief Executive Officer or President of Licensee, setting forth the following for each such License Quarter and the License Year through such period, or for the Sell-Off Period, if applicable: (a) a listing of Licensee's accounts and the accounts of Licensee's Affiliated and third-party distributors in the Territory and the units and description of all the Licensed Products sold and distributed to each such account or otherwise disposed of by Licensee or by Licensee's Affiliated and third-party distributors, to the extent reasonably practicable broken down by SKU # and/or Style #; (b) the computations of Net Sales on all such sales; and (c) the computation of Earned Royalties and the amount of Earned Royalties due and payable. If Licensee fails to submit a Royalty Statement when due, Licensor may terminate this Agreement within sixty (60) Days after the end of such License Quarter as though Licensee had failed to achieve the acquired Minimum Net Sales for the current License Year, except that Licensee shall have the opportunity to cure such default within ten (10) Days after receipt of written notice from Licensor that such Royalty Statement has not been received.

4.3 *Deductions/Returns/Closeouts*

4.3.1 Subject to 6.1.7 hereof, only the following deductions from Gross Sales will be permitted for each License Year for the purpose of calculating Net Sales:

(a) The combined total of Allowances, Payment Terms Discounts and Closeout Discounts shall not exceed twelve percent (12%) of the Gross Sales of Licensed Products sold, with the exception of authorized third-party distributors, for which the combined total of all Allowances, Payment Terms Discounts and Closeout Discounts shall not exceed thirty percent (30%) in the case of third-party distributors who have executed written Distributor Contracts, and twelve percent (12%) in the case of third-party distributors who have not executed written Distributor Contracts; and

(b) Returns of units of Licensed Products shall not exceed ten percent (10%) of the total Licensed Products sold in the applicable License Year.

(c) Gross Sales, all deductions and Net Sales dollar amounts must be clearly identified in Licensee's sales journal.

4.3.2 In each License Year, Closeout units shall not exceed twenty percent (20%) of total Licensed Product units sold in such License Year.

4.3.3 Notwithstanding the foregoing, Licensee shall be allowed to give discounts to employees for personal use as long they do not exceed fifty percent (50%) per Licensed Product purchased ("*Employee Discounts*"); provided, that the combined total of all Employee Discounts shall not exceed one-tenth of one percent (0.1%) of the Gross Sales of Licensed Products sold; and provided further, Licensee shall maintain an accurate listing of all items sold to each employee, by item and by name, and may not sell any unapproved or defective items to employees. Such Employee Discounts shall not be counted toward the Allowances, Payment Terms Discounts and Closeout Discounts limitations set forth above.

4.3.4 Without limitation to any other rights that Licensor may have under this Agreement, if Allowances, Payment Terms Discounts, Closeout Discounts and/or Employee Discounts exceed the permitted percentages described in subsection 4.3.1(a) above for a License Year, Licensor shall have the right in each case to adjust Licensee's Net Sales requirement upward by the amount of the overage, and Licensee shall promptly pay the increased Royalties, Advertising royalties and any other amounts owed as a result thereof.

4.3.5 Without limitation to any other rights that Licensor may have under this Agreement, if Returns exceed the permitted percentage for a License Year pursuant to Section 4.3.1(b) above, Licensor shall have the right to adjust Licensee's Net Sales requirement upward by the amount that is the product of (i) the average price of the Returns during the License Year, multiplied by (ii) the number of units in excess of the maximum percentage of Returns permitted, and Licensee shall promptly pay the increased Royalties, Advertising royalties and any other amounts owed as a result thereof.

4.3.6 Without limitation to any other rights that Licensor may have under this Agreement, if Closeout units exceed the permitted percentage for a License Year pursuant to Section 4.3.2 above, Licensor shall have the right to adjust Licensee's Net Sales requirement upward by the amount that is the product of (i) the average discount given on Closeouts during the License Year, multiplied by (ii) the number of units in excess of the maximum percentage of Closeouts permitted, and Licensee shall promptly pay the increased Royalties, Advertising royalties and any other amounts owed as a result thereof.

4.3.7 Notwithstanding anything contained herein, no deductions whatsoever will be permitted for reserves of any kind, including reserves for bad debts, nor for any actual write-offs of bad debts.

4.3.8 Notwithstanding anything contained herein, Licensee may not manufacture Licensed Products specifically for closeout, off-price and/or discount accounts of any kind, nor may it sell less than first-quality Licensed Products to such accounts. Any closeout, off-price, discount or similar account which may be approved by Licensor (for the limited purpose of Licensee's sales of Closeouts) may only be sold Licensed Products which are actually Closeouts, namely, discontinued merchandise. Each Closeout Licensed Product must retain the original, separate and individual SKU, and the original, separate and individual MSRP (with the applicable discount shown separately in Licensee's records and reports) as each were submitted to Licensor on the Licensed Product Approval Form. Licensee's records and reports must be maintained so as to permit identification of specific, individual Closeouts, as set forth above.

4.3.9 All Gross Sales, Net Sales, Allowances, Payment Terms Discounts and Closeout Discounts shall be listed separately and clearly identified in Licensee's sales ledger used to calculate Net Sales. Any such items not clearly identified, as determined by Licensor or its auditors in their sole discretion, shall not be deductible from the calculation of Net Sales for the applicable period.

4.3.10 Except as otherwise specifically provided in this Agreement, if Licensee sells or otherwise transfers any or all of the Licensed Products to any individual or entity, in whole or in part, directly or indirectly owned or controlled by Licensee, in common ownership with Licensee, an officer, director, member shareholder of Licensee, or otherwise Affiliated with Licensee, at an invoice price that is less than the price that Licensee charges to non-affiliated full-priced customers, then the invoice price charged to the affiliated individual or entity, for purposes of calculating Net Sales, shall be deemed to be the current invoice price charged to nonaffiliated full-priced customers.

4.4 *Price/Liquidation.* Licensee acknowledges that any significant reduction in the Listed Wholesale Price of, or material liquidation of, the Licensed Products would cause serious harm to the quality and goodwill associated with the Licensed Marks, Licensor and Licensor's business activities in the Territory. Should Licensee do so, without Licensor's approval, Licensor may elect, at its sole option, to treat any such occurrence as an incurable default by Licensee under this Agreement and may terminate this Agreement if such goods are not removed from the market within ten (10) Days of Licensee's receipt of written notice from Licensor.

4.5 *Manner of Payment.* All payments due hereunder shall be made in United States currency drawn on a United States bank and payable, at Licensor's election, either by check made payable to Licensor delivered to the address designated by Licensor or wire transfer into an account designated by Licensor, unless otherwise specified by Licensor. No deduction shall be made for income or other taxes without Licensor's written permission, unless Licensee is compelled to do so by law, in which case Licensee shall provide Licensor with evidence in the form of an original tax withholding certificate in the name of Licensor issued by the government taxing authority in the relevant jurisdiction that such tax has been paid in the proper amount. Licensee shall give due notice to Licensor of any such proposed deductions. Licensee shall make no further deductions without prior approval from Licensor based on satisfactory documentation presented by Licensee to Licensor. In the event payments in the manner provided in this Section shall become impossible or illegal by reason of the action of governmental authority, then, at Licensor's option, this Agreement may be terminated; and whether or not Licensor exercises such option, while such restrictions remain in effect, all payments due to Licensor shall be made to an account in the Territory, or elsewhere permitted by law, to be designated by Licensor.

4.6 *Interest on Late Payments.* Any late payments due hereunder, including, but not limited to, all payments of Royalties and shortfalls (whether found on audit or otherwise), shall incur interest at the rate of the greater of the highest amount allowed by law or one and one-half percent (1.5%) per month from the date such payments were originally due to date of payment.

5. Books and Records; Audits

5.1 *Books and Records.* Licensee agrees that it will be keep accurate and complete books and records of account (including, without limitation, utilization of consecutively numbered invoices which reconcile to each Royalty Statement and Licensee's general lender) covering all transactions relating to or arising out of this Agreement in accordance with Generally Accepted Accounting Principles. Such books and records shall be maintained separately from Licensee's documentation relating to other items manufactured or sold by Licensee and shall include manufacturing records, purchase records, and any electronics database, sales, inventory and all other documents and material in the possession of or under the control of Licensee or any of its Affiliates with respect to the subject matter of this Agreement. Licensee will obtain and maintain such accounting, information, communication and operating systems and capabilities as Licensor may require from time to time, including systems or processes that will allow its records to be exportable to Excel to assist Licensor's auditors. At all times during the Term of this Agreement and any time following its termination or expiration, Licensor or

Licensor's auditors shall have the right at all reasonable times during normal business hours and on reasonable notice to Licensee to inspect and make copies of Licensee's books and records at the place or places where such records are normally retained by Licensee or any of its Affiliates. The Licensor's auditors shall not be required to sign a non-disclosure agreement, as the auditors shall be bound by the confidentiality provisions of this Agreement. Receipt or acceptance by Licensor of any Royalty Statement furnished pursuant hereto or any sums paid by Licensee hereunder shall not preclude Licensor from questioning the correctness thereof at any time, and if one or more inconsistencies or mistakes are discovered by Licensor in such Statement, it or they shall be rectified in an amended Royalty Statement received by Licensor no later than ten (10) Days after the date of receipt by Licensee of notice of that which should be rectified. Licensee shall also provide special reports as reasonably requested by Licensor's auditors to properly complete their audit obligations, including, but not limited to, reports showing inventory roll forwards, sales by SKU number and discounts by customer.

5.2 *Discrepancies*. In the event that such inspection reveals a discrepancy in the amount of Royalties or other amounts owed to Licensor under this Agreement from what was actually paid, Licensee shall pay such discrepancy, plus interest, calculated at the rate of the greater of the highest amount allowed by law or one and one-half percent (1.5%) per month, no later than thirty (30) Days after the earlier of receipt of notice or knowledge thereof by Licensee. In the event that such underpayment discrepancy is in excess of twenty percent (20%) in any License Year, then Licensor may elect to treat such occurrence as an incurable default under this Agreement. In the event that such inspection reveals or Licensor or Licensee otherwise discovers an overpayment of Royalties or other amounts paid to Licensor, the amount of such overpayment shall be credited against future payment of any or all of the Guaranteed Royalties and Earned Royalties or, in the event of the expiration or termination of this Agreement and there is no such future payment, such amount shall be paid by Licensor to Licensee no later than thirty (30) Days after the discovery thereof by Licensor or Licensee, subject to Licensor's rights of setoff, recoupment and counterclaim. In the event that such inspection reveals that for any License Quarter covered by such inspection there is a discrepancy of five percent (5%) or more in the amount of Royalties or other amounts owed Licensor under this Agreement from what was actually paid, Licensee shall reimburse Licensor for the cost and expenses of such inspection, including any accounting and/or attorney fees and expenses incurred in connection therewith, and shall pay to Licensor a nonrefundable Ten Thousand Dollar ($10,000) audit administration fee, which shall be payable by Licensee to Licensor no later than ten (10) Days following Licensee's receipt of notice of such discrepancy from Licensor. If such discrepancy is less than five percent (5%), such expenses shall be borne by Licensor.

5.3 *Maintenance of Records*. All books and records, including records of Certificates of Authenticity ("COAs"), relative to Licensee's obligations hereunder shall be maintained and kept accessible and available to Licensor for inspection for at least three (3) years after termination or expiration of this Agreement or, in the event of a dispute between the parties hereto, until such dispute is resolved, whichever is later.

5.4 *Failure to Maintain Records*. Licensee acknowledges that its failure to maintain the appropriate and accurate books of account and records required hereunder will constitute a material breach of its obligations hereunder and will cause substantial damage to Licensor. If an inspection reveals that Licensee's reporting and/or record keeping are not in accordance with Licensor's requirements, including, without limitation, missing sales records or inaccurate inventory records or other records maintained by Licensee, which require Licensor to perform alternative procedures which increase the cost of inspection, Licensee shall pay Licensor for such increased costs. In the event that alternative procedures cannot be performed for missing records or other failure by Licensee to comply with Licensor's requirements under this Section 5, Licensee shall pay to Licensor an amount equal to not less than twenty-five percent (25%) of the Royalties due for the License Year in question and not more than one hundred percent (100%) of such Royalties due, to be determined in Licensor's sole discretion. Licensee shall pay fees charged hereunder within five (5) Days of written demand by Licensor. [Alternative language—If the records kept by the Licensee are insufficient to enable the Licensor to establish the amount of Royalties due from the Licensee to the Licensor under this Agreement, the Licensor shall, in its sole discretion, make a reasonable estimate of such Royalties, based upon such information as its readily available in relation to the relevant market and the Licensee's business, and such estimate shall be binding upon the Licensee."]

5.5 *Disaster Business Resumption Plan*. The Licensee shall, and shall insure that is Manufacturers shall, establish a disaster business resumption plan in respect of any computer systems used by the Licensee or its Manufacturers in relation to the Licensed Products to enable such system to be restored to full operation within seven (7) days of any failure, damage to or destruction of all or any part of such system. The Licensee shall provide a written report summarizing such disaster business resumption plans to the Licensor and, if requested, by the Licensor, demonstrate such plans to Licensor or its representatives.

6. Covenants, Representations and Warranties of Licensee

In addition to its duties and obligations set forth elsewhere in this Agreement, Licensee covenants, warrants and represents the following:

6.1 *Use, Covenants and Obligations*

6.1.1 Subject to Licensor's prior written approval, Licensee shall commence bona fide commercial sales of the Licensed Products as soon as practicable after the Effective Date of this Agreement, but in no event later than two hundred forty (240) Days after the Effective Date. Failure of Licensee to commence sales by such date shall be grounds for immediate termination of this Agreement at Licensor's sole option.

6.1.2 Licensee represents and warrants that: (i) it has the full right, power and authority to enter into this Agreement and to perform all of its duties and obligations hereunder and will not enter into any contract, agreement or understanding with any third party which would in any way restrict or prevent Licensee form the performance of its duties and obligations hereunder during the Term or Sell-Off Period of this Agreement; and (ii) it is financially capable of undertaking the business operations which it conducts and of performing its obligations hereunder.

6.1.3 Licensee agrees that it will, during the Term or any Sell-Off Period: (i) make diligent effort and use its best efforts to promote, develop, manufacture, market, sell, distribute and ship the Licensed Products; (ii) continuously and diligently fill all accepted purchase orders for Licensed Products; and (iii) procure and maintain facilities and trained personnel sufficient and adequate to accomplish the foregoing, all to be determined in Licensor's sole reasonable discretion.

6.1.4 Licensee shall be solely responsible for the design, manufacture, production, sale and distribution of the Licensed Products and will bear all related costs associated therewith.

6.1.5 Licensee shall be responsible for obtaining, at its own expense, any and all licenses, permits, and approvals (including governmental and all other licenses, permits, and approvals) necessary for Licensee to: (a) design, manufacture, advertise, promote, sell and distribute the Licensed Products; (b) pay taxes and the Guaranteed Royalties and Earned Royalties required hereunder; and (c) fulfill any and all other duties and obligations and exercise the rights of Licensee under this Agreement.

6.1.6 During each License Year, Licensee agrees to supply to Licensor or its designee, at no cost to Licensor or its designee, up to and including

$_____$ worth (wholesale) of Licensed Products each License Year for promotional purposes. No royalty will be due on these no cost items provided to Licensor.

6.1.7 Licensee agrees to sell to Licensor and its Affiliates such quantities of Licensed Products as Licensor and its Affiliates may order for their own account for resale or distribution by Licensor or its Affiliates. The price of such Licensed Products shall be at the Listed Wholesale Price, minus the greater of twenty-five percent (25%) or the highest discount provided by Licensee to others (excluding Employee Discounts and discounts to Licensee's approved close-out liquidators) during the previous six (6) months, with sales terms net sixty (60) Days. Such sales shall be included in the calculation of Licensee's Net Sales, subject to the payment of Earned Royalties and included in the Royalty Statement. Licensee shall ship or deliver such Licensed Products either directly to Licensor or its Affiliates, or as Licensor or its Affiliates may direct, to any other person or entity, in reasonable commercial lots.

6.1.8 If Licensee's Licensed Products are considered "accessories" (e.g., hats, sunglasses, jewelry) then Licensee agrees to sell to Licensor and its Affiliates such quantities of Licensed Product accessories as Licensor and its Affiliates may order for their own account for resale or distribution in Licensor shoe and accessory stores. The price for such Licensed Products shall be at the Listed Wholesale Price, minus forty percent (40%), with sales terms net sixty (60) Days. Such sales shall be included in the calculation of Licensee's Net Sales, subject to the payment of Earned Royalties and included in the Royalty Statement. Licensee shall ship or deliver such Licensed Products either directly to Licensor or its Affiliates, or as Licensor or its Affiliates may direct, to any other person or entity, in reasonable commercial lots. Licensor and/or its Affiliates may at its and/or their sole and absolute discretion open Licensor titled shoe and accessory stores, but are in no way obligated to do so.

6.1.9 Without Licensor's prior written consent, Licensee shall not design, manufacture, advertise, promote, distribute, sell or deal with in any way in the Territory any product or material that is, in Licensor's sole and absolute judgment, competitive with or confusingly similar to any or all of the Licensed Products or Materials.

6.1.10 Licensee shall not use color combinations, designs, styles, logo treatments, graphics or packaging unique to any or all of the Licensed Products on or in connection with any product other than the Licensed Products, and Licensee, without charge, hereby assigns, perpetually and irrevocably, to Licensor ownership of all rights that Licensee has acquired or may acquire in such color combinations, designs, styles, logo treatments, graphics or packaging.

6.1.11 Licensee may not sell, directly or indirectly, any Licensed Products on the Internet without the prior written consent of Licensor; provided, that Licensee may advertise the Licensed Products on Licensee's own Web site with a link to Licensor's (or its designee's) Web site; and provided further, that Licensee shall not be considered to be "selling indirectly" on the Internet if Licensee sells to high-end department stores like Barney's, Nordstrom, Saks Fifth Avenue, Neiman Marcus and Bloomingdales, which also offer the Licensed Products for sale online.

6.1.12 Licensee shall use the Licensed Property only in such manner as will comply with the provisions of applicable rules, laws and regulations relating to the Licensed Property and Licensee's use of the Licensed Property. Licensee shall also comply with the procedures, policies and other requirements of Licensor's International Security & Anti-Counterfeiting Program.

6.1.13 Licensee shall not have the right to use Licensee's name on or in connection with the Licensed Products, except with the prior approval by Licensor of the use and placement of Licensee's name. Licensee shall, at the option of Licensor, include on its business materials and/or the Licensed Products an indication of the relationship of the parties hereto in a form approved by Licensor.

6.1.14 Licensee shall not use or permit or authorize another person or entity in its control to use the words of Licensor's name: "_____," "_____" or "_____" as part of a corporate name, trade name (e.g. doing business as name), domain name, or in connection with any Web materials without the express written consent of Licensor and Licensee shall not permit or authorize use of the Licensed Marks in such a way so as to give the impression that the Licensor names "_____," "_____," "_____" or any other Licensed Mark, or any modifications thereof, is the property of Licensee.

6.1.15 All Licensed Products shall be marked with a Certificate of Authenticity ("*COA*") provided by Licensor. All COAs shall be secured to the Licensed Products and inventoried. The Licensee and/or its subcontractor, must account for all COAs provided by Licensor during an audit and must retain damaged COAs for inspection by auditors. Licensee shall maintain records of the number of COAs received from Licensor, number of COAs used on Licensed Products, and number of COAs destroyed, lost or otherwise destroyed. Further, COAs shall be physically counted on a quarterly basis by Licensor and compared to inventory records. Missing COAs of more than one-half of one percent (0.5%) shall be reported to Licensor on each quarterly Royalty Statement. Any discrepancy of more than two-tenths of one percent (0.2%) of COAs shall result in a royalty due to Licensor equal to the average MSRP for Licensed Products sold in the period(s). Licensee shall not sell or otherwise transfer any COAs to third parties.

6.1.16 All of Licensee's activities in connection with the design, merchandising, packaging, promotion, sales and display of any products other than the Licensed Products shall be separate and distinct from Licensee's activities relating to the Licensed Products.

6.2 *Subcontracting*

6.2.1 Licensee may subcontract the manufacture of any or all component parts of any or all of the Licensed Products bearing the Licensed Marks and the Master Licensor Properties pursuant to this Agreement, provided: (i) Licensee notifies Licensor in advance of any intended supplier/ subcontractor and obtain Licensor's prior written approval of such supplier/ subcontractor; (ii) Licensee obtains from each such supplier/subcontractor an executed written agreement in a form acceptable to Licensor, and (iii) furnishes a copy of each such executed agreement to Licensor.

6.2.2 Subject to Section 6.2.3 below, Licensee may subcontract with third-party distributors for the distribution of the Licensed Products in the Territory pursuant to this Agreement, provided: (i) Licensee notifies Licensor in advance of any intended third-party distributor; (ii) Licensee obtains from each Licensor-approved third-party distributor an executed written agreement acceptable to Licensor (the "*Distributor Contract*"); and (iii) Licensee furnishes a copy of each Distributor Contract to Licensor. For purposes of this Section, third-party distributors shall not include any distribution entity which is an Affiliate of Licensee. In addition, Licensee shall be responsible for obtaining from each of its distributors, whether third party or Affiliate, an Inventory Statement of such distributor's inventory and supplying a copy to Licensor of such inventory listing meeting the requirements and within the time frames set forth in Sections 6.3 and 12.2 hereof. Licensor's failure to approve or disapprove of a choice of distributor by Licensee within fourteen (14) Days after Licensor's receipt of written notice of the choice of contractor, Licensor's silence will be deemed acceptance of the distributor.

6.2.3 Licensee may subcontract with third-party international distributors for the distribution of the Licensed Products in the Territory pursuant to Section 6.2.2 above; provided, that Licensee shall offer a right of refusal to Licensor's authorized network of international distributors to distribute the Licensed Products internationally within the Territory.

However, in the event that Licensor's authorized international distributor does not accept the offer on the same terms and conditions as contained in the offer and/or is unable to distribute the Licensed Products, then Licensee may accept the offer of a third-party international distributor of its own choosing. Licensee shall enter into a Distributor Contract with each third-party international distributor pursuant to the terms and requirements of Section 6.2.2 above.

6.2.4 Licensee shall be permitted to allow any manufacturer, distributor or other subcontractor of the Licensed Products to use the Licensed Marks and Master Licensor Property solely to the extent necessary to perform its obligations under the relevant agreement with Licensee. Each such agreement shall contain restrictions on such use consistent with the restrictions contained herein. Nothing contained in this Section 6.2 shall be construed to relieve Licensee of its obligations and responsibility to ensure that its manufacturers, distributors and other subcontractors, whether third-party or Affiliate, perform their duties in accordance with the terms and conditions of this Agreement, including, but not limited to, approved distribution channels and Territory restrictions and Licensee shall remain liable for any breach or default of the applicable terms and conditions of this Agreement by any such persons or entities. In the event of any such violation, Licensor shall have the right, but not the obligation, to do any of the following: (i) require Licensee to immediately terminate, upon receipt of written notice from Licensor, the relevant agreement with such manufacturer, distributor or other subcontractor, at which time Licensee shall immediately and permanently cease selling
to or supplying any or all of the Licensed Products to such person or entity; (ii) declare the License granted under this Agreement to be non-exclusive, or (iii) terminate this Agreement, effective immediately upon receipt by Licensee of written notice from Licensor, by deeming any such violation to be an incurable default by Licensee under this Agreement. No such manufacturer, distributor or subcontractor shall be permitted to sublicense to any other person or entity the rights granted to it with respect to the Licensed Property without the prior written consent of Licensor.

6.2.5 The manufacture, packing and storage of the Licensed Products shall be carried out only at premises approved by the Licensor or its nominee in writing from time to time. The Licensor or its nominee shall be entitled at any time on 72 hours written notice to the Licensee to enter any premises used by the Licensee or its Manufacturers for the manufacture, packaging or storage of the Licensed Products, to inspect such premises, all plant workforce and machine used for manufacture, packaging or storage of Licensed Products and all other aspects of the manufacture, packaging and storage of Licensed Products. The Licensee shall, and shall insure that its Manufacturers shall make any changes or improvements to its premises, plant, workforce, machinery and other aspects of the manufacture, packaging and storage of Licensed Products as the Licensor or its nominee may reasonably request.

6.3 *Inventory*. Insofar as reasonable, Licensee shall at all times during the Term be able to fulfill all orders for the Licensed Products promptly and yet not have an excessive inventory defined as no greater than three (3) months of inventory on hand at the time of the expiration or termination of the License. Licensee shall conduct at least semiannually a physical inventory count of Licensed Products in inventory and shall maintain records reflecting inventory counts and adjustments. Within forty-five (45) Days after each semiannual period and within ten (10) Days of receipt of a request from Licensor or its auditors, Licensee will furnish Licensor with a complete and accurate statement signed by the Chief Financial Officer, Chief Executive Officer, or President of the Licensee, setting forth in detail the quantities and description of each of the Licensed Products in work in process and finished goods inventories of the Licensed Products and the locations thereof. Any missing items of inventory shall be treated as if such items had been sold and shall be included in the calculation of Net Sales at the MSRP of such missing items for purposes of calculating Royalties, Advertising royalties and other payments due by Licensee hereunder. Failure to maintain adequate levels of inventory at all times shall be considered a breach of this Agreement, except that Licensee shall have the opportunity to cure such default within ten (10) business days after receipt of written notice from Licensor that such levels of inventory have not been properly maintained.

6.4 *Distribution Channels*. Licensee shall exercise its best efforts to safeguard the prestige and goodwill represented by the Licensed Marks and Master Licensor Properties and the images associated therewith at the same level as heretofore maintained by Master Licensor and Licensor. Licensee shall use its best efforts to exploit the rights granted hereunder throughout the Territory, including, without limitation, selling commercial quantities of the Licensed Products on a timely basis and maintaining a sales force sufficient to provide effective distribution of the Licensed Products throughout the Territory. Except as otherwise provided herein, the distribution of Licensed Products in the Territory shall be performed only by Licensee. Except as otherwise expressly permitted herein, Licensee will sell the Licensed Products only to quality high-end department stores, high-end boutiques, and retail stores (which have been previously approved by Licensor in writing) offering services and promotions commensurate with the quality of the Licensed Products and the image and reputation of the Licensed Marks and Master Licensor Properties. Licensee shall use its best efforts that the same safeguards apply to its distributors and that its distributors and retail operators agree not to ship any Licensed Products outside the applicable Territory or to an unapproved store or chain of stores. Licensor and Licensee agree to reasonably attempt to settle all differences of opinion as to whether or not a specific store or chain of stores is an acceptable channel for the sale and distribution of the Licensed Products, but Licensor's decisions in this matter shall govern and control. Sales through discounters are prohibited unless otherwise approved in writing by Licensor, although Licensee is authorized to liquidate end of season over-runs, collectively constituting no more than ten (10%) percent of overall annual sales, through Licensor's authorized liquidator(s); provided, that the discount granted to authorized liquidator(s) shall not be greater than fifty percent (50%). The discount granted to other discounters approved by Licensor shall be determined by Licensor in its sole discretion. Failure to remove a store or retail outlet deemed to be unacceptable by Licensor as a channel and its related inventory within thirty (30) Days' written notice shall be deemed an incurable breach of this Agreement.

6.4.1 The Licensee shall not supply Licensed Products for use in promotions, giveaways, free price draws, competitions, fundraisers or sweepstakes or for charitable causes with the prior written approval of the Licensor.

6.5 *Closeouts*. Prior to Licensee's sale of any Closeouts, Licensee shall furnish to Licensor a Licensed Product description of such Closeouts and the proposed selling price. Licensor shall have the option (but not the obligation) to purchase all or any part of such Closeouts from Licensee prior to sale to any third party, upon the following terms: (i) Licensor shall notify Licensee of its intention, if any, to exercise this option and which of the Closeouts are to be purchased, within ten (10) business days after Licensor's receipt of the Licensed Product description of the Closeouts; (ii) the purchase price and terms relating to the Licensed Products for Closeouts shall be the same price and terms relating to the Licensed Products Licensee plans to offer to a discounter approved by Licensor; and (iii) Licensee shall deliver Closeouts purchased by Licensor within fifteen (15) business days after receipt of the notice of Licensor's intention to purchase.

7. Legal Notices, Quality Control and Samples

7.1 *Compliance with Legal Requirements*. Licensee shall fully and completely comply with the marking provisions of the trademark, patent and copyright laws of the United States and other jurisdictions included in the Territory. Licensee also shall design, manufacture, package, sell and distribute the Licensed Products in accordance with all applicable national, state and local laws and regulations. Licensee shall not cause, condone or authorize: (i) the use of any substandard or offensive materials in or in connection with any of the Licensed Products; (ii) any violation of any federal, state, or local law or regulation, including, but not limited to, child labor laws, laws relating to sexual discrimination, and provisions of any law for regulation imposing advertising standards or requiring trade or content description of the Licensed Products; or (iii) the use of Licensed Marks, Master Licensor Properties or any other word, device or symbol associated in any way with any or all of Licensor and its subsidiaries and Affiliates in connection with any product or activity that is not the subject of this Agreement.

7.2 *Legal Notices; Affixation of Licensed Marks and Master Licensor Properties; and SKU Number Affixation*. Licensee shall affix permanently to each Licensed Product a unique SKU number which shall be identical to the SKU number used to identify the respective Licensed Product in all of Licensee's books and records. Each Licensed Product shall bear the Licensed Marks and Master Licensor Properties in the form required by Licensor, and Licensee shall cause to appear on the Licensed Products, as well as all labels, hang tags, inserts, wrappers, packaging, Web sites, and promotional material used in connection therewith, such legends, markings and other legal notices as Licensor may reasonably request from time to time.

7.3 *Quality of Licensed Products*

7.3.1 Licensee recognizes that each of Master Licensor and Licensor has a reputation for high quality and that Licensee must maintain such quality on all Licensed Products. Licensee agrees that Licensor shall have the right to approve or disapprove: (i) the quality, style and design of all Licensed Products (including packaging); (ii) the presentation or style of the Licensed Marks used in connection therewith; and (iii) production samples of all Licensed Products. In connection therewith, Licensee shall notify Licensor of each new seasonal collection of Licensed Products and for each season of each License Year, Licensee shall submit to Licensor (or its designee) for written approval as to quality, samples of Licensed Products ("*Product Samples*") and samples of any other items bearing the Licensed Marks and Master Licensor Properties or intended for use in connection with the Licensed Products, including, but not limited to, photography, cartons, containers, labels, hang tags, inserts, wrappers, packaging, fixtures, displays, artwork and printing, marketing and promotional materials related to the Licensed Products (collectively referred to as the "*Materials*") for approval by Licensor at no cost to Licensor. All such items shall be submitted with a completed Licensed Product Approval Form in the form of *Exhibit A* attached hereto. Such Product Samples and Materials shall be provided to Licensor at each stage of development per season per License Year and shall include, but not be limited to: (a) an initial sketch or photograph; (b) a sample prototype or equivalent acceptable to Licensor; and (c) with respect to Product Samples, two (2) samples as actually manufactured or produced in final form as intended to be sold and distributed by Licensee. Licensee must obtain Licensor's written approval of each stage of development of any Licensed Products or Materials before proceeding to the next stage, and in no event shall Licensee commence or permit the manufacture, advertising, promotion, sale or distribution of any the Licensed Products or the Materials unless and until Licensee has received Licensor's written approval of the samples provided pursuant to this Section. The Licensed Products and Materials each season shall conform to the style approved by Licensor's design department.

7.3.2 Licensor shall have the sole and absolute discretion to approve or withhold approval of any and all of the Licensed Products, the Materials and samples of either throughout each stage of development pursuant to Section 7.3.1 above. Notwithstanding the above, both parties recognize that time is of the essence in obtaining and granting such approvals. Failure of Licensor to approve such Product Samples or Materials within fifteen (15) business days after receipt of such samples will be deemed approval. Once a Product Sample or Material has been approved by Licensor, Licensee shall not materially depart therefrom in the making of future Licensed Products and Materials without Licensor's prior express written consent.

7.3.3 To insure that each of the Licensed Products and the Materials are constantly maintained in conformance with the previously approved samples pursuant to Sections 7.3.1 and 7.3.2 above, Licensee shall, within seven (7) Days after receipt of a request from Licensor, send or cause to be sent to Licensor at Licensee's expense: (a) such actual samples requested by Licensor of the Licensed Products and the Materials Licensee is using, manufacturing, selling, distributing, or otherwise disposing of; and (b) a listing or revised listing of each location where any of the Licensed Products and the Materials or either thereof are designed, manufactured, stored, or otherwise dealt with, except to the extent such listing or revised listing duplicates currently accurate information provided pursuant to Section 7.3.1 hereof. Licensor and its nominees, employees, agents, and representatives shall have the right to enter upon and inspect, at all reasonable hours of the day, any and all such locations(s) and to take, without payment, such samples of any of the Licensed Products and the Materials as Licensor reasonably requires for the purposes of such inspection, subject to two (2) Days' notice to Licensee.

7.3.4 If any of the Licensed Products or Materials sent or taken pursuant to Section 7.3.3 hereof, or which otherwise comes to the attention of Licensor, does or do not conform in Licensor's sole reasonable opinion to the previously approved samples, Licensor shall so notify Licensee, in writing, specifying in what respect such of the Licensed Products or Materials is or are unacceptable. Immediately upon receipt of such notice, Licensee shall suspend all manufacture, sale, and distribution of, and shall obtain back from Licensee's accounts, all such Licensed Products and Materials and shall not resume the manufacture, sale, or distribution thereof unless and until Licensee has made all necessary changes to the satisfaction of Licensor and has received Licensor's written re-approval of each of such Licensed Products and Materials.

7.3.5 Except as otherwise specifically provided in this Agreement, all of the Licensed Products and the Materials that are not approved by Licensor or that are determined by Licensor to be non-conforming or unacceptable shall not be sold, distributed or otherwise dealt with by Licensee. All such Licensed Products and Materials shall be destroyed by Licensee with, if Licensor so requests, an appropriate certificate of destruction furnished to Licensor. Licensor, at its sole option, may elect to treat any and all sales, distribution or use by Licensee of unapproved, non-conforming or unacceptable Licensed Products or Materials as an incurable default under the terms of this Agreement. In the event Licensor elects not to exercise its termination rights pursuant to this Section 7.3.5, all Net Sales from such unapproved, nonconforming or unacceptable sold merchandise shall be payable to Licensor along with Licensee's delivery of its Royalty Statement encompassing such Net Sales pursuant to Section 4.2 above.

7.3.6 Licensee may engage, employ or utilize, at Licensee's sole cost, designers to develop Licensed Products and/or Materials. Licensee must obtain a written assignment, and shall supply Licensor with a copy of such assignment, from any such designer in favor of Master Licensor under which all of such designer's right, title, and interest, including, but not limited to, all rights of copyright, in and to such designer's work product is transferred and conveyed to Master Licensor to the maximum extent permitted by applicable law so that Master Licensor will be the sole owner of all rights therein on a so-called "work-for-hire" basis. Master Licensor through Licensor, in this case, will grant a license back to Licensee pursuant to Licensee's performance under the terms of this Agreement.

8. Intellectual Property Rights

8.1 *Exclusive Rights in Master Licensor*. Licensee acknowledges that, as between Licensee and Master Licensor, Master Licensor owns all right, title and interest, including intellectual property rights, in and to the Licensed

Marks and the Master Licensor Properties, subject to the license granted to Licensor under the Master License and the license granted to Licensee hereunder. Except for the license granted to Licensee hereunder, no other right, title to or ownership of the Licensed Marks or Master Licensor Properties in any form is granted to Licensee. This Agreement shall be deemed inferior and subject to any rights reserved by Master Licensor in the Master License. In the event of any conflict between rights granted hereunder and the rights retained by Master Licensor in the Master License, the Master License shall be deemed controlling. Licensee shall place appropriate notices, including notice of copyright, reflecting ownership of the Master Licensor Properties and the Licensed Marks by Master Licensor, on all plans, packaging, tags, containers, bottles, images, graphic designs, labels and Advertising and promotional materials.

8.2 *Registration*. Licensee shall cooperate fully and in good faith with Licensor and for the purpose of securing and preserving Master Licensor's right in and to the Licensed Marks and the Master Licensor Properties, including, without limitation, in the execution, submission and prosecution of any trademark, service mark, copyright or patent applications and similar applications for registration, and registered user agreements, which Master Licensor may desire to submit at any time and from time to time. Licensee shall not directly or indirectly submit any application to register the Licensed Marks or the Master Licensor Properties for the Licensed Products or any other products or services, or for any other trademark or service mark, copyright, design right or invention of Master Licensor, without the prior written approval of Master Licensor.

8.3 *Rights to the Licensed Marks and Master Licensor Properties*. Subject to the rights of Master Licensor, Licensee acknowledges Master Licensor's exclusive rights in and to the Licensed Marks and Master Licensor Properties. Licensee shall not, at any time during or after the Term of this Agreement, dispute, or contest, or attack the validity of, directly or indirectly, Master Licensor's exclusive right and title in and to the Licensed Marks and Master Licensor Properties, or any other trademarks, copyrights or such other intellectual or intangible property associated or connected with any or all of Licensor, Master Licensor, their Affiliates and licensees and sublicenses or their activities. Licensee shall not seek to avoid its duties or obligations hereunder because of an assertion or allegation by any person or entity that any or all of the Licensed Marks and/or Master Licensor Properties are invalid or because of any contest or dispute concerning the rights of or claimed by Master Licensor. Licensee shall not cause or grant permission to any third party or parties to acquire any copyright(s) or other proprietary right in connection with any word, device, design or symbol used by Licensee in connection with any of the Licensed Products or the Materials.

8.4 *Goodwill and Secondary Meaning.* Licensee acknowledges the great value of the goodwill associated with the Licensed Marks and the Master Licensor Properties and the worldwide recognition thereof; that the proprietary rights therein and goodwill associated therewith are solely owned and belong to Master Licensor; and that the Licensed Marks and Master Licensor Properties and other related words, devices, designs and symbols are inherently distinctive or have acquired secondary meaning firmly associated in the mind of the general public with Master Licensor and the activities of Master Licensor, Licensor and their Affiliates.

8.5 *Benefit.* Licensee agrees that its use of the Licensed Marks and the Master Licensor Properties inures to the benefit of Master Licensor and that Licensee shall not acquire any rights in the Licensed Marks and the Master Licensor Properties.

8.6 *Trademark and Copyright Protection.* Master Licensor and Licensor may seek, in Master Licensor's name and at its own expense, appropriate trademark, or copyright protection for the Licensed Marks. Except with the written consent of Licensor, Licensee shall not directly or indirectly register or attempt to register in any country, state or territory as a trademark or domain name, the Licensed Marks, or any word, name, symbol or design which is so similar thereto as to suggest some association with or sponsorship by Licensor or Master Licensor. In the event of a breach of the foregoing provision, Licensee shall, at its expense and at the request of Licensor, immediately terminate the unauthorized registration activity in question and promptly execute and deliver, or cause to be delivered to Licensor, or at the request of Licensor, to the Master Licensor, such assignments and other documents as it may require to effectuate the assignment and transfer to Master Licensor of all of the rights to the registrations or applications involved.

8.7 *Design Rights.* In addition to the covenants and obligations of Licensee under Section 6.1 hereof with respect to designs, all designs used by Licensee for the Licensed Products shall be used exclusively for the Licensed Products and may not be used under any other trademark or private label without the prior written consent of Licensor during the term of this Agreement. Licensee shall disclose and freely make available to Licensor, and obtain Licensor's written approval of, any and all developments or improvements it may make relating to the Licensed Products and to their manufacture, promotion and sales.

8.8 *Ownership of Copyright.* The parties acknowledge and agree that, as between each other, any copyrights created by or for the Licensed Products under this Agreement in any sketch, design, print, package, label, tag or the like designed and approved for use in connection with the Licensed Products will be the property of Master Licensor if it contains a Licensed Mark or other Master Licensor Properties. Licensee hereby perpetually and irrevocably transfers and conveys to Master Licensor to the maximum extent permitted by applicable law, all of Licensee's right, title and interest in all copyrightable matter (including style copyrights and design copyrights) created by Licensee under or in connection with this Agreement so that Master Licensor shall be the sole owners of all copyrights therein. Licensee may use these copyrights during and under the terms of this Agreement only.

8.9 *Protecting Intellectual Property*. Licensee agrees to execute any documents reasonably requested by Master Licensor and Licensor to effect any of the provisions of this Section 8.

9. Infringements

Licensee shall promptly notify Licensor in writing of each actual, suspect or apparent infringement or imitation of the Licensed Marks, the Master Licensor Properties and/or the Materials that come to the attention of Licensee. Licensor shall take such action in regard to such infringement or imitation as Licensor, in its sole and absolute judgment, deems to be appropriate. Licensor shall, in its sole and absolute discretion, decide whether to assert any claim or undertake or conduct any suit with respect to such infringement or imitation, but Licensee shall, upon receipt of written notice from Licensor, and pursuant to Licensor's instruction, on behalf of Licensor, assert any such claim, or undertake and conduct any such suit, at Licensee's expense, in the name of Licensor or Licensee or in both names as Licensor may direct. Licensee expressly covenants that no discussions whatsoever with the infringing or imitating party or parties, no compromise or settlement of any claim or suit and no negotiations with respect to any compromise or settlement of any such claim or suit shall be had, made or entered into without the prior written approval of Licensor. Licensee may share in fifty percent (50%) of any damage recovery or settlement obtained by Licensor or on Licensor's behalf by Licensee as a result of any such claim or suit only if Licensee notified Licensor in writing upon the initiation of such claim or suit that Licensee agrees to bear all the costs and expenses of such claim or suit. In no event shall Licensor be responsible to Licensee for any consequential or incidental damages that result from such infringement or imitation.

10. Insurance

Licensee shall obtain and maintain, at its own expense, no later than fifteen (15) Days from the Effective Date hereof, product liability insurance satisfactory to Licensor in an amount of Five Million Dollars ($5,000,000) in the aggregate and Two Million Dollars ($2,000,000) per occurrence of primary and umbrella coverage from one or more insurance companies, each with a Best's rating of "A" or better, and qualified to transact business in the Territory. Each such insurance policy shall name Licensor as additional insureds. Licensee shall evidence the insurer's agreement that such insurance shall not be amended, canceled, terminated or permitted to lapse without thirty (30) Days' prior written notice to Licensor and provide Licensor with a certificate of such insurance upon receipt of such policy by Licensee and on each anniversary date of the grant or issuance of each such policy during the Term and the Sell-Off Period, if any, evidencing that each such policy has not been altered with respect to the Licensor Indemnities in any way whatsoever nor permitted to lapse for any reason, and evidencing the payment of premium of each such policy. Licensee shall also cause each such policy to be in full force and effect prior to the commencement of any design, manufacture, advertising, promotion, sale, distribution or dealing with any or all of the Licensed Products whatsoever under this Agreement. Failure by Licensee to obtain the required insurance prior to such commencement or failure by Licensee to adequately maintain such insurance during the Term and the Sell-Off Period, if any, shall be an incurable default by Licensee under this Agreement and Licensor shall be entitled to terminate this Agreement. Regardless of whether Licensor elects to exercise such termination rights, Licensee shall pay to Licensor Thirty Thousand Dollars ($30,000) per License Year for any License Year for which such insurance is not obtained or maintained. Such amount shall be reduced on a pro rata basis for any days within the License Year that Licensee has obtained and maintained the required insurance.

11. Termination

The following termination rights are in addition to the termination rights provided elsewhere in this Agreement:

11.1 *Right of Termination by Licensor*

11.1.1 Licensor shall have the right to immediately terminate this Agreement by giving written notice to Licensee in the event of the occurrence of any of the following:

(a) Licensee files a petition in bankruptcy or is adjudicated as bankrupt or insolvent, or makes an assignment for the benefit of creditors, or an arrangement pursuant to any bankruptcy law, or if the Licensee discontinues its business or a receiver is appointed for the Licensee or the Licensee's business and such receiver is not discharged within thirty (30) Days. If this Agreement is so terminated, none of Licensee or its receivers, representatives, trustees, agents, administrators, successors or assigns shall have any right to sell or in any way deal with any of the Licensed Marks, Master Licensor Properties, Licensed Products or Materials, except with the prior written consent and under the instructions of Licensor, which all of such persons/entities shall be obligated to follow.

(b) Licensee breaches any of the provisions of this Agreement relating to the unauthorized assertion of rights in the Licensed Marks;

(c) Licensee fails, after receipt of written notice from Licensor, to immediately discontinue the distribution or sale of the Licensed Products or the use of any packaging or promotional material which does not contain the requisite legal legends;

(d) Licensee fails to achieve the required Minimum Net Sales during any License Year;

(e) Licensee's independent auditor issues a qualified opinion regarding Licensee's financial statements or an opinion stating that Licensee's financial situation raises substantial doubt about Licensee's ability to continue as a going concern (or the equivalent of such an opinion);

(f) There is a change in control of Licensee;

(g) Licensee at any time shall be in default of payment of any Royalties or other payment required hereunder and such default is not cured within ten (10) Days after receipt of written notice from Licensor specifying such default;

(h) Licensee at any time shall fail to perform any other material obligation hereunder and if such default is not cured within thirty (30) Days after Licensor shall have given Licensee written notice specifying such default; or

(i) Licensee breaches any other obligation under this Agreement which this Agreement expressly deems to be a noncurable breach.

11.1.2 The termination rights set forth in this Section 11.1 shall not constitute the exclusive remedy of Licensor hereunder. Licensor may resort to such other cumulative remedies as it would have been entitled to if this Section 11.1 had been omitted from this Agreement, including the right to seek damages.

11.2 *Termination of Master License.* In the event that the Master License terminates for any reason, this Agreement shall automatically terminate.

11.3 *Loss of Rights to Use Licensed Marks and Master Licensor Properties.* If Licensee's right to use any or all of the Licensed Marks and Master Licensor Properties is adjudged illegal, invalid or restricted and such adjudication has become final and non-appealable or Licensor and Master Licensor, in their sole discretion, choose not to appeal therefrom, or if a settlement agreement is entered into by Licensor, that prohibits or restricts Licensor's or Licensee's right to use the Licensed Marks and Master Licensor Properties, then this Agreement and the license granted hereunder shall automatically terminate without the necessity of any notice whatsoever as of the date such adjudication becomes final and non-appealable, the Licensor makes such choice not to appeal or the execution and delivery of such settlement agreement. Notwithstanding anything to the contrary in this Agreement, Licensee shall have no claim of any nature against Licensor for the loss of any or all right to use the Licensed Marks and Master Licensor Properties. If Licensee's right is adjudicated illegal in a particular geographic region in the Territory, then only the right to exploit the Licensed Marks in that region will be terminated.

11.4 *Termination Upon Impossible Performance*. Licensee and Licensor shall be released from their respective duties and obligations under this Agreement, and this Agreement and the license issued hereunder shall terminate, if governmental regulations or other cause arising out of a state of national emergency or war, or any other similar cause beyond the control of the parties hereto, shall render performance hereunder impossible. Either party hereto shall so notify the other in writing of any such cause and of its desire to be released, and upon receipt by the other of such notice, this Agreement shall terminate and all amounts owed under this Agreement (including, without limitation, all Earned Royalties on sales of the Licensed Products theretofore made) shall become immediately due and payable.

11.5 *Cross-Default*. In addition to, and without derogating from any other rights Licensor may have hereunder or under any other agreement between Licensor and Licensee, or otherwise, any breach or default by Licensee (or its successors or assigns) of any other agreement (collectively, the *"Other Agreements"*), between Licensor (or any Affiliate or assignee of Licensor) and Licensee (or its successors or assigns) may also be deemed by Licensor to be a breach or default by Licensee (or its successors or assigns) under this Agreement, and any breach or default by Licensee (or its successors or assigns) under this Agreement may also be deemed to be a breach or default by Licensee (or its successors or assigns) of any or all Other Agreements, and Licensor (or the applicable Affiliate or assignee of Licensor) shall be entitled to exercise any and all of its rights and remedies under the applicable agreements with respect thereto as if such breach or default occurred under such agreements.

11.6 *Mutual Agreement*. This Agreement may be terminated at any time by mutual written agreement of Licensor and Licensee.

12. Posttermination Rights and Obligations

12.1 *Sell-Off Period*. Upon expiration or termination of this Agreement, except for reason of a breach of Licensee's duty to comply with the quality control or legal notice marking requirements, and so long as Licensee is not in arrears in the payment of any amounts due and owing to Licensor, Licensee shall be entitled, for an additional period of ninety (90) Days, and on a nonexclusive basis, to continue to sell such Inventory in the Territory through Licensee's existing, recognized network of distributors (the *"Sell-Off Period"*). Such sales shall be made subject to all of the terms and provisions of this Agreement and to an accounting for and the payment of Earned Royalties thereon. Such accounting and payment shall be due and paid monthly, in accordance with the terms and conditions of this Agreement as though this Agreement were still in effect. Licensee acknowledges and agrees that the Sell-Off Period shall be considered a separate accounting period for the purpose of computing Earned Royalties due to Licensor for sales during such Sell-Off Period. Sales during the Sell-Off Period shall not be applied against any Guaranteed Royalties due or payable prior to the Sell-Off Period.

12.2 *Inventory Upon Termination or Expiration.* Upon termination or expiration of this Agreement or a Sell-Off Period, as the case may be, Licensee shall provide Licensor with a written statement (the *"Inventory Statement"*) indicating the quantity and description of each model or style number of Licensed Products bearing the Licensed Marks and/or Master Licensor Properties which Licensee had on hand or was in the process of manufacturing or having manufactured as of the date of the expiration or termination of this Agreement (collectively, the *"Inventory"*). Such Inventory Statement shall be delivered by Licensee to Licensor: (i) not more than thirty (30) Days after the expiration of this Agreement, (ii) not more than thirty (30) Days after expiration of the Sell-Off Period (if any), and (iii) not more than ten (10) Days after receipt by Licensee from Licensor notice of termination of this Agreement or a Sell-Off Period or the happening of any event not requiring notice of termination. Licensor shall have the option, at Licensor's own cost, of conducting a physical inventory in order to ascertain or verify such Inventory. In the event that Licensee refuses to permit Licensor to conduct such physical inventory or fails to timely deliver the Inventory Statement, Licensee shall forfeit its rights hereunder to a Sell-Off Period to dispose of such Inventory, and Licensor shall retain all other legal and equitable rights it has under the circumstances, which rights are hereby expressly reserved.

12.3 *Effect of Termination; Freedom to License.* Upon the termination or expiration of this Agreement or the Sell-Off Period, if any:

12.3.1 Except as otherwise provided in this Agreement, all rights granted herein shall immediately revert to Licensor who may use, or license others to use, the Licensed Marks and the Master Licensor Properties.

12.3.2 Unless otherwise approved in writing by Licensor or as permitted under Section 12.2 hereof, Licensee shall thereafter refrain from all further use of the Licensed Marks, Master Licensor Properties and Materials, and any further reference to such marks, direct or indirect, and of any term that is a simulation of the foregoing or is confusingly similar thereto and turn over to Licensor all materials relating to the Licensed Marks, Master Licensor Properties and Licensed Products in Licensee's possession, owned by Licensor or bearing the Licensed Marks and/or Master Licensor Properties, including, but not limited to, all Materials, and other artwork, color separations, prototypes and the like, as well as any market studies or other tests or studies conducted by Licensee at no cost whatsoever to Licensor.

12.3.3 Licensee shall destroy, or cause to be destroyed, all equipment capable of creating the Licensed Marks and Master Licensor Properties, including, without limitation, molds, tools, dies and printing screens.

12.3.4 Licensor reserves the right to purchase all or any portion of the remaining Inventory at Licensee's direct variable manufacturing cost. Licensor shall provide Licensee with written notice of its election or non-election to purchase all or a portion of the Inventory within fifteen (15) Days after Licensor's receipt of the Inventory Statement from Licensee. Any Inventory not purchased by Licensor shall be promptly destroyed by Licensee unless otherwise agreed between Licensor and Licensee, and Licensee shall provide Licensor with a certificate of destruction with respect thereto within ten (10) Days after Licensee's receipt of Licensor's written notice of its election to purchase or not purchase all or any portion of the Inventory.

12.3.5 Within ten (10) Days of after the expiration or termination of this Agreement or the Sell-Off Period, if any, Licensee shall provide Licensor with a written certification, signed by a duly authorized officer of Licensee, certifying that Licensee has complied with the provisions of this Section 12.3.

12.4 *Reserved Rights*. The expiration or termination of the license and this Agreement shall not: (i) relieve Licensor or Licensee, respectively, of any obligations incurred prior or subsequent to such expiration or termination, or (ii) impair or prejudice any of the rights of Licensor or Licensee, respectively, accruing prior or subsequent thereto as provided in this Agreement. Upon expiration or termination of this Agreement, notwithstanding anything to the contrary herein, all of Licensee's royalty obligations, including any unpaid portions of the Royalties, shall be accelerated and immediately shall become due and payable. All Royalties due hereunder for each License Year shall be non-refundable and shall not be credited toward royalties for succeeding License Years. In no circumstances whatsoever will Licensor be required to return to Licensee all or any portion of the Royalties, except as set forth in this Section 12.4 and Section 5.2 relating to overpayment discrepancies. Notwithstanding the foregoing, upon termination of this Agreement pursuant to Section 11.3. or 11.4 hereof, Guaranteed Royalties for the then current License Year shall be prorated based on the ratio that the numbers of days in such License Year prior to termination bears to the number of days in the License Year had the License and this Agreement not been terminated. Earned Royalties due for such License Year shall be the excess of Earned Royalties over such prorated Guaranteed Royalties. Any overpayment of Guaranteed Royalties or overpayment or underpayment of Earned Royalties based on such proration shall be immediately adjusted by the parties.

12.5 *Equitable Relief*. Licensee acknowledges that its failure to cease the use, manufacture, sale or distribution of the Licensed Products bearing the Licensed Marks or the Master Licensor Properties, or any class or category thereof, at the termination or expiration of this Agreement, except as provided for in Section 12.2 above, will result in immediate and irreparable damage to Licensor and to the rights of any subsequent licensee of Licensor. Licensee acknowledges and admits that there is no adequate remedy at law for failure to cease the use, manufacture, sale or distribution of the Licensed Products bearing the Licensed Marks or the Master Licensor Properties, and Licensee agrees that in the event of such failure, Licensor shall be entitled to equitable relief by way of injunctive relief and such other relief as any court with jurisdiction may deem just and proper.

12.6 *Survival*. Sections 1, 4, 5, 6, 8 and 11 through 28 shall survive any expiration or termination of this Agreement.

13. Indemnification

13.1 *Indemnification by Licensee*. Licensee shall defend, indemnify and hold Licensor and its Affiliates, successors, assigns, equity holders, directors, officers, employees and agents harmless against all costs, expenses and losses, claims, demands, damages, liability, causes of action (including without limitation product liability actions and tort actions), judgments, settlement, suits or expenses (including actual attorney fees) claimed, obtained or sustained by third parties in any way related to, arising from or in connection with (i) the design, manufacture, use, marketing, sale, promotion or distribution by Licensee of or any other dealing whatsoever with the Licensed Products or Materials; (ii) any alleged action or failure to act whatsoever by Licensee; (iii) any alleged non-conformity to or non-compliance by Licensee with any law pertaining to the design, quality, safety, advertising, promotion or marketing of any or all of the Licensed Products or the Materials; (iv) any alleged defect in any or all of the Licensed Products; or (v) any breach by Licensee of any of its covenants, representations, warranties, duties or obligations hereunder.

13.2 *Notice; Representation.* No later than ten (10) business days from receipt of notice of a suit or claim which involves the indemnification obligations of Licensee, Licensee shall provide written notice to Licensor of the indemnifiable suit or claim in question, it being understood, however, that Licensee shall have no liability for any delay in providing such notice if Licensor is not materially prejudiced by such delay. Licensor may, at its sole option, elect to assume the defense of any such claim or action, at Licensee's sole cost or expense, or permit Licensee to assume the defense of any such claim or action, at Licensee's sole cost or expense; provided, that if Licensor allows Licensee to assume such defense, Licensor shall have the right to approve any settlement offers, which shall not be unreasonably withheld, and shall not be obligated to consent to any settlement which does not include the delivery by the settling defendant of a full and final release of Licensor and Licensee from any and all liability with respect to the subject matter of such action. Licensor or Licensee, as the case may be, reasonably will assist the other party handling the defense of such claim or action in any settlement, suit or proceeding, provided that such assistance will be at the sole cost and expense of Licensee.

14. Advertising and Trade Shows

In order to protect the Licensed Marks and the Master Licensor Properties, and the quality and reputation of the Licensed Products, Licensee shall at all times maintain the high standards and consistency of the Licensed Products, Master Licensor Products, Licensed Products and image associated therewith in all Advertising, packaging and promotion of the Licensed Products. Licensee therefore agrees as follows:

14.1 *Advertising.* Simultaneously upon execution of this Agreement, Licensee shall execute an Advertising Royalty Agreement with Licensor Brand Management Group, LLC, an Affiliate of Licensor ("*LBMG*"), in the form presented by Licensor Brand Management Group, LLC, whereby Licensee shall pay to LBMG an amount equal to **[five percent (5%)]** of Net Sales for each License Year, payable quarterly, for purposes of advertising and promotion of the image of the Licensed Marks and Master Licensor Properties. Licensee shall also use its best efforts to Advertise and promote the Licensed Products throughout the Territory at its own cost and expense. Licensee shall submit to Licensor for Licensor's approval samples of all advertising and other promotional plans and materials that Licensee desires to use to promote the Licensed Products, the Licensed Marks and the Master Licensor Properties that have not been previously approved by Licensor, other than those developed by LBMG, at least thirty (30) Days prior to the commencement of each License Year.

14.2 *Trade Shows*. Licensee shall be required to attend and maintain a trade booth at all Licensor (or Licensor Affiliate) sponsored trade shows at Licensee's sole cost and expense and shall use its best efforts to attend other trade shows appropriate for the Licensed Products at Licensee's sole cost and expense; provided, that Licensee shall not be permitted to attend any trade shows that occur or are held at the same time as any Licensor (or Licensor Affiliate) sponsored trade show without the prior written consent of Licensor. Licensor recommends that Licensee attend international trade shows but is not required to do so. However, should Licensee attend an international trade show that Licensor is also attending, Licensee is required to purchase a trade booth from Licensor.

15. Assignment; Sublicensing

15.1 *No Assignment by Licensee Without Consent*. Licensor, in entering into this Agreement, is relying entirely upon Licensee's skills, reputation and personnel, including, without limitation, Licensee's officers, managers, directors, and shareholders. This Agreement and all rights, duties and obligations hereunder are personal to Licensee and shall not, without the prior written consent of Licensor (which may be given or withheld in the sole discretion of Licensor), be assigned, delegated, sold, transferred, leased, mortgaged or otherwise encumbered or changed by Licensee or by operation of law. Any attempt to do so without such consent shall be null and void and shall constitute an incurable default under this Agreement. If Licensor in its sole discretion believes that any change in any or all of the officers, managers, directors, and shareholders of Licensee has, will or could materially interfere with or materially and adversely affect Licensee's performance hereunder or the relationship between the parties hereto, Licensor may deem such change to be an incurable default under this Agreement and shall so notify Licensee. The consent of Licensor to any such assignment, delegation, sale, transfer, lease, mortgage, other encumbrance or change shall not be deemed to be consent to any subsequent assignment, delegation, sale, transfer, lease mortgage, other encumbrance or change.

15.2 *Licensor Right to Assign*. Licensor freely may assign this Agreement or assign or delegate any or all of its rights, duties and obligations hereunder to any of its Affiliates or to any third party individual or entity without Licensee's consent.

15.3 *Sublicensing.* Licensee may not, without the prior written approval of Licensor, in Licensor's sole discretion, enter into any sublicense agreement or grant any sublicense for any or all of the rights or obligations of Licensee under this Agreement or the License granted hereunder. The consent of Licensor to any sublicense agreement shall not be deemed to be consent to any subsequent sublicense agreement.

16. Succession

This Agreement shall inure to the benefit of and be binding upon the parties hereto, their heirs, administrators, subsidiaries, divisions, affiliated companies, and, to the extent permitted herein, their successors and assigns.

17. Notice and Payment

Any notice required to be given pursuant to this Agreement shall be in writing and delivered personally to the other designated party at the below stated address or mailed by certified or registered mail, return receipt requested, or delivered by documented overnight delivery service, or, to the extent that receipt is confirmed, telecopy, telefax or other electronic transmission service. Notices will be effective upon receipt.

        If to Licensor, to: _____

                                     _____

                                     _____

                                     Attention: _____

                                     Fax: (___) _____

    and if to Licensee, to: _____

                                       _____

                                     _____

                                     Attention: _____

                                     Fax: (___) _____

Either party may change the address to which notice or payment is to be sent by written notice to the other party in accordance with the provisions of this Section 17.

18. Relationship of Parties

The relationship between Licensor and Licensee is that of licensor and licensee of intellectual property rights. In its capacity as licensee, Licensee shall be acting only as an independent contractor, and not as a partner, co-venturer, agent, employee or representative of Licensor. Accordingly, Licensee shall have no authority, either express or implied, to make any commitment or representation on behalf of Licensor or incur any debt or obligation on behalf of Licensor. Nothing herein contained shall give or is intended to give any rights of any kind to any third persons.

19. Waiver

Failure by either party hereto to enforce any rights under this Agreement shall not be construed as a waiver of such rights, nor shall a waiver of a breach in any one or more instances be construed as constituting a waiver or as a waiver in other instances.

20. Governing Law; Venue

This Agreement shall be governed by and construed and interpreted in accordance with the laws of the State of California without regard to conflict of law principles, and Licensee shall in all cases be deemed to have agreed to submit to the jurisdiction of courts located in Los Angeles County, California and to venue therein.

21. Arbitration

21.1 *Parties' Consent to Arbitration and Waiver of Jury Trial.* Except as otherwise provided in this Agreement, Licensor and Licensee consent and submit to the exclusive jurisdiction and venue of the _____, for the adjudication of any dispute between Licensor and Licensee that arises out of or relates to this Agreement. Except as provided in this Agreement, any dispute, controversy or claim arising out of or relating to this Agreement shall be settled by binding arbitration heard by one (1) arbitrator (who shall be an attorney with experience in trademark matters), in accordance with the Commercial Arbitration Rules ("*Rules*") of the American Arbitration Association. The arbitrator shall be appointed in accordance with the Rules. The parties hereto agree that the venue of such arbitration shall be the _____. EACH OF THE PARTIES HEREBY KNOWINGLY AND PURPOSEFULLY WAIVES ITS RIGHT TO A JURY TRIAL RELATING TO ANY

DISPUTE, CONTROVERY OR CLAIM ARISING OUT OF OR RELATING TO THIS AGREEMENT.

21.2 *Powers*. The arbitrator shall be bound by the terms and conditions of this Agreement and shall have no power, in rendering the award, to alter or depart from any express provision of this Agreement, and the failure to observe this limitation shall constitute grounds for vacating the award. Except as otherwise may be provided in this Agreement, the arbitrator shall apply the law specified in Section 20 above. Any award of the arbitrator shall be final and binding upon the parties and judgment may be entered in any court of competent jurisdiction, including, without limitation, the courts of _____ or any federal court in _____. The award and judgment thereon shall include interest at the legal rate from the date that the sum awarded to the prevailing party was originally due and payable, and costs as set forth in Section 21.4.

21.3 *Provisional Remedies*. All provisional remedies shall be within the exclusive jurisdiction of the courts. The parties may seek and obtain provisional remedies prior to or contemporaneously with arbitration as permitted under the Rules. Licensee acknowledges and admits that the Licensed Marks and Master Licensor Properties possess a special, unique and extraordinary character, which makes difficult the assessment of monetary damages that Licensor might sustain by any use which is inconsistent with this Agreement, and that irreparable injury would be caused to Licensor by any use of the Licensed Marks and/or Master Licensor Properties that is inconsistent with this Agreement, such that injunctive and similar relief would be appropriate. Accordingly, without prejudice to any other right and/or remedy Licensor may have under this Agreement or the law, if, after notice by Licensor, Licensee fails to take any action that Licensee is obligated to take under this Agreement pertaining to the Licensed Products, the Licensed Marks, and/or the Master Licensor Properties, then Licensor shall be entitled to an award of injunctive relief, specific performance to compel such action, and/or other provisional relief.

21.4 *Entitlement to Costs*. If any legal action or dispute arises under this Agreement, arises by reason of any asserted breach of it, or arises between the parties and is related in any way to the subject matter of this Agreement, the prevailing party shall be entitled to recover all costs and expenses, including reasonable attorneys' fees, investigative costs, reasonable accounting fees and charges for experts. The "prevailing party" shall be the party who obtains a provisional remedy such as a preliminary injunction or who is entitled to recover its reasonable costs of suit, whether or not the suit proceeds to final judgment; if there is no court action, the prevailing party shall be the party who wins any dispute. A party need not be awarded money damages or all relief sought in order to be considered the "prevailing party" by the arbitrator(s) or a court.

22. Integration

This Agreement and the Schedule to the Agreement constitutes the entire Agreement between the parties concerning the subject matter hereof, and revokes and supersedes all prior agreements between the parties and is intended as a final expression of their agreement. No other agreements, understandings, representations or discussions are included in this Agreement except as expressly noted herein.

23. Force Majeure

It is understood and agreed that in the event of an act of the government, or war conditions, or fire, flood or labor trouble in the factory of Licensee or in the factory of those manufacturing parts necessary for the manufacture of the Licensed Products, which prevent the performance by Licensee of the provisions of this Agreement, then such nonperformance by Licensee shall not be construed as grounds for breach of this Agreement.

24. Modifications

This Agreement may not be modified except by a written instrument, signed by both parties, making specific reference to this Agreement by date, parties and subject matter; provided, that notwithstanding the foregoing, the policies and procedures of Licensor may change from time to time, and this Agreement and the License granted hereunder may be amended by those additional policies and procedures by Licensor in its sole and absolute discretion, as long as the policies and procedures apply to licensees of Licensor as a whole rather than targeting only Licensee.

25. Severability

The invalidity or unenforceability of any provision of this Agreement, or the invalidity or unenforceability of any provision of this Agreement as applied to a particular occurrence or circumstance, shall not affect the validity or enforceability of any of the other provisions of this Agreement or any other applications of such provisions, as the case may be.

26. Other Provisions

26.1 *Counterparts*. This Agreement may be executed in one or more counterparts, each of which shall be deemed an original and all such counterparts together shall constitute one and the same Agreement.

26.2 *Further Assurances.* The parties hereby covenant and agree to execute and deliver all such documents, make such governmental filings, and do or cause to be done all such acts or things as may reasonably be necessary to complete and effect the transactions contemplated hereby.

26.3 *No Strict Construction.* The language used in this Agreement shall be deemed to be the language chosen by both parties to express their mutual intent, and no rule of strict construction shall be applied against either party as drafter.

26.4 *Headings.* The headings used in this Agreement will be used only for the purpose of reference and shall not be deemed to govern, limit, modify or in any other manner affect the scope, meaning or intent of the provisions of this Agreement or be given any legal effect whatsoever.

27. Warranty Exclusion and Waiver

LICENSOR GRANTS NO WARRANTIES HEREUNDER, EXPRESS OR IMPLIED, AND LICENSOR SPECIFICALLY DISCLAIMS, AND LICENSEE SPECIFICALLY WAIVES, ALL WARRANTIES, WHETHER EXPRESS OR IMPLIED, ORAL OR WRITTEN, OR ARISING BY TRADE USAGE OR OTHERWISE, INCLUDING, BUT NOT LIMITED TO, EXPRESS OR IMPLIED WARRANTIES OF MERCHANTABILITY AND FITNESS FOR A PARTICULAR PURPOSE.

28. Confidentiality

The parties each agree that during the term of this Agreement they may receive information regarding the other party's affairs that the disclosing party considers confidential. Each party receiving such confidential information agrees not to disclose it to a third party except to its own employees and agents and only as necessary to perform its obligations or exercise its rights under this Agreement. This Section 28 is not applicable to any information which: (i) the receiving party is authorized in writing by the disclosing party to disclose; (ii) is generally known or becomes part of the public domain in the trade through no fault of the receiving party; (iii) is independently developed by the receiving party or its agents without any use of the confidential information; or (iv) is required to be disclosed by law or regulation or by proper order of a court of competent jurisdiction after adequate notice to the disclosing party to seek a protective order, the imposition of which protective order the receiving party agrees to approve and support. The terms of this Agreement are deemed confidential information under this Section 28; provided, however, in the event that any portion or all of this Agreement shall be required to be disclosed pursuant to any rule or regulation, either party shall be permitted to disclose such portion, or all of this Agreement, as applicable; provided, further, that in any such event, the disclosing party shall provide written notice to the other party, and at the request of such other party, take such action as may reasonable or necessary, at the discretion of the disclosing party, to seek confidential treatment of the material governing provisions hereof with the government agency. In the event that any such confidential treatment request, or any portion thereof, is denied by the staff of the government agency, the disclosing party shall be permitted to disclose such portions, or all of this Agreement, as may be required.

IN WITNESS WHEREOF, the parties hereto have signed this Agreement by their duly authorized representatives as of the date first set forth above.

LICENSOR:

[LICENSOR NAME]

By:_____

Name:_____

Title:_____

LICENSEE:

[LICENSEE NAME]

By:_____

Name:_____

Title:_____

I.2. Exhibit A—Licensed Product Approval Form

[LICENSOR'S NAME]

NAME OF LICENSEE: _____

LICENSED PRODUCT:_____

SEASON:_____

SKU#:_____

COMMENTS:

_____

_____

_____

_____

_____

[PLACE PHOTO HERE]

[ ] NEW SUBMISSION [ ] CARRYOVER

WHOLESALE $ _____

RETAIL $ _____

SIZES _____

START TAKING ORDERS _____

END TAKING ORDERS _____

START SHIP _____

END SHIP _____

_____   _____

SIGNATURE OF LICENSEE   SIGNATURE OF LICENSOR

[ ] APPROVED [ ] APPROVED WITH CHANGE [ ] DISAPPROVED

I.3. Schedule to Trademark License Agreement

THIS SCHEDULE TO TRADEMARK LICENSE AGREEMENT is made as of the Effective Date (as defined in the Agreement) of the Trademark License Agreement (the *"Agreement"*).

S.1. *LICENSOR:*
[NAME]
[ADDRESS]

S.2. *LICENSEE:*
[NAME]
[ADDRESS]

S.3. *THE "LICENSED MARKS":*
   [LIST BRANDS]

S.4. *THE "MASTER LICENSOR PROPERTIES":*
   Artwork and designs created by Licensor and provided to Licensee in a digital or otherwise easily reproducible form.

S.5. *TYPE OF LICENSE:*
   Exclusive, except as set forth in the Agreement, including, without limitation, Section 2 of the Agreement.

S.6. *THE "LICENSED PRODUCTS":*
   [LIST PRODUCTS]

S.7. *THE "TERRITORY":*
   [LIST TERRITORIES]

S.8. *THE "EFFECTIVE DATE":*
   _____, 20__

S.9. *THE "EXPIRATION DATE":*
   _____, 20__

S.10. *"MINIMUM NET SALES":*

License Year	Amount
Year 1 period ending _____, 20__	$_____
Year 2 period ending _____, 20__	$_____
Year 3 period ending _____, 20__	$_____
Year 4 period ending _____, 20__	$_____
Year 5 period ending _____, 20__	$_____

S.11. *"GUARANTEED ROYALTIES":*

Year 1 period ending _____, 20__	$_____
Year 2 period ending _____, 20__	$_____
Year 3 period ending _____, 20__	$_____
Year 4 period ending _____, 20__	$_____
Year 5 period ending _____, 20__	$_____

* Guaranteed Royalties for Year 1 shall be payable as follows: [$_____,_____) shall be payable upon signing the Agreement. Guaranteed Royalties for each of the subsequent License Years (as defined in the Agreement) shall be payable in four (4) equal installments, each equal to 25% of the Guaranteed Royalties for the License Year in question, payable at the beginning of each License Quarter (as defined in the Agreement) of each License Year. During each Annual Period, Licensee shall pay to the Licensor Royalties that are equal to the greater of (A) the royalties based on Licensee's net sales during each such year, or (B) the minimum amount of Royalties set forth as the Guaranteed Minimum Royalties for each annual period. Advances of Minimum Guarantees for any annual period will be payable only to the extent not earned by Royalties or Advances otherwise paid to Licensor for that Annual Period. In no event will Royalties payable for any annual period which are in excess of the Guaranteed Minimum Royalties for that period be applied to reduce Guaranteed Minimum Royalties for any other Annual Period.

S.12. *"EARNED ROYALTIES":*

Ten percent (10%) of Net Sales—FOB In (as defined in the Agreement) Twelve percent (12%) of Net Sales—FOB Out (as defined in the Agreement)

S.13. *THE ADDRESS WHERE BOOKS AND RECORDS SHALL BE KEPT:*
The address set forth in Paragraph S.2. above.

S.14. *LICENSE FEE:*
*[_____ **Dollars (US $**_____*], *nonrefundable, nonrecoupable fee as "Key Money" due upon signing.*

S.15. *ADVERTISING:*
Licensee shall pay five percent (5%) of Net Sales (as defined in the Agreement) to Licensor's designee per Section 15 of the Agreement. Licensee shall also comply with the other terms and conditions of Section 15 of the Agreement.

The parties acknowledge and agree that this Schedule to the Agreement contains a summary of certain material provisions of the Agreement for the convenience of the parties and that to the extent any provision of this Schedule conflicts with any provision of the Agreement, the provision of the Agreement shall apply.

LICENSOR:

[LICENSEE NAME]

By:_____

Name:_____

Title:_____

LICENSEE:

[LICENSOR NAME]

By:_____

Name:_____

Title:_____

II

Registration of Manufacturer

Registration of Manufacturer

Licensee must obtain and submit to Licensor(s) this executed approval form of any third party manufacturer of any of the Licensed Product(s), as set forth in Clause 10.1.2 of the Merchandise Licensee Agreement.

LICENSED PRODUCT(S): _____

BRAND:

MANUFACTURER INFORMATION (List all addresses including headquarters and factory locations):

Company Name	Street Address	City	State/Province	Country	Zip Code/ Postal Code
Company Name	Street Address	City	State/Province	Country	Zip Code/ Postal Code
Company Name	Street Address	City	State/Province	Country	Zip Code/ Postal Code
Company Name	Street Address	City	State/Province	Country	Zip Code/ Postal Code
Company Name	Street Address	City	State/Province	Country	Zip Code/ Postal Code

The undersigned ("Manufacturer') understands that Licensor(s) has licensed Licensee to manufacture or have manufactured for Licensee the Licensed Product(s) utilizing the Brand. To induce Licensor(s) to consent to the manufacture of the Licensed Product(s) by Manufacturer, Manufacturer agrees, for the benefit of Licensor(s), that it will not manufacture and/or sell the Licensed Product(s) utilizing the Brand for anyone but Licensee or its wholly-owned subsidiaries; that Manufacturer will not manufacture the Licensed Product(s) in any territory other than the above-named Territory; that

Manufacturer will not (unless Licensor(s) consents in writing) manufacture any other merchandise utilizing any of the Brands; and that when Licensee ceases to require Manufacturer to manufacture the Licensed Product(s), Manufacturer will deliver to Licensor or Licensee all artwork, drawings, software, molds, plates and other materials used in connection with the manufacture of the Licensed Products or which reproduce the Brands or will give satisfactory evidence of the destruction thereof. Licensor(s) shall be entitled to invoke any remedy permitted by law for violation of this Manufacturers Agreement by Manufacturer. Manufacturer agrees to keep for a period of three (3) years after the term of this Agreement reasonable record covering the manufacturing and other transactions authorized in this Manufacturers Agreement. Licensor and Licensee and their duly authorized representatives shall have the right to examine such records and to make copies of them.

MANUFACTURER:_____   **LICENSEE:**_____

By: By:

Title: _____   Title: _____

Date: _____   Date: _____

LICENSOR:_____

Title: _____

Date: _____

APPENDIX

III

Royalty Statement

QUARTERLY ROYALTY REPORT	
QUARTER END DATE:	

SUMMARY

Royalty calculation

Number of unaccounted for/lost/stolen units in the quarter	
Value of unaccounted for/lost/stolen units in the quarter	$
Number of free products in the quarter	
Whole-sale arm's-length Value of free products in the quarter	$
Royalty Due this Quarter	$
Offset: Minimum Guarantees paid to offset royalty due	$
Total Due this quarter:	$

Signature _____   Title _____   Date _____

I certify the information in this report is correct and complete to the best of my knowledge.

[To be signed by the Chief Financial Office or other substitue executive when the CFO is not available.]

DETAIL

Product Description	Invoice Number (if applicable)	Customer Name (if applicable)	Style No.	# of Units Sold or otherwise disposed	List/Gross Price	DEDUCTIONS								Net Sales Price	Royalty
						Volume Discount	Close-Out Discount	Sales Incentive Discount	Taxes Offset w/ Licensor Credit	Returns actual/ Received	Early Payment Allowance	Invoiced Freight	Total Deductions		

Settlement Letter (California)

December 25, 2008

Joe Licensee
Licensed Bags Incorporated, LLC.
123 South Flower Street, Suite 230
Los Angeles, CA 90013

Re: Licensee Audit Report September 30, 2008

Dear Philippe,

In accordance with the "Records and Audit" provisions of the Licensing Agreement dated January 2, 2007 between Licensor and Licensee, our auditors recently completed a thorough audit of your records for the XYZ® and ABC® brands.

As you know, our auditors completed a final report that includes a breakdown of monies owed to Licensor, based on several contractual obligations that were not fulfilled during the scope period of January 2, 2006 to June 30, 2008. These findings were presented to you during the fieldwork, and we have reviewed the comments you made regarding the findings with the auditor. Should you need additional information regarding the report findings, please contact the auditor, Sidney Blum, directly at sblum@sjaccounting.com.

In accordance with the Licensing Agreements, you are required to remit payment of the amounts due from the audit within thirty (30)days of the discovery of the audits. It has been more than thirty (30) days since the auditors identified their findings to you. As a reminder, these findings are:

Section M-1	Underreported royalties and late payments equal prior to interest	$84,922
Section M-2	Advertising Expenditures	$719,060
Section M-3	Excessive trade discounts more than 10%/30%	$8,629
Section M-4	Missing Inventory	$19,447
Section M-5	Excess samples to related party	$7,625
Section M-7	Audit costs	$35,000
Total		$884,240

Of the above finding and cost recovery amounts, we can confirm you have paid $74,765, resulting in a remaining balance of $809,475. As a sign of our valued relationship with you and in order to resolve this matter quickly, if you make payment by January 10th, 2009, we are willing to forego the interest that has accumulated between September 30, 2008 and today's date in addition to foregoing one-half of the Advertising Expenditures finding for $359,530. We are also willing to amend the agreement, reducing your Advertising Expenditures requirement to 5 percent from the current 10% percent effective as of June 30, 2008, an additional substantial savings to you in excess of several hundred thousand dollars. This results in a net amount currently due by December 10th of $449,945.

Please keep in mind that this offer should not be construed as a starting point for further negotiations. This letter contains a settlement offer that is subject to the settlement privilege and is not admissible as evidence in any dispute resolution proceeding pursuant to evidence code Section 1152 and other applicable law. If the $449,945 is not paid by January 10th' we retain the right to seek the entire $809,475 plus the full 10 percent of Advertising Expenditures plus interest until the balance is paid in full.

I would like to thank you for your cooperation with our auditors and let you know we value our relationship with you. Please call me directly should you have any questions.

Kindest regards,
Director of Licensing

Non-Disclosure Agreement

This Non-Disclosure Agreement (the "Agreement") made and entered into as of XXXXX, 20XX by and between AUDITORS having a place of business at _____, _____, _____, United States of America (hereinafter, "AUDITOR") and _____ ("Disclosing Party"), having a place of business at _____.

As consideration for the Disclosing Party agreeing to disclose such information to AUDITOR and for other good and valuable consideration, the receipt and sufficiency of which are hereby acknowledged, AUDITOR and Disclosing Party agree as follows.

Confidential Information may be used by AUDITOR for the purpose of providing certain contract compliance professional services ("Services") to AUDITOR's client, _____. ("Client"). The Confidential Information received by AUDITOR from the Disclosing Party will provide AUDITOR with the necessary information to perform its Services on behalf of its Client.

1. "Confidential Information" means all documents, software, reports, data, records, forms and other materials obtained by AUDITOR from Disclosing Party in the course of performing the Services (including, but not limited to, client records and information): (i) that have been marked as confidential; (ii) whose confidential nature has been made known by Disclosing Party to AUDITOR; or (iii) that due to their character and nature, a reasonable person under like circumstances would treat as confidential. The confidentiality restrictions and obligations imposed by this Agreement shall terminate three (3) years after the expiration or termination of this Agreement.

2. AUDITOR may disclose certain Confidential Information AUDITOR receives from Disclosing Party to its Client in performing the Services for the Client. The disclosure of such Confidential Information shall include sufficient information required for AUDITOR to report to Client sufficient specific information regarding underreporting or overclaiming as may be required as findings from the Services. Such reporting may not include profits, cost of goods sold, or gross margins unless specifically mentioned as reportable or a component of a reportable amount in the agreement between the Disclosing Party and the client. No limitations shall be placed on the reporting of product quantity differences, sales, net sales, discounts, credits, returns, advertising expenditures, including, but not all inclusive, the reasons for those differences.

3. Notwithstanding the foregoing, the obligations of confidentiality under this Agreement shall not apply to Confidential Information that:

a. is already known to AUDITOR at the time it is disclosed to AUDITOR;

b. has been independently developed by AUDITOR;

c. becomes or has become publicly known through no wrongful act of AUDITOR;

d. has been or is received by AUDITOR from a third party without a restriction on disclosure; or

e. is required by law, court or administrative order to be disclosed.

4. The Disclosing Party agrees that it shall not disclose any information to AUDITOR in violation of the proprietary rights of any third party.

5. AUDITOR shall retain all Confidential Information in confidence, exercising the same standard of care used by AUDITOR to protect its own confidential and proprietary information, to prevent the disclosure of Confidential Information to any third party. AUDITOR shall not use Confidential Information for any purpose not allowed herein or other than in furtherance of the provision of Services for the Client.

6. The provisions of this Agreement shall not be construed as preventing AUDITOR from:

i. conducting its engagements for the Client in accordance with firm policies and professional standards; or

ii. conducting its normal review and quality assurance processes with regard to engagements for the Client.

7. Any waiver, modification or amendment of any provision of this Agreement shall be effective only if in writing in a document that specifically refers to this Agreement and such document is signed by both parties.

8. This Agreement constitutes the full and complete understanding and agreement of the parties hereto with respect to the subject matter covered herein and supersedes all prior and contemporaneous oral or written understandings and agreements with respect thereto.

9. This Agreement shall be governed by and construed in accordance with the laws of the State of California.

10. All notices or reports permitted or required under this Agreement shall be in writing and shall be by personal delivery, nationally recognized overnight courier service, facsimile transmission or by certified or registered mail, return receipt requested, and shall be deemed given upon the earlier of actual receipt or one (1) day after deposit with the courier service, receipt by sender of confirmation of electronic transmission or five (5) days after deposit in the mail. Notices shall be sent to the addresses set forth at the end of this Agreement or such other address as either party may specify in writing.
IN WITNESS WHEREOF, the parties intending to be legally bound, have executed this Agreement as of the later date set forth below.

AUDITOR LLP   Disclosing Party's Name

By: By:

Title: Principal   Title:_____

Date: XXXXX x, 20XX   **Date:**_____

APPENDIX
VI

Third-Party Risk-Ranking Matrix

The following should be placed into an Excel spreadsheet and based on each target. Those targets with the highest number represent the highest risk and are often subject to an earlier visit. Special consideration should be made for a third party whose right-to-audit period is near expiration.

Annual Royalty Revenue

> $10,000,000	10
5,000,000–9,999,999	8
2,500,000–4,999,999	6
1,000,000–1,499,999	4
250,000–999,999	2

Royalty Trend to Sales Trends

Significantly Less Growth	5
Slightly Less	4
Comparable	3
Slightly More	2
Significantly More	1

Audited Before

Never	10
Over 3 years ago	5
Between 2–3 years ago	3
Between 1–2 years ago	2
Within a year	0

Primary Reasons for Monetary Findings

Inadequate Management Control	5
Manual Processes/Mergers	4
Foreign Locations/Multiple Amendments and/or Products	3
Foreign Exchange	2
Other, e.g., personnel change	1

Size of Audit Findings

> $5,000,000	7
1,000,000–999,999	5
500,000–999,999	3
100,000–499,999	2
0–99,999	0

Skill of Prior Auditors

Low-skilled (i.e., internal staff)	10
Moderate-skilled (internal accountants)	7
Financial auditors/nonspecialist	5
Unproven royalty auditors	3
Royalty audit experts	0

Contract Expiration Date

Expired	5
Within 1 year of expiry	4
Within 2 years of expiry	3
Within 3 years of expiry	2
More than 3 years before expiry	1

Number of agreements

One point for each agreement covering the review period up to 10 points.

Number of Amendments or Side Letters affecting products or royalty rates.

One point for each amendment/side letter, up to 10 points.

Calculation Complexity (1. Ambiguous terms, 2. Many variables, 3. Detail of calculation not on royalty statement, 4. Performed by clerk or nonsenior accountant, 5. Consolidation from different regions)

All four of the above concerns	5
First two and either of next two	4
One of the first two and either of the next two	3
Both of the last two	2
One of the last two	1

Contract Geography & Licensee Operating Structure

Worldwide License/Multinational	5
Worldwide License/International	4
Regional License/International	3
Local License	2

Licensee's Location

Asia/Africa/Middle East, India	7
Europe/South Africa/South America	4
Other not North America	2

Number of Licensed Products

More than 5	5
Between 4–5	4
Between 3–4	3
Between 2–3	2
Between 1–2	1

Number of Licensee's Products

More than 20	5
Between 15 to 19	4
Between 10 to 14	3
Between 5 to 9	2
Between 1 to 4	1

Third-Party Involvement (1. M&A, 2. Sub-licensing, 3. Outsourcing)

More than one of the above	5
One of the above	3
None	1

Royalty Reporting Elements (1. Timely, 2. Errors, 3. Complete, i.e., all info required by contract)

All of the above	5
Two of the above	4
Consistently one of the above	3
One of the above	2
None of the above	1

Average of late payments for review period

More than 180 days	5
90 to 179 days	3
30 to 89 days	2
1 to 29 days	1

Disputes/Litigation

Licensor and licensor are in litigation	5
Licensor and licensee have threatened Litigation or are pending litigation	4
Hostile relationship between licensor & licensee	3

Right-to-audit period expiring within:

90 days	7
6 months	5
1 year	3
1.5 years	1

VII

Notification of a Third-Party Audit Program

Dear DSP:
I am writing to advise you that **COMPANY** has initiated a worldwide Contract Compliance Program. The purpose of the Program is to improve COMPANY'S support and service of its products and to ensure that the amount of usage of those products is consistent with that agreed to in your license agreement. As a part of the Program, COMPANY will conduct random licensing reviews of its customers. We have engaged a team of specialists from AUDITOR to conduct these reviews, and you may be receiving a letter from us indicating that AUDITOR will be contacting you in this capacity.

The Program has three main objectives. First, we desire to increase COMPANY'S understanding of the challenges encountered by the customer in the management of full compliance or reporting of usage of our licensed music.

Second, we want to ensure that proper systems and processes are in place to accurately and efficiently monitor the usage of your licensed PRODUCT. Accordingly, we will need to ascertain whether your actual usage (both on a node count and geographic basis) conforms with the original usage rights purchased by your Company as specified in LICENSE AGREEMENT.

Finally, we want to strive to educate and share best practices with your organization to help you become more efficient in managing and monitoring your software assets.

In anticipation of this review, you may wish to do an internal examination of the usage of your licensed COMPANY software and ongoing support needs. If you determine any deviations or needs, we would be happy to assist you.

Please contact me at (123) 456-7890 if you have any questions regarding COMPANY'S License Compliance Program, resolving issues associated with undercompliance or obtaining additional licensing rights for our products.

Sincerely Yours,

Gabriella Marissa
License Compliance Manager

VIII

Notification of an Audit

(Date)
(Name)
(Title)
(Company Name)
(Address)

Dear *(Name)*:

Dear:

We would like to inform you of our desire to review your books and records relating to the sale of XXXXX products in accordance with the licensing agreement between XXXX and xxxxxx. Our review will also include testing your compliance with all aspects of the agreement inclusive of validating the accuracy of contractual payments made to XXXXXX for all sales from
_____ through _____.

Our review will be performed by Auditors under the supervision of Sidney Blum, Principal. All requests made by Auditors will be made on behalf of and with the prior approval of XXXXXX. They would like to begin this review by July 10, 2008 and will contact you shortly to confirm the engagement date and provide a list of documents to be available prior to the and during the review.

If you have any questions, do not hesitate to contact me or Sidney Blum at 818-631-3192 (mobile).

Very truly yours,

Rachel Jessica
Director—Royalty Licensing

Index

A

Accounting departments
  in-house lawyers and, 4.3.3.1.
  lists of third party relationships, 4.3.3.1.
  monitoring of royalties,
    disincentives, 4.3.1.1.
  operation of Contract Monitoring
    Programs, 5.1.7.
  review of financial agreements by, 1.3.2.
Accounting Information and Management
  System (AIMS), 2.5.2.
Accounting systems
  changes in
    consequences of, 2.5.2.
    depth of monitoring and, 4.3.2.
    notification of, 3.9.3., 6.20.
    periodic reports and, 2.1.6.
    as selection criteria for
      inspection, 5.1.9.3.
    underreporting and, 5.1.13.
  for construction contracts, 3.2.2.
  digital content and, 2.3.
Advance and minimum guarantees
  contract language for, 6.13.
  in royalty/licensing monitoring, 1.1.,
    3.9.2., 4.3.2., 5.1.13.
Adverse publicity
  contracts with foreign governments
    and, 3.6.1.
  IP licensees and, 3.9.1.1.
  joint ventures and, 3.6.2., 3.6.3.
  recalls and, 3.8.2.
Advertising
  contract language for, 6.1.–6.2.
  in franchise agreements, 3.5.2.
  media specialized expenditures, 3.1.1.
Advertising agency self-reporting contracts,
  reporting risks, 3.1.–3.1.4.
  audit terms and conditions, 3.1.2.
    agency compensation, 3.1.2.

agency obligations, 3.1.2.
agency services, 3.1.2.
commissions, 3.1.2.
exhibits, 3.1.2.
fees, 3.1.2.
proof of performance, 3.1.2.
retainers, 3.1.2.
right to audit clause, 3.1.2.
  contract description, 3.1.1.
  documents for external monitoring, 3.1.4.
  reporting areas and risks, 3.1.3.
Aerospace industry, IP examples
  of, 3.9.1.2.
Africa, monitoring trends in, 2.4.3.
Agreed Upon Procedures (AUP), 3.2.2.,
  5.1.10.1., 5.1.10.1.7., 5.1.10.1.9.
AIMS (Accounting Information and
  Management System), 2.5.2.
All-you-can-eat agreements/enterprise
  license agreements, 3.10.1.
Amendments, contract
  in construction contracts, 3.2.1., 3.2.2.
  in-house lawyers and, 4.3.3.1.
  licensee records of, 6.18., 7.1.
  royalty audits and, 2.1.5.
American Institute of Certified Public
  Accountants (AICPA)
  Attestation Standards, 3.2.2., 5.1.10.1.,
    5.1.10.1.7., 5.1.10.1.9.
  Audit standards of, 3.2.2., 3.8.2.,
    5.1.10.1., 6.30.
  Consulting Standards, 3.2.2., 5.1.10.1.
  IT systems and, 5.1.2.
  mission of, xvi
Annual reminders, of Contract Monitoring
  Program, 5.1.18.
Apparel industry
  anticounterfeiting stickers, 6.4.
  automatic license renewal options, 1.3.5.
  cost recovery in, 4.3.1.1., 4.3.2.

Asia, monitoring trends in, 2.4.3.
Attestation Standards (AICPA), 3.2.2.,
 5.1.10.1., 5.1.10.1.7., 5.1.10.1.9.
Attorneys. See also Contract terms and
 conditions, writing of
 franchise agreements and, 3.5.1.
 in-house, role in third party
  monitoring, 4.3., 4.3.1.1.,
  4.3.4., 5.1.7., 5.1.15, 5.1.15.1.
  accounting departments and, 4.3.3.1.
  contract amendments and, 4.3.3.1.
  outsourcing vs., 5.1.15.1.
 litigation monitoring audits and, 1.3.4.
 writing of contracts, 1.3.2.
Audit, use of term, 1.3.4., 3.2.2.
Auditing Standard No. 5 (SOX), 2.5.2.
Auditors
 as expert witnesses, 1.3.4.
 financial statement vs. royalty
  auditors, xviii, 2.1.5., 2.5., 5.1.10.,
  5.1.10.1.5., 5.1.15.1.
 indemnification of, 5.1.10.1.8.
 independent, 3.2.2.
 internal vs. external, 2.1.5., 5.1.15.1.
 non-disclosure agreements and, 3.7.4.,
  4.3.3.1., 6.16.
 outsourcing and, 5.1.10.1.5., 5.1.15.1.
 qualifications of, 3.2.3., 4.3.2., 5.1.10.
 review of contracts by, 1.3.2., 2.1.1.
 right to audit clauses and, 1.3.2.
Audit rights. See Right to audit
AUP. See Agreed Upon Procedures
Automatic renewal options, 1.3.5.

B
Bankruptcy, 3.5.2., 6.20.
Best practices, for licensees, 7.1.–7.8.
 avoidance of audits, 7.8.
 communication with licensors, 7.6.
 internal controls, 7.7.
 IP inventory monitoring, 7.3.
 listing of, 7.1.
 non-disclosure agreements, 7.5.
 reasons for underreporting
  royalties, xix, 7.2.
 royalty audit preparation, 7.4.
Black-and-grey markets. See Grey
 Market activity
Books and records. See Record retention
 requirements; *specific types*
Bundling
 digital distribution and, 3.3.4.

royalty calculations and,
 5.1.10.1.3.2., 6.23.
underreporting of royalties and, 3.9.1.2.,
 4.3.2., 5.1.13.
Business development departments, 4.1.,
 4.3.1.1., 4.3.3.1.
Business Software Alliance (BSA), 7.1.

C
California, interest penalties, 6.11.
Certificate of Authenticity (COA), 6.4.
Certified Public Accountants (CPA)
 as contract auditors, 5.1.10.,
  5.1.10.1., 5.1.15.1.
 cost recovery audits and, 3.2.2.
 right to audit provisions and, 1.3.4., 6.22.
Change-order process, 3.2.3.
Channels, in distribution/reseller contracts
 overview, 3.4.1.1.
 incentive/rebate programs, 3.4.1.3.
 monitoring process, 3.4.1.4.
 retailer to OEM reporting, 3.4.1.2.
Checklists, royalty statements and, 2.1.2.
Chief Financial Officer (CFO)
 third party monitoring, role of,
  4.1.–4.3.1.1.
China, counterfeiting in, 6.4., 7.1.
Civil penalties. See also Penalties
 under SOX, 1.3.6.
 for using unlicensed software, 3.10.1.
Clickwrap agreements, 3.10.1.
Client access licenses, software, 3.10.1.
Closeouts
 advertising expenditures and, 6.1., 6.2.
 contract language for, 3.4.1.1., 6.3., 6.9.
 as deductions, 3.9.2.
CMP. See Contract Monitoring Program
COA (Certificate of Authenticity), 6.4.
Commissions, in advertising
 contracts, 3.1.2.
Committee of Sponsoring Organizations
 of the Treadway Commission
 (COSO), 2.5.2.
Computer hardware industry, IP
 examples of, 3.9.1.2.
Conflict checks, in selection of
 auditors, 5.1.10.1.5.
Construction self-reporting contracts,
 reporting risks, 3.2.–3.2.5.
 audit terms and conditions, 3.2.2.
  accounting systems, 3.2.2.
  cost allocation, 3.2.2.

cost recovery, 3.2.1., 3.2.2.
  on-site visits, 3.2.2.
  work-in-progress monitoring, 3.2.2.
contract description, 3.2.1.
  cost-plus contracts, 3.2.1.
  fixed-fee contracts, 3.2.1.
  overcharges, 3.2.1.
  variable fee contracts, 3.2.1.
documents for external monitoring, 3.2.5.
timing of self-monitoring and
    audits, 3.2.4.
  right to audit clause, 3.2.4.
variable cost monitoring process, 3.2.3.
  cost allocation, 3.2.3.
  cost-plus contracts, 3.2.3.
  duplicate charges, 3.2.3.
  government contracts, 3.2.3.
  labor costs, 3.2.3.
  materials usage/overorders, 3.2.3.
  overhead charges, 3.2.3.
  prepayments, 3.2.3.
  rebates, 3.2.3.
  right to audit clause, 3.2.3.
  subcontractors, 3.2.3.
Consulting Standards (AICPA),
    3.2.2., 5.1.10.1.
Consumer Price Index, 3.8.2.
Consumer products, IP examples of, 3.9.1.2.
Content aggregators, digital products, 3.3.1.
Content creators, digital products, 3.3.1.
Content distributors, digital products, 3.3.1.
Content owners, digital products, 3.3.1.
Contingency fees, auditor, 5.1.10.1.7.
Contract amendments
  in construction contracts, 3.2.1., 3.2.2.
  in-house lawyers and, 4.3.3.1.
  licensee records of, 6.18., 7.1.
  royalty audits and, 2.1.5.
Contract execution, 1.3.2.
Contract management, 1.3.3.
Contract Monitoring Program (CMP),
    5.1.–5.1.18.
  annual reminders to self-reporting
    parties, 5.1.18.
  audit reports, 5.1.16.
  board adoption resolutions, 5.1.6.
  department operations and, 5.1.7.
  establishing, 5.1.1.
  information to auditors, 5.1.14.
  justification for, 5.1.2.
  lawyers role in third party audits,
    5.1.7., 5.1.15.

in-house vs. outsourcing, 5.1.15.1
notification letters to third parties
  annual reminders, 5.1.18.
  on establishment of CMP, 5.1.11.
  on impending audits, 5.1.12.
objectives, 5.1.4.
overcoming objections to, 5.1.8.
policy statements, 5.1.5.
reports to management, 5.1.17.
scope of, 5.1.3.
selection/contracting with auditors,
    5.1.10.–5.1.10.1.9.
  auditor qualifications, 5.1.10.
  conflict checks, 5.1.10.1.5.
  contract provisions, 5.1.10.1.–5.1.10.1.9.
  deliverables, 5.1.10.1.4., 5.1.10.1.8.
  engagement fees, 5.1.10.1.7.
  engagement teams, 5.1.10.1.6.
  fieldwork, 5.1.10.1.3.
  objectives, 5.1.10.1.1.
  other auditor responsibilities,
    5.1.10.1.9.
  scope of work, 5.1.10.1.2.
  work plans, 5.1.10.1.3.
selection of third parties for
    monitoring/audits, 5.1.9.
  criteria for, 5.1.9., 5.1.9.3.
  depth of monitoring, 5.1.9.2.
  frequency of inspections, 5.1.9.1.
  number of licenses to inspect, 5.1.9.3.
  red flags, 5.1.9.5.
underreporting indicators, 5.1.13.
Contract terms and conditions, writing
  of, 6.1.–6.30. See also Appendices
  overview, xix-xx, 1.3.2.
  advertising
    external expenditures, 6.1.
    as payment to licensors, 6.2.
  closeouts, 3.4.1.1., 6.3., 6.9.
  cost recovery, 6.5.
  counterfeiting protection, 6.4.
  deduction limitations, 6.6., 6.15.
  discount limitations, 6.6.
  exchange rates, 6.7.
  granting rights, 6.8.
  gross sales, 6.9., 6.15.
  insurance, 6.10.
  interest penalties, 6.11.
  inventory, 6.12.
  minimum guarantees, 6.13.
  most-favored-nation pricing, 6.14.
  net sales, 6.9., 6.12., 6.15.

Contract terms and conditions (*cont.*)
 non-disclosure agreements, 6.16.
 post termination rights, 6.27.
  effect of termination, 6.27.1.
 price controls, 6.17.
 product returns, 6.6., 6.15., 6.21.
 record keeping, 6.18.
 related party sales, 6.19.
 reporting, 6.20.
 right to audit, 6.22.
 royalty calculations, 6.23.
 royalty payments, 6.24.
 tax deductions
  as a reduction from gross sales, 6.29.
  on royalty payments, 6.28.
 termination, 6.26.
 territory, 6.25.
 unauthorized use of licensed
  products, 6.30.
Copyrights, in royalty/licensing
 contracts, 3.9.1., 3.9.1.1., 3.9.1.2.,
 3.9.2., 5.1.13.
Cost allocation
 in construction contracts, 3.2.2., 3.2.3.
 in right to audit clauses, 3.1.2.
Cost/benefit assessments, 5.1.2., 5.1.10.
Costello, James, xvi
Cost-plus contracts, 3.2.1., 3.2.3.
 cost plus award fee, 3.2.1.
 cost plus fixed fee, 3.2.1.
 cost plus incentive fee, 3.2.1.
 cost plus percentage of costs, 3.2.1.
Cost recovery
 in apparel industry, 4.3.1.1., 4.3.2.
 in construction contracts, 3.2.1., 3.2.2.
 contract language for, 6.5.
 CPAs and, 3.2.2.
 in entertainment industry, 4.3.2.
 in license monitoring programs,
  2.1.4., 2.4.2.
 reactive vs. proactive audits, 1.3.4.
 in royalty/licensing monitoring, 3.9.2.,
  4.3.1.1., 4.3.2.
 in software industry, 4.3.1.1., 4.3.2.
Cost-reimbursement contracts, 3.2.1.
Costs
 of extensive audits, 1.3.4.
 of litigation audits, 1.3.4.
 recoverable, 1.3.4.
Counterfeiting, 2.4.3., 6.4., 7.1.
CPU/server based licensing, 3.10.1.
Criminal penalties. See also Penalties

 under SOX, 1.3.6., 2.5.3.
 for using unlicensed software, 3.10.1.

D

Damage and defective allowance, 6.21.
Deduction limitations, in contract
 language, 6.6.
Desktop monitoring audits, 1.3.4.
Destruction records, inventory, 6.12.
Digital content, global royalty market, 2.3.
Digital distribution self-reporting contracts,
 reporting risks, 3.3.–3.3.4.
 contract description, 3.3.1.
  advertising, 3.3.1.
  content aggregators, 3.3.1.
  content creators, 3.3.1.
  content distributors, 3.3.1.
  content owners, 3.3.1.
  digital rights management, 3.3.1.
  OEMs, 3.3.1.
 internal controls for areas of
  concern, 3.3.2.
  approvals on product usage, 3.3.2.
  channels, 3.3.2.
  new digital products, 3.3.2.
  new distribution sublicensees, 3.3.2.
  ownership rights, 3.3.2.
  precontract accounting review, 3.3.2.
  quality of reporting, 3.3.2.
  revenue sharing, 3.3.2.
  subscription and streaming service
   royalties, 3.3.2.
 monitoring of agreements, 3.3.4.
  bundling, 3.3.4.
  disaster recovery plans, 3.3.4.
  subdistributors, 3.3.4.
 risk summary, 3.3.3.
Digital life cycle, 3.3.1.
Digital rights management (DRM), 3.3.1.
Disaster recovery plans, 3.3.4.,
 3.6.2., 3.10.3.2.
Discounts
 limitations on, contract language for, 6.6.
 volume, 3.4.1.3.
Distribution/reseller self-reporting
 contracts, reporting risks, 3.4.–3.4.3.
 audit terms and conditions, 3.4.2.
 contract description, 3.4.1.
  channels, 3.4.1.1., 3.4.1.2., 3.4.1.3.
  closeouts, 3.4.1.1.
  distribution agreement sample, 3.4.3.
  distribution channels, 3.4.1.1., 3.4.1.2.

incentive programs and controls,
  3.4.1.1., 3.4.1.3.
information exchange methods, 3.4.1.1.
point of sales, 3.4.1.2.
POS Instant Rebates, 3.4.1.3.
price protection incentives, 3.4.1.3.
rebates, 3.4.1.1., 3.4.1.3.
retailer reports to OEMs, 3.4.1.2.
revenue sharing, 3.4.1.1.
tracking requirements
  incentives, 3.4.1.1.
volume discounts, 3.4.1.3.
distribution agreement sample, 3.4.3.
Distributorships, franchise
  agreements, 3.5.2.
DNS Audit, self-monitoring tool, 3.10.3.3.
Double charging, of direct costs, 3.2.2.
Dumping, of inventory, 6.12.
Duplicate charges, 3.2.3.

E
Eastern Europe, 2.4.3.
Einstein, Albert, xix
Electronic data interchange (EDI), 3.4.1.2.
Employers Cost Index, 3.8.2.
End user license agreement (EULA), 3.10.1.,
  3.10.3., 6.4.
End user license contracts. See
  Software/end user license
  self-reporting contracts
Engagement fees, auditor, 5.1.10.1.7.
Engineers, construction contracts
  and, 3.2.3.
Entertainment industry. See also Digital
  distribution self-reporting contracts
cost recovery in, 4.3.2.
IP examples, 3.9.1.2.
monitoring companies in, 3.3.1.
Environmental compliance, manufacturing
  contracts, 3.8.2.
Europe, monitoring trends in, 2.4.3.
European Union, IP protection in, 2.4.3.
Evergreen licenses, 1.3.5.
Exchange rates
contract language for, 6.7.
in royalty statements, 2.1.3.
sales records and, 3.9.2.
sources of, 3.9.3., 6.7.
underreporting of royalties
  and, 3.9.1.2., 5.1.9.
Exhibits, in advertising contracts, 3.1.2.
Exit strategies, 1.3.5.

Expert witnesses
author as, 2.5.
neutral party as, 1.3.4.
outsourced auditors as, 5.1.10.1.5.,
  5.1.15.1.
Extensive monitoring audits, 1.3.4.

F
Fees
in advertising contracts, 3.1.2.
auditors, engagement fees, 5.1.10.1.7.
contingency fees, 5.1.10.1.7.
value-based fees, 5.1.10.1.7.
in franchise agreements, 3.5.1., 3.5.2.
in most-favored-nation contracts, 3.7.5.
Finance departments, 4.3. See also
  Accounting departments
Financial statement auditors
materiality and, xv-xviii, 3.6.2., 5.1.10.
royalty auditors vs., xviii, 2.1.5., 2.5.,
  5.1.10., 5.1.10.1.5., 5.1.15.1.
Financial statements
margin of error, xv-xviii
materiality, xv-xviii, 3.6.2., 5.1.10.
restatement of, xvi, 2.5.
Finished goods, inventory roll forwards,
  3.9.2., 4.3.3.1., 6.12.
Fixed-fee contracts, 3.2.1., 5.1.10.1.7.
Fixed rate interest penalties, 6.11.
Floating rate interest penalties, 6.11.
Foreign governments, contracts with, 3.6.1.
Franchise self-reporting contracts, reporting
  risks, 3.5.-3.5.4.
audit terms and conditions, 3.5.2.
  advertising, 3.5.2.
  designated supplier, 3.5.2.
  distributorships, 3.5.2.
  fees, 3.5.2.
  financial statements, 3.5.2.
  insurance, 3.5.2.
  key money, 3.5.2.
  lease agreements, 3.5.2.
  net worth, 3.5.2.
  noncompete clauses, 3.5.2.
  royalties, 3.5.2.
  sales register systems, 3.5.2.
  subfranchisees, 3.5.2.
  territory, 3.5.2.
  working capital, 3.5.2.
contract description, 3.5.1.
  franchisor goodwill, 3.5.1.
  key money, 3.5.1.

Franchise self-reporting contracts (*cont.*)
  revenue sharing, 3.5.1.
  royalties, 3.5.1.
  up-front fees, 3.5.1.
  documents for external monitoring, 3.5.4.
  misreporting of royalties, 3.5.4.
  sales register systems, 3.5.4.
  reporting areas and risks, 3.5.3.
  surprise audits, 3.5.4.
Franchising, IP examples of, 3.9.1.2.
Franchisor goodwill, 3.5.1.
Free goods
  in calculating royalties on licensed
    products, 2.1.1., 6.9.
  contract language for, 6.15.

G

Generally Accepted Accounting
  Standards, 6.19.
Generally Accepted Accounting
  Principles, 6.18.
Generally Accepted Accounting Procedures
  (GAAP), 3.6.2., 6.18.
Generally Accepted Accounting
  Standards, 1.3.4.
Global compliance
  COSO and, 2.5.2.
  emerging regional monitoring trends
    in Africa, 2.4.3.
    in Asia, 2.4.1.
    in Europe, 2.4.3.
    in Middle East, 2.4.3.
    in North America, 2.4.2.
  intellectual property, 2.2., 2.4.3.
  unsophisticated accounting systems
    and, 4.3.2.
  U.S. SOX impact on, xvi, 1.3.6.
Global economy, risks, 1.2.
Government Accountability Office, U.S.
  (GAO), 3.2.2.
Government Auditing Standards
  (GAO), 3.2.2.
Government contracts, for construction
  projects, 3.2.3.
Government inspections, 3.8.2.
Grey market activity
  challenges to right to audit
    provisions by, 2.2.
  contract language, protection against, 6.4.
  depth of monitoring and, 5.1.9.2.
  exit strategies and, 1.3.5.
  product value and risks in, 3.4.1.1.

underreporting of royalties
  and, 2.2., 5.1.13.
Gross sales
  contract language for, 6.9., 6.15.
  in royalty/licensing contracts, 3.9.2.,
    6.6., 6.9.
  tax deductions and, 6.29.

H

Healthcare industry, IP examples of, 3.9.1.2.
Honesty system, 2.4.1.

I

Incentives, in distribution/reseller
  contracts, 3.4.1.3.
  POS Instant Rebates, 3.4.1.3.
  price protection, 3.4.1.3.
  for tracking requirements, 3.4.1.1.
  volume discounts, 3.4.1.3.
Information exchange methods, contract
  language for, 1.3.1., 3.4.1.1.
In-house lawyers. See also Contract
  Monitoring Program
  accounting departments and, 4.3.3.1.
  contract amendments and, 4.3.3.1.
  third party monitoring, role of, 4.3.,
    4.3.1.1., 4.3.4., 5.1.7., 5.1.15., 5.1.15.1.
  outsourcing vs., 5.1.15.1.
Institute of Internal Auditors (IIA), 3.2.2.
Insurance
  contract language for, 6.10.
  in franchise contracts, 3.5.2.
  in joint venture contracts, 3.6.2.
  in manufacturing contracts, 3.8.2.
  penalties for failure to maintain, 3.8.2.
  worker's compensation, 3.5.2.
Insurers, ratings of, 3.5.2.
Intellectual property (IP). See also Digital
  distribution self-reporting contracts
  contract language errors, 6.1.
  copyrights, 3.9.1., 3.9.1.1., 3.9.1.2.,
    3.9.2., 5.1.13.
  digital content, 2.3.
  global compliance, 2.2., 2.4.3.
  industry examples of, 3.9.1.2.
  internal use of, 2.1.1.
  penalties for unlicensed use
    of, 3.10.1., 6.7.
  preapproval of new product
    usage of, 4.3.3.1.
  protection of, in royalty/licensing
    contracts, 3.9.2.

royalty audits and, 2.1.5., 2.2.,
4.3.3.1., 5.1.13.
sublicensing of, 3.9.2., 4.3.2., 5.1.13.
trademarks, 3.9.1., 3.9.1.1., 3.9.2.
Interest penalties, on late payments, 3.7.2.,
3.7.4., 5.1.18., 6.11.
Internal monitoring. See Contract
Monitoring Program
*International Standards for the Professional
Practice of Internal Auditing* (IIA), 3.2.2.
Internet. See also Web sites
monitoring advertisers on, 3.3.1.
monitoring digital distribution on, 3.3.1.
Inventory records
contract language for, 6.12.
destruction records, 6.12.
dumping and, 6.12.
licensee best practices and, 7.3.
otherwise disposed of inventory, 3.9.2.,
4.3.3., 6.12.
percentage of inventory
shrinkage, 4.3.3.1.
roll forwards, 3.9.2., 4.3.3.1., 6.12.
in royalty/licensing contract monitoring,
3.9.2., 4.3.3.1.
Investors, joint ventures. See Joint ventures/
partner self-reporting contracts
IP. See Intellectual property
IT systems, CMP Program and, 5.1.2.

J
Japan
royalty audits, 2.4.1.
SOX compliance, 1.2.
Joint ventures/partner self-reporting
contracts, reporting risks, 3.6.–3.6.3.
audit terms and conditions, 3.6.2.
accounting standards, 3.6.2.
adverse publicity, 3.6.2., 3.6.3.
books and records, 3.6.2.
capital outlay, 3.6.2.
disaster recovery plans, 3.6.2.
insurance, 3.6.2.
JV operator duties, 3.6.2.
legal compliance, 3.6.2.
rebates, 3.6.2.
revenue sharing, 3.6.2.
right to audit clause, 3.6.2.
contract description, 3.6.1.
Oxy example, 3.6.1.
documents for external
monitoring, 3.6.3.

K
Key money, franchising, 3.5.1., 3.5.2.
Key performance indicators (KPIs)
in CMP reports to management, 5.1.17.
in manufacturing contracts, 3.8.2.
Kickbacks, defined, 3.2.1.

L
Labor costs, 3.2.3.
Language, contract. See Contract terms
and conditions, writing of; Weak/vague
contract language
Language barriers, outsourcing and, 1.3.1.
LanGuard, self-monitoring tool, 3.10.3.3.
Late payments
construction audits, 3.2.4.
depth of monitoring, 4.3.2.
in franchise contracts, 3.5.2.
interest accrual on, 3.7.2., 3.7.4.,
5.1.18., 6.11.
underreporting of royalties and, 5.1.13.
Lease agreements, franchising, 3.5.2.
Letters of notification, to third parties
annual reminders, 5.1.18.
on establishment of CMP, 5.1.11.
on impending audits, 5.1.12.
Licensees. See *specific contracts*
Licensees, best practices, 7.1.–7.8.
avoidance of audits, 7.8.
communications with licensors, 7.6.
internal controls, 7.7.
IP inventory monitoring, 7.3.
listing of, 7.1.
non-disclosure agreements, 7.5.
reasons for underreporting
royalties, xix, 7.2.
royalty audit preparation, 7.4.
License monitoring programs. See also
Contract Monitoring Program
cost recovery provisions, 2.1.4., 2.4.2.
goals of, 2.1.4.
License period, 3.9.2.
Licensing. See *specific industry types*
Licensing, defined, 3.9.1.
Licensors. See *specific contracts*
Liquidated damages, 2.1.2., 6.11.
Listed wholesale price, defined, 6.9.
Litigation. See also Attorneys
audit reports and, 5.1.16.
expert witnesses, 5.1.10.1.5., 5.1.15.1.
in manufacturing contract
monitoring, 3.8.2.

Litigation (*cont.*)
    reports and release of liability, 3.2.2.
    self-reporting relationships and, 1.3.2.
    weak contract language and, 6.1.
Litigation monitoring audits, costs of, 1.3.4.

M

Major event notification, 6.20.
Manufactured Suggested Retail Price
    (MSRP), defined, 6.9.
Manufacturing self-reporting contracts,
    reporting risks, 3.8.–3.8.3.
    audit terms and conditions, 3.8.2, 3.8.2.
        books and records, 3.8.2.
        cost of raw materials, 3.8.2.
        environmental compliance, 3.8.2.
        insurance, 3.8.2.
        KPIs, 3.8.2.
        minimum orders, 3.8.2.
        OEMs and, 3.8.2.
        packaging and labeling, 3.8.2.
        payment terms, 3.8.2.
        production delays, 3.8.2.
        raw materials, 3.8.2.
        recalls and adverse publicity, 3.8.2.
        reporting periods, 3.8.2.
        right to audit clause, 3.8.2.
        special events notification, 3.8.2.
        unit pricing, 3.8.2.
        variable pricing, 3.8.2.
    contract description, 3.8.1.
        OEMs, 3.8.1.
        outsourcing, 3.8.1.
    documents for external monitoring, 3.8.3.
        listing of, 3.8.3.
    reporting areas and risks
        OEMs and, 3.8.3.
Margin of error, financial statements, xv-xvi
Market changes, termination clauses
    and, 1.3.5.
Marketing fees, in franchise
    agreements, 3.5.2.
Materiality
    under AICPA standards, 3.8.2.
    financial statement auditors and, xv-xviii,
        3.6.2., 5.1.10.
    financial statements and, xv-xviii,
        3.6.2., 5.1.10.
    joint ventures and, 3.6.2.
    risk ranking of licensees and, 4.3.1.1.
    under SOX guidelines, 2.5., 2.5.2.
Materials usage/overorders, 3.2.3.

Media advertising expenditures, 3.1.1. See
    also Digital distribution self-reporting
    contracts
Metadata accuracy, of digital content, 2.3.
Microsoft Certificates of Authenticity
    (COAS), 6.4.
Middle East, monitoring trends in, 2.4.3.
Minimum guarantees
    contract language for, 6.13.
    in royalty/licensing monitoring, 1.1.,
        3.9.2., 4.3.2., 5.1.13.
Minimum orders, manufacturing
    contracts, 3.8.2.
Minimum per article royalty (MPAR),
    defined, 6.9.
Misreporting of royalties, overview, xv-xx,
    1.1. See also Royalties
Monitoring, of self-reporting contractees,
    2.1.–2.5.3. See also Self-reporting
    contracts, reporting risks
    digital content, 2.3.
    emerging regional trends
        in Africa, 2.4.3.
        in Asia, 2.4.1.
        in Europe, 2.4.3.
        in Middle East, 2.4.3.
        in North America, 2.4.2.
    intellectual property and global
        compliance, 2.2., 2.4.3.
    licensees and, 2.1.–2.1.7.
        calculating royalties on licensed
            products, 2.1.1.
        internal records, maintenance of, 2.1.2.
        monitoring programs, 2.1.4.
        periodic reports, 2.1.6.
        royalty audits, 2.1.5.
        royalty statements, 2.1.3., 2.1.4.
    SOX and third-party
        monitoring, 2.5.–2.5.3.
        assessment of internal control, 2.1.4.,
            2.5., 2.5.2.
        civil penalties, 1.3.6.
        criminal penalties, 1.3.6., 2.5.3.
        internal control certification, 2.5.1.
        proactive monitoring programs, 1.3.4.
Monitoring of third parties, roles in, 4.1.–
    4.3.6. See also Third party relationships,
    planning for
    accounting departments, 4.3.3.1.
    CFOs, 4.1.–4.3.1.1.
    contract control, 4.3.
    controllers, 4.3.

decision-makers, 4.2.
depth of monitoring and, 4.3.2.
determining roles, questions/answers
    for, 4.3.3.
in-house legal counsel, 4.3., 4.3.1.1., 4.3.4.,
    5.1.7., 5.1.15, 5.1.15.1.
licensees' role in audits, 4.3.6.
licensors' role in audits, 4.3.5.
licensors' role in monitoring
    programs, 4.3.1.1.
outside financial auditors, 4.3.
program coordination, 4.3.5.
Monitoring programs. See Contract
    Monitoring Program; *specific aspects
    and industries*
Most-favored-nation self-reporting
    contracts, reporting risks, 3.7.–3.7.5.
audit terms and conditions, 3.7.2.
    government agencies, 3.7.2.
    minimizing rebate risks, 3.7.2.
    time periods, 3.7.2.
contract description, 3.7.1.
    pricing incentives, 3.7.1.
contract language sample, 3.7.5.
    annual based fees review and
        adjustment, 3.7.5.
    audit disputes, 3.7.5.
    favored-nation status, 3.7.5.
    for pricing, 6.14.
    right to audit provisions, 3.7.5.
documents for external
    monitoring, 3.7.4.
    non-disclosure agreements, 3.7.4.
reporting areas and risks, 3.7.3.
    confidentiality clauses, 3.7.3.
    noncompliance, conditions of, 3.7.3.
MSRP (Manufactured Suggested Retail
    Price), defined, 6.9.

N
Negative reinforcement, incentives, 3.4.1.1.
Negotiations, post audit reports, 5.1.16.
Net sales
    contract language for, 6.9., 6.12., 6.15.
    in royalty/licensing monitoring, 3.9.2.
Network and device manufacturers, digital
    products. See OEMs
Network Inspector, self-monitoring
    tool, 3.10.3.3.
Net worth, in franchising, 3.5.2.
Nmap, self-monitoring tool, 3.10.3.3.
Noncompete clauses, franchising, 3.5.2.

Non-disclosure agreements (NDA)
    auditors and, 3.7.4., 4.3.3.1., 6.16.
    contract language for, 6.16.
    in-house lawyer approval of, 4.3.4.
    licensee best practices, 7.5.
North America, monitoring trends
    in, 2.4.3.
Notification letters. See Letters of
    notification, to third parties
Numerical terms in contracts, 1.3.2., 6.1.

O
Occidental Petroleum (Oxy), 3.6.1.
OEMs (original equipment manufacturers)
    defined, 3.3.1., 3.8.1.
    distribution/reseller contracts and, 3.4.3.
        distribution agreement sample, 3.4.3.
        distribution channels, 3.4.1.1., 3.4.1.2.
        incentive programs and controls,
            3.4.1.3.
        retailer reports to, 3.4.1.2.
    manufacturing contracts and
        KPIs, 3.8.2.
        record keeping, 3.8.1., 3.8.3.
        right to audit clause, 3.8.1.
    software licenses, 3.10.1.
On-site visits
    in construction audits, 3.2.2.
    internal controls vs., 4.3.
    by licensor, 4.3.3.1.
    remote monitoring vs., 6.20.
Operating manuals, franchising, 3.5.2.
Operations departments, monitoring
    disincentives of, 4.3.1.1.
Outsourcing
    of contract auditing, 5.1.10.1.5., 5.1.15.1.
    language barriers and, 1.3.1.
    of legal counsel, 5.1.15.1.
    of manufacturing, 3.8.1.
Overhead charges, common abuses
    in, 3.2.1., 3.2.2., 3.2.3., 3.6.2.

P
Packaging and labeling, manufacturing
    contracts, 3.8.2.
Partners, joint ventures. See Joint ventures/
    partner self-reporting contracts
Penalties
    contract language for, 1.3.2.
    for digital distribution without
        ownership, 3.3.2.
    for failure to maintain insurance, 3.8.2.

Penalties (*cont.*)
for failure to notify of litigation or outside
inspection, 3.8.2.
for late payments, 3.2.4., 3.7.2.,
5.1.18., 6.11.
for misreporting, 3.4.1.1.
for selling in unauthorized
territory, 6.25.
for selling to unauthorized
retailers, 3.4.1.1.
under SOX, 1.3.6., 2.5.3.
for substandard products/materials/
people, 3.2.3.
for unauthorized distribution of licensed
products, 6.30.
for unlicensed use of intellectual
property, 3.10.1., 6.7.
for using unlicensed software, 3.10.1.
Periodic monitoring audits, 1.3.4.,
4.3.2., 4.3.3.1.
Periodic reports, 2.1.6.
Personnel turnover, monitoring and, 3.2.3.,
4.3.2., 4.3.3., 4.3.3.1., 5.1.13.
Pharmaceutical industry, 3.8.2., 4.3.1.1.
PingSweep, self-monitoring tool, 3.10.3.3.
Point of sales (POS)
franchisee sales register systems,
3.5.2., 3.5.4.
Instant Rebate programs, 3.4.1.3.
retailer to OEM reports, 3.4.1.2.
Positive reinforcement, incentives, 3.4.1.1.
Post termination rights, contract
language for, 6.27–6.27.1.
Precontract audits, 3.3.2.
Prepayments, 3.2.3.
Price controls, contract language
for, 6.17.
Price protection programs, 3.4.1.3.
Pricing structures, for contracting with
auditors, 5.1.10.1.7.
Proactive monitoring programs, 1.3.4.
Producer Price Index, 3.8.2.
Production delays, manufacturing
contracts, 3.8.2.
Product returns
in calculating royalties on licensed
products, 2.1.1.
contract language for, 6.6., 6.15., 6.21.
Profit and loss allocation, joint
ventures, 3.6.2.
Proof of performance, in advertising
contracts, 3.1.3.

Public accounting firms, SOX guidance
for, 2.5.2.
Public Company Accounting Oversight
Board (PCAOB), 2.5.
Auditing Standard No. 5, 2.5.2.
Public Company Accounting Reform and
Investor Protection Act (2002). See
Sarbanes-Oxley Act, U.S.

R
Raw materials
approved vendors in agreements, 4.3.3.1.
contract language for inventory
records of, 6.12.
costs of, manufacturing contracts, 3.8.2.
inventory roll forwards, 3.9.2.,
4.3.3.1., 6.12.
Reactive monitoring audits, 1.3.4.
Reasonable, use of term, xix, 3.9.2.
Rebates
in construction contracts, 3.2.3.
in distribution/reseller contracts,
3.4.1.1., 3.4.1.3.
in movie production joint ventures, 3.6.2.
Recalls, manufacturing contracts, 3.8.2.
Record retention requirements, 2.1.2., 2.1.7.,
3.2.2., 3.8.2., 3.9.2., 6.18.
Records. See *specific types and contracts*
Red flags
continuous internal monitoring
and, 1.3.3.
selection of third party for
monitoring, 5.1.9.5.
underreporting of royalties and, 5.1.13.
Related third parties
contract language for sales
limitations, 6.19.
as subcontractors, 3.2.3.
Remedies
overview, 1.1., 6.1., 6.26.
contract language for, 6.8., 6.11.
termination and, 6.26.–6.27.1.
in digital distribution contracts, 3.3.2.
in franchise contracts, 3.5.2.
in manufacturing contracts, 3.8.2.
Renewal of contract audits, 4.3.2.
Reorganizations, of companies
monitoring and, 4.3.3.1., 5.1.13.
Reporting risks. See Self-reporting
contracts, reporting risks
Reports
contract language for, 6.20.

KPIs in CMP reports to
   management, 5.1.17.
   periodic, 2.1.6.
   post audit and negotiations, 5.1.16.
   release of liability and, 3.2.2.
   retailer to OEMs, 3.4.1.2.
   survey questions for, 6.20.
Reseller contracts. See Distribution/reseller
   self-reporting contracts, reporting risks
Retailers, authorized, 3.4.1.1.
Retainers, in advertising contracts, 3.1.2.
Retention of records. See Record retention
   requirements
Return on investment (ROI), extensive
   audits and, 1.3.4.
Returns, sales
   contract language for, 6.6., 6.15., 6.21.
   sales records and, 3.9.2.
Revenue sharing, monitoring of
   in digital distribution contracts, 3.3.2.
   in distribution/reseller contracts, 3.4.1.1.
   in franchise agreements, 3.5.1.
   in joint venture agreements, 3.6.2.
Review, use of term, 1.3.4.
Right to audit
   contract clause for, 1.3.2., 4.3.3.1., 6.22.
     in advertising contracts, 3.1.2.
     in construction contracts, 3.2.3., 3.2.4.
     cost allocation and, 3.1.2.
     expiration dates, 4.3.3.1., 5.1.9.
     in franchise agreements, 3.5.2.
     in joint venture contracts, 3.6.2.
     in manufacturing contracts, 3.8.2.
     in most-favored-nation contracts, 3.7.5.
     non-disclosure agreements and,
        6.16., 7.5.
     in royalty/licensing contracts, 3.9.2.
     writing of, 6.22.
   CPAs and, 1.3.4., 6.22.
   grey markets and, 2.2.
   periodic monitoring audits, 1.3.4.,
     4.3.2., 4.3.3.1.
   third party distributors and, 2.3.
Risk/benefit assessment, for monitoring
   programs, 4.3.1.1., 5.1.9.
Risk ranking, of licensees, 4.3.2.,
   5.1.9., 5.1.13.
ROI (Return on investment), extensive
   audits and, 1.3.4.
Roll forwards, inventory, 3.9.2.,
   4.3.3.1., 6.12.
Royalties

audits of, 2.1.5.
   contract amendments and, 2.1.5.
   cost recovery in, 3.9.2., 4.3.1.1., 4.3.2.
   intellectual property and, 2.1.5., 2.2.,
     4.3.3.1., 5.1.13.
   in Japan, 2.4.1.
   preparation for, 7.4.
calculations of
   accuracy in, 5.1.10.1.3.2.
   on all licensed products, 2.1.1., 6.9.
   contract language for, 6.9., 6.23.
on digital subscription and streaming
   services, 3.3.2.
due dates
   contract language for, 6.24.
   in royalty/licensing monitoring, 3.9.2.
in franchise agreements, 3.5.1., 3.5.2.
misreporting of, 1.1., 2.1., 2.1.4., 2.1.5.
   digital content, 2.3.
   in franchises, 3.5.4.
   IP and global compliance, 2.2.
   reasons for, xix, 2.4.2., 3.9.1.2.
   underreporting, xix, 2.2., 3.9.1.2.,
     4.3.2., 5.1.9., 5.1.13., 6.5., 7.2.
payments
   tax deductions on, 6.28.
   timeliness of, 3.3.2.
   web-based, 6.24.
sublicensing and, 5.1.13.
timeliness of reporting and
   payment, 3.3.2.
Royalty auditors, financial statement
   auditors vs., xviii, 2.1.5., 2.5., 5.1.10.,
   5.1.10.1.5., 5.1.15.1.
Royalty/licensing self-reporting contracts,
   reporting risks, 3.9.–3.9.3.
   audit terms and conditions, 3.9.2.
     advance and minimum guarantees,
        1.1., 3.9.2., 4.3.2., 5.1.13., 6.13.
     closeouts as deductions, 3.9.2.
     copyrights, 3.9.1., 3.9.1.1.,
        3.9.1.2., 3.9.2.
     cost recovery, 3.9.2.
     exchange rates, 3.9.2.
     gross sales, 3.9.2.
     intellectual property protection, 3.9.2.
     interest rates, 3.9.2.
     inventory records, 3.9.2.
     inventory roll forwards, 3.9.2.
     IP notices, 3.9.2.
     net sales, 3.9.2.
     record retention requirements, 3.9.2.

Royalty/licensing self-reporting
  contracts (*cont.*)
    right to audit clause, 3.9.2.
    royalty payment due dates, 3.9.2.
    sales records, 3.9.2., 3.9.3., 4.3.3.1.
    sales returns, 3.9.2.
    sublicensing, 3.9.2.
    territory, 3.9.2., 5.1.13.
    trademarks, 3.9.2.
    unsold units at termination, 3.9.2.
  contract description, 3.9.1.
    bundling, 3.9.1.2.
    copyrights, 3.9.1., 3.9.1.1.
    licensee role, 3.9.1.2.
    licensor role, 3.9.1.1.
    trademarks, 3.9.1., 3.9.2.
    underreporting, 3.9.1.2.
  documents for external monitoring, 3.9.3.
    changes in accounting systems, 3.9.3.
    sales records, 3.9.3.
    tax withholding certificates, 3.9.3., 6.28.
Royalty statements
  checklists for, 2.1.2.
  components of, 2.1.3., 4.3.3.1.
  exchange rates and, 2.1.3.
  movement of licensed property in, 2.1.3.
  in short audits, 1.3.4.
  in third party monitoring, 4.3.1.1.

S

Sales catalogs, 4.3.3.1.
Sales records
  exchange rates and, 3.9.2.
  gross sales deductions, 3.9.2.
  returns, 3.9.2.
  in royalty/licensing contracts, 3.9.2.,
    3.9.3., 4.3.3.1.
  sales register systems, 3.5.2., 3.5.4.
Sales tax recovery, 3.2.3.
SamSpade, self-monitoring tool, 3.10.3.3.
Sarbanes-Oxley Act, U.S. (SOX, 2002)
  enactment of, xvi, 1.2., 2.5.
  global impact of, xvi, 1.3.6.
  on materiality, 2.5., 2.5.2.
  third-party monitoring and, 2.5.–2.5.3.
    Auditing Standard No. 5 (SOX), 2.5.2.
    civil penalties, 1.3.6.
    proactive monitoring programs, 1.3.4.
    Section 302, internal control
      certification, 2.5.1.
    Section 404, assessment of internal
      control, 2.1.4., 2.5., 2.5.2.
    Section 802, criminal penalties,
      1.3.6., 2.5.3.
Securities and Exchange Commission, xvi,
  1.3.6., 2.5., 2.5.2., 5.1.2.
Self-reporting contracts, overview. See also
  specific aspects
  economics of, 1.2.
  by industry, 3.1.
  misreporting
    environment of, 1.1.
    penalties for, 3.4.1.1.
  third party relationships, planning for,
    1.3.–1.3.6.
    business strategies, 1.3.1.
    continuous internal monitoring, 1.3.3.
    contract execution, 1.3.2.
    contract management, 1.3.3.
    exit strategies, 1.3.5.
    future planning, 1.3.6.
    periodic monitoring audits, 1.3.4.
Self-reporting contracts, reporting risks,
  3.1.–3.10.3.
  advertising agency contracts, 3.1.–3.1.4.
    audit terms and conditions, 3.1.2.
    contract description, 3.1.1.
    documents for external
      monitoring, 3.1.4.
    reporting areas and risks, 3.1.3.
  construction contracts, 3.2.–3.2.5.
    audit terms and conditions, 3.2.2.
    contract description, 3.2.1.
    documents for external
      monitoring, 3.2.5.
    timing of self-monitoring and
      audits, 3.2.4.
    variable cost monitoring process, 3.2.3.
  digital distribution contracts, 3.3.–3.3.4.
    areas of concern, 3.3.2.
    contract description, 3.3.1.
    monitoring of agreements, 3.3.4.
    risk summary, 3.3.3.
  distribution/reseller contracts, 3.4.–3.4.3.
    audit terms and conditions, 3.4.2.
    contract description, 3.4.1.
    distribution agreement sample, 3.4.3.
  franchise contracts, 3.5.–3.5.4.
    audit terms and conditions, 3.5.2.
    contract description, 3.5.1.
    documents for external
      monitoring, 3.5.4.
    reporting areas and risks, 3.5.3.
  joint venture/partner contracts, 3.6.–3.6.3.

audit terms and conditions, 3.6.2.
contract description, 3.6.1.
documents for external
    monitoring, 3.6.3.
manufacturing contracts, 3.8.–3.8.3.
    audit terms and conditions, 3.8.2
    contract description, 3.8.1.
    documents for external
        monitoring, 3.8.3.
most-favored-nation contracts, 3.7.–3.7.5.
    audit terms and conditions, 3.7.2.
    contract description, 3.7.1.
    contract language samples, 3.7.5., 6.14.
    documents for external
        monitoring, 3.7.4.
    reporting areas and risks, 3.7.3.
royalty/licensing contracts, 3.9.–3.9.3.
    audit terms and conditions, 3.9.2.
    contract description, 3.9.1.
    documents for external
        monitoring, 3.9.3.
software/end user license contracts,
    3.10.–3.10.3.
    audit terms and conditions, 3.10.2.
    contract description, 3.10.1.
    reporting areas and risks, 3.10.3
Self-reporting economy, size of, 1.2.
Self-reporting party, defined, xv
Short monitoring audits, 1.3.4.
Shrink-wrap agreements, 3.10.1.
Singer, Isaac, 3.5.1.
SKU numbers, 3.3.1., 6.12., 6.20.
Software asset management programs,
    3.10.3., 3.10.3.3.
Software/end user license self-reporting
    contracts, reporting risks, 3.10.–3.10.3.
    audit terms and conditions, 3.10.2.
        software management systems
            and, 3.10.2.
    contract description, 3.10.1.
        clickwrap agreements, 3.10.1.
        client access licenses, 3.10.1.
        CPU/server based licensing, 3.10.1.
        enterprise license agreements, 3.10.1.
        EULA agreements, 3.10.1.
        OEMs and, 3.10.1.
        penalties for using unlicensed
            software, 3.10.1.
        shrink-wrap agreements, 3.10.1.
        tier based licenses, 3.10.1.
        user based licenses, 3.10.1.
        value unit based licenses, 3.10.1.

volume agreements, 3.10.1.
documents for external monitoring,
    3.10.3.3.
    self-monitoring software tools
        and, 3.10.3.3.
reporting areas and risks, 3.10.3
    causes of contract violations, 3.10.3.1.
    disaster recover plans, 3.10.3.2.
    EULAs, 3.10.3
    problem areas, 3.10.3.2.
    software management systems
        and, 3.10.3
Software industry
    cost recovery in, 4.3.1.1., 4.3.2.
    IP examples of, 3.9.1.2.
South Korea, emerging trends in, 2.4.1.
SOX. See Sarbanes-Oxley Act, U.S.
Special event notification, 6.20.
Stockholder governance, xvi-xvii
Stonefield Josephson, Inc., 2.4.1.
Street date, 3.4.1.1.
Strong contract language. See Contract
    terms and conditions, writing of
Subcontractors, monitoring of
    approval of related parties, 3.2.3.
    in construction contracts, 3.2.3.
Subdistributors, digital products, 3.3.4.
Subfranchisees, franchise
    agreements, 3.5.2.
Sublicenses
    of intellectual property, 3.9.2.,
        4.3.2., 5.1.13.
    royalty underreporting indicators
        and, 5.1.13.
Subscription and streaming services,
    digital products, 3.3.2.
Substandard products/materials/
    people, 3.2.3.
Suppliers, franchise agreements, 3.5.2.
Surprise audits
    drawbacks of, 5.1.12.
    in franchising, 3.5.4.
Survey questions, for reports, 6.20.

T

Taxes
    deductions on royalty payments, 6.28.
    as gross sales reduction, 6.29.
    in license agreements, 2.1.1., 6.6.
    sales tax recovery, 3.2.3.
    value added (VAT), 6.29.
    withholding certificates, 3.9.3., 6.28.

Technology companies, 3.3.1.
Telecommunications. See Digital
distribution self-reporting contracts
Termination provisions
contract language for, 6.26.
exit strategies vs., 1.3.5.
post termination rights, contract
language for, 6.27–6.27.1.
risk management and, 1.3.6.
unsold units and, 3.9.2.
Terms and conditions. See Contract terms
and conditions, writing of
Territory
contract language for, 6.25.
in franchise monitoring, 3.5.2.
national security restrictions on, 6.25.
penalties for selling in authorized, 6.25.
in royalty/licensing monitoring,
3.9.2., 5.1.13.
Third party monitoring. See Monitoring of
third parties, roles in
Third party relationships, planning
for, 1.3.–1.3.6.
business strategies, 1.3.1.
continuous internal monitoring, 1.3.3.
contract execution, 1.3.2.
contract management, 1.3.3.
exit strategies, 1.3.5.
future planning, 1.3.6.
periodic monitoring audits, 1.3.4.
Tier based licenses, software, 3.10.1.
Time and material costs, 1.2., 3.1.1., 3.2.1.
Timeliness, of reporting and payment,
3.3.2. See also Late payments
Trademarks, in royalty/licensing contracts,
3.9.1., 3.9.2.
Transactional attorneys. See Attorneys
Trends, in global monitoring
in Africa, 2.4.3.
in Asia, 2.4.1.
in Europe, 2.4.3.
in Middle East, 2.4.3.
in North America, 2.4.2.
Trust, but verify system, 1.3.2., 2.4.1.
Turnover of personnel, monitoring and,
3.2.3., 4.3.2., 4.3.3., 5.1.13.

U

Uniform Franchise Offering Circular
(UFOC), 3.5.1.
Unit pricing, manufacturing
contracts, 3.8.2.

Units, definition of, 3.8.2.
Up-front fees, franchising, 3.5.1.
User based licenses, software, 3.10.1.

V

Value added taxes (VAT), 6.29.
Value-based fees, auditor, 5.1.10.1.7.
Value unit based licenses, software, 3.10.1.
Variable cost contracts
construction overcharges and, 3.2.1.
monitoring process, 3.2.3.
Variable pricing, manufacturing
contracts, 3.8.2.
Volume agreements, software
licenses, 3.10.1.
Volume discounts, 3.4.1.3.

W

Wall Street Journal, 6.7.
Weak/vague contract language. See also
Contract terms and conditions,
writing of
audit, use of term, 1.3.4., 3.2.2.
normal, use of term, 1.3.2.
obsolete, use of term, 3.4.1.1.
reasonable, use of term, xix, 3.9.2.
review, use of term, 1.3.4.
Web sites
Business Software Alliance (BSA), 7.1.
clickwrap agreements, 3.10.1.
COSO, 2.5.2.
for electronic royalty payments, 6.24.
exchange rates, 6.7.
review of products on, 4.3.3.1.
Weekly Gross Sales statement (WGSS),
franchising, 3.5.2.
Witnesses. See Expert witnesses
Worker's compensation insurance, in
franchising, 3.5.2.
Working capital, franchising, 3.5.2.
Work-in-progress monitoring, construction
contracts, 3.2.2.
Writing contracts. See Contract terms and
conditions, writing of

Y

Yellow Book Standards (AICPA), 3.2.2.